KU-845-298

Politics as Development

POLITICS AS DEVELOPMENT

The Emergence of Political Parties in

Nineteenth-Century Serbia   GALE STOKES

Duke University Press   Durham and London 1990

© 1990 Duke University Press
All rights reserved
Printed in the United States of America
on acid-free paper ∞

Library of Congress Cataloging-in-Publication Data
Stokes, Gale, 1933–
Politics as development : the emergence of political parties in
nineteenth-century Serbia / by Gale Stokes.
Includes bibliographical references.
ISBN 0-8223-1016-3
1. Political parties—Serbia—History—19th century.
2. Serbia—Constitutional history.   3. Serbia—Politics and
government—1804–1918. I. Title.
JN9659.A45S86 1990
324.2497′1′009—dc20   89-39903 CIP

1004401064

To the memory of my mother
Ida Jane Bassett Stokes

CONTENTS

ACKNOWLEDGMENTS

Financial support from many organizations enabled me to carry out the research for this book and to write a good part of it. A National Endowment for the Humanities summer fellowship allowed me to do preliminary research in Belgrade in 1977. In 1980 I conducted the basic research in Belgrade with a Fulbright-Hays grant administered by the Council for the International Exchange of Scholars and an International Research and Exchanges Board grant, funded by the National Endowment for the Humanities and the Ford Foundation. In 1983 I was able to write the bulk of the book under a grant from the Joint Committee on Eastern Europe of the American Council of Learned Societies and the Social Science Research Council, using funds provided by the National Endowment for the Humanities and the Ford Foundation. During that same semester I also held a Mellon Fellowship from the Dean of Humanities, Rice University. In the summer of 1984 a travel grant from the American Philosophical Society enabled me to spend two weeks using the Nikola Pašić collection in Toronto. I would like to extend my heartfelt thanks to all these agencies.

Many individuals both in Yugoslavia and elsewhere helped me in many ways. Vasilije Krestić of the History Department of Belgrade University was my mentor on the occasion of several visits to Belgrade and was of unfailing assistance. Dragan Živojinović, also of the Belgrade University History Department, has been a great help, and Milorad Radević of the Historical Institute assisted me greatly in using the Archive of Jovan Ristić. The personnel of the Archive of the Serbian Academy of Sciences, the Archive of

Serbia, and the National Library were particularly helpful. Work in Belgrade would be inconceivable without the truly unrepayable hospitality of Radivoje and Milena Lukić, two of the finest people it has been my pleasure to know. Outside of Yugoslavia, Dimitrije Djordjević of the University of California at Santa Barbara kindly permitted me to use works from the Nikić Collection, sent me papers and other scholarly works, and provided good friendship and guidance for more than twenty years. Nikola Pašić of Toronto, Ontario, permitted me to use the collection of his grandfather's papers as collected and edited by Sofija Škorić. Several colleagues read earlier versions of this manuscript, and I thank them each and all for their assistance. In particular, however, I would like to thank John A. Fine, Jr., of the University of Michigan, who went over the manuscript with a fine-tooth comb and provided the most thorough and useful reading that any manuscript of mine, long or short, has ever received. I deeply appreciate his comments and advice. Naturally, whatever faults remain are my responsibility alone.

Finally, I would like to thank Adam Osborne, inventor of the portable computer. Even though his company went bankrupt early, my version of the sturdy little machine he produced has been almost as indispensable to me as the person usually thanked last in acknowledgments such as these, my wife Roberta.

FOREWORD

The Serbian Orthodox calendar in the nineteenth century was twelve days behind the calendar in use in Western Europe. All dates in the text are given in full in the Western style but in the footnotes dates are presented in telegraphic format. If a single date is shown in a footnote, the document in question was originally dated according to the Western style. When both an old style and a new style date are shown in a footnote, the document was originally dated according to the Orthodox calendar.

The terms "Radical," "Liberal," and "Progressive," as well as "Conservative" and "Young Conservative" are capitalized throughout. The reader should realize, however, that in the earlier parts of the book, these terms do not apply to fully formed political parties, but rather to groupings, tendencies, and shifting alliances.

I have used the term "Ottoman" instead of "Turkish" for the Serbian term *turski*, except in a few instances where flavor in a direct quotation seemed to demand "Turkish." Serbs routinely use "Turkish" to refer to the Ottoman Empire, but in English this lends an improper ethnic connotation to a state organized on a completely different principle. In fact, most of the "Turks" the Serbs came in contact with were not ethnically Turkish.

The term to use in referring to what was called the Dual Monarchy after 1867 is not easy to find. Technically the Habsburg lands constituted an empire only from 1806 to 1867, but in this study the terms Austria, Austria-Hungary, the Dual Monarchy, the Habsburg Empire, Vienna, and the Habsburgs are used more or less interchangeably to refer to the same entity.

ABBREVIATIONS

AJR: The archive of Jovan Ristić, held by the Historical Institute, SANU.

ANUBIH: Akademija nauka i umetnosti Bosne i Hercegovine (Academy of Arts and Sciences, Bosnia and Hercegovina).

AS: Arhiv Srbije (Archive of the Republic of Serbia, Belgrade), followed by the specific collection:
  MG papers of Milutin Garašanin
  MPS Ministarstvo prosvete i crkvenih dela (Ministry of education and church affairs)
  NS Narodna skupština (national legislature)
  PO Pokloni i otkupi (gifts and accessions)
  Varia Miscellaneous
  Vš Velika škola (Belgrade academy)

Crveni barjak: Blagoje Bitković and Živomir Spasić, eds., *Crveni barjak u Kragujevcu 1876* (Kragujevac: Istorijski arhiv Šumadije, 1976), 2 vols.

Dnevnik Kalaja: Andrija Radenić, ed., *Dnevnik Benjamina Kalaja* (Belgrade and Novi Sad: Istorijski institut and Institut za istoriju Vojvodine, 1976).

DSS: Društvo srpske slovesnosti (Serbian Literary Society—predecessor to SKA).

FO: Foreign Office files of the British Public Record Office, Kew.

IAB: Istorijski arhiv Beograda (Belgrade Historical Archive).

Protokoli: Protocols of the national skupština for the year under discussion.

SANU: Srpska akademija nauke i umetnosti (Serbian Academy of Arts and Sciences).

SB: *Stenografske beleške* (Stenographic record of the national skupština) published in volumes available at AS.

SKA: Srpska kraljevska akademija (Royal Serbian Academy, predecessor of SANU).

Škorić collection: collection of the papers of Nikola Pašić owned by Nikola Pašić of Toronto but held in the library of the University of Toronto, where they have been organized and edited into a manuscript volume by Sofija Škorić.

TB: Milen M. Nikolić, ed., *Timočka buna 1883* (Belgrade: Državna arhiva NR Srbije, Gradja, 1954), 2 vols.

VMO: Slobodan Jovanović, *Vlada Milana Obrenovića* (Belgrade: Geca Kon, 1934), 3 vols.

Zbornik zakona: Zbornik zakona i uredaba kneževine (kraljevine) Srbije (Collection of Laws and Regulations of the Principality [Kingdom] of Serbia), volumes and years as cited.

Politics as Development

SERBIA IN 1880

INTRODUCTION

By most standards Serbia in the nineteenth century was a backward country. Almost completely undeveloped economically, Serbia had only 571 kilometers of railroad by 1900 and, out of a population of over 2 million, fewer than 4,000 "industrial" workers.[1] The overwhelming majority of Serbs were smallholding peasants living in villages of fewer than 1,500 persons. Land was remarkably evenly distributed. Peasants owning between 2 and 20 hectares (1 hectare equals about 2.5 acres) constituted 68.7 percent of Serbian landowners and they held 79 percent of the land. The 1897 Serbia boasted only three landowners with properties larger than 300 hectares, whereas at the other extreme only about 10 percent of Serbian rural households were landless.[2] What trade existed consisted mainly of the export of live pigs to Austria—since Serbia had no packing plants of its own with which to produce packaged meats—and a modest export trade in grain. Only 2 towns larger than 10,000 persons existed, and only 3 percent of Serbia's population lived in them. In the larger towns the literacy rate for males was almost 50 percent (23 percent for females), but in the countryside the literacy rate for males was only about 10 percent. For peasant females the rate was less than 1 percent.

Despite this utterly undeveloped situation, however, the Serbian political system, especially in the decade just preceding the First World War, had every appearance of being modern. Serbia had a constitution, a reasonably independent court system, and a powerful and well-organized bureaucracy. A parliamentary system functioned with significant freedom of the press, active political parties, and a broad franchise. Of course, the system did not work perfectly. The king remained strong, as did the military, and Serbia was deeply in debt to more economically developed states. But the fact remains that this almost completely peasant nation, without the complex socioeconomic structure that we associate with functioning democracies, had built a relatively sophisticated political structure based on the best models of the nineteenth-century liberal state.

Simply to designate Serbia as backward, therefore, hides an interesting anomaly: that politically Serbia was not backward, but had a political system at least as advanced as many economically more developed states. Serbian political development in the absence of concurrent social and economic change goes against our tendency to understand political structures as reflections of social and economic ones. Serbia had a social structure very different from that of the societies that originated the ideas of constitutionalism, popular sovereignty, and nation, but once these concepts were introduced into Serbia they developed a momentum of their own. Serbia became modern politically, but not in other spheres. The purpose of this study is to show how this modern political system in Serbia began, how constitutionalism led to the development of a party system—even though Serbia did not enjoy the pluralist socioeconomic system that a party system seems designed to reflect—and how an increasingly emotional nationalism became the standard form of Serbian political discourse.

In an earlier study on nineteenth-century Serbian liberalism I investigated the coming to Serbia of the ideas of nation, popular sovereignty, and parliamentarianism.[4] In part as an effort to make their country recognizable to the great powers of Europe, in part because of the idealism of youth, and in part because they wanted to exercise the power of the state themselves, the young Serbian Liberals of the 1850s and 1860s found a way to outflank the previously preeminent claim of the prince to be the sole legitimate political actor by proposing that they represented another source of legitimacy, the people. In doing so they fundamentally transformed Serbian political possibilities. These liberals did not achieve political power in the 1860s but they did prepare the way for sharing power in the 1870s on the basis of the idea that the right to rule was connected with popular sovereignty. The transformational quality of this idea became apparent when the Liberals came to power and introduced reforms reflecting their views, like an annual legislature. In this new environment other groups emerged almost immediately with counterclaims that they too represented the people, and represented them better than the Liberals. The 1870s and early 1880s, therefore, beside being the era when Serbian independence achieved de jure recognition by the Great Powers, was also an era when the implications of the idea of popular sovereignty were thrashed out in Serbian politics, a period of struggle for control of the discourse of nation.

More specifically, this study concerns the struggle among three groups and one individual from 1869 to 1883 over how Serbia's constitutional regime was to be organized. The first of these contestants was Milan Obrenović, who came to the Serbian throne as an adolescent of fourteen in 1868. The three groups were the political parties and their predecessors: the Liberals, the Progressives, and the Radicals. The first represented the generation of the 1860s in power through most of the 1870s, and the original creative element of Serbian politics. The second made up the next generation, educated abroad, typically lawyers, more liberal than the Liberals but not in any sense democrats. The Progressives opened up Serbian politics in the early 1880s by permitting the legal formation of political parties. But it is the third group, the Radicals, that was the most important. The Radicals took the legitimating idea of the Liberals and the legal opportunity offered them by the Progressives and created the first political party in the Balkans characterized by organizational continuity, regular links between local and national levels, the ability to take power, and organized efforts to mobilize the electorate.[5] By developing the rhetoric of nation and by successfully taking that rhetoric to the Serbian countryside, the Radicals mobilized the people for whom others had claimed to speak. For that reason, the development of the early Radical Party constitutes a main theme of this book.

This is a study in political history, because it seems to me that the dynamics of creating a state with a functioning party system is the main problematic of nineteenth-century Serbian history. For that reason, then, the first chapter concerns the beginnings of parliamentary life, which did not happen because of any social imperatives but because of the chance convergence of an assassination, an underage prince, and a strong political leader. But once introduced, parliamentary life very quickly developed its own momentum. Public debate created a space for political conflict that had not existed earlier, and before long groupings emerged to occupy portions of that space. Chapter two introduces the most important of these, the Radicals, whose populist socialism hinted at future possibilities by using nationalist rhetoric to mobilize the people who made up the nation, the peasantry.

But before parliamentary life could mature very far, Serbia faced a war with the Ottomans. Chapter three discusses how the left-Liberals and young socialists used this crisis to introduce reforms, but how war fever submerged their efforts in the end. The military and diplomatic course of the wars of 1876 and 1877–78 have been discussed often, but chapter four concentrates on the implications of the war for the development of internal politics. The final three chapters constitute the core of the study. The first of them shows how coherent political alliances consolidated themselves once parliamentary life was restored after the war, whereas the next chapter concentrates on the originality of the Radical Party. Under the intellectual leadership of Pera Todorović and the practical leadership of Nikola Pašić, the Radicals pushed the level of nationalist rhetoric to a new level, created a strong party organization throughout the country, and mobilized peasant support in an unprecedented measure. But their success threatened both the king and the other parties, especially the Progressives.[6] Therefore, as we see in the final chapter, when the king refused to accept a Radical electoral victory, the result was Serbia's last major peasant revolt. Its defeat closed the initial stage of the development of a modern political system in socially and economically backward Serbia.

1 : THE BEGINNINGS OF PARLIAMENTARY LIFE

To do things according to our own circumstances would be better than all these great forms brought in from foreign lands.—Ilija Garašanin

The moment when Serbia began its transformation from an oriental land to a Western one can be fixed with considerable precision. It was in 1804 when the Serbs rose in revolt against the renegade janissaries that were seizing their crops and killing their headmen. This First Serbian Uprising, as it is called, failed, although it did bring Serbia to the attention of the great powers, especially Russia, for the first time. In 1813 its great leader, Karadjordje, along with thousands of his countrymen, had to flee before the reconquering Ottomans. But from 1815 to 1830, Miloš Obrenović, who assumed leadership of the Serbs after Karadjordje, created an autonomous Serbian principality by methods Ottoman administrators understood and appreciated: absolute loyalty, ruthless self-aggrandizement, and shameless bribery. In 1830 the sultan recognized Miloš as hereditary prince of an autonomous province of the Ottoman Empire.

Autonomy was the fundamental first step in beginning Serbia's movement out of the Ottoman orbit into a European one, but Miloš's reign had little in common with the parliamentary system that Serbia adopted in the second half of the nineteenth century. Miloš was one of several local warlords who rose in Southeastern Europe in the early nineteenth century to carve out domains for themselves. Ruthless and boisterous men, their unself-conscious principle of rule was personal gain. Miloš discouraged trade except through his own companies, appropriated the income from ferries and import duties, and murdered not only his enemies, but even men who would not loan him money. If Miloš had a political model it was not any system influenced by the French Revolution and its aftermath, but the "well-flourishing, absolute domain of the House of Osman."[1] Contemporaries referred to his reign wryly as the sultanate, and, just as in the Ottoman Empire, under Miloš the source of authority was simply the ruler himself.

But even in Miloš's time Serbia possessed some indigenous political traditions not directly inherited from the Ottomans. The first was the skupština (the term is derived from the word for gathering), an amorphous body that met occasionally to ratify important changes during the First Serbian Uprising. Miloš ran roughshod over the tradition that the adult males of the community should be consulted when important undertakings were under consideration, but a strong sense that in the end only decisions ratified by such a body were authentic remained a part of the Serbian folk ethic. Even Miloš had to call skupštinas from time to time to lend fig leaves to his autocratic rule. A second tradition was the idea that the prince should govern with the help of a council of advisors. Karadjordje had established such a council, which, despite the opposition of local strongmen who might have served on it, he controlled completely. Miloš was even cruder than the none too subtle Karadjordje; he simply murdered his opponents, appointed local leaders loyal to him, and put down the resultant uprisings by force.

But when the sultan recognized Miloš's special position in 1830, demands became more and more insistent that he create a government appropriate to Serbia's new dignity. After a stirring call for a constitutional government by Serbia's greatest intellectual figure, Vuk Karadžić, and, more important, a widespread conspiracy and rebellion by his main advisors, Miloš promised a constitution to Serbia in 1835. By doling out some formal appearance of power to the State Council, which was composed mainly of his opponents, Miloš hoped to maintain real power for himself. The new law also called for a skupština (assembly), but one with no important functions.

Besides formally instituting the main Serbian political institutions, the constitution of 1835 occasioned foreign powers to take a direct interest in Serbian affairs. The Austrians feared the constitution was too liberal and received permission from the Porte to send a consul to Belgrade. When England and Russia followed suit, the international competition between Russia and England became reflected in Serbian politics. The English consul took Miloš's side, for no better reason than the fact that the Russian and Austrian consuls had allied themselves with Miloš's opponents. Miloš's defeat by these forces came when the Porte agreed in 1838 to issue a new fundamental statute for Serbia that turned over power to the State Council, which consisted mainly of Miloš's opponents. The skupština was not even mentioned. The Defenders of the Constitution, as the victors in this struggle were called, set the seal on their victory when they chased Miloš's son Michael, who had succeeded him, into exile in 1842 and set up the weak grandson of Karadjordje, Alexander, as their figurehead prince.

During the era of the Defenders of the Constitution, the State Council overshadowed both the prince and the skupština, which met only once. At the same time, however, a fourth political element emerged, the bureaucracy, or the government itself. In a country like Serbia, almost totally peasant in structure, without a middle class, and without an intelligentsia, the state and the church were the sole permanent employers. Bureaucrat or priest—these were the options for anyone talented or tenacious enough to get an education. Of the two, the former had at least two important advantages. State service provided not only good and steady pay, prestige, a special uniform, and social standing, it also provided an opportunity to exercise power. Furthermore, as Serbia turned more and more toward Western styles of government the growing size of the state created a constantly expanding number of jobs. Although the number of state employees during the period of the Defenders of the Constitution was very small—perhaps one thousand—many of them had crossed over from Habsburg lands, bringing with them the Central European science of administration of cameralism, which reserved the dominant position in society to the government bureaucracy. Cameralists believed that initiatives in public affairs, whether this meant declaring war or simply setting up a scale at a local market, were the responsibility of state officials, not of popular organs of government. The prince—in actuality the State Council—decided the direction of movement, the bureaucracy provided the resources through administering the tax structure and keeping order, and the people supplied the wherewithal by paying taxes. Ilija Garašanin, the founder of the Serbian bureaucracy during these years, believed in rigid lines of authority and absolute obedience from inferiors. In his view the people were the "incompetent wards of the state." "Tell all of them simply to consider minding their own business instead of concerning themselves with what government is charged with doing," he said.[2] The Defenders of the Constitution no longer called the peasantry cattle—that was an Ottoman term *(reaya)*—they just treated them that way. The strongly centralized and growing bureaucracy they created became, along with the State Council, the unquestioned and indeed unchallengeable directors of local and national *affaires d'état*.

The Defenders of the Constitution lasted sixteen years. Finally, in 1858, ineptness on the part of Prince Alexander Karadjordjević, intrigues by Ilija Garašanin, and excited agitation by young Liberals returning home with new ideas from their educations in Western Europe led to the calling of the first truly national skupština in Serbian history. In a small-scale analogy to the French National Assembly of 1789, the St. Andrew's skupština sent both Prince Alexander and Ilija Garašanin packing. But instead of establishing a republic, the Liberal leaders of the assembly could think of nothing better to do than recall old Prince Miloš to the throne. Despite this failure of imagination, the successes of the St. Andrew's skupština in changing rulers and in introducing new ideas gave the idea of the skupština as an important player in the political game a fundamental boost. For this reason, and because of its enunciation for the first time of demands for constitutional government and civil liberties, Serbian historians consider the St. Andrew's skupština the locus classicus of nineteenth-century Liberal aspirations in Serbia. When Miloš finally died in 1860 and was once again succeeded by his son Michael, the new prince could not abandon the idea of a skupština, as the Defenders of the Constitution had. When he restructured the Ottoman Constitution of 1838 he kept the skupština, but only as an advisory body, since the State Council retained its formal legislative functions. Still, by accepting the principle that the skupština should meet once every three years, he assured it a regular place in the state apparatus. Michael was no Alexander Karadjordjević and would not let himself be dominated by a State Council or anyone else. Recalling Ilija Garašanin to be his main minister, Michael ruled with an iron coldness over a bureaucracy from which he expected no arguments, a state council he dominated, and a skupština he treated like the window dressing it was.

In mid-1868, in the prime of his life, Michael was struck down by assassins. This dark event was a disaster for Michael's ambitious plans for Serbia, but it presented the new political forces that had been fermenting since 1858 with an unprecedented opportunity for change. The first quick-witted response to the assassination did not seem very progressive. Colonel Milivoje Blaznavac solved what at first seemed like a thorny problem of succession by calling the small Belgrade garrison out to swear allegiance to Milan Obrenović, the unruly and poorly educated grandson of Prince Miloš's brother. For a moment, it appeared that Serbia was in for a military regime, at least during the minority of Milan. But at the same time Blaznavac was making his move, a craftier intriguer, Jovan Ristić, began to make his.

Ristić was, along with Ilija Garašanin, Serbia's greatest statesman of the nineteenth century. Born of poor parents in Kragujevac in 1831, Ristić's brilliance in grammar school convinced a family friend to send him to the gymnasium in Belgrade. There he excelled, becoming prominent in the quasi-political activities of the "Družine mladeži srpske," an organization of students that flourished for a few years in the heated atmosphere of 1848. Having turned down the opportunity to study religion in Russia (the person who accepted the scholarship in his stead later became Metropolitan Michael, Ristić's ally as the relatively liberal leader of the Russophile faction in the second half of the century), in 1849 Ristić went to study law in Germany. Starting his studies in Berlin, in 1852 he received his doctorate from Heidelberg. After two years of further study in Paris, Ristić returned to state service in Prince

Alexander's government. A frugal man with very strong work habits, Ristić quickly became identified as an able young administrator in the ministry of foreign affairs. In 1861 Michael appointed him representative to Istanbul, a most sensitive and important post. In 1867, when Michael changed the direction of his foreign policy, lessening his dependence on Russia and dismissing Ilija Garašanin, he invited Ristić to become minister of foreign affairs. But Ristić refused to serve in a government that still contained several ministers from the Old Conservative school of Garašanin. Unless he could appoint persons with whom he agreed in principle, such as Jevrem Grujić, leader of the St. Andrew's Liberals—that is, unless he could install a cabinet—he would not serve. Finding this request insulting and outrageous, Michael appointed instead Filip Hristić, a Conservative war-horse (who was Ristić's brother-in-law), to the position.[3]

In 1868, therefore, Ristić was one of Serbia's most prominent politicians. He was also very well connected, having married into the Hadži-Tomić family, one of the two wealthiest and most powerful families in Belgrade. Accordingly he became, along with Colonel Blaznavac and Jovan Gavrilović—a political nullity—one of the three regents for the fourteen-year-old Milan. Blaznavac was not a politician, either by profession or by temperament. He had the loyalty of the handful of officers and men that constituted Serbia's army, and he considered that enough. Ristić, however, had thought a good deal about what sort of government Serbia should have and he used the opportunity presented by Michael's death to put these thoughts into effect.

The liberalism that Ristić was to bring to Serbia had been defined originally by men much more radical than he, like Vladimir Jovanović and Ljubomir Kaljević.[4] These more extreme Liberals were the first to propose a solution to the fundamental problem facing Serbia's young educated elite. Having seen as students the material prosperity of Germany, England, and France, and having tasted the intoxicating ideas of freedom and equality produced by the French Revolution, they had returned home in the 1850s and 1860s to a country whose poverty was matched only by its low cultural level. Was it even possible to imagine that Serbia could raise itself to the levels of wealth and sophistication these young men experienced abroad? The Liberals of the 1860s were the first to provide an affirmative answer to this question. Having staked out their claim to political legitimacy by putting themselves forward as representatives of the nation, they constructed a theory of Serbian history that purported to show why the Serbian people, appearances to the contrary, were capable of becoming modern. They held that the germs of democratic experience could be found deep in the Serbian past and were reflected in harmonious parliamentary-like behavior characteristic of the Serbian extended family (zadruga). The overwhelming majority of Serbs might be illiterate peasants, unlikely to create an industrial economy, but—the left-Liberals argued—Serbs were uniquely suited by their history and customs to become constitutional democrats. The place that the naturally democratic people could most effectively exert their influence was in the national skupština, which is the title that Vladimir Jovanović and Milovan Janković gave to their opposition newspaper in the early 1860s. If Serbia were to become modern, they argued, it would have to be first in the political arena, and only later, through enactment of the proper political program, through economic development.

Jovan Ristić agreed with the general line of argument that Serbia could be made politically modern, but, unlike Liberals such as Vladimir Jovanović, his model was not England or France but Prussia. Whereas he agreed with the left-Liberals that Serbia should have the legislature that its traditions demanded, a skupština, his twofold plan for Serbia had a distinctly patriarchal flavor rather than a democratic one. Externally, Ristić wanted Serbia to unify its scattered people much as Italy or Germany had done and to become an independent state under the domination of neither Austria nor Russia. This would give Serbia a place among undeniably modern companions, the sovereign states of Europe. Internally, though Ristić spoke a good deal about the nation and the people, in actuality, much like liberals throughout Europe during the middle third of the nineteenth century, he believed that society should take its lead from the government, not vice versa. More precisely, Ristić thought that leadership should come from the minister president, a dignity to which he aspired.[5]

In the five years following Michael's assassination Ristić was able to take advantage of the youth of the prince and the maladroitness of his co-regent Blaznavac to create the kind of governmental organization be believed would stabilize Serbia at the same time that it gave him the opportunity to dominate its politics. The Grand National Assembly (*Velika narodne skupština*) that formally elected Milan as prince in 1868 had, without considering it at all, approved a program of seventeen points, including several Liberal demands from the days of the Saint Andrew's skupština. Ristić understood immediately that he could seize on the authority of this resolution to reshape the form of Serbia's government. Using it as justification, in December 1868 he convened seventy-five delegates from around the country to discuss whether Serbia should adopt a new constitutional arrangement to replace the Ottoman law of 1838, which Michael had rewritten in 1861. With little discussion and only one dissent, the Nikoljski odbor, as this group was called, adopted Ristić's view that a change was needed. The question of just what the new constitution should include was more controversial. The main point of disagreement—one that concerned Ristić very much—was whether the skupština, which everyone agreed should have an important role, should be unicameral or bicameral. Ristić proposed that an upper house consisting of the State Council plus members appointed by the government for limited terms meet with the elected skupština while it was in session. His left-Liberal opponents proposed a unicameral skupština entirely elected by the people. The principle involved was fundamental; would the ultimate power lie in the hands of the skupština or in the hands of the government? When Ristić used the opportunity presented by the king's minority to write a new constitution in 1868, he took this issue out of the realm of oppositional rhetoric and placed it on the agenda of actual politics. Rescued from abstraction, it remained a central issue of Serbian politics for the rest of the nineteenth century.

After meeting for two weeks, the Nikoljski odbor broke up without deciding how the skupština should be structured but having at least provided Ristić with what he wanted: a formal call for a new constitution. Using this justification, Ristić had no great difficulty in getting the other two regents to agree to convening a Grand National Assembly in mid-1869 in Kragujevac, Miloš's traditional capital. Ristić held three trump cards at this constitutional convention. First, it met far away from the relatively liberal political currents of Belgrade. Second, the delegates were mostly local peasant patriarchs, unfamiliar with the niceties of constitutional theory and prone to accept whatever came from above.[6] Third, Ristić wrote the draft constitution himself. It came as no surprise, therefore, that Ristić's draft sailed through the Kragujevac skupština with only desultory discussion, despite the fact that under Michael's laws of 1861 a constitution could not be adopted during the minority of a prince.

The introduction of the constitution of 1869 was a crucial moment for the development of Serbian politics. It could not have happened except by a series of accidents—Michael's assassination, Blaznavac's impetuous swearing in of Milan Obrenović, and the appearance on the scene of a determined Jovan Ristić. This was not a constitution that emerged out of any social movement. But once it was in place, the imperatives it contained began to work even without a social engine. Despite Ristić's efforts to create a tutorial system in which the head of state would be able to manipulate the body politic, adoption of the constitution ensured that a public political life would ensue—at first in the skupština and then outside of it—that arguments over the limits of public speech would fester, and that political groupings would emerge. As long as the constitution was permitted to operate, Serbian political life was pushed willy-nilly toward ever greater differentiation and definition.

When it was passed, the constitution of 1869 seemed to produce an arrangement amenable to Ristić's hopes for himself and agreeable to his view of government. The prince, of course, remained sovereign: he commanded the army; he appointed the members of the bureaucracy; he conducted foreign affairs; and he promulgated laws.[7] The State Council, on the other hand, lost its legislative function. It became an administrative court, with certain rights to advise the government on financial matters. The legislative authority lost by the State Council technically passed into the hands of the skupština, but, as we shall repeatedly see, in such a way as to maximize the ability of the government to control legislation, not only while the skupština was in session, but throughout the rest of the year. Ristić budged slightly on the question of the upper house. The prince received the right to appoint one representative to the unicameral skupština for every three who were elected popularly, but there would be no senate. Ristić hoped, doubtless, that the government's quarter, along with its ability to influence the election of regular delegates, would be more than sufficient to control the skupština. To make this even more certain, any person receiving a salary from the state—including professors, teachers, and pensioners—was ineligible for election, although governmental representatives could be picked from this group. This rule had the effect of inhibiting opposition by ensuring that the most educated members of the skupština would be friendly to the government. With this provision Ristić felt confident enough to permit the skupština to meet every year, even though this tripled the opportunities for controversy and conflict from Prince Michael's time.

But controversy was not what Ristić anticipated, and, for a while, it was not what he got. Late in 1870 he called a special skupština to complete writing the laws that had not been specified in 1869. This session produced—with somewhat more debate than that of the previous year—an electoral law, skupština by-laws, a law on ministerial responsibility, by-laws for the State Council, and a law on the press, all in the spirit of dirigisme. Under these laws ministers could be indicted for crimes, but they were accountable politically to the prince, not to the skupština. Elections to the skupština, which were to be held once every three years, were public and, for the peasantry, indirect. Every adult male Serb who paid property taxes could vote, but in the countryside the voting was indirect. Peasants elected representatives who then went to the administrative town of the district to vote publicly in the presence of the local authorities. Legislators were immune from arrest only if a majority of the skupština opposed a government request to arrest them.

Other provisions of 1870 strengthened the government's position as well, most importantly the new press law. The demands for press freedom that swept the rest of Europe in 1848 had come to Serbia a decade later at the St. Andrew's skupština, but they had not produced a change. In 1870 Serbia was still operating under a law of 1841 by which all publications had to be approved by a state-appointed censor. Ristić's new law was, if anything, a step backward. Based in part on the Prussian law of 1851, the new law took its most repressive feature from Alexander Bach's Austrian press code of 1852.[8] This provision, much favored by conservatives in Central Europe, required the publisher of any newspaper or periodical to present a copy of his publication to the local police at least one hour before beginning its distribution. If the police disapproved of an article or even a phrase, they could insist on its deletion by informing the publisher that he would be subject to some combination of fine, imprisonment, or confiscation if he went ahead with distribution. If the police felt a paper was simply too critical, they could, after two warnings, suspend it for three months. Furthermore, it was not just the author of an offending piece or the publisher who was considered responsible, but all who produced the publication, including even the typesetter.[9] This chilling law, which was characteristic of the period of repression following 1848 rather than the more liberal era of the late 1860s, but which Ristić characterized nonetheless as a "complete success," gave the regency more than enough authority to stifle the Serbian press during the rest of its term.[10]

Ristić was not a reactionary. He wanted Serbia to be as independent a state as it could be in the difficult geopolitical situation in which it existed and to model itself on the obviously powerful and successful states he knew from his student days. He understood that after the French Revolution the people had to be represented in a legislature, and that in a modern state the legislature should confirm the actions of the government. Therefore, despite his reputation for calculation and his predilection for controlling things himself—and despite building mechanisms into Serbia's constitutional system that would help him achieve this control—he also felt driven to introduce certain institutions and practices that undermined his system. The basic innovation that might do this, of course, was the skupština itself, which now began to meet annually.

Even such a fundamental innovation might have remained stillborn had Ristić continued Prince Michael's tradition of considering skupštinas closed consultations between the delegates and the government. Instead, Radivoje Milojković, one of Ristić's closest allies and later his minister of the interior, in 1870 announced that "it is the government's wish that the work of the skupština be public."[11] Ristić believed that public discussion would promote stability. "In place of underground channels for internal struggle," he said later, "it was time to create a popular organ to vent that hot air which is the normal fruit of friction among passionate peoples."[12] But this was all Ristić believed the skupština should be, a vent. With the reins of authority in his own hands, Ristić was sure he could control the largely illiterate peasant delegates.

The first test of how well Ristić could do this came in 1871. Having gotten his constitution and enabling laws onto the books in the first two years of the regency, the time had come to begin actually governing Serbia under the new rules. These rules called for the convening of the regular skupština once a year after the election of delegates for a three-year term. Already Ristić's strict interpretation of the new press law, along with bitter internal struggles among the Liberals, had resulted in the demise of the main Liberal newspaper, Ljubomir Kaljević's *Srbija*. Even during the 1871 elections government pressure at the public polling places prevented the return of any oppositionists. Nonetheless, it was still possible for a controversy to emerge at the very beginning of the skupština over what the address to the throne should contain. (In nineteenth-century parliamentary practice the sovereign opened the legislature by outlining his government's program in a speech from the throne, and the legislature answered in turn with an address to the throne.) Ristić believed that the government and the skupština should work in harmonious concert. The government should respect the members of the skupština as prominent men of the people, while the skupština should recognize the government's superior wisdom in public affairs. His position, therefore, was that the address to the throne should simply paraphrase the prince's speech. But some members of the skupština, notably Kaljević, believed the skupština should present its own program in the address.

Care had been taken to exclude possible oppositionists when the regency appointed the one-fourth of the skupština members the new constitution allowed. The center-Liberal Alimpije Vasiljević had been dropped, for example, after he had spoken up vigorously for broader guarantees of civil rights in the legislative skupština of 1870. But Kaljević was an elected delegate, not a government appointee, and he was a relatively radical Liberal. Therefore, he demanded that the address to the throne include three new proposals: to reduce control by the central bureaucracy over the smallest local unit of government, the opština, which would increase local spontaneity and initiative; to introduce free trade into the countryside, which would allow peasants to open village shops; and to enact a new tariff law, which would protect Serbian merchants. In years to come these proposals were to lead to bitter and protracted debate, but in 1871 Ristić so completely controlled the skupština that Kaljević could find only three cosponsors for his proposed additions to the address, and they failed.

Later in the session Ristić gave the skupština a strong warning that he did not expect to hear any reform proposals from the floor. When Kaljević proposed a liberalization of the press law, Ristić responded by having one of his supporters introduce a law for preventive detention. Although the government finally let this threat die without actually proposing any legislation, Minister President Radivoje Milojković told the delegates ominously before the skupština closed that "the government will use all means to hinder the work of 'troublemakers,' knowing that it can count on the help and support of the skupština."[13]

This first skupština under the new constitution seemed to show that a determined leader would have little trouble controlling the Serbian political process. Ristić was having equal success in his personal struggle with his co-regent, Colonel Milivoje Blaznavac, who aspired at least as high as did his rival. Ristić was a great deal more supple than the heavy-handed Blaznavac. Each step in the construction of Ristić's system seemed a logical extension of an earlier mandate of the nation, starting with the proposals of the Grand National Assembly of 1868, but each step also strengthened the civil government's control of the political process and lessened the potential impact of the few officers that led Serbia's tiny professional army. Any whenever Ristić and his ally Milojković needed to thwart some initiative of Blaznavac, they simply told him that the skupština would never go along with his idea.

In foreign policy, too, Ristić's true vocation, Blaznavac found himself outmaneuvered. Blaznavac was an Austrophile, whereas Ristić was a pragmatist who hoped to place Serbia in an independent position exactly between Russia and Austria. The appointment of Blaznavac to the regency had satisfied the Austrians that the pro-Austrian stance adopted by Prince Michael in his last year would be continued, but quite naturally this made the Russians unhappy. Their candidate for prince in 1868 had been Nikola of Montenegro, a grown man and staunch Russophile. Moreover, the constitution of 1869 was a direct affront to the Russian principle of autocracy. But Ristić, undeterred by this antipathy, kept seeking ways to let the Russians know he distrusted Austria, in order to edge Serbia away from complete dependence on the Habsburgs. When an opportunity rose for the still underage Prince Milan to visit Tsar Alexander II at his Crimean estate at Livadia in the fall of 1871, Ristić convinced Blaznavac that their popularity and future ability to remain in power depended on cultivating the Russian link.[14] Blaznavac acquiesced, but it was Ristić who gained the appreciation of the Russians and even some grudging respect from the Austrians.

If the struggle for personal power had remained one between Blaznavac and Ristić, there is no doubt who would have won out. But in 1872 a new and quite formidable contender entered the arena, Prince Milan himself, who came of age in that year. The eighteen-year-old prince was not particularly happy with the way his regents had managed affairs for him. He said later that he had felt like sending them to prison for introducing the constitution of 1869, but had held back because he realized that "as a young unknown man he might ruin himself instead."[15] One of Milan's first acts was to appoint his own cabinet to take the place of the caretaker regime that Ristić had dominated. The obvious candidate for minister president was the man whose control of the Belgrade garrison had made Milan the prince. So, despite being outmaneuvered at every turn by Ristić, Blaznavac suddenly found himself Milan's first minister president, while Ristić became minister of foreign affairs.[16]

Before the character of the new government became firmly established, however, it was over: early in 1873 Milivoje Baznavac died unexpectedly of a heart attack.[17] Now, with his military leader gone, Prince Milan faced a more difficult decision in seeking a minister president. His favorite was Jovan Marinović, a protégé of Ilija Garašanin, the creator of Serbia's bureaucratic system and leader of the conservative faction. But the young Milan knew he could not ignore Ristić, now Serbia's most important political figure. Therefore, he asked Marinović to form a government, but suggested that it include Ristić as minister of internal affairs. Ristić, however, would not accept that portfolio, which he considered a demotion. This irritated Marinović, who actually did not want to bring Ristić into the government at all, since he considered him responsible for destroying the power of the State Council that Marinović and Garašanin had created in the 1840s and 1850s. Rather than go against the prince's wishes that Ristić be included, Marinović decided to step aside. The retired Garašanin, who agreed with Marinović that Ristić's constitution had inappropriately introduced "forms from foreign lands" into Serbia, nonetheless urged Marinović to forget "that old reserve, which no one will understand, and try to help in a loyal but more energetic way." But Marinović refused. "Let Ristić fix what he has broken," he pouted.[18]

Reluctantly, Milan turned to Ristić, but in doing so took care to ensure that military affairs would continue to be under the prince's control. "Please outline for me a short program of the direction you will follow," he wrote to his foreign minister, "and name for me the men who will help you in effecting your thoughts. It is even more important for me to know these things since I have decided in the future to concern myself more with military affairs, and for that reason I insist that the minister of war be as little responsible to the ministry as possible, and that he work mainly in agreement with me."[19] But just because Milan wanted to keep control of military affairs did not mean he intended to stay out of politics. When Ristić tried to create a strong Liberal ministry that included his friend and ally, Radivoje Milojković, and the important Liberal from 1858, Jevrem Grujić, whom Ristić had unsuccessfully proposed to Prince Michael for a ministerial position in 1867, Milan refused to accept the list.[20] Ristić eventually was forced to put together a ministry of lesser persons with which he himself was not satisfied, but which gained his major objective.[21] On April 5, 1873, the first Ristić government took office.

Ristić's accession to power as head of a regular government set two important precedents. For the first time in Serbian experience the entire ministry represented one political grouping under the leadership of someone other than the prince. This kind of ministerial government was exactly what Ristić had sought to create by the reforms of the regency period. The new government was not a parliamentary one since it remained responsible to the prince, but neither was it a simple reflection of the patrimonial power of the prince or a cabal of opponents to him. The second significant development was that Milan explicitly established his personal control over the army. In 1873 the small size of the officer corps did not permit Milan to turn this control to immediate use, but over the years his interest in creating a support for the crown in a country that had no landholding aristocracy had, by 1900, led to the creation of a new, powerful element in the political equation, the officer corps.[22]

Ristić knew what his first task had to be: to reestablish good relations with Austria, which had grown increasingly hostile since Prince Milans' trip to Livadia. The Austrians had begun to use a tool they were to find useful for the next thirty years: economic pressure. When relations had been friendly under the regency, Austrian steamships on the Danube had begun calling at Serbian ports. After the Livadia trip they stopped.[23] Austria's new foreign minister, Gyula Andrássy, now even hinted that Austria might halt Serbian livestock exports into the Habsburg Empire. Ristić's answer to this pressure was analogous to the one he used to improve relations with Russia: a trip by Milan, this time to Vienna. Two weeks after being appointed minister president in April 1873, Ristić was off to make the arrangements for the trip, albeit with "the greatest disgust."[24]

Milan's trip to Vienna was very successful from the point of view of Serbia's foreign relations but a serious setback for Ristić's personal ambitions. Austro-Serbian relations improved markedly, but during the journey the prince's traveling companion, Filip Hristić, Ristić's conservative rival from the 1860s as well as his brother-in-law, began to undermine Ristić's position with the impressionable Milan by accusing Ristić of permitting the former minister of war, Jovan Belimarković, to follow questionable procurement practices. Rumors in Belgrade claimed, among other things, that Belimarković had allowed his close relative Zivko Karabiberović to obtain army contracts, by which he supplied goods of poor quality for high prices. As an officer, Belimarković had been close to Blaznavac and Milan, and it was not difficult to suggest to the prince that Ristić was somehow undermining the prince's authority with the officer corps. Additional fuel was added to the fire by accusing Ristić of condoning the losses suffered by the First Serbian Bank, of which Karabiberović had been the head. The bank had failed, causing the loss of all its capital, after two Austro-Hungarian enterprises in which it invested most of its money collapsed in the crisis of 1873. Some claimed that this happened because of Karabiberović's incompetence or corruption, and they demanded restitution.

Hristić—who had been Serbia's representative at the Porte during the regency—had irritated Ristić several times since Blaznavac's death by advising him to bring Jovan Marinović into the government, and Ristić had told him to mind his own business.[26] Now, by filling Milan's ear with proposals for change, proposals that Milan, who hated the cold and imposing Ristić, was none too reluctant to hear, Hristić had his revenge.[27] Realizing that he was in a difficult position, Ristić tried to clear the air by submitting his government's resignation immediately upon Milan's return. After writing four different letters accepting the resignation, ranging from nasty to coldly polite, Milan finally let Ristić go and appointed Marinović to head the new government.[28] Ristić's departure signaled the true end of the regency period. The time of transition was over, and the parliamentary period of Serbian politics began.

Jovan Marinović was by birth a Bosnian who came to Serbia as a child, the story has it, when an uncle who was fleeing Bosnia impulsively grabbed him up, put him in one of his saddle baskets, and carried him off to Kragujevac. Excelling as a young student in what was then the capital of Serbia, Marinović entered Prince Miloš's service at the tender age of sixteen. In 1841, when he was twenty, Marinović went abroad to study, but, with the outbreak of the crisis of 1842 that brought Alexander Karadjordjević to the throne, he chose to return and quickly became a moderately high official for the State Council. By the 1850s Marinović had mastered the refined language of diplomatic French and transformed himself from a Bosnian orphan into a cultured European. Marinović not only spoke like a gentleman, he lived like one. Having married the daughter of Miša Anastasijević, who, as Belgrade's richest man in the nineteenth century, is still celebrated in Serbian nursery rhymes, Marinović maintained one of the largest houses in Belgrade, pursuing an elegant and restrained life-style. His marriage also put Marinović in contact with Ilija Garašanin, Serbia's dominant politician through the 1840s, 1850s, and 1860s. The two men became not only political allies, but close friends.[29]

In 1861, under Prince Michael, Marinović became president of the State Council. Working closely with Michael and Garašanin, he emerged as a public servant of the most valuable kind. Skilled in his assigned diplomatic missions, his lack of ambition posed no threat to those above him. Despite his passive character, when Ilija Garašanin left public life in 1867 Marinović became the leader of the Old Conservatives, as historians now call them. Unlike Garašanin, Marinović was not a fighter. For example, when approval of the State Council had been necessary to permit the introduction of the constitution of 1869, Marinović, as president of that body, simply gave Ristić approval to go ahead, even though his personal view was that the constitution was a mistaken step toward democratization and liberalization.

When he came to power in 1873, therefore, Marinović had neither the inclination nor the ambition to run a narrow party government like Ristić's. He hoped to preside, as he put it, over an administration without "party aspirations" or "personal pretensions."[30] To demonstrate his approach, he appointed two Liberals to the State Council and included two surprises in his cabinet. The first was his new minister of finance, Čedomil Mijatović, a Liberal, who had been Serbian representative in London and minister of finance in the last months of Ristić's government, and of whom we shall hear more later. [31] Even more surprising was the appointment of Aćim Čumić, one of the more unstable political figures in Serbian history. [32] A professor of criminal law who had a reputation of lecturing in a preposterously loud voice, Čumić had been one of the most extreme opponents of the regency and particularly of Ristić. He created a sensation in the Nikoljski odbor in 1869 when he opposed the government's proposal for an appointed upper house and suggested members should be elected for life. [33] Late in 1870 he was elected "kmet" (that is, president) of the Belgrade opština, despite heavy opposition from the police. [34] His election not only irritated the government, it led to a student revolt in the Velika škola (Belgrade Academy) when the government appointed a professor to take Čumić's place who did not have the approval of the faculty senate. [35] Ristić stepped in, expelled some of the boycotting students, and deposed Čumić from his job as kmet as well. Čumić became so outraged that, as Slobodan Jovanović put it, he forgot he was a conservative and went over temporarily to the socialists. [36] Only enormous government pressure and chicanery prevented his election to the regular skupština of 1871. [37] Prone to citation for contempt for his outrageous statements in court, cuckolded by the Austrian consul, hating Ristić, but considered more a demagogue than a real conservative, Čumić entered Marinović's government as minister of the interior, that is, head of the police. [38]

Čumić's first public act set the tone for the remarkable changes that this ostensibly conservative government was to undertake, and set the stage for some of its contradictions as well. It demonstrated also how the introduction of a Western constitution had created a logic of its own that implied the expansion of the space in which political life occurred. Only a few days after the composition of the government was announced, Čumić publicly instructed all police officials to permit the press to discuss issues freely. When a skupština member complained that two newspapers were writing articles that were much too critical, Čumić responded that the government could only close papers that were convicted of a breach in the press law by a court, not just those it disagreed with. Even though Čumić did not follow his own advice and quickly began using his powers against the press, his declaration was a first in Serbian public life. The minister of justice, Mita Cenić, also usually identified today as an Old Conservative, followed this with an instruction to all judges that henceforth they should reach their decisions not according to wealth, and especially not according to political affiliation, but according to the merits of the case at hand.[39] These two announcements indicate how misleading it is simply to refer to Ristić as a Liberal and Marinović as a Conservative. Serbian political life was still very unformed and ideological positions had not yet solidified. Ristić introduced the constitution of 1869, but since he believed the rightful holders of state authority were the ministers, he had ruled in an arbitrary and ruthless way. Marinović hated the constitution of 1869, but since he believed in moderation, compromise, and the rule of law rather than faction, his administration was notable for its restraint, at least at first. Contemporaries criticized this trait in Marinović as weakness, but Serbian politics would surely have taken a much less stormy course had his accommodating style penetrated Serbian public life a bit more deeply.

Marinović had very little time to get his government on its feet before the skupština of 1873 convened, the third session of its three-year mandate of 1871. Three weeks after Marinović took office the prince addressed the opening session in Kragujevac, and immediately the question re-emerged of how the skupština should respond.[40] As in the past two years, Ljubomir Kaljević argued in favor of a statement about ministerial responsibility and a free press law, while most delegates, elected under Ristić's tutelage, argued that to place proposals in the address to the throne offended the dignity of the prince's sovereignty. In 1871 and 1872 Ristić had refused to hear of any initiatives in the skupština's address. But this year the new minister president said, "The government will not make a question of this point, nor will it . . . request the skupština not to place new matters in the address."[41] With this encouragement from the top, the skupština included an extra sentence in its address to the throne, saying it hoped that the laws on ministerial responsibility and the press could be improved.[42] With such small successes the creation of a parliamentary system built on European models proceeded.

Though the two issues of ministerial responsibility and freedom of the press may sound bland, in fact they constituted two of the most burning issues of the day, and Marinović was unwilling—some would say unable—to sweep either of them under the rug. In fact, Marinović ensured that contentious issues such as these would be raised in the skupština through another procedural innovation, permitting interpellations, or questions from the floor. Ristić had opened up Serbian political life significantly by making skupština sessions public. Now Marinović permitted the skupština to become a real force for contrasting views.

In the freer atmosphere produced by these changes, Ljubomir Kaljević was able to get thirty-eight delegates to sign his proposal to delete the provisions of the press law that required showing a copy of a newspaper to the police at least one hour before publication. This contrasted strongly with the three delegates he had gotten to support his suggestion for a substantive address to the throne in 1871. The legislative committee to which the press proposal was sent waited until the very last day of the session, December 31, before recommending against Kaljević's proposal. According to Nikola Krstić, spokesman for the majority, it was better to prevent poisoning the people than to have to find remedies after the fact. "We know from experience what it means to give the police leeway," Kaljević responded. "Mr. Krstić says the authorities are not permitted to [abuse their authority], but that is not true. There is nothing that is not permitted to the authorities."[43] One of Kaljević's supporters queried how dangerous the press could be. "It never killed a man nor burned a haystack."[44] But since Kaljević could not muster a majority and time was running out, he finally withdrew his proposal, ending the question for the time being.[45]

Despite the skupština's unwillingness to support a liberal law on the press, and despite the fact that the government was ostensibly in the hands of the Old Conservatives, the skupština of 1873 produced some of the most dramatic reforms ever enacted by a Serbian legislature. Many of these changes reflected the new sense of inferiority that educated Serbs felt when they contemplated Europe. Other changes suggested how the smallholding structure of the Serbian countryside acted to limit European innovations to the political sphere, about which most peasants had little knowledge or interest, and to hinder changes that might permit Serbia to develop economically at the expense of the interests of ordinary peasant households.

Several innovations indicated that Serbian politicians were acutely aware of their deficiencies in comparison with Europe. On December 23 the skupština abolished corporal punishment, long the administrative right of any local policeman, accepting the assessment of the subcommittee that the law would "erase the memory of that time when we were far below the European peoples, and place us . . . in the ranks of the rest of the cultivated European states."[46] When the skupština allocated funds for building new jails, it did so with the hope that Serbia would get "modern prisons such as existed in western Europe."[47] In order to turn Serbian mercantile practice away from Ottoman standards and folk measurements toward European ones, the skupština adopted the metric system, to be fully implemented by 1880, and it authorized the minting of silver money (although this proved impossible until after independence).

Some Liberals wanted to push Europeanization further by promoting industry in Serbia. One obvious way to do this would have been to introduce a protective tariff, but as a vassal state of the Ottoman Empire Serbia was bound by Ottoman conventions with Austria that limited duties to 3 percent ad valorem. Unable to change this, Marinović, who agreed with the Liberals that home industries needed encouragement, proposed a scheme of concessions by which the government could grant monopolies for up to fifteen years, waive tariff payments for ten years, and even grant the use of government land for up to thirty years.[48] The proposal made foreigners eligible for these concessions, and for that reason Ristić's allies opposed the law, because they knew the only ones with the money and skill to take advantage of it would be Austrian subjects.[49] Nevertheless, after some debate the skupština adopted Marinović's scheme.

If the above reforms indicated a conscious effort to modernize by Europeanizing, even by industrializing, by far the most important legislation of this skupština, the Law on Six Days Plowing, as it was called, pointed in a different direction. A "day of plowing," also called a "morning" (jutro), was a standard unit of traditional measure equivalent to about 1.4 acres. Thus six "days of plowing" equaled about 8.5 acres.[50] The new law forbade a peasant from pledging that much of his holding as security for a loan and prohibited any sale or alienation of his homesite and garden. Prince Miloš promulgated the initial law of this sort, but this is the first instance in the period we are considering that the government acted to ensure that Serbian peasants would continue to live according to their smallholding traditions.

Surprisingly enough, Prince Milan was one of the few who recognized that this meant committing the government to a policy of underdevelopment. He believed that the atrocious rates of interest, which he said reached as high as 1 percent per day in the villages, were a good thing because they weeded out the weak producers and consolidated the land in holdings that were big enough to permit modern forms of agriculture.[51] Some Liberals agreed, arguing that the new law infringed on the rights of property and hindered the development of a national credit system by preventing the peasantry from borrowing on their homesteads. Most members of the skupština, however, favored the law. For the twentieth-century observer this does not seem consistent with their short-term interests. As the more successful of the smallholders, including many who lent money at interest, the members of the skupština might well have favored squeezing the smaller peasant in order to increase their own holdings. But as Michael Palairet has shown, they did not think in this market-oriented way.[52] Although some of them sold livestock at market, they were still intimately linked with an ethic of protecting the forest lands on which Serbs of an earlier generation had produced pigs. The most successful Serbian peasants, therefore, maximized their ownership of open land and forest, rather than arable land, and considered production of grain for sale unethical. In their view the Law on Six Days Plowing would help make sure that most Serbian peasants would not have to resort to the demeaning practice of selling grain for cash, which they denigrated as "gypsying."

Marinović, as was his habit, took a hands-off attitude to the proposal, letting the skupština work out the law on its own, although he did propose a response to the criticism that the law hindered the development of a credit system. Under this amendment, which the skupština approved, a peasant could mortgage the protected portion of his lands, but only to the government, which would lend him money in small amounts at modest interest rates. Thus the peasant could have his land and eat from it too.

The Law on Six Days Plowing constituted the government's half of an implicit bargain reached between the peasantry and the state. The bargain was essentially this: the state would encourage, or even force, the peasants to retain immediate access to their means of social reproduction. Put another way, the state promised not to threaten the traditional life-style of the smallholders, even though economic development could come only with severe dislocation in the countryside. In return, the peasants would let the intellectuals who operated the state introduce as many European-style political changes as they wanted. This deal ensured that efforts to industrialize, such as the law on subsidies to industry, would not work. Without incentives to enter into uncertain market relations, the growth of these relations would be difficult to initiate and sustain. On the other side, if the unspoken bargain could be maintained, the intelligentsia would have neither incentive nor need to approach the peasantry politically. The constitution made possible an opening up of the political system, but exploitation of this new public space would be left to the educated.

There remained one person who was not happy with appeasing the peasantry, and that was Prince Milan. But Milan was not left without a victory of his own. During the regular session of the skupština two liberal delegates, Jovan Bošković and Aleksandar Nikolajević, used the new right of interpellation from the floor introduced by Marinović to touch off an acrimonious debate on the question of ministerial responsibility by again raising the question of nepotism and fraud by former minister Jovan Belimarković, who seemed on the verge of getting off scot-free. A decision by the

Court of Appeals that, as minister of the government, Belimarković could not stand ordinary trial upset the delegates. Under the constitutional provisions for ministerial responsibility, a minister could only be indicted by the skupština itself, and so Bošković and Nikolajević called for such action. After a certain amount of outrage had been vented against the court for seemingly exonerating Belimarković on a technicality, Marinović convinced a reluctant prince to authorize a special session after the regular one closed to consider indicting the accused former minister; Marinović, moreover, agreed to bring a proposal for improving the law on ministerial responsibility to the next session of the assembly in 1874.[53]

When the regular session of the 1873 skupština closed on the last day of the year, Milan immediately ordered the special session to convene on January 14. After considering the budget it had not passed in the regular session—and for the first time effecting some relatively minor changes in the government's proposal—the skupština immediately made it clear that it was very unhappy about Belimarković. It even refused to list Belimarković's relative, Živko Karabiberović, who had been president of the 1873 skupština, on its list of candidates for skupština president for the special session.[54] Nevertheless, after a full discussion in which Belimarković admitted he broke the law but defended himself by claiming that this had saved the government money, the skupština voted 56 to 22 not to indict him. This decision not only satisfied Milan, who had lobbied heavily for Belimarković both personally and through his ministers, but it also showed why the left-Liberals were so thoroughly dissatisfied with the law on ministerial responsibility. The only way a minister could be removed from office was through a criminal conviction; yet, even if the minister had committed a crime the courts would not touch him without skupština approval. The relative ease with which Belimarković escaped was proof of how successfully Ristić had built ministerial inviolability into his constitution of 1869.

The explanation of the fruitful activity of the 1873 skupština in comparison with those of 1871 and 1872 can be found to a significant degree in Marinović's style, which was so antithetical to the stereotype of fiery Serbian behavior. Marinović was conservative. For example, he ensured that a new press law did not pass, and he vigorously supported Belimarković. But he did not take the tutorial approach institutionalized by both Garašanin and Ristić. Ideas that came from the skupština floor were not illegitimate for him simply because his government did not initiate them. Marinović also believed that all the nonsocialist political factions should have their representatives in the skupština, and even on the State Council, although he preferred to appoint them himself rather than see them popularly elected. Marinović knew that a skupština elected without government interference would favor the opposition, but he believed also that a government that must rely on force was not legitimate.[55] This attitude might have helped Serbian politics mature had Marinović been able to stay in office as long as, say, Robert Walpole. But he could not. Friends as well as enemies considered him pusillanimous, a perception that hampered his popularity and ability to lead.[56]

Even in the area in which Marinović was considered most expert, foreign affairs, he did not project strength. A diplomat in the narrow sense of the term, a good negotiator and an elegant phrasemaker, Marinović was not a statesman. Worse, he seemed too accommodating to foreigners. It was because of this perceived weakness that Marinović's popularity began to wane by mid-1874. As we have seen, Ristić had tried to keep Serbia balanced between Austria and Russia by sending Prince Milan on judiciously chosen trips to Livadia and Vienna. Now, however, those powers, having allied themselves in the Three Emperors' League (Dreikaiserbund) to maintain stability in Southeastern Europe, insisted that Milan pay a visit to his suzerain, the Ottoman sultan. Ristić had not wanted Milan to do this unless the promise of a visit could be used to wring some concessions from the Porte before departure, but Marinović felt it might be possible to achieve a territorial concession on Mali Zvornik or an agreement on railroad-building through personal negotiations on the spot.[57] Accordingly, without prior agreement on the resolution of any outstanding questions, in the spring of 1874 Milan and his Minister President Marinović paid an official visit to the sultan.[58] The visit could have been seen as merely a meaningless courtesy call, required by Serbia's formal allegiance to the Porte. However, the last visit a Serbian prince had made to Istanbul occurred only after the Turks had turned over all their fortresses on Serbian soil to the Serbian government (Prince Michael in 1867), so expectations were high that Milan would also achieve some important gain. Needless to say, Jovan Ristić, always undermining those in power when he was not, did everything he could to encourage this hope, which he knew could not be fulfilled.[59] As Ristić anticipated, the Ottomans conceded nothing, and Marinović returned with only "two sheep and a horse," as one contemporary put it.[60]

Milan did not seem particularly concerned by this failure. Having spent the entire month of May with Marinović on the trip to Istanbul, the prince now proposed that the two depart on a grand tour of Europe as soon as possible. Marinović's friends advised him against leaving home when it seemed his strength was ebbing, but Marinović believed he could recoup his failure in Istanbul by taking the case for Mali Zvornik and the railroad concessions to foreign governments in person. After a delay, during which Milan tried to raise the money he needed to travel in the extravagant mode to which he was accustomed, the two departed with a large entourage on July 10.[61]

Before Marinović left, however, he began preparations for the elections to the next skupština. Expiration of the three-year terms of 1871 made new elections mandatory. Benjamin Kállay, the Austrian consul, advised Marinović to hold them before he left, but Marinović decided to hold them only a week or so before the skupština convened in order to prevent potential opposition from influencing or organizing the delegates.[62] But he must have left instructions with his minister of the interior, Aćim Čumić, to make the necessary preparations, because already in June Čumić was replacing local officials appointed by the regency with persons loyal to the conservatives. Čumić also started financing new village dram shops from a secret fund, thereby ensuring that the place local peasants gathered would be in the hands of government supporters.[63]

Much more importantly for the fate of Marinović's government, and much more ominously for the future of Serbian politics,

Čumić went after the two men who had reopened the accusation against Belimarković at the 1873 skupština, Jovan Bošković and Aleksander Nikolajević. The attack on the latter became notorious, for in June a minor government official who had been caught embezzling claimed he had given the proceeds to Nikolajević. Nikolajević denied the charge but was hauled off in chains and thrown into the murky and filthy Požarevac jail, which was usually reserved for serious offenders. Many persons offered to stand bail for Nikolajević, one of the richest and most respected men in Požarevac. But Čumić did not let him out until August 11, after a month in prison, and then only after the embezzled money was found at the home of a relative of the original accuser and it became apparent that the entire affair was a plot to discredit the man who raised the uncomfortable Belimarković issue. Čumić's pursuit of Nikolajević only further discredited a government that already, by Čumić's own analysis, had suffered a loss of prestige when it had been unable to contain the public squabbling over the Belimarković affair.[64] Milan and Čumić got their short-lived revenge on Nikolajević, but the real consequences were paid by Marinović.

In June 1874 another cloud appeared on Marinović's horizon, the formation of a new political newspaper, *Istok* (The East), under the influence of Jovan Ristić.[65] The paper's program, which it claimed in its first issue was well known to its readers, called for the formation of a "liberal-national party" (*slobodnjačko-narodna partija*) which would seek "freedom at home and a national policy abroad."[66] "Freedom at home" referred to a restricted list of ordinary liberal demands, including a free press, progress in education, and separation of the police from the courts; all of which sounded considerably better in print than some remembered them from Ristić's earlier practices. More threatening to Marinović, however, was the call for a "national policy abroad." *Istok* proposed that Serbia assume the role in the Balkans that Piedmont/Sardinia had taken in Italy fifteen years earlier. This meant two things: first, not relying on Austria, or indeed on any other power, and second, aggressively agitating among the Serbs and other south Slavs beyond the borders of the principality for their integration into an independent Serbian state. Both of *Istok's* policies were calculated to be popular with ordinary literate Serbs, but neither could be accepted by Marinović, who understood better than most Serbia's weakness in the midst of strong neighbors.

Prince Milan and his minister president arrived back in Serbia on September 30 after a leisurely twelve-week promenade through Europe.[67] Almost immediately Marinović called for elections on November 5 and announced the skupština session for two weeks thereafter. This was the first election in Serbia to be fought relatively openly, although that was in part simply a result of confusion and bungling. Čumić had installed loyal local officials but he had not instructed them clearly on what they were supposed to do. Most supported government candidates, but a number of them did not. Čumić's naive notion of how to obtain a majority for the government was simply to defeat anyone identified as a trouble-maker. He did not foresee the potentially fatal consequences of the outrageous measures he had taken in attempting to defeat Nikolajević and his colleague Bošković, nor did he grasp how much frustration his strenuous efforts against Jevrem Marković, the brother of Serbia's leading socialist, would engender. If Čumić was a primitive administrator over the long haul, he had a high degree of short-term energy. Throwing himself into the election, he made it a much more emotional affair than the temperate Marinović probably wanted, and a much less successful one as well.[68]

Despite the emotional heat generated by the elections, neither Ristić nor Marinović took effective steps toward running their own candidates or organizing local supporters. Lack of desire did not prevent them. Both Conservatives and Liberals spoke as if parties existed, and *Istok* claimed its main goal was the formation of a "liberal-national" party. But organizational inexperience and lassitude hindered them, as did the lack of guarantees protecting freedom of assembly in Ristić's constitution of 1869. More importantly, neither the Liberals nor the Conservatives had a concrete vision of what an electoral party would be like, and neither felt any necessity to approach the electorate directly. If in actuality Serbian political factions were based on the leadership of strong individuals, in theory these same individuals professed to believe that political parties were built around abstractions. Governments organized bureaucracies, perhaps, but parties were organized around correct principles.[69] The Conservatives considered themselves educated guardians of the prince and of high culture, and believed in a passive foreign policy. They dismissed the nation as a mass of ignorant peasants for whom those with knowledge (*znanje*) were destined to provide guidance. Ristić's Liberals, on the other hand, professed the principles of 1858 and were much more vigorously nationalistic than the Conservatives. Only the extreme left wing of the Liberals rejected the idea of paternalism, which remained the common denominator of most educated Serbs. At this early stage in the reorientation of Serbian politics, no politician had yet grasped the possibilities for mobilizing the electorate. In fact, quite the opposite was true. Although the Liberals talked a good deal more about the nation than did the Conservatives, they did not think of the Serbian peasant as ready for real participation in the sophisticated game of politics. Power meant for them a strong leader backed by correct opinion, not the support of an organized electorate. Therefore, despite reference to Liberal and Conservative, and despite the use of the term "party" in political discourse, candidates to the skupština ran locally on the basis of their personalities and reputations, rather than on the basis of their political philosophies, which remained loose and changing. And once in the skupština representatives did not see themselves as part of any extra-parliamentary organization, but rather voted according to their personal preferences and passing allegiances. There were no parties, only tendencies; there were no organizations, only loyalties to strong individuals.

Nevertheless, the elections were hard fought at the local level. Even before their conclusion the Liberals were predicting Marinović's government would fall, and when the results came in *Istok* called the election a complete victory for the "liberal national-freethinking party."[70] "So far as we can see at this moment," the paper wrote the day after the election, "we [are] . . . completely satisfied." *Istok* cited only one absolute victory for the Conservatives, the election of Milutin Garašanin, son of the late Ilija Garašanin, and went on to list eighteen persons whose election the Liberals found particularly satisfying.[71] The list indicates how unformed and tentative political boundaries were at this time. It contains several names that later were associated with vigorous opposition to the Liberals, such as Adam Bogosavljević, the populist-socialist, and Miloš Glišić, a leader of the Progressives in the 1880s. But in 1874 only two directions were generally recognized, government and opposition, which translated loosely into Conservative and Liberal. It was enough not to be a government man to be considered a Liberal.

Appointment of the government's quarter to the skupština provided a chance for Marinović to redress his losses. However, Marinović had not abandoned hope of creating a government "without party aspirations." When he came to power in 1873 he had disheartened his supporters by appointing a few Liberals to the State Council. Now he outraged them by proposing that Ristić be included in the government's delegation. "The prince needs people who have a party," he was reported to have said, "and Ristić represents a force that cannot be ignored." "What then of our principles?" his ministers asked. What principles? Marinović responded: "The most important thing is to protect the crown and in some way get things moving."[72] Thwarted by his colleagues from taking this accommodating step toward Ristić, Marinović tried to make a deal with the 1858 wing of the Liberals, led by Jevrem Grujić, whom he appointed to the skupština. Once again his supporters objected. In their none-too-sophisticated view a "fusionist" or coalition policy was a sign of intolerable weakness. Marinović appointed Grujić anyway. "From this it follows," observed Dr. Nikola Krstić, a conservative judge and legal specialist, "that this year's skupština can be interesting."[73]

Krstić was right. By the time the skupština opened on November 20, excitement was running high, helped along by Marinović's decision to hold the assembly in Belgrade, rather than in the traditional Kragujevac, which was a long, one-day trip from the capital. The first test of the government's strength, the election of the six candidates out of which the prince would choose the president and vice president of the assembly, went smoothly. Jovan Krsmanović, a Conservative who had been the strongest candidate from Belgrade, received the greatest number of votes; but as part of the plan of cooperation worked out by Marinović the prince chose Djordje Topuzović of Šabac, a Conservative who was acceptable to the Liberals, as president and Jevrem Grujić as vice president.[74] The prince did his part in attempting to defuse the electric mood by delivering a calm, indeed dull, address from the throne in which he reported on his visit to Istanbul and apologized that the government would not be able to present a new law on ministerial responsibility since, in the formula worked out by the Conservatives to avoid the issue, this was covered by the constitution.[75]

The restless skupština did not take this last announcement in good grace, and other signs pointed to the likelihood of a serious confrontation. Even though Marinović had gotten the president and vice president of the skupština he wanted, no bureaucrats from the government's delegation received much support in the elections to standing committees when the skupština began organizing itself.[76] The selection of four left-Liberals as secretaries clearly demonstrated the inability of the government to control events, and the membership of the skupština's Finance Committee confirmed it.[77] The skupština had three standing committees: legislative; finance; and petitions and complaints. The night before elections to these committees Čumić gathered some of his supporters to discuss how to prevent any Liberals from getting onto the finance committee. In his typically erratic and heavy-handed way he proposed getting rid of Uroš Knežević, one of the most vigorous oppositionists, by arresting him on a charge of theft. His friends dissuaded him from using this mode of attack on the opposition, but apparently he had no better plan, because the next day not only was Ljubomir Kaljević, the main person Čumić wanted to exclude from the committee, elected to it, but so was Knežević.[78]

The next struggle came over seating the socialist Jevrem Marković, who, against all odds, had been elected delegate from Jagodina (today Svetozarevo), even though the prince had let it be known that he considered a vote for Jevrem as a personal insult. Despite this clearly expressed attitude of the prince, the committee looking into the election recommended seating Marković since there was little question he had been fairly elected, even though the polling place did close slightly early. But the government insisted on a roll call vote by the full skupština. With few delegates willing to identify themselves as a personal enemy of the prince, the skupština voted 87 to 14 with 9 abstentions to invalidate Jevrem's election and call for a new one in that district.[79] Perhaps to balance matters, the skupština also decided that the election of the delegate who had defeated Jovan Bošković, another of Čumić's enemies, should also be repeated.

All of these indicators gave the government little hope that it would be able to push through a purely formal response to the prince's address from the throne. Since the debate was clearly going to be a difficult one, the skupština decided to select a special committee of eighteen persons to consider its response. By this time the election to this committee of a majority of Liberals came as no surprise.[80] Equally expected, but more controversial than anything yet to appear before a Serbian skupština, was the committee's report, which constituted what amounted to a full statement of the Liberal position. A minority report, favored by the government, held out for a courteous and uncontentious reply.

The proposed address to the throne was written by Milan Kujundžić, a philosopher of the Omladina in the 1860s and 1870s, in the style and spirit of that liberal and nationalistic movement. The most inflammatory portions of his draft were not the standard demands for a free press, freedom of assembly, educational reform, and reform of the army—although the latter was a suggestion likely to bring Milan onto the warpath.[81] The portion of the proposed address Marinović could not accept concerned foreign policy:

From Your Highness's remarks on the trip to Istanbul the national assembly has realized that not only have all those solemn undertakings toward the Serbian people that the powerful Sultan has established in the past by sworn oath been forgotten for a considerable time, but no account is taken in Istanbul of our holiest and most natural rights and duties. Our brothers by language and our comrades by history are raising ever greater complaint about our cold loyalty. . . . Even worse, we do not see that Istanbul is showing any good will toward

correcting that unjust situation. . . . Gathering together our
scattered people in conscious joint effort, understanding, and
cooperation among brotherly peoples who have the same aspirations, the same interests, and the same dangers—that is the
road toward which the national assembly with enthusiasm
wishes to direct the gaze of its Holy Ruler, that is the only
national policy.[82]

At this point in the history of Serbia, when it was still formally
part of the Ottoman Empire, the government was in no position
to accept a formal statement from the skupština couched in the
tone of injured nationalism that the left-Liberals used in the sixties,
even if Kujundžić's statement was quite modest in comparison with
the appeals that were to come within a few years. But, despite the
government's fears about the reaction of the Sublime Porte, the
majority report was accepted. So, rather than fight the foreign
policy statement on its merits, Marinović claimed that placing an
"entire program, an entire series of questions from foreign policy
to internal affairs," in the address was unconstitutional.[83] This
position was difficult to defend for two reasons: the previous year
Marinović had permitted a sentence to be added to the address
concerning ministerial responsibility, and this year he himself had
included political matters in the prince's speech.[84]

The Liberals responded to Marinović's claim that their address
was unconstitutional by pointing out that legislatures in all constitutional states made formal proposals to their governments, and so
this should be the case in Serbia too. The Liberals saw the address
issue not only as a short-term struggle over particular policy points,
which in fact were not debated, but also as part of their long-range
plan to make Serbia into a parliamentary state.[85] The Conservatives
believed the characterization of Serbia as a constitutional state was
ludicrous. Instead they stressed Serbia's dependent international
position. "We are a small people, we are a new state, and we have
many needs for which the sympathy and friendly disposition of
other more powerful countries are unavoidably necessary," argued
Milutin Garašanin. The skupština must do everything possible to
avoid giving others an excuse to take advantage of Serbian weak-

ness. "We can never forget that we are always, even this very day, before the eyes of powerful lands, who carefully follow and evaluate our every move."[86]

The debate was the most heated yet experienced in the Serbian legislature. At one point Uroš Knežević, the excitable editor of *Budućnost* [The Future], a new liberal paper, brought the proceedings completely to a halt. "I hold," Knežević said, "that a ruler is not insulted when the people tell him what is needed. A ruler cannot know everything, cannot be the best judge of everything. Our prince too cannot see and hear everything, nor can he know all the national needs. He is still young. . . ." At this point the ministers jumped up from their chairs, a great hubbub arose, and skupština president Topuzović adjourned the session until the next day, at which time the delegates excluded Knežević from their midst for thirty days for violating the constitutional prohibition on criticizing the prince.[87]

In the end Marinović won his battle over the address, but at the cost of losing the war. On December 3 the skupština rejected the committee's proposal for the Liberal address by a vote of 61 to 58, with three abstentions, and adopted the government's bland minority report as its address to the prince.[88] Marinović himself considered this adequate and sought now to present various aspects of his program to the skupština, for example, a revision to the press law.[89] But his ministers were not satisfied. Aćim Čumić, in particular, had been threatening to resign for months over various real and imagined failures of the government, and after this close call his colleagues joined him. That evening all of them, including the complaisant Marinović, went to the prince and presented their resignations. To everyone's surprise, except probably that of the scheming Čumić, Milan asked Čumić to stay behind when the ministers left.[90] By three o'clock the next morning Milan offered Čumić the new government.[91]

If Marinović's resignation was a surprise, Čumić's elevation was a sensation.[92] No one believed the unstable Čumić could last, but Milan liked the way he had gone after the accusers of Belimarković and he believed Čumić was loyal to him personally, even though shortly before the skupština opened his new minister president had demanded reforms that sounded suspiciously like those proposed by the Liberals.[93] Almost as startling was Čumić's inclusion of two left-Liberals in his cabinet. Milan met with Čumić and his proposed colleagues on December 5. The prince asked his new ministers if they would now be assured of a majority in the skupština, or whether at least they could forestall any major demonstrations against them. When they could not give the prince that assurance, Milan Piroćanac, Čumić's foreign minister, suggested that the inclusion of Ljubomir Kaljević might ensure skupština support.[94] Kaljević had been one of Ristić's main critics and opponents, was no friend of Piroćanac, and had attempted to introduce reforms with which Prince Milan can not have been entirely comfortable. Furthermore, Čumić, who had always criticized Marinović for his "fusionist" tendencies, vigorously opposed adding him. But Prince Milan liked Kaljević, whose style typified the gregarious and accommodating personality Serbs associated with his native Užice. He had proven to be very good at smoothing over difficulties in the skupština and at politicking with any and all factions. In addition, the prince was attracted to his wife. For these reasons, and because, as Milan put it, Kaljević controlled fifty votes, the prince took Piroćanac's advice and included this unusual man in his cabinet, and Serbia had its first coalition cabinet created specifically to minimize friction with the skupština.[95]

Čumić's cabinet was the first Prince Milan considered his own. Blaznavac, Ristić, and Marinović had all been obvious, almost prescribed, choices. But Čumić represented his own decision. In choosing Čumić, the still very young Milan hinted at the kind of destabilizing decisions he was to continue to make throughout his career, for Čumić was certainly not the best possible choice for minister president. Those who hoped to make Serbia into a more strictly constitutional monarchy found it a discouraging appointment. It could easily have seemed to them that the only outcome of the 1874 skupština was to discredit the moderate Marinović government and to permit Milan to install the unpredictable Čumić, a meaningless political charade of ins and outs dominated by a young and unpredictable prince.

But the skupština of 1874 signified more than that. Before it met, the role of the skupština remained in doubt. How active would it or could it be in a political culture shaped by an Ottoman past, Miloš's patriarchalism, Michael's authoritarianism, and Ristić's paternalism? With such a heritage, the introduction of Ristić's constitution was of utmost importance; for whatever its faults, it not only implied a line of liberalizing development, but it provided for an annual skupština in which that development could occur. When Marinović permitted discussion in the skupština to expand, the possibility of actual parliamentary activity in Serbia became apparent, especially to those in the opposition. The skupština of 1874 was the first to bring down a government; elections to it had been contested; debate was open and vigorous; and even the prince himself had come to realize that under the constitution of 1869 workable government required taking into account political realities in the skupština. In the five years that had passed since the installation of the new constitution the Serbian political system had opened up enormously, despite the continuing power of the police to intimidate opponents of the regime. In the new atmosphere inchoate Liberal and Conservative groupings established themselves, and both sides began to speak of forming "parties," although usually in abstract terms. A few years would pass before these vague sensations were transformed into well articulated parliamentary politics, but in contrast to the moment when Prince Michael had been assassinated, the possibility now existed. The Radicals eventually took best advantage of the opportunity. Gathered around the personality of Svetozar Marković and located in the only city in Serbia with any pretentions to industry, they began to find each other at just the moment that Serbian political life became able to receive them.

2 : THE RADICALS FIND EACH OTHER

Everyone wants to be among those who eat rather than among those who are eaten.—Adam Bogosavljević

The father of Serbian radicalism was Svetozar Marković.[1] Born in the Timok region and brought up in the heart of Šumadija, Marković—like most of his eventual allies and enemies—was a superb student, first in the Kragujevac lower schools and then in Belgrade, where he entered the gymnasium in 1860.[2] Completing both the gymnasium and the Belgrade Academy (*Velika škola*) with excellent results six years later, he won a fellowship to study engineering at the Institute of Ways and Communications in St. Petersburg. Like many perceptive young men of his time, Marković had become interested in politics while a student in Belgrade. His ideological mentor was the great Liberal opponent of Prince Michael, Vladimir Jovanović. In St. Petersburg, however, Marković came into contact with the ideas of what are today called the revolutionary democrats, especially Chernyshevsky, and adopted them as his own. In 1869 Marković transferred his studies to Zürich, both for health reasons and because he wanted to get closer to the sources of European socialism.[3]

Shortly after arriving in Zürich, Marković published his first major article, "Serbian Deficiencies," in which he criticized the opposition Liberals of the 1860s, including his former mentor Vladimir Jovanović, for accommodating themselves to the regency after Michael's murder. The young Marković believed in the Lavrovian principle that an enlightened intelligentsia could lead the masses to socialism.[4] In Serbia, he said, the intelligentsia—those sons of peasants whom the state had educated abroad—had not enlightened the masses at all, but instead had created a "bureaucratic party," a self-perpetuating group of state administrators that treated the people as merely the objects of its rule. What Serbia needed, he said, was to destroy the bureaucratic system.[5]

This article cost Marković his scholarship, and in the summer of 1870 he had to return to Serbia. But the year in Zürich had been decisive for the young socialist. In March 1870 the General Council of the International Working Men's Association officially recognized the formation of a Russian section of the International that Nikolai Utin had begun to form in November 1869. One of the privileges granted the section was the right to appoint agents-correspondents in the various Slavic countries. The only one ever appointed was Svetozar Marković. Marković's first step in his new capacity was to use the occasion of the visit of his friend Djura Ljočić to Zürich in May to discuss the formation of a political party, which he insisted be called "Radical."[6] Besides Marković and Ljočić, the other two initial members of this "radical party" were Pera Velimirović and Nikola Pašić.[7] Each of the four agreed to draft his own version of a program and to meet in the fall to work out a definitive statement.[8] The fall meeting never took place, but in August Marković and fourteen other supporters presented a proposal to the fifth annual meeting of the Omladina (Youth), which was a nationalist cultural association of Serbian intelligentsia from both Habsburg and Ottoman lands. The young Radicals proposed solving the Eastern Question on the basis of the principles of human liberty, by which they meant that, whereas they favored the liberation of the Balkan peoples still directly ruled by the Ottomans—just as did Jovan Ristić—they did not want the regency simply to conquer new territory and expand its oppressive regime. Instead, they hoped the liberation of the Balkans would be a revolutionary struggle that would produce fundamental reforms: the reorganization of the state into a union of free opštinas (that is, local governmental units) and the introduction of direct democracy.[9] Although these proposals were not adopted by the Omladina, Marković became a member of the organization's governing committee, as well as its representative in Belgrade.[10]

In the fall of 1870 Marković tried to put his ideas into practice in Belgrade by establishing cooperatives of producers and consumers and by publishing a newspaper. Both endeavors engendered serious opposition, the first from merchants and guilds, the second from the government, and both undertakings were short-lived. The cooperatives were ahead of their time in terms of the maturity of Serbian social conditions but the newspaper, call *Radenik* (The Worker) to stress the class orientation of Marković's radicalism, succeeded. At one point its paid circulation reached 1,500, a very high number for Serbia at this time and quite sufficient to make it a viable business proposition. But the contents of the paper, which was actually edited by Djura Ljočić and to which Marković submitted surprisingly few articles, were much too radical for the government from the beginning, when Marković had published a series of articles praising the Paris Commune. Marković's outspoken socialism, as well as his agitation among the students of Belgrade, made the regency increasingly hostile. In March 1872 he had to flee into exile in Novi Sad to avoid arrest.[11] Shortly thereafter the regency shut down *Radenik*.

Marković's chief interests in the year and a half he spent in Belgrade were ideological. The article that secured his reputation, which he had already established by "Serbian Deficiencies" and his polemics with the Liberals, was entitled "The Realist Direction in Science and Life," the first part of which appeared in May 1871.[12] The constant refrain of this lengthy two-part article was the phrase "science teaches." Basing his thought on Darwin and Haeckel, Marković espoused a rather crude social Darwinism in which victory in the "rivalry for the acquisition of the necessary means of existence" came to those enjoying higher levels of development.[13] But higher development was to be understood in terms of understanding, of education, of scientific knowledge, rather than in terms of the stage of development of capitalism or in personalized terms of individual status. Marković's underlying demand was for fairness, which he believed revolved around rewarding members of society for their work, not for the positions they held. In other words, Marković's socialism had a moral basis: however, since he believed that Darwinism showed all morality to have a scientific basis, he considered his view that society should be organized on a moral postulate to be a scientific view as well.[14] In particular, he argued that only a society in which there was no private property—by which he meant large accumulations—could be just.

If "The Realist Direction" was Marković's profession of faith in materialism and communism, as Woodford McClellan has suggested, his longer essay "Serbia in the East" was his profession of faith in Serbia's national future.[15] In a manner reminiscent of both the Liberals' whig theory of Serbian history and the Russian populism from which he took many of his ideas, Marković suggested that two institutions common among Serbs during Ottoman times, the zadruga and the opština, actually reflected socialist principles. The Liberals believed a democratic spirit was at work in these institutions that made constitutional government possible, but to Marković the zadruga exemplified the principle of association and the opština the principle that land belongs to those who work it.[16] Unlike the Liberals, who traced Serbia's democratic traditions far into the misty past, Marković stressed the active role of the people, especially in the First Serbian Uprising. He held that the people had established the State Council (*Sovjet*) as a democratic organ representing the zadrugas and opštinas, but during and after the First Serbian Uprising its rightful power had been usurped by a bureaucracy that did not labor and a prince who had outlived his usefulness.[17] These were not agencies of the people, Marković claimed, but only a ruling class that wanted to perpetuate itself. Worse, when these rulers spoke of unifying all Serbs into one Great Serbia, they actually sought simply to expand the arena of their authority. All Serbs must be united, Marković agreed; indeed, all Balkan peoples should be liberated through a revolutionary uprising against the Ottomans; but this revolution could be completely successful only if it also toppled the Serbian state and established in its place an administration based on the principles of association and work that typified the inherent institutions of Serbian civilization. In this way Marković translated the Liberals' concept of the people into a legitimating vision appropriate to his socialist views.

Marković published "Serbia in the East" from exile in Novi Sad, to which city he had repaired after his forced departure from Belgrade. There, working with the prominent Liberal Svetozar Miletić and with radical members of the Omladina, he laid plans for a popular uprising in Bosnia and Hercegovina. After the Hungarian government forcibly disbanded the Omladina in 1871, a few of its more excitable members—not including Marković—traveled to the Montenegrin capital of Cetinje and formed a "Society for Serbian Unification and Liberation" with a similar purpose. When this group's hopes that Prince Nikola of Montenegro would assist them proved ill placed, they did not give up but formed small chapters in Belgrade and Kragujevac, the latter group being organized by Marković's brother, Jevrem. Their strategy called for armed bands of volunteers to create peasant uprisings on the model of the First and Second Serbian Uprisings, whereupon the Serbian government would mobilize its national army and liberate the Balkans.[18] Svetozar Miletić even produced a formal statement of this plan for the consideration of Blaznavac, but the Serbian regent rejected it. Despite Marković's criticism of the regency and his belief that internal reform must accompany any Balkan wars, his work in Novi Sad convinced him that the solution of the Eastern Question was an essential first step to liberating the Serbs, "whatever sort of Serbian state might emerge from the uprising."[19] Ideally, the Radicals wanted to organize the uprisings themselves, since they feared that if the Serbian government ran the entire liberation effort, democratic reforms would become more difficult; but even Marković was willing "to leave the practical solution of internal questions for later, when the war for liberation is finished."[20]

The regents did not adopt the Radicals' plan, but in April 1873, suffering from tuberculosis and discouraged by the difficulties of promoting his plans abroad, Marković decided to return to Serbia anyway. He wrote to Nikola Pašić saying there was no point in forming student societies abroad. The purpose of going abroad was to learn what was new there, and if one wanted practical work, one should return home. *"My work is in Serbia."* Marković fully expected to be arrested as soon as he set foot in Belgrade, and in fact he was.[21] But Ristić, with no desire to make the returning revolutionary any more notorious than he already was, soon released him. Marković went to the spa at Arandjelovac to recover his health, and then home to Jagodina.

While Marković rested, Jovan Ristić's first government was nearing its end and the skupština of 1873 was preparing to meet in Kragujevac, not far from Jagodina. Even today, despite the ravages of prestressed concrete, a visitor to Kragujevac can get a sense of the remote charm that this small city must have had in the nineteenth century. Two-story shops, streets newly planted with young trees, Miloš's *konak* (residence)—it was not up to Zürich perhaps, but Kragujevac was, nevertheless, a city that already had a special place in Serbian tradition.[22] Miloš had made it his capital, and it was in Kragujevac that the first Serbian gymnasium, the first theater, the first pharmacy, the first library, and the first lyceum (the precursor to Belgrade University) all opened their doors. In 1841 the Defenders of the Constitution moved the capital to Belgrade, since it made contacts with foreign consuls easier, but Kragujevac retained its importance both because it remained the seat of the skupština and because it was, from 1850, the site of Serbia's only real factory, the State Munitions Works.[23] The addition of the approximately six hundred employees of the State Munitions Works to the relatively developed crafts and trades of the old capital made Kragujevac perhaps the most socially complex city in Serbia, although with a population of about five thousand it remained small by European standards. It was, nevertheless, the most sophisticated of Serbia's provincial cities, boasting a small intelligentsia second only to Belgrade's.

Perhaps in part because of this diversity, Kragujevac had been a center of opposition since Miloš's time. There the uprising of 1842 that brought Alexander Karadjordjević to the throne had begun. And there in the early 1870s a cadre of oppositionists formed around Jevrem Marković, Svetozar's older brother. Jevrem was behind the socialist manifesto of 1871 that had temporarily attracted Aćim Čumić, and during 1871–72 he was one of the leaders in the efforts to work out a plan for a Balkan uprising,

organizing a "Committee for Liberation" that contemplated con-
tacting radicals of similar mind in Bucharest and Greece.[24] These
initiatives did not work out, but when Ristić fell in early November
1873 and Čumić, the new minister of the interior, instructed local
officials to permit more freedom of the press, a group of Liberals
and leftists in Kragujevac, who earlier that year had founded a
cooperative printing venture, decided to start a Radical newspaper.
Two officers from the State Munitions Works were among the
founders of this Kragujevac Social Printing Works, and one of
them, Sava Grujić, became its president. Other organizers included
Todor Tucaković, a well-known Liberal, Pavle (Paja) Vuković, the
president of the town council, and Prota Jovan Jovanović (no relation to Vladimir), who had been an outspoken exponent of freedom
of speech in Prince Michael's otherwise docile skupštinas.[25] The
organizers asked Svetozar Marković, then resting at home in Jagodina, to join them as "administrator," which actually meant editor.[26]
He accepted with alacrity, and in a remarkably short time the first
issue of *Javnost* (The Public), Serbia's second socialist newspaper,
was in the hands of its subscribers.

Unlike *Radenik*, which had tended toward the theoretical, *Javnost* turned its attention immediately to current political issues.
Marković had realized in the more than a year he had spent in exile
that practical political activity was just as necessary as theoretical
work, maybe more so. He may have exaggerated when he said, "All
my work from the very beginning has been in error," but he was
right when he continued, "Now a new foundation must be laid."[28]
That foundation was active participation in the hurly-burly of Serbia's fledgling parliamentary politics. From 1873 onward the Radicals, who took their initial inspiration from Marković, were never
far from the center of Serbian political events again.

In private Marković advocated a position that might be called
revolutionary socialism. In a personal letter to the Ninković sisters
in November 1873 he called for "the complete abolition of today's
administrative system by decision of the skupština" followed by "a
take-over by a temporary committee, elected from the skupština,
of the central administration." In the same letter he advocated that
police administration be given over to the opštinas, that the court

system be replaced with a system of elected judges, that all debts of those who worked the land be canceled, and, "to prevent the proletarianization of the Serbian people," that eventually all land be changed from private ownership to ownership by the opština, although he did admit that no present way to do that existed.[29]

In public, however, Marković stuck to the somewhat less dangerous line of a radical democrat, pushing for the sovereignty of the skupština and for legal guarantees of civil liberties. *Javnost* immediately jumped into the politics of Marinović's skupština, which began its work only one week after the first issue of the paper appeared. Since the elections for the 1873 skupština had taken place in 1871 under the regency, no Radical delegates sat in the assembly. Jevrem Marković had been elected from Jagodina, but his election was annulled. *Javnost*, therefore, supported Ljubomir Kaljević's outnumbered faction, favoring a substantive address to the throne and supporting Kaljević's efforts to revise the law on freedom of the press. Marković turned to personal invective as well. He attacked the government's delegates as a "miserable intelligentsia . . . seeking by their complicated questions to confuse ordinary people." "*Simple courtesy*," Marković said, with a rare, if moderate, touch of humor, "*demands that the government's representatives restrain themselves when it is a question of speaking about national aspirations. They themselves should know how much their participation in the national skupština degrades the Serbian legislature before all the educated world.*"[30]

In discussing the utter defeat of Kaljević's proposals for changes in the press laws, Marković defended the skupština as the proper forum for national politics. He did not really expect much freedom of speech from the new government, and its promises would be no better than those of any earlier government. "They are all freethinking, but they do not tolerate opposition," he continued. "*There are some who criticize us for defending this skupština, which passed through the school of Radivoj* [Milojković, Ristić's minister of the interior], *which threatened every honorable defender of national freedom and progress with a beating, and which until yesterday bowed down before everything that came from the government. . . .* [But] by raising up the national skupština we simply want to raise its importance and its dignity. . . . We simply do not want freedom as a *favor* of the ruler, but we seek it as a national right."[31]

In a third article Marković drew the logical conclusion of these ideas about Serbia's political system by hinting that the skupština should get rid of the prince on its own. In Western Europe, he said, constitutions that regulate the relations between ruler and people emerged as grants extracted by the people from their rulers. But in Serbia, rulers have always been placed on their throne by "free popular election. Accordingly, they have no other rights than those which the people themselves give. . . . *The nation has always believed that it has the right to throw out a prince who is evil, and to establish another who seems more likely to do good.*"[32] Sometimes, he said, laws are not written to further the national interest, but to hinder it. "*And if an individual often does not have the strength or does not dare to take the moral responsibility on himself to break such laws, the national representatives both can and dare and must extinguish the dead formulae of the law whenever it is a question of salvaging justice. . . .*"[33]

Inflammatory newspaper articles were not the Radicals' only weapons. During the second week in December the skupština was discussing the Law on Six Days Plowing. Marković opposed this law, not because it infringed on the right of property or hindered the development of the national credit system, but because it guaranteed entirely too little land to the peasantry.[34] Marković believed that the national welfare depended on a strong peasantry, Serbia's only producer, and the enormous interest that the peasants themselves took in the debate gave the first hint that politics based on such a view might have possibilities. On December 24 a large group of peasants gathered in Kragujevac to demonstrate for a halt to lawsuits against peasants and for a moratorium on the selling of farms for debt. Since many of the peasants came from the Jagodina area the government suspected Jevrem Marković of being behind the demonstration.[35] Both Milan and Marinović took the event very seriously, believing that the appearance of such an organized group of peasant protestors could presage a seizure of power and the overthrow of the regime, possibly even the dynasty. Milan sent his minister of war, Kosta Protić, to investigate. Protić reported to Milan early in January the alarming news that some military men were involved in publishing *Javnost,* which seemed to be the rallying point for the opposition. To stop this trend Milan took the unprecedented step of removing from state service artillery captain Sava Grujić, who was in fact a Radical. Marković answered quickly, both with an uncharacteristically conciliatory article that included the words "Long Live Prince Milan," and with a personal attack on the vain Protić. "When someone groundlessly attacks another publicly as a violator, then he himself is the slanderer and violator, even if he be minister of war."[36]

Under suspicion of fomenting peasant unrest, identified as a vigorous antigovernmental polemicist, and having insulted both the excitable minister of the interior and the proud minister of war, Marković was clearly a marked man. Early in January 1874 he was arrested, charged with defaming the prince and the national skupština by the statements italicized above, and put in jail. The government put every obstacle in the way of releasing Marković on bail and when he was quickly convicted it rejected his appeals. On April 26 Marković entered the Požarevac jail, as he had predicted he would a year earlier. For the sickly Marković, who was in the advanced stages of tuberculosis and actually collapsed in court while presenting his defense, entrance into the dank prison was widely considered a death sentence. When he emerged seven months later, his health was completely broken. Despite a final effort to obtain medical help in Vienna, he died in Trieste en route to a milder climate early in 1875.

Today, Svetozar Marković is remembered and praised as the greatest Serbian socialist of the nineteenth century.[37] In the final analysis Marković did seek the abolition of private ownership of land. In his private correspondence he suggested that eventually all land in Serbia would have to come under the administration of the opština, and he considered the Russian commune as the best example of cooperative ownership because it included the periodic redistribution of land according to need. It is in this sense that Marković can be considered a socialist. But during the last year of his life especially, Marković's main interest was in political reform, not social or economic change. This has been obscured by the understandable and even correct emphasis given to Marković's use of the Serbian extended family as the model for his socialism.[38] Woodford McClellan has called Marković's position "zadruga socialism," emphasizing the centrality of the patriarchal ethic, and Ellen Claire Hadidian also stresses the zadruga in Marković's ideas. But it was precisely Marković's confidence in the patriarchal ethic of the Serbian peasant that made him almost romantically opposed to social change and pushed him in the direction of political reform. He wished to maintain the traditional style of Serbian life—the fundamental aspect of which he believed was equality—not to create the conditions for development, the unfortunate result of which was inequality. Marković was not a modernizer. He was a populist who believed in the wisdom, virtues, and right to govern of the common people, who in Serbia were made up of self-sufficient peasants. No Serb was far from the peasantry, and when Marković combined personal knowledge of the village with the socialism he learned from books he was able to hypothesize, much as the Liberals had done, that Serbia's traditional institutions made the peasant a natural democrat. The changes in Serbia's political system begun by Ristić's constitution gave Marković an opportunity to turn this rather abstract idea into practical plans for political reform. The operational bent of Marković's late writings differentiates them from the less practical (and more suppressed) Russian narodniki he admired, and provides an excellent example of how, in the social situation of smallholding Serbia, even Serbia's first socialist turned to the political sphere when he contemplated how Serbia should be reformed.

The slogan under which Marković worked out his ideas, and which was later adopted by the Serbian Radical Party, was "samouprava," which may be translated self-administration, or self-government. Since this is the same word used by today's Yugoslav government to describe its version of market socialism, modern scholars have found it easy to construct linkages between Marković's theories and current practice. But for Marković, self-administration did not mean social ownership and administration of capital, but rather a democratic politics of equality, especially at the local level. For this reason, during the last year of his life most of his writings emphasized proposals for the reform of local administration.[39] Briefly, Serbia had three levels of local government in the 1870s, and in all of them, even the lowest level, the central government either appointed or approved the responsible administrator. This supervision from the center was what Marković wanted to break. He realized that the smallest unit, the opština, could not raise enough in taxes to pay for the schools, hospitals, bridges, and flood control that he saw as the main activities of local self-administration; therefore, he proposed dividing Serbia into about fifty mid-sized units (srezes), each with about twenty thousand people organized, as he put it, like a big opština. In each of these units an annual skupština of about fifty directly elected delegates would select a council to administer affairs during the year. Each srez would also elect its own judges. Marković preferred popular justice over a system of "paragraphs," as he styled formal law codes. In his system there would be no possibility of an appeals court reversing the judgment of an elected court. Appeals courts would exist, but they could only approve judgments, send them back for reconsideration, or perhaps remand them to the local srez council for more extended consideration. They could not reverse.

Marković's articles on local reform reaffirmed his confidence in the self-governing abilities of the Serbian peasant, but they did not deal in a practical way with national affairs. For him, the most important body at the national level—indeed, the only possible agent of the sovereign people—had to be the national skupština, to which he would give unconditional powers, including the right to establish constitutional changes without the signature of the prince.[40] Naturally, for such a body to be truly representative of the nation, elections would have to be open, freedom of association guaranteed, and freedom of speech assured. Marković fully supported the left-Liberals around Kaljević who were seeking these reforms in the skupštinas of 1873 and 1874.

An elaboration of what reform at the national level would look like, not written by him but reflecting his views, appeared in the Radical newspaper *Oslobodjenje* at the same time as his detailed articles on local government. The main proposal of this series, the most important of which was entitled "The National Question," was to make the skupština sovereign by the following measures:

abolishing the State Council, establishing complete freedom of the press and freedom of association, prohibiting ministers from participating in skupština debates, and permitting state employees to be elected to the skupština.[41] A skupština thus constituted would be able to rule directly on behalf of the people, *Oslobodjenje* believed, rather than become involved in the party squabbles of the "gentlemen." When Nikola Pašić later referred to the program of Svetozar Marković and *Oslobodjenje* published in 1875 as the ideological basis of the Radical Party, in all likelihood he was referring to these proposals, rather than to the local reorganization schemes Marković put forward. Nevertheless, these articles were fully consistent with Marković's belief in the necessity for absolute sovereignty of the skupština.

In sum, even though Marković had a socialist notion of why the Serbian peasants remained poor, he focused his attention on a radically democratic plan for equalizing them politically. The peasants were the real producers of wealth, but nonproducing bureaucrats of the centralized state had seized control of the levers of power, which they then manipulated for their own benefit. The peasant was not merely left out but actually suppressed. Marković's plan would rid the Serbian peasant of the heavy hand of the bureaucracy by abolishing the requirement that the central government approve elections to local governments and by reorganizing local units into viable self-governing entities. His purpose was not to free the productive capacities of the more intelligent or harder-working peasants so that market forces could produce economic development, but rather to preserve the peasant smallholding culture—which he felt contained its own sound traditions of equality and fairness—from exploitation by the state bureaucracy. Explicitly calling himself a socialist and believing in the eventual community of property, during 1874–75 Marković in actuality pursued a political program of radical democracy and populism without much thought to its conservative social and economic implications. In this he was perfectly consistent with the main direction of nineteenth-century Serbian development, which remained political rather than social or economic.

Svetozar Marković was the most influential Radical in Serbia in 1874. His trial drew large crowds, his imprisonment united hundreds of people in opposition to the government, his writing in *Javnost* and its successors inspired young Serbs throughout the principality. But Marković was not the only important figure of the movement, nor of the opposition in general. Two of his closest collaborators of this period, Pera Todorović and Nikola Pašić, deserve special mention.

Pera Todorović was one of the most fascinating figures of Serbian public life.[42] A dandy who kept both his fingernails and his shoes highly shined, he was a vigorous conversationalist, a scintillating journalist, a morphine addict, and perhaps a homosexual. Six years younger than Marković, Todorović was a spottier student than his colleague. Brilliant in subjects he liked, he paid no attention to the others. Todorović found it difficult to concentrate, and his father found it difficult to head him in the direction of the pig trading business, which, along with modest landholdings, had made the family prosperous. When Pera entered the Belgrade gymnasium he was soon ejected for refusing to take communion, and his father packed him off to trade school in Pest. Failing also to get a diploma there, Todorović ended up in Zürich in 1870, where he fell in with Nikola Pašić and Svetozar Marković. A good cook, he opened his apartment to friends and pursued his education through passionate discussions with them. He read quickly and widely, talked endlessly with Russian revolutionaries—from whom he picked up Russian—and frequented leftist cafés, where friends admired his ability to talk about Marxism in a "highly interesting way."[43] Familiar as well with Darwin and Haeckel, and influenced by Lavrov's notion of the indebted intellectual, Todorović became a socialist.

In 1873, disgusted with mere formal schooling, Todorović returned to Kragujevac to put into action some of the ideas that burned in his breast. When Ristić fell it was Todorović who turned over 2,500 ducats of his inheritance, a significant sum, to the Kragujevac Social Printing Works so that it could begin operation. The society not only published *Javnost* but other brochures and pamphlets as well, including a book by Captain Sava Grujić urging the reorganization of the army into a national militia.[44] The Social

Printing Works continued its work after Marković went into prison, and when the government banned *Javnost* Todorović and the others simply restarted the paper under the new name *Glas javnosti* (The Voice of the Public). But without the personality of Marković to keep the group together, conflict arose over the editorial direction of the paper. Some thought it should tone down its articles to keep itself from being banned, whereas Todorović wanted to pursue a more aggressive editorial policy. When the moderates won, Todorović left and set up his own socialist newspaper in Belgrade, entitled *Rad* (Labor). The now much paler *Glas javnosti* lost so many subscribers that it lasted only two months.[45] Todorović kept *Rad* going as best he could, but it too stopped publication early in 1875.

The other significant collaborator with the Radicals in 1874 was Nikola Pašić, later the dominant political figure in Serbia and in the new state of Yugoslavia after World War I. Pašić was born in 1845 of a respected family in Zaječar, the same town in the Timok region of eastern Serbia where Svetozar Marković was born about nine months after Pašić.[46] Marković moved to Jagodina in childhood, but Pašić remained in Zaječar, where he began the standard route to success by excelling in school.[47] Progressing through grammar school in his hometown, lower school in Negotin, and the gymnasium in Kragujevac, in the fall of 1865 Pašić took up studies in the technical faculty of the Velika škola in Belgrade. Arriving one year before Svetozar Marković departed for St. Petersburg, Pašić had a chance to become acquainted not only with him, but with several others who were later associates, including Pera Todorović. Little is known of Pašić's life in Belgrade except that he was a good student and an impecunious one. His father died in 1862 and Pašić had to make ends meet by tutoring. In the fall of 1867 he was selected as a state stipendist to study railroad engineering at the Eidgenössische technische Hochschule, or Polytechnikum, in Zürich.[48]

Zürich was an exciting city when Pašić arrived there in the spring of 1868. Capital of one of Switzerland's most liberal cantons, Zürich had been dominated since 1830 by a liberal party that had reorganized the canton's administration on the principles of representative government, separation of powers, and direct election. The liberals had also modernized the city, built railroads, and created an atmosphere in which a vigorous economic expansion could take place. By the late 1860s, however, having been in power continuously since 1848, the liberals had become complacent. Their paternalistic method of governing left them open to attacks by radical democrats. Shortly before Pašić's arrival in the city, these opponents had forced the convening of a constitutional convention and had won a majority of the seats in that convention. One year after Pašić's arrival, therefore, in April 1869, Zürich adopted a new constitution that called for referendums on all laws at two-year intervals and special referendums on laws requiring expenditures in excess of 250,000 francs, as well as other important innovations. The agitations that the struggle over these reforms produced led to changes in other Swiss cities as well and eventually to the adoption of a new federal constitution for Switzerland in 1874. For a young man interested in radical politics, no city in Europe outside of Paris itself could have been more stimulating.[49]

No evidence exists concerning the impact of Zürich's exciting democratic transformation on Nikola Pašić, although one might speculate that at the very least the atmosphere did not inhibit his political thinking. When Pašić first arrived, he probably was not able to understand German well enough to enter into political debates directly, and in any event he discovered, as Marković was to find later, that one could only enter the Polytechnikum's regular program in the fall. He asked to be sent to Freiburg, because "in Zürich they speak very bad German and a person has no occasion to talk with anyone," but he was turned down.[50] In Zürich Pašić lived in the same neighborhood as the other Serbian students, near the present Stadtarchiv, and entered rapidly into Radical affairs.[51] He knew Bakunin, was involved in the affairs of the International, and spoke about revolution, but even at this early date Pašić was more an organizer than an ideologue.[52] Fragmentary notebooks that have survived from the Zürich period show him as the meticulous secretary/treasurer of the miniscule group of Serbian Radicals.[53] When the Radicals managed to buy a Slavic press in Geneva and bring it to Zürich it was Pašić who organized the effort, and when Svetozar Marković lost his stipend Pašić was the one who gathered contributions to support him.[54] A letter of 1870 reveals that he already had a keen nose for the tactics of political opposition. Ristić had forced three opposition newspapers out of existence in 1870. Pašić argued in a letter to Djura Ljočić that the editors of the three papers had erred in not using the moment to undermine Ristić. Instead of just stopping publication, they should have awaited the new press law Ristić was introducing and then simultaneously stopped publication with a protest. Since the papers were banned anyway, why not make the cost in public opprobrium as high as possible? Pašić also had heard that Ljočić was being transferred to Aleksinac as part of the regency's program of suppressing the opposition. He proposed that all the opposition bureaucrats resign at the same time, protesting that they were forbidden to work in the national interest. This would have much more impact than individual firings or resignations.[55]

Pašić was a serious student. His Zürich notebooks list many books on technical subjects as well as a good many works on socialism, including Buonarotti on Babeuf, the works of Marat, a study of the Paris Commune, and *Etude sur le mouvement Communiste* by Adolphe Clémence. In his course work, too, Pašić went beyond the required subjects of his specialization. In particular, he attended the lectures of two German professors, Johannes Scherr and Karl Victor Böhmert, both of whom were popular with the Serbian students. Scherr was a forty-eighter, but like many of his liberal colleagues who remained in Germany, in the 1860s Bismarck won him over.[56] Böhmert and Scherr were members of a strong faction of pro-German professors at the Polytechnikum and at Zürich University. Pašić took twelve lecture courses from Scherr, concentrating mostly on German history and contemporary events, including the war of 1870–71, and two courses in socialism and the worker's question from Böhmert.[57]

As this selection of courses suggests, Pašić's socialism in his student days was shaped much more by the German experience than by Russian populism or by Marx. Significantly, his notebooks list sixteen works by Ferdinand Lassalle. The notebooks do not indicate which of Lassalle's works Pašić actually read, but his friend Vlada Ljotić, who published a translation of the Communist Manifesto in *Pančevac* in 1870, also published translations of Lassalle's "Das Arbeiterprogramm" and "Über Verfassungswese" in the Omladina journal, *Mlada Srbadija*, in 1871.[58] The characteristics of Lassalle's socialism make Pašić's interest in him significant in light of Pašić's later career. Lassalle emerged from the 1848 tradition of democratic radicalism.[59] Even though he took most of his ideas on socialism directly from Marx, Lassalle emphasized democratic reform within Germany, even if it meant negotiating with Bismarck himself, which he did. He believed that the main goal of the working class in Germany should be to form a party whose strength would force the introduction of free speech, universal suffrage, and direct elections. Once these reforms had been achieved, large-scale producers' cooperatives could enlist the help of the state in accumulating capital and thereby reorganize the means of production. Lassalle's commitment to creating a political party from Germany's working class for the purpose of democratizing Germany has an obvious parallel with Pašić's later organizational efforts as leader of the Serbian Radical Party, which sought in the 1880s to organize a party around the Serbian working class—the peasantry—and to democratize Serbia.[60] Like Lassalle, Pašić was a strong leader, and like Lassalle he emphasized work in his own country rather than internationalism.[61]

Other notes from Pašić's student days, made for his presentations at meetings of the Radical group, show that Pašić was essentially a materialist. Some people believe, he wrote, that the existence of self-consciousness indicates there is a general spirit or consciousness in the world, and that "people have a little spark of that force. . . . In my opinion I consider that totally false. Self-consciousness is a product of our bodies. It does not exist outside of the body." Nevertheless, Pašić believed that good manners and honesty, which in practice meant "respect for what the majority of all the people respect," were essential for civilized human intercourse. In notes for another talk he struck out against "that old student evil," foul language and argumentativeness. He criticized those whose mode of argument consisted of saying "Eat shit" to which another responded "You eat two." "When two or more persons discuss something it should be assumed that they indeed think about it, that their speeches are reflections of their thoughts."[62]

Pašić completed his four-year course of study in the spring of 1872.[63] In March of that year he requested and received assignment of an extra year of practical field work in Hungary. His petition for that assignment presents a fascinating contrast with the vision of Svetozar Marković.

> Serbia is a state which, if it wants to live, must enter into the flow of European industry and civilization. If it does not do so, it will be sentenced to a completely peripheral and station-ary life and always will have to be defending itself from a flood of European industry and civilization. It will never be certain that European events will not force the entry of European transportation methods. The railroad is nothing more than an extension of the contemporary method of production— industry. It is the necessary concomitant of today's industry. Factory production is replacing manual production to such an extent that even when long-range transportation costs are included industrial products can still compete with manual labor. The more developed the machines, the more thor-oughly the power of nature can be harnassed, and the larger the market these products can reach. They have succeeded in making the world their market and are beginning to overcome the hindrances of time and space. The tendency of today's industry is to transform all human labor into factory labor, and to use natural resources (water and coal) in place of human resources (this is the main characteristic of our century), from which it follows that factories are constantly multiplying and that railroads are rolling from the northwest to the southeast like a flood. No region can prevent (and it is not a question of forbidding, since the struggles go on over the division of natu-ral riches) railroads from passing through it and factories from being built on it, since these things are useful. The waves of European trade are already lapping at the borders of Serbia.
>
> Serbia has shown on various occasions that it is seriously interested in this aspect of national progress. Railroads will

cross Serbia as soon as it enters into trade with the rest of the industrial world. The task of every government then is to bring the progress of industry into agreement with the national interest, that is, not to permit industrial enterprises on which the well-being of the people depends to fall into the hands of the kind of entrepreneur whose interests are diametrically opposed to those of the people. In building its own railroads or granting the concession to an outside organization, Serbia must be careful to make as its first and greatest condition that the railroad damage neither national liberty nor national well-being. The most care must be exercised with foreign companies. The first principle of the foreign enterprise is to profit as much as possible without the least regard to how much it damages the interests of others. The capitalist concern is rarely humanitarian toward its own citizens and even more rarely toward foreign citizens. To insure a profit to foreign capital and to guard the national interest at the same time is very difficult.

Besides railroads, which in any event will be built by enterprises that find them closely linked with their own progress, there are other necessities as well, such as regulating the rivers, dredging them, and making them navigable, as well as regulating tributary rivers and streams to prevent flooding. Also Serbia needs to undertake an exact survey of the country and to complete a cadaster.

All these undertakings Serbia must accomplish, and in a short time without giving them to foreign companies, because if that happens Serbia will be subjugated to foreign capital forever.[64]

Pašić's remarkable analysis shows his practical nature very clearly, and is clear evidence that he understood Serbia's dependent economic position better than most. Pašić realized that Serbia would not be able to resist the enormous power that capitalism had created when it learned how to substitute steam and iron for wind and muscle. The only hope, he thought, was for Serbia itself to undertake the economic projects it required before it was forced to hand them over to exploitative foreign firms. This was a much more realistic assessment than Marković's hope that Serbia might be able to avoid the worst features of capitalism by organizing itself around the zadruga and opština, although Pašić's hope that Serbia could manage these projects with the tiny handful of inexperienced engineers and specialists at its disposal may also have been unrealistic. From Pašić's early understanding of Serbia's economic needs it might be predicted that he would be a modernizer in the sense of seeking such things as subsidies for industry, protective tariffs, and a progressive income tax, all of which in fact he later favored. But, whereas ideas such as these continued to be important to him, they never dominated his thought, or the thought of the Radicals in general. For Pašić politics always came first.

Completing his year of field work in Hungary in the spring of 1873, Pašić returned to take up a position as assistant engineer second class for the ministry of works: as one of Serbia's only surveyors, he was put to work surveying the route for the projected Belgrade-Aleksinac railroad that Ristić and Marinović were attempting to negotiate with the Porte.[65] His assignment put him conveniently close to where Svetozar Marković was resting, and the two met often. The intellectual style of the two Radicals differed, but Pašić remained a friend and coworker of Marković until Marković's death, and an admirer long afterward. Pašić became an active participant in the Kragujevac Social Printing Works, and even though prose writing was not his greatest talent, the group chose him to organize the newspaper they unsuccessfully tried to begin in Belgrade after the loss of *Glas javnosti* late in 1874 (Todorović started *Rad* instead).[66] Pašić must have been more than competent professionally, because in February 1874 he was promoted to assistant engineer first class and sent on a special mission to Ottoman Bulgaria to study the terrain for a possible Niš-Pirot-Sofia railroad.[67] In May 1875 he became engineer sixth class for the Kruševac district. But at this point, events began to overtake Pašić, as they did the rest of the Radicals, both in internal Serbian politics and in the volatile international situation.

As we have seen, the failure of the Liberal address to the throne by only three votes late in 1874 led to the fall of the Marinović government and the coming to power of Aćim Čumić, who post-poned the skupština sessions for two months in order to formulate his government's program. During these two months Čumić's personal instability fostered an atmosphere of complete political confusion. Čumić himself set the tone by proposing to get Ljubomir Kaljević out of his government by falsely accusing him of taking a bribe.[68] Kaljević's Liberal allies, on the other hand, were delighted that Prince Milan, having tired of his most recent mistress, was taking an interest in Kaljević's wife, an affliction they hoped to find useful.[69] Jovan Ristić, lurking always in the wings, kept saying such a government could not last, and in January 1875 rumors were flying that the prince had been talking to Ristić about returning.[70] Marinović too, infuriated with the way Čumić had betrayed him, remained a frequent visitor of the prince, whose willingness to talk with all sides frustrated everyone. On top of these problems, at the turn of 1875 fears swept the foreign community that the Kragujevac Radicals might be preparing an uprising to overthrow Milan. The Austrian consul, Benjamin Kállay, was so worried that he recommended Vienna place cannon across the Danube in Zemun to counter the expected rioting.[71] And widespread rumors about the activity of the Karadjordjević faction and possible links of the left-Liberals with Prince Nikola of Montenegro completed the chaotic picture.[72]

In this unstable atmosphere of intrigue and personal animosities, the skupština reconvened on January 26, 1875. Immediately Čumić came under a barrage of interpellations and complaints, the most dramatic of which concerned the election of Jovan Bošković from Loznica, who had been re-elected to the skupština even though he had been in jail on trumped-up charges at the time of the election. Conservatives, too, criticized Čumić's blatant use of police power against Bošković, and the skupština declared the election valid by a large majority.[73] With a tide of feeling running against him, and with little political fortitude, on February 3 Čumić suddenly—without consulting his colleagues—asked the skupština if all this agitation and confusion meant it had no confidence in the government. When the vote was taken, no delegate proved willing to vote against the government; nevertheless, that evening Kaljević and Piroćanac resigned, saying they could not maintain solidarity with ministers that jailed people.[74] Čumić responded by going straight to the prince and resigning himself.

Once again without a government, Milan turned to Marinović for advice. "Only when a government has a true and complete majority in the skupšina can it do anything," Marinović told him, "but as long as the majority consists of people without principles and direction, inclined to reject rather than to help create something, the government's hands will be tied. . . . It is absolutely impossible to govern in a constitutional country without the help of a skupština majority."[75] Taking this advice would mean appointing Jevrem Grujić, who had the support of a majority in the skupština, but after talking to Grujić twice Milan could not bring himself to let Grujić form a government from Liberals who sought reforms that would diminish his power.[76] Instead, he took the alternate route advised by Marinović and appointed a government of nonpolitical figures headed by a lifelong bureaucrat, Danilo Stefanović, or Uncle Danilo, as the peasant members of the skupština took to calling him. Stefanović immediately announced a government of "reconciliation and harmony," but since all of the ostensibly neutral ministers were, in fact, allies of Marinović, the expectation was that as soon as the skupština was over Marinović would return.[77]

The antagonisms between the Liberals and the Conservatives that became increasingly overt during Čumić's brief and chaotic tenure shaped the debates when Uncle Danilo reconvened the skupština. The newly open atmosphere within the skupština created opportunities for clash after clash. Apparently destructive and without underlying benefit to the society, these debates permitted, even forced, the two groups to define themselves more clearly than had been necessary under the regency or before. Still, despite a call in *Vidovdan* by Milutin Garašanin for "political meetings, programs for skupština candidates, and so forth," the groupings, though more distinct, remained informal.[78] At the abstract level, the conflict centered once again on the role granted the skupština by the constitution. The Conservatives hated the constitution of 1869. Marinović had hinted in the speech from the throne in 1874 that constitutional changes might be in order, and one of the first proposals offered to the reconvened skupština was Milutin Garašanin's recommendation that a constitutional convention be held in order to establish an upper house and increase the prince's prerogatives. The Liberals countered by producing a constitutional proposal of their own that abolished the government representatives to the skupština, excluded from election only police and similar officials—rather than all state employees—and gave the skupština authority to initiate legislation.[79]

The really heated debates, however, were personal. The gigantic gulf between Danilo Stefanović, who, as a member of the old school of bureaucracy, could barely endure even friendly questions, and the majority Liberal faction exacerbated an already difficult situation in which the skupština was accomplishing very little. After being in session for two months, the delegates' main energies continued to be absorbed by personal accusations against old ministers brought up by each side to embarrass the other. The hoary tales of Liberal participation in the assassination of Prince Michael provided grist for the Conservatives, while the Liberals accused Marinović of misappropriating funds. A particularly nasty affair brought the mutual accusations to a climax and provided an unfortunate precedent for the inexperienced skupština. In October 1874 a certain Pavle Grković was murdered on the night of his election to the skupština. His widow claimed that Čumić arranged the murder. Her petition to the skupština was sent to the committee on petitions, and on March 23 Aksentije Kovačević, a Liberal opponent of Čumić, reported that the committee accepted the complaint as valid and recommended it be sent to the government for appropriate action. Immediately several delegates jumped up to say that the committee had not discussed the issue yet and that Kovačević was lying. Confronted, Kovačević admitted his mistake, saying he had inadvertently gotten the petition into the wrong pile. When the Conservatives insisted on excluding Kovačević from the skupština many of the Liberals walked out, preventing a quorum, the first time obstructive methods were used in a Serbian legislature. The next day two votes were taken, and Kovačević's Liberal supporters won them both. A proposal to exclude Kovačević from the skupština lost 63 to 44 and a proposal to reprimand him but let him

decide on his honor whether he should stay in the skupština failed
58 to 47. When a Liberal proposal simply to vacate his committee
seat came up a crisis erupted. As *Istok* described it, Marinović
and several other Conservatives "throw their mandates on the
president's table. A roar. Marinović mashes his hat on his head and
storms out, about thirty after him. Clamoring. Shouts: 'Pleasant
journey!' "[80]

Stefanović's government had been talking about proroguing
the skupština for some time, but now, even with this uproar, the
inexperienced and indecisive ministers could not make up their
minds to act. It was the resolute refusal of the Conservatives to
return to the skupština that forced Milan's hand. When Milan
learned that thirty three Conservative delegates refused to return
if Kovačević was not excluded he exercised for the first time his
right to send the skupština home. New elections were set for three
months hence.[81]

In this heated atmosphere the activities of the Radicals remained something of a sideshow. No members of their intimate
group were in the skupština elected in 1874, although Uroš Knežević, the delegate ejected for insulting the prince, was a close ally,
and they were in contact with Ljubomir Kaljević. But since Aćim
Čumić's method of running the 1874 election was haphazard at
best, quite a few delegates had been elected who found the Radical
position congenial. The most important of these was Adam Bogosavljević, who, unlike the Radicals, was a completely homegrown
populist.[82] Bogosavljević started his career like many other successful Serbian political figures. Born in eastern Serbia, the grandson
of the richest man in his opština, Bogosavljević's brilliance in lower
schools eventually brought him to Belgrade and by 1864 into the
Velika škola. Little data exists to link Bogosavljević directly with his
soon-to-be Radical schoolmates, although his biographer says he
was a member of a student group *Srbadija*, which was banned in
the mid-1860s. It is unlikely that Bogosavljević missed the currents
swirling around the creation of the Omladina in 1866, but he was
not overwhelmed by them. Adam had a mind and a conscience of
his own that led him to a completely original decision. In 1867,
with only a few examinations left in order to graduate, Bogosavljević quit the Velika škola and returned to his village to till the soil.

In itself, returning to the village was not an unusual thing to do. Many Serbian students dropped out along the educational route, just as students do today, never to be seen again on the broad stage of public life. But Bogosavljević did not go back to the village to drop out. Instead, he was determined to devote his life to the direct improvement of the peasant's economic situation. Unlike the vast majority of bright young Serbs who left the village via the route of education, Adam did not become a member of the state class. Believing that if individuals did not strive to improve the way peasants actually worked their land Serbia would never prosper, he set out to create a model farm. Much to the amazement of his peasant neighbors, he began to use a factory-built metal plow, a metal harrow, a mechanical reaper, and a mechanical thresher. The last two were relatively sophisticated machines, among the first to be used in Serbia, but even such a basic instrument as the metal plow caused astonishment among the local peasants. They did not want to switch from their homemade wooden plows because they were afraid they would not be able to get the metal plow repaired if it broke, since the nearest smith was in Negotin, about twenty kilometers from Adam's village. Undaunted, Adam continued his work, becoming an active member of the Society for Agricultural Improvement—which was founded early in 1869 in Belgrade—helping to organize agricultural fairs and competitions, and encouraging the use of fertilizer and systematic animal breeding.[83]

At first, Adam's efforts were met with jokes and sneers from the peasants, but soon his goodwill, his education (he owned a library valued at 400 ducats), his farming success, and his lack of pretention (he and his wife plowed their fields together) won them over and they elected him kmet (president) of the opština, a position he held for life after first obtaining it in 1871. Adam's political ideas were totally shaped by his belief in the centrality of the peasant to Serbia's future. Very much like Svetozar Marković, he believed that the only true producers were the peasants, but that their possibilities for economic progress were limited by the nonproducers, the bureaucrats who treated the creators of their own wealth as second-class citizens.[84] His political program, therefore, was simple: thwart, hinder, and, if possible, eliminate the bureaucracy. Adam did not have a thoroughly worked out scheme for reconstituting

Serbia around the srez as did Marković, but he had one big advantage over Marković: in the election of 1874 he was sent to the skupština as the representative of his opština of Koprivnica.

Already well known as the "peasant philosopher," a contradictory concept not only to most Serbs but to most Europeans as well, Bogosavljević made a vivid impression in the 1874 skupština when in one of his very first speeches he spoke out against those who opposed the Liberal address to the throne.[85] "I see in [such opposition] only that the government does not want to give the people what it wants [murmuring in the skupština]." He proposed "that the bureaucratic system be completely abolished [laughter and murmuring in the skupština]."[86] This sentence sums up Adam's political program. Adam was not a theorist like Svetozar Marković, nor a journalist like Pera Todorović, nor an organizer like Nikola Pašić. He simply expressed the widespread peasant feeling that the bureaucrat received a lordly, guaranteed salary for keeping his hands clean and not working. The lowest bureaucrat was a gentleman, the richest peasant was a peasant still. The Radicals had many supporters among students and the educated young, but it was the Serbian peasant who could best appreciate Bogosavljević's visceral hatred of the representatives of the state. Eventually, the Radicals were able to tap this deep reservoir of peasant resentment that Adam was the first to articulate, but Adam himself was not sophisticated enough yet to use this resource fully, nor was the party system sufficiently developed yet to take advantage of his populist vision. Nevertheless, his understanding of peasant grievances attracted a small group of like-minded delegates around him into the first Radical faction in a Serbian skupština.

One of these was Ranko Tajsić, newly elected delegate from the mountainous region south of Čačak called Dragačevo.[87] At age eleven Tajsić had attended only three years of grammar school when his mother died and he had to return home to perform the women's duties in an all-male zadruga. When his father died, Ranko, then twenty-three, became head of the family. Being literate brought him the respect of his peasant neighbors, and Ranko was a talented manager as well. Helped by a wife who was a devoted companion and dedicated supporter, he became prominent enough to be elected kmet of his opština. Meanwhile, he was reading Renan's life of Jesus, Ranke on the Serbian Revolution, and most importantly, Svetozar Marković. "I began to think about natural laws," he later wrote, "about poverty and why people were poor, about the gentlemen and why they had so much pay and so little work."[88] In a letter to *Javnost* he said "all the ordinary people hope that this usury, high interest, fraud, and robbery will be stopped." In 1874 Tajsić decided to run for the skupština. When he successfully brought a complaint against the local authorities for their inefficiency and for keeping people in jail for no reason, he gained enormous popularity and was elected easily.[89]

Ranko Tajsić was not the only newly elected member of the skupština who was ready to respond to the populist appeals of Adam Bogosavljević. Dimitrije Katić and Miloš Glišić also established themselves as members of the Radical clique. Close to them, but still considered left-Liberals, were such delegates as Uroš Knežević and Milan Kujundžić. All of them supported the regular Liberal program and participated in the criticism that brought Čumić down, but they could not count on widespread support in the legislature for their most radical suggestions. The most dramatic of these was Adam's proposal to place a ceiling of 1,000 talirs per year (500 in retirement) on the salaries of all state employees. "When in our nation men and women, young and old, work, sweat and are driven like cattle for years, and none the less don't even have enough bread, then it is not justice that one bureaucrat is paid enough for four or five hours of easy work a day that he can not only support himself, but also provide his wife and children, who do not produce anything, with fine wool and silk clothes and the best food."[90] "Everyone wants to be among those who eat rather than among those who are eaten," Adam added.[91] Despite this impassioned plea, the proposal, which would have slashed some salaries by four-fifths, was defeated by a vote of 100 to 3. Proposals more in line with traditional demands of the skupština could generate considerable support. For example, a proposal to abolish local administrators received thirty signatures requesting it be placed on the agenda, not enough to pass, but a sizable number in a skupština in which sometimes forty-five or fifty votes could win an issue.[92]

The skupština of 1874–75 was important to the Radicals simply because they found each other. No members of the faction came to the session knowing any of the others, but when they left in March 1875 they took with them an encouraging sense of solidarity and mutual support. While the Liberals and the Conservatives fought each other and smirked at Bogosavljević's and Tajsić's naive proposals, the Radicals were building a psychological bond that sustained them and permitted them to hope for success in the future.

The Radical press played the most important role in building this sense of solidarity during the first months of 1875. As soon as Svetozar Marković got out of jail in November 1874 he proceeded directly to Kragujevac and began yet another newspaper, *Oslobodjenje* (Liberation), the first issue of which appeared on January 13, 1875 (New Year's Day in the nineteenth-century Orthodox calendar). The program of the paper, Marković said, did not need much introduction to those who knew his work, although, in a change from his policy in 1873 and probably more in line with his true feelings, he did not propose that national liberation take place first and then reform. "We do not have to 'liberate our brothers' in Bosnia and Hercegovina," he said. "We have to liberate ourselves. . . . We want to go from freedom to unification, not vice versa," and this meant placing all power in the hands of the people. Borrowing from the Abbé Sieyès to heighten the impact of what he was saying, Marković ended his introductory article with the words "the nation until now has been nothing—it should become everything."[93]

When Marković died, his friends were able to continue *Oslobodjenje* only until the proroguing of the skupština in March 1875, when the government closed the paper down. Its successor, *Staro oslobodjenje* (Old Liberation), was able to keep publishing until February 1876. During their brief lives *Oslobodjenje* and *Staro oslobodjenje* cast the Radicals in a heroic mold that magnified their importance and helped spread knowledge of their activities widely. *Oslobodjenje* relished the moment, for example, when Ranko Tajsić got into an argument with Minister of Education Stojan Novaković, a debate that Tajsić by no means lost. That an ordinary man with three years schooling could stand up to one of Serbia's leading intellectuals had an electrifying effect on the peasants who heard about it. More dramatic was the lengthy article in *Staro oslobodjenje* describing in great detail Adam Bogosavljević's struggles with the authorities during the occasion of Prince Milan's visit to Negotin (described below). For the first time word began to reach a few peasants that the skupština contained people like them who sought goals they could understand. Their ability to bring this message to the Serbian countryside eventually became the basis of the success of the Serbian Radical Party.

Danilo Stefanović's bungling efforts to increase his government's prestige helped the process along. After Čumić's naive mistake in the election of 1874, when he believed it was only necessary to defeat troublemakers to ensure a government majority, Stefanović's government took more positive measures to ensure success in the August 1875 election made necessary by the proroguing of the skupština. The most dramatic of these was a trip through the country by Prince Milan in order to lend prestige to the government and help elect its candidates. On trips such as these, local delegations met with the prince to present formulaic and ritualistic greetings. Despite the government's efforts to prevent it, the local delegation from the Timok area selected Adam Bogosavljević to present the region's greeting to the prince when he visited Negotin.[94] Adam, whose relatives and friends had already been harassed by local officials during the skupština, was not prepared to go along with the government's efforts to evoke a display of popular affection for the prince.[95] On the contrary, he saw the visit as an opportunity to present the prince with a list of grievances. For this reason Adam was forcibly prevented from joining those greeting the prince. When another member of the delegation tried to pass the petition of grievances to the prince during the formal reception, he was rudely hustled off by the police in full view of the public. The result was to enhance Adam's reputation and to make the government and the prince look crudely foolish. The government compounded its error by arresting Adam, because, as the local official candidly noted, "the stupid people here look on him as their savior."[96] Two days later, sixty men proved the official correct by riding for seven hours from Adam's native village into Negotin to rescue him. Never had such a large group of horsemen been seen in peacetime in this part of Serbia. Converging on the jail, the sixty horsemen forced the local officials to free Adam, whereupon they returned home with their leader, telling everyone they met on the way of their success. Word of the great event spread throughout eastern Serbia in a way that no government-inspired newspaper article could ever counter.

Adam's victory was only one of the political misfortunes Milan suffered on his tour. In visiting Čačak, for example, the local officials had to confine Ranko Tajsić to his home to prevent him from participating in the greetings. Minister President Stefanović's statement to the Čačak delegation that "Ranko shouldn't be elected because he is lucky not to be expelled from the country" only confirmed to the assembled peasants that Tajsić must be good, since the government hated him so much.[97] Instead of helping the government's prestige, Milan actually gave the Radicals word-of-mouth publicity among the peasantry that they could never have gained without his trips, and the Radical press seized on every instance of it. Stefanović himself realized the futility of the government's position in Bogosavljević's case. His minister of interior wanted to send cannon to the Timok region to seize Adam and crush resistance. But when the minister of education, in a personal visit, failed to get the villagers to give up Adam, Stefanović wisely decided to call off any further harassment.

The government did not limit itself to these primitive methods of mobilization in its efforts to ensure victory in the elections. It began identifying (but not firing) persons on the state payroll not supportive of the government, and not only banned *Oslobodjenje* after the close of the skupština, but even put the editor of *Istok* under house arrest for three months and began heavily censoring Ristić's paper.[98] As August approached, the conservative *Vidovdan* gave vent to the fears of the Conservatives. "To elect these people [oppositionists, particularly the Radicals] again would mean to set the national house on fire; it would mean to expose the land to the most unfortunate eventualities; it would mean, and we choose this word carefully, committing patricide."[99] *Istok* joined the call for the election of politically mature persons, because "the intelligentsia is the blood of our organism," and accused the Radicals of being "false radicals," because they wanted to "abolish marriage and the family, and to institute a wild, bestial state."[100]

These exaggerated fears made it clear that by mid-1875 the young Radicals had begun to have an impact on Serbian politics. The logic of constitutionalism as Ristić introduced it and Marinović expanded it made it almost certain that a group like the Radicals would emerge. Public political debate opened the possibility of questioning whether the government was actually committed to the principles of free elections and open debate that increasingly constituted the terms of public discussion, and more significantly, made it inevitable that at some point someone would expand the definition of nation to mean not only the educated, but the peasants as well. It was only one small jump from this redefinition to mobilizing the peasantry at election time, and from there to creating a political party to organize the mobilization.

In mid-1875 this line of development was not yet plainly seen by any of the participants in Serbian politics, although it is clear that the elements for it were in place. Taking advantage of the minority of Prince Milan, Ristić had introduced a constitution he thought would make Serbia recognizable to the European powers he wanted to emulate, but with the intention of creating a tutorial style of government he and his associates could dominate. The Liberals' whig theory suggested that history and experience inclined Serbs toward liberal government, but not that the uneducated among them should participate directly in the affairs of the state. Ristić also successfully introduced the notion of cabinet government, by which it quickly became customary for the prince to appoint a coherent set of ministers. Already by 1875 the combination of open debate in a regularly meeting skupština with the cabinet idea had produced the fall of one government and increasing pressure on the prince to appoint governments that could work with the skupština.

The elections of 1874, the second under Ristić's constitution, brought into the skupština a handful of men prepared to raise questions about the adequacy of Ristić's system. Adam Bogosavljević in particular challenged the bureaucracy. At the same time Svetozar Marković and his allies were propagating a different interpretation of the role of the people, making them the active creators of democratic institutions that were being perverted by the prince and the bureaucracy. Self-administration became the byword of these Radicals, a term they opposed to the Liberal idea of paternalistic government. The Radicals took the ideas of nation and democracy that constituted the rhetorical basis of the Liberal innovations and began to invest them with substantial content. These development had little or nothing to do with social change. In fact, the Law on Six Days Plowing, which passed with widespread support during this period, helped ensure that the Serbian peasant would remain a smallholder, thus hindering any more complex social transformations. The logic of constitutionalism and the rhetoric that surrounded it is what drove Serbian politics.

In mid-1875, fears of increasing Radical coherence and the passions it might produce in the peasantry could easily be seen as premature. The Radicals were few in number, they were not organized, and their penetration into the countryside was only beginning. But before the elections could be held in August a new factor intervened that interrupted the development of Serbian politics and gave the left-Liberals and Radicals a unique opportunity. In June 1875 the long anticipated and hoped for peasant uprising broke out in Hercegovina, an Ottoman province populated in part by Serbs. For many the revolt seemed the spark that might ignite a general uprising and clear the Balkans of the Ottomans, freeing the Christian peoples of Southeastern Europe. The conflict between this aspiration and Milan's fear that a war with the Ottomans might end disastrously, both for Serbia and for him personally, produced a strange political interlude in which the most extreme government Serbia experienced in the nineteenth century created the free press and local self-administration that the Radicals had been advocating. But since the Radicals did not have the organization and support that were needed to sustain such broad-ranging innovations, the changes proved to be temporary.

3 : REFORM AND THE RED BANNER

The bureaucracy has accused me in the name of the throne. I accuse
it in the name of our naked, hungry, and oppressed people. — Pera
Todorović

Initially, Prince Milan and Danilo Stefanović both reacted similarly
to the insurrections that broke out in Hercegovina and Bosnia in
the summer of 1875. Acting emotionally rather than calculatingly,
they created a secret fund to smuggle armed bands and guns to the
rebels. However, since the spontaneous uprisings were centered
in Hercegovina, which had no border with Serbia, and northern
Bosnia, whose main border was with Croatia (the Habsburg Empire), it proved difficult to get supplies and men to the rebels.
Stefanović sent two armed bands of about three hundred men each
into the region of eastern Bosnia that was accessible to Serbia;
however, not only did the leaders of these prove as inept at soldier-
ing as they were skilled at plundering, but the peasants had to be
driven to revolt at gunpoint.[1] Without an open commitment from
the Serbian government, which pressure from the Great Powers
prevented, only a few of the Bosnians bordering on Serbia were
willing to enter the field against the Ottomans.[2]

If Stefanović's active policy evoked a weak response from the
Bosnians, it provoked the opposite reaction from ordinary Serbs
and from the Great Powers.[3] Milan had tried to prevent news of
the uprising from reaching the Serbian public, but this proved
impossible. When an emotional current of pro-war sentiment began to sweep through Belgrade, he hurried off to Vienna with a

Conservative entourage headed by Jovan Marinović to seek advice.[4] Both Foreign Minister Andrássy and E. P. Novikov, the Russian ambassador in Vienna, told Milan that the Three Emperors' League was intent on keeping the peace and therefore Serbia must not encourage unrest in Bosnia. Milan agreed to change his hasty decision to aid the rebels on the condition that his princely rival, Nikola of Montenegro, not intervene either.[5] After two weeks in Vienna, Milan returned to Belgrade and told Stefanović to stop sending armed bands into Bosnia. Stefanović, unwilling to agree, resigned.[6]

Stefanović's resignation, which—according to his own account—came about solely because of the conflict between the prince's wish to reduce tension and Stefanović's desire to continue clandestine aid to the rebels, occurred, by chance, on the day after the August election.[7] Despite heavy pressure against the main Radical and Liberal candidates, the voters returned a skupština that was even more solidly oppositionist than the one Milan had prorogued earlier in the year.[8] When Stefanović resigned the next day it appeared that electoral defeat had brought the government down. "The Stefanović cabinet evaluated the significance of the recent elections best when it gave its resignation the same day," exulted *Istok*. "The reactionaries are morally buried." Rather than calming the war fever that was beginning to grip some elements of the population, Stefanović's resignation encouraged the Liberals to believe that the war of liberation they had dreamed of was at hand. "We will finish with the Ottomans in the same way [as we did with the Conservatives]," *Istok* predicted.[9]

With the exception of Stefanović, most Conservatives supported Milan's rejection of an activist policy. Marinović, for example, uncongenial to popular uprisings in the first place and inclined to follow the advice of the Great Powers in any event, pointed out prophetically that "the country is not prepared, the people have no money, and the state has not the means to conduct war like a Great Power."[10] But the elections made it impossible for Milan to appoint a Marinović government. The new skupština, which was already called into session in Kragujevac by Stefanović before Milan named a new government, was overwhelmingly non-Conservative.

Milan hesitated. He found the necessity of appointing a Liberal government, as Marinović once again advised, not only distasteful, but dangerous. The certainty that the Liberals intended to follow an aggressive policy toward the Ottomans would place Milan in a false position with Austria, to whom he had promised moderation, and, in the worst case, defeat in war might even threaten his throne.[11] Furthermore, neither of the two main Liberals, Jevrem Grujić, who looked back to the St. Andrew's skupština of 1858, and Jovan Ristić, who looked back to the constitution of 1869, would consent to serve in a cabinet led by the other. Finally, after delaying for two weeks, Milan—realizing he had no choice but to appoint a Liberal government—found a solution by naming Stevča Mihailović, an old war-horse from 1858, as minister president, Ristić as foreign minister, and Grujić as minister of the interior. Ristić, who considered himself senior to the other Serbian politicians because of his term as regent from 1868 to 1872, agreed to serve only because it could be argued that Mihailović was his senior by virtue of having been a regent himself briefly in 1858. Despite these niceties, Ristić was the dominant figure in the new government.

No more revolutionary in a social sense than Marinović, but much more aggressive in the pursuit of what *Istok* called "national policy," Ristić saw the possibility of using the revolts in Bosnia and Hercegovina to extract concessions from the Ottoman Empire that would be acceptable to the Great Powers. For this reason historians call his government the First Action Ministry. Ristić's eventual goal was to obtain Bosnia, but first he had to get the skupština to agree to help the insurgents, which might mean accepting the risk of war.

This time there was no question of whether there would be new information introduced into the address to the throne. There would be. Prince Milan's moderate speech from the throne, in which he characterized the uprisings as having broken out "in spite of the mild and generous intentions of His Highness the Sultan," did not correspond to the mood Ristić was promoting. After electing Ljubomir Kaljević its president, the skupština selected an unusually large committee of thirty-five persons to work out its response. When an initial poll of the committee showed almost unanimous support for helping the insurgents—although opinion was divided on whether that support should be continued if it meant war—Prince Milan left Kragujevac and returned to Belgrade, frustrated with a skupština so unwilling to follow his lead.[12] In a formal vote taken after his departure, the committee voted 21 to 12 with 2 abstentions to advise the government to assist the rebels, even if it meant war.[13] The same day two subcommittees were established; one to write the public address to the throne, the second to write a secret one. The first subcommittee included both Adam Bogosavljević, who had voted for giving aid but against risking war, and Jovan Ristić, who later accused Bogosavljević of lack of patriotism for this vote, a combination that must have made for some piquant, although unfortunately unrecorded, exchanges.[14]

The public address to the throne adopted by the skupština on September 19 was not at all conciliatory toward the Porte. It asked each Serb to make whatever sacrifices might be needed "to stand as one man in the defense of his beloved homeland."[15] Perhaps under Bogosavljević's goading, the address also expressed satisfaction that the government had promised in the speech from the throne to bring forward laws on reorganizing the opštinas, freeing the press, and guaranteeing civil liberties, but added that the skupština "would from its own side make certain proposals, particularly . . . those relating to ministerial responsibility, the transformation of our legal system in the national spirit, . . . and simplifying our courts and administration."[16] The assertive tone with which these by now almost traditional demands of the opposition were made indicate how far the skupština had come in only three years from a time when it hesitated to venture even a modest addition to the formal phrases of response to the prince.

The secret address authorized the practical steps needed to prepare for the possibility of war. Ristić well knew that an aggressive foreign policy, whatever its diplomatic potential, was useless without money and without improvements in Serbia's poorly prepared military machine. Having received approval in principle to support the insurgents in Bosnia, he now demanded that the skupština approve a loan of 24 million dinars to make that support feasible. The Radicals, along with many Liberals, insisted that if the skupština were to authorize such an unprecedented amount it would have to have a continuing voice in how the money was spent. Adam Bogosavljević proposed that the skupština stay in session as long as the emergency that called for the loan was in effect, but the final compromise was to create a standing committee of the skupština to consult with the government on spending the emergency funds. Bogosavljević also used the crisis to push his pet scheme, reducing bureaucrats' salaries. He proposed to eliminate all state salaries in case of war. The skupština did not go that far, but it did decide to reduce the wages of the bureaucracy 20 percent or to 300 talirs, whichever was less, when the time came. And finally, the secret address suspended the enforcement of debt collection for the duration of the emergency, a victory for peasant debtors with which the Radicals were very satisfied.[17]

The main reason the Radicals under Bogosavljević's leadership were able to shape the secret address to the degree that they did in a skupština technically dominated by the Liberals was that in the still embryonic Serbian political arena, the lines of demarcation separating the three main political forces were not as distinctly drawn as they were to become by 1880. When Bogosavljević's ideas provoked sympathy from delegates, they were not restrained by any sort of party discipline from voting for them. The Radicals also showed a more mature sense of parliamentary tactics in this skupština than they had the previous year. Adam Bogosavljević and Milutin Garašanin, ideological opposites, voted together in an effort to elect as many non-Liberals to the skupština's standing committees as possible. This cooperation, which did not go unnoticed in *Istok*, was perhaps the first parliamentary coalition in Serbian experience.[18] Since both the Conservatives and the Radicals were much less numerous than the Liberals, their strategy usually did not work. Bogosavljević was elected as one of the skupština secretaries, but neither he nor Garašanin were elected initially to any of the standing committees, all of which were dominated by either Ristić or Grujić supporters.[19] But the two continued to cooperate. Later, when both were elected to fill positions that had become vacant on the Finance Committee, *Istok* complained that "all the miserable radicals voted for Garašanin."[20]

When the full skupština, meeting in closed session, accepted the secret address on September 18, it wholeheartedly agreed to grant the government the standby special powers it had asked for, to authorize 24 million dinars in loans, and to create the standing skupština committee.[21] The skupština's decisiveness surprised Prince Milan, who had thought the delegates would not go so far as to risk war, especially since Ristić took care to explain to them that Serbia could not count on any help from the Greeks, the Bulgars, or the Romanians, and only a little from the Montenegrins.[22] When the package sailed through anyway, Ristić immediately dispatched Radivoje Milojković from Kragujevac to Belgrade to present the address to the prince, but Milan refused to sign it. He not only opposed Ristić's active policy, he abhorred the idea of the standing skupština committee, which he called "unconstitutional and revolutionary" and some sort of "Committee of Public Safety."[23] When Ristić stood his ground Milan summoned him to Belgrade immediately for consultations.[24] Shortly thereafter, he ordered the skupština to leave Kragujevac and reconvene in Belgrade, which it did on September 28.

Still adamantly opposed both to the direction and to the form of Ristić's policies, Milan decided at this point to take measures into his own hands. The skupština reconvened in the main hall of the Velika škola on October 4, but before debate could move very far word came that the prince was on his way. The ministers gathered in their conference room. Milan confronted them. "I hear that you are accusing me of being afraid of war and of being unfaithful to the banner of the heroic leader of Rudnik [Miloš]. I have come to tell the skupština all that is a lie." The ministers pointed out it was unconstitutional for the prince to appear in the skupština without his ministers. "If you wish," Ristić said, "please enter the skupština with us." When Milan angrily refused, Ristić, "white as a sheet," offered his government's resignation.[25] The infuriated Milan signed the resignations on the spot and entered the skupština to tell the astonished delegates that Serbia was not ready diplomatically, militarily, or financially for war.[26]

After this bold step the prince invited all the delegates to his palace, where he lined them up and asked each one individually if he was for war. Intimidated in the presence of a prince who was against war, most delegates waffled, saying they favored war only if it were possible.[27] "See how the peasant is clever and flexible," Milan said to Kaljević later. "He runs around the streets and cafés taking about war, praising the Novi Sad articles that are for war, and when you drive him into a corner and put the question to him unequivocably he finds some sort of formula that neither stinks nor smells (*koja niti smrdi niti miriše*). His 'if possible, sir,' means: if you are brave go to war—if you win, glory; if you lose, disgrace."[28]

Victorious over the war party by means of his personal confrontation with the skupština, Milan now had to face yet again the question of who would form a government. At first he tried to install the Conservatives, turning to Marinović of course, then to the old standby Nikola Hristić, and finally to an even older one, Djordje Cenić, but they all refused. In desperation, he approached Ljubomir Kaljević, president of the skupština and a man on good terms with almost all factions. After talking over the offer not only with his left-Liberal allies and with Ristić's faction, but with Aćim Čumić and Milutin Garašanin, Kaljević accepted. Respecting the wishes of the prince in regard to foreign policy, he installed Djordje Pavlović, a most moderate man, as foreign minister, and Tihomilj Nikolić, a military specialist, as minister of war. But for minister of education he appointed Stojan Bošković, who had made his reputation as Vladimir Jovanović's close ally in the 1860s, and most surprisingly of all, the fiery Milovan Janković as minister of finance, another of Jovanović's early associates.[29] Janković was the most radical Serbian ministerial appointee up to this point in Serbian history, but also one of the most unstable.

Kaljević's appointment greatly diminished the possibility that Serbia would take a rash step in the diplomatic or military spheres. The new government stopped the unsuccessful policy of sending armed bands into eastern Bosnia, although it continued the search for major foreign loans and took steps to beef up the army.[30] The Three Emperors' League was satisfied. But Milan paid a significant price for this success. Kaljević favored internal reforms that Milan had always opposed and had enough backing in the skupština to get them enacted. On the surface it might appear as a mark of

Milan's lack of political skills that he was willing to pay for temporarily getting rid of the war party by permitting domestic changes that, if they became permanent, would fatally undermine the authority he insisted he should retain. Milan's cleverness lay in his confidence, which proved justified, that he could manipulate Serbian politics sufficiently to ensure that Kaljevic's ministry would remain a short-term one and that any untoward results could be nullified. Kaljević put the prince to the test immediately by turning his attention to precisely the reform that Svetozar Marković and his allies, the opponents Milan most feared, had been demanding for several years, the introduction of self-administration to the opštinas.

In order to understand the importance of this reform and why the left-Liberals and Radicals attached so much importance to it, it is essential to know how local administration in Serbia actually worked. Under the Ottomans the adult males of each village or group of villages chose one of their number, the kmet, to represent them to the local Ottoman authorities. There were no special electoral rules. A kmet was simply the most respected peasant of his village. Above the village level the centralized Ottoman hierarchy ruled. The pashaluk that encompassed traditional Serbia was divided into several subunits called nahijas, and when the Austrians conquered part of Serbia in 1718, they divided each nahija into kneževinas, which were administered by native Serbs called knezes. Serbian national mythology to the contrary, there was nothing particularly democratic about this system, except perhaps at the lowest level, but knezes were at least Serbs, so that during the eighteenth century a modest stratum of native leaders began to develop.

During the First Serbian Uprising, emerging military leaders in each kneževina overshadowed the knezes, and under Miloš knezes were simply Miloš's personal representatives. But after Serbia became autonomous in 1830 Miloš had to define lines of local authority more precisely. He abolished the title knez and renamed the kneževinas srezes. The head of a srez, whose formal title was simply načelnik, or headman, became known popularly as the kapetan. Below the srez the local units of government began to be called opštinas.[31] According to Ružica Guzina, the term opština probably was introduced into the principality after the First Serbian Uprising by Austrian Serbs, who derived it from the Russian-influenced Slaveno-srpski literary language. The word "opština" had only minimal connotations of collective ownership, meaning simply "smallest unit of organization." It could refer, for example, to a school district (školska opština) or church parish (crkvena opština). The head of an opština retained the title kmet, but under Miloš he was given two assistants and expanded authority. The kmets rented out the opština's forests, which Miloš declared national property, for pig grazing and they served as a small claims court, replacing the traditional trial by hot iron still in use in the first third of the century.[32]

The Defenders of the Constitution, who threw Miloš out and began to establish their Balkan version of a *Rechtsstaat*, used legislation to bring local government under direct control of the central authorities. Their law on local government in 1839, along with its many later amendments and modifications, established the opština as the lowest level of local government, but its definitions of the institution and its function remained extremely vague. Local residents (*mesni žitelji*) were to elect persons who held the respect of the people and who were "naturally bright" (*od same prirode bistri*). When unspecified important issues came up, the leaders were to call together "the necessary number" of elders "according to the former custom."[33]

The main point of the laws concerning opštinas under the Defenders of the Constitution was to subordinate the opštinas to the central government. No term of office was specified for the kmet, nor was any method prescribed for changing a kmet once he got into office. Furthermore, all elections had to be approved by the srez kapetan. When an opština did select a new kmet after the incumbent died or was dismissed by the kapetan, it could only select one approved by the government. Since the kmet apportioned taxes, approved the rental of public land, regulated grazing rights, and granted the right to open taverns and shops, the kapetan and the kmet had ample scope for cooperative corruption. When a dishonest or brutal kmet had the support of his kapetan the peasants could do little, except perhaps revolt. On the other hand, cooperation between the kmet and the kapetan could lead to short-term benefits for the peasantry. For example, the Defenders of the Constitution introduced restrictions on cutting down the forests in an effort to keep this ancient asset of the Serbian pig farmer intact. Serbian agriculture, however, was in transition from population-extensive transhumance to population-intensive field cropping, so the peasants wanted to clear new land. Relative peace reigned as long as the kmet, perhaps for a small remembrance to be sure, winked when peasants, usually his friends and relatives, broke the rules they did not like.

Zealousness in enforcing the government's well-intentioned rules could lead to outright revolt. Two practices, in particular, aroused peasant dissatisfaction with local administration. The first was that the central government had the right to create new opštinas by either joining or splitting existing ones. The peasants' lack of say in these reorganizations, in which great emotions could be generated, was a constant source of complaint. The second was that the kmet had the authority to punish local wrongdoers with twenty-five strokes on the spot. When a kmet was installed the kapetan would gather the villagers and in front of them instruct the new kmet more or less as follows: "Whoever you see not working, beat him like you would a bull that's gotten into the cabbage or a goat in the bean patch. If you don't, you won't last long as kmet."[34] Eventually appeals against arbitrary beatings became possible, but only after the beating had already been administered. For years after the abolition of corporal punishment in 1874 peasants well remembered how easily and often the power to flog had been abused.

These dissatisfactions were raised first in the skupština of 1848 and then again at the St. Andrew's skupština of 1858. Not until the 1860s, however, were changes introduced, and then only to regularize practices, not to increase local autonomy. The law on opštinas of 1866 specified rules for two types of opštinas, ones consisting of town residents, and ones consisting of village residents. Both types were to have three agencies of local government: the opština meeting (zbor), the opština council (odbor), and the opština court (sud). The court, which consisted of the kmet and his two assistants, who were also called kmets, administered the opština on a day-to-day basis. The council consisted of the court (the kmet and his two assistants), plus eight other elected members. It had the task of supervising the work, especially the financial affairs, of the kmets. The zbor, or opština meeting, codified by this law for the first time, consisted of adult male heads of households. It elected the council and the court. The main difference between town and village opštinas lay in the method of electing the opština court and council. In town, members of the zbor gathered and voted directly; but in the countryside, villages sent delegates to the zbor, which then elected the court and council. As in the past, elections had to be approved by the kapetan and his superiors in Belgrade, and the government retained the right to join and split opštinas.

From the beginning this law was extremely unpopular. Even the man who got the blame for it, Nikola Hristić, Prince Michael's minister of internal affairs, admitted that it might need some adjustments. A new opština law was one of the main demands at the Grand National Assembly of 1868, and the issue came up again and again in succeeding skupštinas. Even Conservatives had to respond. One of Marinović's main accomplishments was getting rid of corporal punishment. Aćim Čumić promised a new opština law, but fell from power before he could introduce one. Danilo Stefanović was forced to promise one too, but he also left power before he could do anything about it. The First Action Ministry actually introduced a draft law based on skupština recommendations only two days before it resigned in 1875. The proposal was under discussion when Milan made his dramatic entry into the skupština. Therefore, when Ljubomir Kaljević came to power the question of the self-administration of opštinas had been a basic issue of Serbian politics for years. The difference was that Kaljević paid more than lip service to the need for reform. It took his new government only one month to completely revamp the law on local administration.

The law of October 1875 freed the opštinas from almost all control by the central government. The institutions of meeting, council, and court were retained, as was the title kmet, and electoral rules were laid down in great detail, but the right traditionally possessed by higher authority of confirming electoral winners was eliminated. Victory in the election was the only mandate needed to assume office. The new law prohibited the kapetan even from attending an election without an invitation from the opština authorities. Elections were direct and public, although the right to vote remained restricted to adult males who paid the full head tax (danak). Each listed voter approached the election committee and publicly stated his choices. Once elected, the kmet and his court had considerably increased power. The monetary limits on civil law suits they could ajudicate was raised and the limits on the amount of money the opština could tax and spend for its own purposes were removed entirely. The joining and splitting of opštinas also became purely the choice of the opštinas involved. To balance these increased powers, kmets and their courts were restricted to a one-year term of office (reelection was possible) and voters were given the right of recall. In villages, as few as twenty voters could petition for a new election if they were dissatisfied with their kmet, whereas in towns fifty signatures were required.[35]

Passage of the opština law, which gave Serbia the most open system of local government it has ever had, before or since, set the tone for Kaljević's ministry. Kaljević was an excellent tactical politician with lines out to all camps, but, perhaps because of his skills at accommodation, he was not strong enough as minister president to restrain the Radicals once they got the bit in their mouth. For the rest of the skupština session, which ran with one break until February 2, 1876, Adam Bogosavljević and his associates continued to push Kaljević and the Liberal skupština toward populist measures, generating several new laws that reduced the power of the police and the bureaucracy in the same spirit as the opština law had done. A law on personal security, despite many flaws, imposed restrictions on jailing citizens, and two laws on civil and criminal procedures increased the power of the opština courts.

The most important among these new regulations was a liberalized press law, which, after many years of agitation, passed and was promulgated by the end of 1875. During the debates on this law, Adam Bogosavljević and his associates, including in this case his sometime Conservative ally, Milutin Garašanin, proposed that the new law consist of only one sentence: "The press is unlimited, free." Such an extreme position convinced some Conservatives that a moderately liberal law would be the lesser of two evils. The new law abolished the requirement that published material be shown to the police one hour before publication and lifted the restriction on selling newspapers on the streets or through means other than mail subscriptions.[36] The police could seize a paper only for a bona fide illegal act, like insulting the prince or fomenting revolution, and even then the authorities had only one day to take the case to a judge, who was enjoined to dispose of the matter expeditiously. And the police could no longer suspend publication of a newspaper on their own authority. Under the old law the authorities could ban a paper for up to three months without a court order. Kaljević's law also stated that if editors were convicted of a violation and could not pay a court-imposed fine, they could serve a jail sentence and the paper could continue to publish. Not all the rules were liberal. Voluntary contributions could not be sought to pay fines, for example, and attempted violations could be punished as well as ones that succeeded. But by and large, the new law was by far the most liberal press law nineteenth-century Serbia experienced.[37]

Kaljević's successes were often, in fact, compromises to prevent passage of even more radical suggestions coming from the populists, the purpose of which was to emasculate the bureaucracy, which included the army, the church, and even the schools. Not only did Bogosavljević and his group propose abolishing the office of srez kapetan, but they called for cutting state assistance to the agricultural/forestry school, the agricultural society, the national theater, and the teachers' school. They wanted to lower the pay of the Metropolitan, lessen the number of bishops, close all but six monasteries, abolish the ministry of public works, do away with Serbia's representatives in Vienna and Bucharest, and stop the granting of stipends to students for study abroad. This was populism with a vengeance. Bogosavljević was not against religion, nor was he against education as such. What he opposed was the expenditure of tax money on persons who did no physical work. He opposed stipends for students because they merely came back to work for the bureaucracy. He wanted to simplify church structure because he thought too many nonworking priests lived off their state-collected tithes without producing any social benefits. In one of his most famous interpellations he attacked the bishop of Negotin for not having made the required annual round of his parishes for three years. Bogosavljević greatly angered some delegates by saying that, whereas the bishop should make his rounds, he personally would not seek the bishop's blessing.[38] This sort of dramatic phrasing kept Bogosavljević's constant interjections in the forefront of the skupština's consciousness and put Kaljević in the position of always having to react rather than lead. Usually Kaljević was up to the mark, but sometimes not. In the case of the salary of state councillors, for example, which Bogosavljević was constantly trying to reduce, it took all the authority Kaljević could muster to limit the cuts imposed by a successful Radical campaign to only 25 percent.

Whereas Kaljević had to fight off extreme populist proposals, his basic reforms were still consistent with the fundamental faith of the left-Liberals, as well as of the Radicals, that the nation had to be a participant in Serbian public life. This view was based on the Liberals' whig theory of history, or on Svetozar Marković's ideas of the role of association and work, or on faith in the necessity of incorporating the pluralist norms of democratic life into Serbian politics. The proposals that all sides produced to deal with the Bosnian uprisings clearly reflected these varieties of incipient national ideologies.

The Radicals were ecstatic about the revolts in Bosnia and Hercegovina. Now that the uprising they had plotted for in 1872 had broken out without their assistance, they ascribed enormous importance to it. In 1875 the Radicals in Kragujevac had begun to try out the principle of self-administration in their personal lives by creating what amounted to a small commune. Two of the most interesting participants in this avant-garde life were Milica and Anka Ninković, daughters of the director of the Novi Sad gymnasium, who had trained to be teachers in Zürich. The two sisters were good friends and admirers of Svetozar Marković, and after his death in 1875 they emigrated with their mother to Kragujevac to set up a woman's school along progressive principles. Danilo Stefanović's government ruled it was illegal for them to do this since they were not Serbian citizens. To save the two young women from deportation, and perhaps inspired by Lopukhov in Cherny-shevsky's *What is to be Done?* the Kragujevac Radicals arranged marriages with two willing bachelors to give them Serbian citizen-ship. Sreta Andjelković, formerly the responsible editor of *Oslobo-djenje*, married Anka, and Pera Todorović married Milica.[39]

These two couples formed the nucleus of a communal living arrangement to which young Radicals from elsewhere in Serbia repaired. Nikola Pašić had tried to resign his position as railroad engineer in Kruševac in order to run for the skupština in 1875, but his resignation was not accepted. However, as soon as the election was over, Ristić's new government fired him for his presumptuous-ness and he decided to go to Kragujevac.[40] Another young Radical who joined the group was Avram Petrović. In June 1875 Petrović, during one of his periodic forced hiatuses from state service due to political activities, had traveled through Serbia on foot gathering subscriptions for *Staro oslobodjenje*. Later that year he astonished his local kapetan by accurately predicting the victory of the opposi-tion in the 1875 election and the resultant resignation of Danilo Stefanović. In the fall Petrović moved in with the Ninković sisters and their husbands, who had rented a large house for their printing press, editorial offices, and women's school. "There everyone lived like brothers and members of a family or zadruga," said Petrović. "That was the ideal Radical period."[41]

The Kragujevac commune was enthusiastic about the revolt in Bosnia. Nikola Pašić's interpretation was one of the most extreme, but it indicates both the nationalist excitement the revolt inspired and the socialist tenor of the commune's thinking. "The fate of all Serbdom depends in good measure on the outcome of the Hercegovina uprising," Pašić wrote shortly after the outbreak of hostilities. Pašić believed that those who said it was some kind of conspiracy were mistaken, and he did not consider it primarily a national or religious struggle. Instead, Pašić called the revolt a social rising against the Ottoman "gluttons who make up the ruling class . . . that lives parasitically on the body of the subjugated people, as does the bourgeoisie in the west."[42]

This highly ideological interpretation was not typical of Pašić, whose strength lay in practical political suggestions. That side of him became more apparent when in the fall of 1875 the Kragujevac Radicals chose him to take money they had collected for the rebels to Hercegovina.[43] Traveling through Croatia to the Dalmatian coast, by October he was in touch with one of the leaders of the uprising and had visited a rebel camp. On the spot, he realized that rhetoric about the bourgeoisie was not what the rebels needed. Their deficiencies were coordination, legitimacy, and acceptance abroad. Wanting to have an impact by surmounting these shortcomings, Pašić also wanted the rebellion to achieve a democratic result favorable to the unification of Serbs. To accomplish these goals he suggested the rebels create a provisional government, a proposal almost unknown at that time but today common practice in national liberation struggles. This twelve-person provisional government would consist of six Hercegovinians, and two members each from Montenegro, Croatia, and Serbia.[44] The basic idea of a provisional government was sound, but since Pašić's plan required not only cooperation among the feuding Hercegovinian rebel leaders, but agreement among Austria-Hungary, Montenegro, and Serbia as well, it was doomed to failure. Pašić spent several months in contact with various rebels, until in February 1876 a crisis in Kragujevac drew him back to Serbia.

Pašić's proposal for a Hercegovinian provisional government was perhaps the most original solution proposed for ending the uprisings, but far from the only one. Jovan Ristić had a peculiarly contradictory view of how to achieve Serbian aims in Bosnia even before the uprisings. He had spoken of a "national program" in *Istok* for years, but for Ristić "national" meant control of the state apparatus by Liberals on behalf of the people, not direct democracy. And yet, Ristić believed the Balkan peasantry was fully capable of rising up and throwing off the Ottoman yoke. During the regency Ristić had tried, without great success, to establish a network of agents in Bosnia who would help in case of an uprising, but he organized it around merchants and other notables whom he saw as potentially educated allies, not by proselytizing among the peasantry. His network collapsed as soon as he left office, in part because Ristić did not grasp the contradiction between his faith in the revolutionary tradition of the peasantry and his plans for organizing Bosnia under the privileged classes, who were the natural enemy of that same peasantry.

When the uprising of 1875 actually broke out, Ristić seems to have realized that his earlier scheme was contradictory, because his surprising new idea was to induce the Ottomans to create a system of local self-administration for Serbs in Bosnia. By permitting each local region to elect its own councils and headmen separately from the Ottoman administration, and by having each district elect its own bishop, who would be subordinate ecclesiastically to the Metropolitan of Belgrade, Ristić hoped to increase Serbian self-consciousness in Bosnia and create internal pressure for its eventual incorporation into Serbia.[45] Averse to self-administration in Serbia because it would threaten his tutorial methods of rule, Ristić was willing to propose it for Bosnia if it would improve Serbia's chances of expanding its territory and thereby increasing its prestige.

Quite naturally, the Radicals favored self-administration in Bosnia. The most interesting Radical proposal was published in January 1876 by Vaso Pelagić, a Bosnian priest who had come in contact with Chernyshevsky's ideas while in Russia and had also been heavily influenced by Svetozar Marković. Pelagić called for organizing Bosnia into srezes and opštinas that would be run under the principles of self-administration.[46] There would be a court system of unpaid judges and an overall national militia. A Bosnian skupština would hold the legislative power, but the prince of Serbia would become the sovereign and the Bosnian skupština would meet with its Serbian counterpart every third year. In an earlier program from 1874 Pelagić had also talked of ensuring a free press and doing away with the legal profession, a standard populist demand.

The various programs and proposals put forward by the Radicals and by Ristić share one thing in common.[47] They show very little appreciation for the actual situation in Bosnia. Only Pašić's proposal for a provisional government took into account what the rebels really needed, which was some practical way to organize

themselves for negotiation and eventual rule, but even his suggestions were unrealistic, given the views of the Great Powers. Pašić's
initial reaction that the uprising should be seen as an anti-bourgeois
revolt, or Pelagić's and Ristić's quite differently perceived proposals
to introduce self-administration into Bosnia, were even more unrealistic. Whereas the proposal put forward by the Radicals in the
skupština may have made some sense in Serbia and may have begun
to reach a few Serbian peasants through Adam Bogosavljević and
Staro oslobodjenje, in Bosnia such proposals were far removed from
the mentality of the peasants who had launched the revolt. In a
country that had a literacy rate of less than 1 percent and did not
boast of a single bookstore, even in its largest city, the burdened
peasantry sought simply the lowering or elimination of feudal dues.
The Bosnian peasant not only had little notion of self administration, skupštinas, lawyers, or freedom of the press, he even had
difficulty with the notion of property as it was thought of in Europe.
"It is fruitless to search the archival data for information about a
general underlying peasant program," Milorad Ekmečić tells us.
"The uprising was not the result of certain programs—it was itself
the program."[48] Neither official Serbia nor the Radicals understood
this basic fact about the uprisings they were both so interested in,
the former counting on the forces of order in the notables, the
latter bemused by relatively sophisticated and abstract plans for
political reform. In any event, plans for introducing self-administration in Bosnia were plans spun in thin air, since there was no
chance that Austria would permit Serbia to annex a territory that
the Habsburgs themselves had set their sights on.

More significant for the development of internal politics in
Serbia was the new law on the self-administration of opštinas.
Although the continuing efforts of Jevrem Marković and others to
improve on it indicate that the Radicals did not think it went far
enough, the law was a great triumph for them and for the left-
Liberals. It introduced direct democracy to the countryside and
made the peasantry responsible for its own local affairs. But the
law had one serious and, as it turned out, fatal flaw: just as the
Bosnian peasant was not prepared for sophisticated and abstract
reforms, so in Serbia not every peasant was as competent as Ranko

Tajsić, as interested in politics as Adam Bogosavljević, or as adept at political analysis as Svetozar Marković. The myth that the Serbian peasant had been schooled in the traditions of democracy through the Ottoman oppression and was merely waiting to be kissed on the lips by populist reform turned out to be just what the Sleeping Beauty story was—a fairy tale. Democracy, like nationalism, is not a natural phenomenon. It must be learned, and the Serbian peasant was, as the Conservatives of the time were fond of saying, not ready for it yet. Had opština self-administration been given a chance to work under the leadership of a wise ruler and a tolerant but firm government, it might have developed into a vigorous and healthy social organism. But unfortunately for Serbia, it lacked both those prerequisites.

The new opština law, passed in October 1875, decreed that elections to fill the opština courts and councils be held forthwith, on November 13. The order was met with satisfaction in a few places, such as Belgrade and Kragujevac, which were relatively mature politically. But in most opštinas only a handful of voters turned out, in some cases fewer than there were positions to be elected.[49] Not only were few peasants as interested in taking part in local affairs as some of the more educated Radicals believed, but many of them suspected a trick. With a good sense born of generations of conflict with governmental officials they preferred to make sure the authority of the kapetan was really broken before they did anything that might come back to haunt them later. Inexperience was also a factor. Many peasants were not sure just what a treasurer did, for example. And the recall provision of the new law proved to be too lenient. It was all too easy to disrupt local government by getting together enough signatures to force an election, even when the new opština government had been in office only a few days or weeks. In Smederevo four new courts were elected in the first four months the law was in effect.[50] Kaljević, who believed in the law in principle if not in every paragraph, nonetheless persisted. He told local officials not to interfere (not always successfully) and pressed forward with his reform program in the skupština.[51]

The main place where the opština law had an impact was

Kragujevac, the Radicals entering into the November 13 election there with great enthusiasm.[52] Their main electoral strategy was to win the support of the workers in the Kragujevac munitions plant, Serbia's only bona fide factory. This aim fitted well both with the Radicals' socialism and with the new opština law, which for the first time permitted factory workers to vote if they had paid their head tax, as most of them had. The Liberals who had held power up until this point in Kragujevac, such as Todor Tucaković, found it difficult to attract workers' votes. Although the Liberals representing the merchants and wealthier stratum succeeded in electing the two assistant kmets, thus attaining a majority on the three-person court, the Radicals attained a majority of the sixteen-person council and elected Paja Vuković president (kmet) of the court and council. Shortly thereafter, however, a by-election had to be held since one of the assistant kmets, incensed at having to serve under a president elected by what he considered the town's disreputable elements, resigned and Paja Vuković himself went off to Belgrade as a delegate to the national skupština. This by-election, held on December 12, elected two Radicals. Thus, after a month of confusing campaigning, the Radicals attained a majority on the court to go with the majority they already held on the council and began their first experiment in the exercise of political power.[53]

Despite these changes, however, the one assistant kmet the Liberals still retained was the only one who had any previous public service. Therefore, in the absence of Vuković—who was by rights the chairman—the acting chairmanship of the court passed to Milenko Petrović, a tailor, but a Liberal nevertheless, and the representative of the old ruling group. Almost immediately Petrović began obstructing the Radical majority. First, at a meeting of the council on December 14 he gave a false report on the price of flour in the local market. Since bread was the fundamental element in the diet of all Serbs, town opštinas closely regulated its price in the local markets by correlating it with the price of flour. Using Petrović's false price of flour, the council, in its inexperience, raised the regulated price of bread almost 25 percent, causing a tremendous outcry against the Radicals, just as Petrović had intended. Then, as presiding officer, he refused to call another meeting of the council to remedy the situation until December 22. Petrović also angered the Radicals by trying to unseat two of their members from the council for alleged conflicts of interest and by stating incorrectly that Pera Velimirović had no real property and therefore could not be a kmet. Finally, on December 23, when Petrović refused to bring to order a meeting of the council that was about to reseat the two ousted members, the council simply convened itself on its own authority and began ignoring him.

Meanwhile, the Radical victory created considerable stir in Belgrade. *Istok* reported that "in Kragujevac one hears a majority of sans culottes were elected, or as the Turkish *Oslobodjenje* itself calls them, the pantless ones [*bezgaćnici*]. . . . By this careless act the people of Kragujevac have really put a bone in their throats to choke on. It will not be long before they will angrily repent, and their repentance will cost them plenty."[54] Kaljević sent a new kapetan immediately after the election with instructions to keep the situation under control, which he did by putting both the editor of *Staro oslobodjenje*, Pera Todorović, and its printer, Ilija Todorić, in jail for alleged infractions of the press law.[55] But, as was possible under the new law, *Staro oslobodjenje* continued to publish, complaining bitterly about the attacks on the Radicals in *Istok* and accusing the Liberals of bringing back "intellectually bankrupt" people like Vladimir Jovanović to attack Svetozar Marković and ridicule the Kragujevac council.[56]

Despite harassment, by the end of December the council was working satisfactorily on its own, conducting such ordinary business as periodically resetting the price of bread, buying fire fighting equipment, investigating construction of a road to Kruševac, seeking twice weekly mail service for packages, and turning down payment to a street paver who had not satisfied them.[57] In February the reckoning came. On February 14 a group of eighty-seven liberal and conservative citizens petitioned for a vote of no confidence in the council. Since the petition had more than the required fifty signatures, the court had to call a town meeting for February 23, a Wednesday. This was a bad day for the Radicals, since all the workers in the munitions plant would be at work; so when the requisite numbers of voters did not appear, the court reset the date to Sunday, February 27, despite Petrović's cogent objection that the normal procedure was to continue the election on the next day.

Already by 8:00 A.M. on the appointed Sunday several hundred citizens had gathered in front of the unpretentious two-story opština hall. From the beginning they divided themselves into two parties, the "poor" and the "rich," as Pera Todorović says they called themselves.[58] When agreement on an electoral committee to count the no-confidence vote proved impossible, the three presiding kmets (two Radicals and one Liberal), who were standing on the small balcony of the opština hall, asked the sides to divide. The "rich" moved to a side where many other people, including women and children, were gathered. Since this side looked like a majority the kmets signified that the delegates of the "rich," Todor Tucaković and Milenko Nešković, were selected to tabulate the vote. The Conservatives and Liberals broke into raucous cheers, but the Radicals started shouting the division had been unfair. When Tucaković and Nešković tried to take their places on the balcony they were forced down to cries of "Down with the rich." The kmets themselves descended into the crowd, and, after considerable confusion, restored order. Eventually, the vote of no confidence was taken, with two Radical delegates doing the counting, but not before the "rich" left the meeting place. They left, they said, because the kmets had closed the meeting due to disorder. They left, said the Radicals, because once order was restored they saw they were in a minority and their vote of no confidence would fail. The Radicals were right about the vote, at least. By the suspiciously overwhelming count of 402 to 1 the town meeting voted to retain the Radical council and went on to deprive Milenko Petrović of his office of assistant kmet by acclamation.

Their work finished, the Radical leaders signaled to a band they had brought to the square for the occasion to strike up a patriotic song and someone unfurled a large red flag with the word "Self-Administration" sewn on it in white letters.[59] Emotionally charged by their dramatic and overwhelming victory, the jubilant crowd of more than three hundred persons proceeded to march through the city shouting "Long live self-administration" and singing *La Marseillaise*. The parade, which wound through the town for two hours, finished up by hanging the red flag on the opština hall. By three P.M. everyone went home for lunch, only to gather again about five P.M. in front of the main café in town to begin singing and dancing again. The celebration went on until eight P.M. when the standing army, always the nemesis of the Radicals, appeared at the behest of the local kapetan and cleared the streets. It was a fine party, but the hangover was enormous.

The appearance of a red banner in Kragujevac, along with reports that the crowd had shouted "Long live the republic," sent Prince Milan into near hysteria. Milan, who had not yet reached his twenty-second birthday, greatly feared for both his life and his throne, and not without reason. Right at the beginning of his reign, the regent Blaznavac had cultivated Milan's insecurity by emphasizing the violent fate of his predecessor, even to the extent perhaps of planting a false bomb in Terazije in 1871. The most humorous event in those early days occurred when an outhouse collapsed on Milan in Smederevo. In a panic the young prince started firing the revolver he always carried with him.[60] Milan also believed that some of the Liberals in the Kaljević government had participated in the plot against Michael, and he was prepared to believe even worse about the Radicals. He had already received one report that Jevrem Marković's society of 1872 was actually a conspiracy to murder him and establish a republic with Adam Bogosavljević as president, and he constantly received less credible reports of rumors and plots of all kinds.[61]

Milan's first thought on hearing of the demonstration was to occupy Kragujevac militarily and subject all participants in the affair to the harshest punishments, "cutting them to bits" if necessary.[62] Kaljević was able to moderate the prince's excitement, but Milan proceeded with firmness, arresting thirty of the most important participants in the event within ten days and asking his kapetan to reconstitute the opština government. Accordingly, Milenko Petrović was reinstalled and called an election for March 15, which, under pressure from the authorities, returned Todor Tucaković and the Liberals to power. *Staro oslobodjenje*'s complaints that the interfering of the central government in local elections was illegal under the new opština law were disregarded.[63]

The Red Banner Affair immediately became a cause célèbre. Radical lawyers from throughout Serbia rushed to volunteer their services. The accused hoped that the left-Liberals in Novi Sad, whom they asked to send volunteer lawyers, would also spring to their assistance too, but surprisingly their appeal was met with an extremely critical article in *Zastava* accusing the Radicals of wanting to do away with private property, marriage, canon law, and the family, and worse, of being supporters of the Karadjordjević dynasty (*Kara-dinastijaši*).[64] The Radicals could not respond publicly under the circumstances, but a shocked and dismayed Nikola Pašić wrote a heated letter to Miša Dimitrijević, an editor of *Zastava*, that not only made an effective complaint, but produced an excellent brief summary of the tenets of Serbian radicalism.

> The program of the Radicals is simple and consists approximately of this: the nation [*narod*] is sovereign and to it belong all political rights, including the right to organize the land economically. The political rights of individual citizens can be best preserved when the opština, srez, and okrug, indeed all Serbia, is organized on the basis of self-administration. Economic freedom, by which I mean independence, can best be arranged if we adopt the method of association and if the means for building industry and agriculture are not given to *one person* but to *an association* [*zadruga*] that can show it is in a position to administer capital and develop productivity. In other words: we want democratic freedom and decentralization. We want to preserve the nation from the mistakes of western industrial society, which has produced a proletariat and infinite ostentatious wealth [*bogatašluk*], and instead to raise up industry on the basis of associated labor [*na osnovi zadružnoj*]. We do not agitate to prohibit private property, but to bring the peasants into association and to work the land by machinery, because without association [*zadruge*] steam engines cannot be used efficiently. On what basis these associations will be made is a local question, and cannot be done by a recipe.[65]

The Radicals were not against the church, Pašić went on, but simply wanted to separate the church from the state. It was for this reason they advocated civil marriage. Pašić did not consider this a measure that threatened the family, but a step toward softening the tyranny of Serbian husbands over their wives and children and introducing greater humanity into the family. The Radicals also believed everyone should be taught to read and write at society's expense. And as for foreign affairs, Pašić used the word revolution to describe how he believed the liberation of the Serbian people and a union of the Bulgarian and Serbian people should be accomplished, naturally, he added, always "on the basis of self-administration."

Pašić's private communication was one of the most passionate and yet clearest defenses of his youthful socialism that he ever wrote. It came, of course, at a moment when the entire movement was under intense pressure and when rejection by people he had considered friends had provoked him. Not often did Pašić, publicly or privately, commit himself to views such as those expressed in this letter. They are clearly based in good measure on Svetozar Marković's idea that association was the ideal method of social labor. But it is also easy to see in them Pašić's clearer vision of Serbia's need to confront the problem of development. Pašić was not a romantic believer in the virtues of peasant life, although on occasion he made use of the idea. He knew better than most that someday, sooner or later, Serbia would have to face up to the challenge of the steam engine, and he knew that the smallholding Serbian peasant would not be up to it unless he could be raised to a higher level of productivity. Associated labor was the device the Radicals believed would provide this. Whether his proposal that the steam engine could be harnessed by associated labor is correct or not, Pašić's letter to Dmitrijević is consistent with his letter from Hungary in 1873 and again shows him as one of the few Serbs in 1876 who was trying to reason his way to an understanding of development that went beyond politics.

The trial of the Red Banner Affair produced a second important programmatic statement of perhaps more importance than Pašić's, if only because it was public. The main charge against the thirty men imprisoned in the affair was "preparing traitorous undertakings," the particulars of which included gathering under the red flag of revolution, shouting "Long live the republic," and singing *La Marseillaise*. Four of the accused were also accused of specific crimes, even though all of these actually occurred at some time other than the demonstration. For example, the charges of breaking the press laws lodged against Ilija Todorić and Pera Todorović in November were dusted off and reinstated for this trial.

The actual trial, which took place in June 1876, provoked Pera Todorović to a defense that stirred many Serbs. "I do not stand to *defend* myself," Todorović said, "I stand to *accuse*. . . . The bureaucracy has accused me in the name of the throne, and I accuse it in the name of our naked, hungry, and oppressed people."[66] "I will smash the state's accusation into pieces, grind the pieces into dust and ashes, and blow these ashes into the eyes of the state prosecutor." Serbia was not prosperous and homogeneous, as the prosecutor asserted. It actually was in decline, with its livestock population falling, the number of lawsuits increasing, and the wealth of large landowners growing at the expense of the landless. Todorović reveled in the description of himself as a socialist. The most sublime principle of social organization was "from each according to his ability, to each according to his need," he said, and economic relationships ideally should be based on common work and common ownership of tools. Advocacy of these ideas was certainly not a crime, and in fact the socialists were the only ones who advocated true justice. From the practical point of view, however, Todorović agreed that the most important task was to break the power of the bureaucracy, which in impoverished Serbia constituted the oppressive class. It was not the Radicals who put the rich and the poor at each other's throats, Todorović said, it was the bureaucracy—the class in power—which refused to make the reforms that would create a harmonious society. Only the people know what is right for themselves, he said. Once "morally and intellectually raised up . . . [by] information, acquaintance with the truth, purification of popular temperament, strengthening of character and cultivation of virtues . . . the people . . . will find the way to create what is in their own view good and useful for themselves."[67]

Todorović's speech in his own defense was designed for a different audience than Pašić's private letter and therefore contained more rhetorical flourishes, but its underlying themes were similar. Todorović emphasized common work and common owner-ship of tools, blamed the bureaucratic class for Serbia's problems, and called for more democratic control by the people. Naturally he legitimated his position with the argument that he represented not the bureaucracy or the prince, but Serbia's "naked, hungry, and oppressed people." More interesting for the question of political legitimation, however, is the end of his speech. A close reading of his final words provides an accurate forecast of how the Radicals actually were to go about achieving their goals in the years to come: raise up the peasants morally and intellectually by bringing radical ideas to the countryside, and then use the support thus generated to authenticate the creation of what is good and useful; that is, what the Radicals proposed in the first place. Circular though this argument may be, it is precisely what is meant by the abstract term mobilization—convince the masses of your program, and then argue that you are legitimate because your program represents the masses. The great success of the Radicals was that in the next seven years they did exactly what Todorović hinted they would do.

Most of the defendants were not able to articulate their cases with the precision of a Pašić or the vitality of a Todorović. They generally used three tactics to deflect the accusations against them. First, they tried to minimize the importance of the red flag and point out that no law prohibited carrying one. "Red flag! My heav-ens, is red such a terrible color? Are not the majority of our church banners red, do not our peasants make banners out of red scarfs, do not the police wear red clothing?"[68] Another tactic was to point out that *La Marseillaise* was no longer a revolutionary song. "In 1872 on the anniversary of the transfer of the [Ottoman] fortresses [to the Serbs in 1867] *La Marseillaise* was played and sung in a Belgrade theater in the presence of the prince. The Pančevac Singing Society sang *La Marseillaise* [on that occasion], after which they received flowers, as well as gifts and awards from the prince."[69] And finally, they tried to show that the police informants were lying, and in any case that no one could actually name a person who had committed acts in preparation for treason. "When one witness accused Dušmanović of consorting with the rabble, of carry-ing the red flag, and of shouting 'Long live the commune, long live

the poor, down with the rich,' the president of the court asked him
if he knew Dušmanović. The witness answered that he knew him,
because he had been a comrade of his for years. At that the president of the court asked the witness to show him which among the
people in the courtroom was Dušmanović. The witness turned and,
pointing a finger at someone said, 'There, that's him.' 'What is your
name,' the president asked the indicated person. 'Jovan Rogulić.'
'And where are you from?' 'From Irig' [which was not in Serbia at
that time]."[70]

These defenses proved to be well chosen. When the trial ended
early in July, all thirty indictments for "preparing a traitorous
undertaking" were dismissed for lack of evidence, a good indication
of the relative fairness and independence of Serbian courts, even
when the prince was vitally interested in convictions. The innocent
verdict was sustained even on appeal, although fifteen persons
were directed to remain "under police surveillance" for one year,
which was a harsher penalty than it sounded, since the Kragujevac
kapetan, supported by the government, interpreted surveillance to
mean that the fifteen men had to spend each night in jail. The four
men that Milan considered the most dangerous, on the other hand,
were all eventually convicted of relatively minor charges. Todorović was sentenced to nine months in jail for the press charge from
1875, a sentence lengthened to three years and nine months by
the appeals court in 1877. His coworker on *Staro oslobodjenje*, Ilija
Todorić, fared worse for the same charge, getting four years,
which was lengthened to five years on appeal. One other defendant
received a jail sentence for defaming the prince, and Pera Velimirović received three years, but only after intense efforts by the government to find a formula by which he could be imprisoned.[71]

The Red Banner Affair today is remembered with pride in
socialist Yugoslavia as the first politically significant outbreak of
worker protest in Serbia.[72] It had symbolic importance for contemporary Radicals as well, uniting them behind Svetozar Marković's
ideal of self-administration. But there is no denying the fact that
at the time the Red Banner demonstration was a serious defeat for
the Radicals. The Kaljević skupština, which closed only two weeks
before the demonstration, had just completed enacting some of

the most important planks in the Radical platform, including a new opština law and a liberalized press law. The Red Banner Affair gave the Conservatives and Liberals more than enough ammunition to claim the new laws were bringing Serbia to the brink of revolution and that Kaljević and his reforms would have to go.

And go he did. But it was not internal politics that brought Kaljević down, it was war, or, to be precise, the threat of war. Prince Milan had opposed war in the fall, and both his Conservative friends and the Great Powers supported him. During the winter, however, every other political force in Serbia became increasingly seized with patriotic enthusiasms, led by the Liberals. Jovan Ristić believed that if Serbia was to have a future, it must be as large as possible, as strong as possible, and as independent as possible. "Only an aggrandized, powerful Serbia will possess the requirements for independent national life," *Istok* editorialized.[73] Unlike his conservative counterpart, Marinović, Ristić did not care particularly what foreign diplomats thought of him personally, as long as he could achieve freedom of action for Serbia. And, unlike his Liberal colleague Jevrem Grujić, he had the energy and audacity to pursue risky but potentially fruitful policies. For two years *Istok* had been calling for a "national policy abroad," saying that Serbia should "carry the torch of freedom to the enslaved brethren" and continually comparing Serbia's mission in the east to Piedmont's mission in Italy.[74] When uprisings actually broke out in 1875 the Liberals intensified their calls for action: "Now or never! Help brothers! Serbia must be larger in order to secure her future."[75] By the beginning of 1876 the Radicals were taking up the call. "It is time for the organization of . . . a general Balkan movement against the Ottoman state," wrote *Staro oslobodjenje* a few days before the Red Banner demonstration.[76] The Conservatives too began to come around. Their new and short-lived paper, *Šumadija*, became perhaps Serbia's most strident advocate of war, and even the staid *Vidovdan* said, "Any government that wants to decide on [war] . . . can be sure of our support."[77]

Milan wilted under the pressure. In September he had been outraged when some of the standing army had been sent to the border without his knowledge, but in November he consented to a rapid rearmament effort, and in January he named a commission to begin planning a spring offensive. The most respected Serbian military strategist, Antonije Orešković, had already worked out a plan of action and by February the prince was saying his mind was made up to go to war.[78]

Diplomatically Serbia remained isolated. It had no allies among the Balkan states, even Montenegro refusing to enter into an agreement. Worse, all the Great Powers were pursuing an official policy of preventing war. Indeed, had the Powers maintained a united front Serbia would never have attacked the Ottoman Empire. But Russian policy, in particular, was beset by contradictions between the firm official line taken by the tsar and his foreign minister and the belligerent unofficial line propagated by the Pan-Slavists in the Asiatic department. The Russian consul in Belgrade explicitly passed these contradictory signals on to Milan and his ministers as "official" and "unofficial" views, so that the Serbian government believed that whatever Russia's public policy might be, when war actually began help would come. This impression was confirmed late in April when General Mikhail Grigorevich Cherniaev, Russian conqueror of Tashkent, arrived "privately" in Belgrade and offered his services. Impressed by Cherniaev's reputation and the cadre of volunteer officers he brought with him, Milan immediately granted the Russian general Serbian citizenship and placed him in charge of the Serbian army.

Despite the failure of his efforts to prepare for war, Kaljević realized that Milan was now set on attacking the Ottomans and that his government, consisting of secondary figures, would have to make way for Ristić and Grujić, the two leaders who could unify the government and skupština behind the war effort. On May 6, 1876, he resigned. Accepting that it probably meant war, Milan replaced him with what became known as the Second Action Ministry, nominally headed once again by Stevča Mihailović but, in fact, dominated by Ristić and Grujić. At first Grujić seemed the most aggressive of the new ministers, as Ristić put up a smoke screen of diplomatic activity to show Serbia's pacific intentions. But in actuality the government immediately turned its attention to the military issue. Only a week after coming to office it dropped Orešković's war plan and adopted one drafted by Major Sava Grujić, a Radical now restored to favor because of his military expertise. One week later the skupština committee, which had been working with the government since early February, approved the emergency plans they hoped would mobilize Serbia for war.

When the standing skupština committee had been first formed it appeared that it would be yet another Radical thorn in the side of the government. Many of the members of the committee were left-Liberals or Radicals, including Adam Bogosavljević, Uroš Knežević, and Paja Vuković. Its president, of all persons, was Jevrem Marković.[79] The committee began its work in early February by refusing a request by the minister of war to come and view the new rifles being procured, informing the minister that the rifles should be brought to the committee instead; but as it began to take a closer look at Serbian finances and war preparations the committee got more and more serious. The most difficult problem was the government's inability to float a loan. The only alternative seemed to be a forced internal loan, which the Radical majority on the committee did not want to sanction without some corresponding concession. Finally the committee approved an internal loan of 24 million dinars to be announced the moment the government declared war, on the conditions that a simultaneous moratorium on payment of debts be instituted and that bureaucrats' salaries be lowered.[80]

In this tense situation word of the April uprisings in Bulgaria arrived, as did the news in June that Sultan Abdul Aziz had been overthrown in Istanbul. The first encouraged the belief that the age-old dream of a Balkan-wide uprising to free the Orthodox Christians from their Ottoman yoke was beginning; the second convinced the government that confusion at the Sublime Porte made it a good time to attack, even though the new Ottoman government seemed initially to be inclined toward reform. Jevrem Grujić began to batten down the hatches for war by suspending the new law on freedom of the press, as he had the right to do by Article 38 of the constitution of 1869, and Ristić began to negotiate seriously with Montenegro about a military alliance. The former action brought a protest from the skupština committee since *Staro oslobodjenje* was closed down, whereas *Istok* continued to publish blatantly political articles; but when on June 16 a military convention with Montenegro was achieved all protests became secondary.[81] As official Russia sat on its hands and the Slav committees of Moscow and St. Petersburg enthusiastically began raising money and sending arms to their "Serbian brothers," Prince Milan made his final decision. On July 2 Serbian troops crossed the border into Ottoman territory, Nikola of Montenegro's troops did the same, and rebel groups in Hercegovina and Bosnia renounced the suzerainty of the Ottoman sultan in favor of either Nikola or Milan, as their inclinations moved them. The time for opposition, temporarily at least, was over.

4 : WAR AND POLITICS

If you win, glory; if you lose, disgrace.—Milan Obrenović

When their country went to war in 1876 Serbs of all parties believed
that the Serbian peasant, relying on his natural fighting abilities
and assisted by spontaneous revolts of his brothers throughout the
Balkan Peninsula, would defeat a decaying Ottoman Empire. The
idea that the Christian peasant secretly nursed a passion for rising
up against his Muslim overlords was an old one, and it is not dead
even today.[1] As early as 1597 a certain Father Athanasium claimed
in a request to the Roman curia that 200,000 Christian warriors
were waiting in the mountains for his signal to march on Constantinople, and in 1981 Stephen Fischer-Galati and Dimitrije Djordjević
argued that the fundamental ingredient of Balkan history was a
revolutionary tradition that lived among the peasantry.[2] "The history of the Serbian nation for the last five centuries is nothing other
than a series of bloody struggles against the Turks," is how Ristić
put it in 1878.[3] Many Serbs looked upon the uprisings that led to
Serbian autonomy in the early part of the nineteenth century as
proof that the peasant was a natural warrior on whom an otherwise
weak nation could build an anti-Ottoman policy. In 1804 Serbs
who had learned their military methods in the Austrian *Freikorps*
led an untrained (and often unwilling) peasantry against the cor-
rupt Ottoman janissaries and spahis. Self-taught but able hajduks
(bandits) made rough and ready military commanders, and in the
confused and relatively primitive fighting conditions of the central
Balkans the peasants they routed out of the villages to do the

fighting often did a good job of it. Eventual defeat did not detract from the many successes, the memory of which was kept fresh by a cycle of oral epic poetry that glorified the actions of the natural leaders and their equally natural troops. As Miloš Obrenović put it, "the whole Serbian people is under arms and a soldier"; a verdict confirmed by a powerful tradition of wearing arms. In 1876 Milan Dj. Milićević described this custom. "Earlier a peasant, well-dressed, armed, riding upon horseback with a long rifle over his shoulder, a pistol at his belt, and pair of embroidered gloves over the saddle was a real delight to the eye."[4] The tradition of the armed peasant, ready to come alive at the presentation of a threat to his independence, formed the basis of both the whig theory of liberal nationalism and the Radicals' faith in the peasant capacity for self-administration.

Outside of this tradition, indeed, opposed to it, stood Serbia's professional army, which had grown out of the personal guard that Miloš Obrenović created in the 1830s.[5] Serbia's first army law, promulgated in 1839, set the size of this force at 4,000 men, which had not increased by 1876, and 63 officers, which by 1876 had increased to 450 officers, many of whom, however, were commissioned just before the outbreak of hostilities from the gendarmes. In the 1840s and 1850s this "army" got together for training at the most only one month a year. Otherwise it acted as a border patrol, an internal police, and a personal escort for the prince. The troops received arms, but for a uniform the state provided only a cap.[6] Serbia's only other military experience came from individual participation in the Serbo-Hungarian wars of 1848, which produced a few heroes but little lasting impact on military development.

When Michael Obrenović came to the throne in 1861 he realized that a force of this magnitude was totally inadequate. It was too small to be a military factor in the unification of the Balkans—which he intended to make his main goal—and it did not accord with the national myth of the martial Serbian peasantry. Almost immediately upon coming to the throne, therefore, he created a national militia (*narodna vojska*) of seventeen regiments, one for each okrug.[7] Each regiment consisted of battalions from the srezes, which in turn were made up of companies from each opština. As

in the First Serbian Uprising of sixty years earlier, each soldier had
to provide his own shoes, food, and weapons, which were to include
a rifle and bayonet or, in the absence of the latter, a yatagan (a long
curved knife). He even had to provide himself with sixty shells for
his rifle and fodder for his horse if he had one; after 1864 a general
surtax provided uniforms for recruits.[8] Michael calculated that the
first reserve of this militia, men between the ages of twenty and
thirty-five, would provide a force of 50,000 soldiers. Supplemented
by the second reserve of men up to age fifty, the national militia
actually numbered 125,000 men when Milan ordered it across the
border into Ottoman territory in July 1876.

The officer corps that had to lead these troops, though much
too small for the size of the task, was well trained. In 1850 the
creation of the State Munitions Plant at Kragujevac necessitated
the formation of an artillery academy in Belgrade.[9] On the recommendation of Stefan Knićanin, Serbian hero in the anti-Hungarian
fighting of 1848, Prince Alexander appointed Franjo Zach director
of the academy, which became, in effect, an officer training school.
A Czech, Zach had been Adam Czartoryski's emissary to Serbia in
1844, when he had drafted the famous statement of Serbian policy,
Načertanije, for Ilija Garašanin. In his new position Zach created a
rigorous curriculum for officer training that included not only
military subjects, but many subjects designed to make the Serbian
officer a cultivated man as well, such as Serbian history, general
history, French, German, Turkish, hygiene, and dancing, and others to introduce him to modern science, such as physics, chemistry,
and mathematics. This five-year course was at least as demanding
as the curriculum of the Velika škola, so that the Serbian officer
corps constituted a significant portion of the intelligentsia of Serbia.
By 1876, 186 officers had received training in this school, and the
best of them had studied at military academies abroad as well. Later
observers considered them the equal in their training to officers of
the Great Powers.[10]

The increasing professionalization of the standing army and
its officer corps, small though they were, disturbed the Radicals,
especially from the moment of Milan's majority, when the young
prince began to assert more and more control over the officer

corps. Milan considered the standing army his personal tool, the one pillar on which he could rely in a country lacking the aristocracy that in Austria and Prussia provided the class support for monarchy, and the one area of Serbian life that reasonably could have some pretention to modernity. But the Radicals, not unlike the Prussian liberals who opposed the professionalization of the *Landwehr* in 1862 and precipitated the appointment of Bismarck, feared that the professionalization of the national militia was undermining Serbia's most potent democratizing force, the natural drive of the peasant for self-administration.

The peasants themselves were none too pleased with the militia. The original army law stipulated a naively optimistic training schedule. All able-bodied men between the ages of twenty and thirty-five were to train in their local companies on Sundays and holidays; the battalions supposedly trained two days every two weeks, and the regiments two weeks every year. Professionals from the miniscule standing army assisted militia noncoms and officers in the larger training exercises, but training at the company level was placed in the hands of local notables. The indifference of the peasants to unpaid training, coupled with the high frequency of the training, made it a certainty that the system would not work. When this became apparent, the government tended to blame the notables at the opština level. To bypass them, the government began to give militia duties to the local bureaucracy, that is, to the načelnik or kapetan, so that in the mind of the peasant the militia became simply one more bureacuratic obligation imposed from outside.

The solution, the Radicals thought, was not to abandon the idea of a national militia, since it best captured the healthy, if untutored, spirit of the naturally democratic peasant, but, as Adam Bogosavljević proposed, to abolish the standing army or, at least, as most Radicals suggested, to fold the standing army into the national militia. Failing in their efforts to do this, the Radicals continued to put roadblocks in the way of professionalization of the army, even as late as 1876, when Serbia obviously was at risk of war. They failed in their effort to cut the budget of the ministry of war by over 4 million groš, a sizable amount, but their proposal to shorten the time of service for those called up for special training from two years to one year proved very popular, losing by only two votes, despite strong objections from the minister of war, and their proposal to prohibit kapetans from serving as officers in the militia passed easily, despite Kaljević's objections.[11] Their idea of an army led by natural peasant commanders was part and parcel of the Radicals' concept of self-administration, as was their confidence that the Balkan peasant wanted political liberation and would fight for it.

It is easy to see how the Radicals could believe this since it fitted their ideology so well. But even the Liberals, who wanted the peasants to have no active part of governing, believed in the possibilities of mass revolt. Almost all Serbs of the state class entered the war of 1876 with a strong faith in the revolutionary élan of the peasantry, even though Russian advisors had warned as early as 1867 that the militia would not perform well in a modern war.[12] Clearheaded analysis of the failures of the armed bands that Danilo Stefanović sent into eastern Bosnia in 1875 also should have indicated that reliance on national revolution was a vain hope, all the more so since the networks of Bosnian agents established by Garašanin and restructured by Ristić had collapsed after 1873. In addition, the Serbs were not aware of the enormous changes that had taken place in the technology and tactics of warfare from 1860 to 1875, changes that made an untrained peasant force obsolete, even in the Balkans. Serbian military thinkers had not yet learned the lessons of the Crimean War, the wars of Italian and German unification, and the American Civil War, all of which demonstrated that firepower concentrated in good defensive positions could withstand heavy assaults, and that only very well-trained, highly disciplined troops carrying first-class weapons could have a chance at offensive success.[13]

Confident in the myth of peasant eagerness and blind to military realities, most Serbs were shocked when the offensives of July 1876 went poorly from the very beginning.[14] Relatively minor pushes into the Sandžak and Bosnia collapsed in two days or less, while the offensive toward Niš, which was designed to engage and defeat the main Ottoman force, failed within a week. To make things worse, a strong Ottoman counterattack in the Timok River region overwhelmed the Serbian flank. The Ottomans withdrew after their initial victories, but in October they invaded again, crushing the Serbian defenders, devastating large portions of southeastern Serbia, putting thousands of families to flight, and opening the road to Belgrade. At this point the Russians stepped in with an ultimatum that quickly produced an armistice. A peace was eventually signed in February 1877.

Even though for many Serbs this humiliating defeat was not expected, a dispassionate analysis of the situation sustains Milan's judgment of 1875 that Serbia was not prepared for modern war. The Serbs had almost no money and found it extremely difficult to raise any. The 24 million dinar loan authorized by the skupština could not be placed abroad, and the similar amount authorized by the skupština committee as an internal loan only generated slightly more than 1 million dinars. The forced internal loan produced only about 3 million more, and a semiprivate loan finally contracted through the Slav committees in Russia added only an additional 6,800,000 dinars, all of which fell far short of the need. The Serbs were poorly armed as well. Michael Obrenović had obtained about 30,000 smoothbore muzzle loaders in the 1860s which had been retrofitted into none too reliable breech-loading weapons with rifled bores. The militia also disposed of 55,000 Peabody rifles produced under license at the Kragujevac State Munitions Works, and a large number of obsolete Greens, which had the tendency to foul after only seven to eight rounds. Such weapons compared very poorly with the Ottoman equipment, which included Martini-Henry rifles of advanced design for the infantry, and Winchester repeaters for the cavalry, both of which had greater accuracy, range, and rate of fire than the Serbian weapons.[15] In addition, the Serbs were almost totally deficient in support groups, such as a commissariat, a medical corps, and a veterinary corps. When the troops left for the front their wives and families simply followed, bringing food and supplies to their husbands and relatives as best they could. The national militia was essentially untrained, and, most important, ineptly led by General Cherniaev and the approximately seven hundred Russian officers he had brought with him to conduct the war. In addition, the Russians did not understand the changes in military tactics that had been introduced in the previous fifteen years. When the inexperienced and poorly armed Serbian troops could not sustain massive frontal charges against superior Ottoman firepower coming from well-chosen defensive positions and fled in confusion—sometimes throwing down their obsolete and jammed rifles in the process—Cherniaev did not blame his tactics; he blamed the Serbian peasant, whom he believed was cowardly and unwilling to fight. After his final defeat at Djunis, Cherniaev fled the country in disgrace, wiring the tsar: "The Serbs all fled, the Russians all perished." Cherniaev's petulant assessment was a gross injustice to the Serbs, who actually lost over four hundred dead in the final battle compared to a handful of Russians, but is well indicates Cherniaev's hostility toward the Serbs, which was heartily reciprocated.[16] In actuality, when the Serbian militia was provided with decent arms and native commanders, and when it took up sound defensive positions, it fought well, considering its handicaps.[17]

Nonetheless, the greatest disappointment of the war for the Serbian state class was similar to that suffered by Cherniaev: the failure of the peasantry to confirm the national myth of the efficacy of the natural peasant soldier, although neither the Liberals nor the Radicals felt called upon to change their understanding of peasant virtues accordingly. Just as the opština law confused most peasants, so did the war against the Ottomans. "Why does our prince need these rugged and deserted rocks?" asked one peasant from fertile Mačva when he surveyed the canyons of Javor mountain. Peasants would defend their own village, and did so with great tenacity. But peasants from one region felt little concern about other regions. Let those who lived in these places protect their own homes, they said. "Why should we do it for them?"[18] Later Cherniaev recalled telling Prince Milan, after an initial inspection trip, that he was "struck by the popular antipathy to the imminent war. I had not noticed even the slightest enthusiasm among the mustered militia."[19] Moreover, the Bulgarian peasant failed as greatly as did the Serbs. Eventually some 3,000 Bulgars served with the Serbian army as volunteers, but the massive uprising expected by the Serbian planners did not occur. The main offensive had been taken in the direction of Niš with the expectation that the Bulgars would rise in revolt, which they had done in May 1876. Advanced guards were even sent into Bulgaria to distribute weapons. But the Bulgars did not rise. A substantial number of Bulgars who found themselves across the border in Serbia when the war started also refused to fight, and more than 500 of them had to be put to work on the roads instead. When Bulgars in Ottoman territory did not refuse Serbian weapons entirely, some actually turned them over to the Ottomans.[20] "It is especially disconcerting to our troops that there is no uprising in Bulgaria," the minister of war reported on August 18, 1876, "and even more that the Serbs in Turkey have not risen in arms."[21] "The participation of the Christians, particularly of the Bulgarians, failed in a manner which amazed everyone," said Jovan Ristić.[22]

If the peasant did not understand the war, he certainly understood its consequences. Serbia was left economically and physically exhausted. Technically still under Ottoman suzereignty and therefore without its own currency, Serbia could not resort to the printing press to offset its inability to secure sufficient loans, but the government took every other measure of fiscal restraint it could think of.[23] It put off paying bills, lowered the pay of all government employees (as the skupština, prodded by Adam Bogosavljević, had decreed), spent all its ready cash (including the cash behind such funded reserves as the Widows and Orphans Fund), promulgated special war taxes in the form of forced loans, and, most importantly, simply requisitioned peasant property as needed for the war effort. Requisitions produced substantially more resources than any other device, including the Russian loan, but it also produced the greatest hardship, as draft animals, carts, and food supplies simply disappeared over the horizon. And, despite all these efforts, by October 1876 the Serbian army was in desperate condition. Ammunition had almost run out and the Kragujevac factory had exhausted its supplies of lead and iron. The soldiers were very poorly clothed, many of them barefoot and in the light summer clothing, by now often in tatters, which they had originally worn to the front.[24] And these were among the survivors. By modern standards

the Serbs did not suffer great casualties. Out of a total force estimated at 125,000 men, approximately 5,000 were killed and 9,500
wounded.[25] But when this was coupled with an estimated 200,000
persons from the southeastern region of the country made homeless by the Ottoman invasion and destruction, it is clear that many
families in Serbia suffered great personal or family loss in this short
war.

Such a complete defeat had to have its political consequences,
or so it seemed. Milan, always sensitive to potential threats to his
throne, feared that the unrest caused by the disaster portended
not simply a political change, but an end to his dynasty. Mobilizing
himself for action, the young prince showed every devious characteristic that made him both a clever politician and an erratic leader.
His first reaction was to find a scapegoat, which was not difficult,
since Jovan Ristić had advocated the war and helped push Milan
into it. Ristić's potential culpability suited Milan well, because his
political favorite remained Jovan Marinović, with whom he would
be much more comfortable as minister president. The prince first
considered the possibility of a coup d'état in which he would suspend the constitution for seven years and rule as an autocrat. But
it seemed to Marinović and his close supporter, A. N. Kartsov, the
Russian consul, that the Conservatives' best course of action would
be to disgrace Ristić by forcing him to account for the defeats of
1876, and then to replace him. The plan on which Milan, Marinović, and Kartsov finally agreed was to use the Grand National
Assembly (*Velika narodna skupština*) that would have to ratify the
peace treaty to accomplish this end.

Grand national assemblies were elected separately from regular skupštinas and had twice as many members. The three plotters
preferred going to the trouble of a special election over calling the
regular skupština into session, even though its mandate was still in
force, because the regular skupština was dominated by Liberals
who supported Ristić. Naturally, for precisely the same reason,
Ristić opposed calling a Grand National Assembly which probably
would not have a Liberal majority. When Milan insisted, Ristić,
unaware of Marinović's machinations, decided to tender the government's resignation in the belief that no one could be found who

would risk an election at a time when Ottoman troops still occupied portions of southern Serbia. But just at the last minute, after a letter of resignation had been prepared, Ristić heard that Marinović had already formed a cabinet and was ready to step in.[26] Forewarned that his Conservative enemy was unexpectedly prepared to accept power, Ristić changed his mind and suppressed the government's resignation. Milan's surprise at this turn of events became concern when the results of the election, held on February 13, 1877, returned many oppositionists, including, ominously enough, some supporters of the rival Karadjordjević dynasty. Aware of what had happened when the St. Andrew's skupština got out of control, Milan now calculated that his own safety lay not in installing Marinović, which risked involving the assembly, but in ensuring that no sudden breaks occurred in the continuity of authority. Without telling Marinović and Kartsov about his change of viewpoint, he worked out a plan that kept both Ristić and himself in power.

Belgrade was buzzing as the members of the Grand National Assembly began to gather for the special session. On the night before the skupština opened, the cafés were full of delegates, both Conservatives and Radicals, who believed that their moment of reckoning with Ristić and his failed policies was at hand. The next day troops surrounded the National Theater, where the skupština was being held, to keep the crowds at a distance. After being blessed by the Metropolitan, the delegates went on to elect a Conservative, Djordje Topuzović of Šabac, as president, and a Liberal, Todor Tucaković of Kragujevac, as vice president. In Milan's opening speech, which the government carefully specified was not a "speech from the throne" that would require a response from the assembly, the prince set the task of the assembly as deciding on war or peace.[27] Filip Hristić and Dimitrije Matić had negotiated a treaty with the Ottomans that would restore the *status quo ante bellum*, which meant that the Ottoman troops occupying Serbia would withdraw. Milan put the question: Shall we accept the treaty or return to war? After Milan withdrew and Ristić reviewed the treaty article by article in secret session, the assembly accepted the inevitable and ratified the treaty by acclamation.

At this point the members of the assembly, including the Conservatives who believed they were about to overthrow Ristić, expected to go on to a second piece of business: assessing responsibility for the defeat. Instead Milan, who had been waiting in an anteroom, reappeared. Thanking the assembly, he accepted their decision and reported that the peace would be signed the same day. As soon as Milan stepped down, Minister President Mihailović took the rostrum and read the prince's proclamation declaring that since the assembly had ended its business successfully, it was closed. The ministers filed out of the theater and the lamps were turned off. When the stunned legislators finally walked out into the square, the captain of the local guard told them that since the assembly was over they were no longer immune from arrest. If they wished to avoid that fate, they were to leave Belgrade immediately. Police guards even accompanied assembly president Topuzović to his home in Šabac to ensure he did not attempt to rally the population against the government.[28] Abandoning his friends the Conservatives and cleaving to his enemy Ristić, Milan accomplished his main goal: avoiding the political consequences of defeat and maintaining himself on the throne.

Milan's coup ended Marinović's aspirations to become minister president again and interrupted the career of consul Kartsov as well. In 1879 Marinović became ambassador to Paris, never to play a central role in Serbian politics again, and a few months after the skupština Milan contrived to get Kartsov recalled for meddling in Serbian internal affairs, which of course he had been doing in cooperation with the prince himself!

The Radicals were equally as shocked as the Conservatives, but not equally subdued. They immediately began laying plans for the next session of the regular skupština, which eventually convened in Kragujevac on July 1, 1877. Once again, as in the previous session, Adam Bogosavljević and his colleagues worked out an arrangement with the Conservatives in an effort to overcome the Liberal majority. Milutin Garašanin probably passed documents from his Conservative contacts to Bogosavljević for use in formulating embarrassing interpellations. For example, in the military court proceedings following the Topola Mutiny that took place later in 1877, a witness testified that Garašanin had passed to Bogosavljević a telegram given him by Kartsov's secretary in which Russia advised the Serbian government against entering the 1876 war. Bogosavljević was supposed to use the information to write an interpellation that would discredit Ristić's war policy.[29] In the elections for officers of the skupština a Radical/Conservative coalition of about forty delegates voted for two Radicals most likely to get support from marginal Liberals (Uroš Knežević and Pavle Vuković), two left-ward-leaning individuals, the first of whom was close to the Liberals and the second of whom had an affinity toward the Conservatives (Nikola Krupežević and Miloš Glišić), and two Conservative opposi-tionists (Milutin Garašanin and Djordje Topuzović). Bogosavljević himself received only seven votes for president, far fewer than he had in the previous session, but it is likely this was because of the tactical decision in which he himself took part to maximize the voting strength of the opposition.[30]

But Ristić, unlike his weaker and less organized predecessors, was prepared for the new organizational tactics of the opposition. Having found a way to stay in power despite the defeats of 1876, Ristić was determined to keep this skupština strictly under control. He began by restricting permission to enter Kragujevac and by expelling ten Radicals, including Avram Petrović, from the city as a precautionary measure.[31] When he received a report that dele-gates of the opposition, including Adam Bogosavljević, had arrived in Kragujevac one week early to work out their strategy, Ristić called the Liberal delegates together to instruct them on the gov-ernment's goals.[32] By whipping his delegation into line, Ristić pre-vented the sort of individual decisionmaking that had characterized the elections for officers and committees in previous skupštinas. Instead of voting for persons they respected as individuals, in this skupština both the government and the opposition delegates, for the first time, voted for prearranged tickets. Ristić did not push party solidarity, however, to the extreme of absolutely excluding the opposition from committees, although he had the votes to do so. The opposition did not see this as a concession, but by the standards of a few years later Ristić's unwillingness to press the Radicals and Conservatives to the wall was actually a relatively benign policy. Still, block voting in this skupština was an important development in the evolution from informal parliamentary factions to disciplined political parties.[33]

When those who hoped to use the regular session of the skupština to call Ristić to account became aware that they would have little hope of doing so, they determined at least to restore Kaljević's opština and press laws, which had been suspended because of the wartime emergency. Therefore, after officers were elected and Milan opened the skupština with the normal address, a serious battle ensued over the skupština's response. The main struggle, if we discount accusations of irregular behavior during the war and the continuing demands to censure the Liberals, centered on whether to reinstate the laws on opština organization and press. Ristić had opposed both laws when they were originally passed, for neither was compatible with his idea of ministerial autonomy and his goal of a complaisant skupština. He now maintained, therefore, that in the current state of crisis (Russia had declared war against the Ottoman Empire in April) it would be inappropriate to return to a situation that would weaken the unity of the country. The opposition disagreed and demanded a return to the prewar laws. One draft proposal written by Nikola Pašić (who was not a member of this skupština) included other standard populist proposals as well, such as cutting the gendarmes, abolishing three bishoprics, and, naturally, cutting the pay of the bureaucracy.[34] It took the committee on the address and the skupština meeting in secret session five days to come to its decision: approval of the government's conduct of the war and continued suspension of the opština and press laws.

When the skupština's Liberal majority approved these decisions, the opposition took a fateful step that created a mischievous precedent for the development of Serbian parliamentary politics. Inexperienced in the workings of government by accommodation and compromise, frustrated by the government's possession of a guaranteed one-quarter of the skupština through the prince's appointees, angered by the abrupt closing of the Grand National Assembly in what seemed a clear thwarting of the will of the elected delegates, and believing strongly in the rightness of their cause, on July 9, twenty-two members of the opposition—including Adam

Bogosavljević, Ranko Tajsić, and several Conservatives—resigned their seats in the skupština.[35] They gave ten reasons for their act, among them that the government would not lift restrictions clearly intended only for emergency use, and that "national desires and needs" did not enter into the address. The idea behind this action was not solely to dramatize the opposition's principles. The constitution of 1869 stated that a skupština quorum consisted of three-quarters of the elected and appointed delegates. By resigning, the opposition believed they could prevent a quorum and thereby render the skupština helpless. Presumably they believed that this would paralyze the government and force it to call for new elections that would elect an anti-Liberal skupština.

But the ploy did not work. Ristić's tough old ally, Radivoje Milojković, minister of the interior, took quick and decisive action. Elections for the vacated spots were decreed for July 12 in the hope that in three days the dissidents would not have time to take their case to the electorate. Milojković directed local officials to use the "full severity of the law" against any efforts to assist the opposition.[36] The Radicals moved quickly too. Jevrem Marković and Avram Petrović organized students from the teachers' school in Kragujevac to copy over the statements of resignation. Overnight three hundred copies were made and given to the resigned delegates to use in their campaigns. Two who actually did so, however, were arrested and eventually ended up spending two years in jail for "insulting the government."[37] Ristić also ordered all soldiers, many of whom were still on active duty due to the seriousness of the international situation, to vote for government candidates. As a result of these tactics, only ten of the delegates who resigned in protest over the failure to restore the more liberal prewar laws were reelected. Adam Bogosavljević had no difficulties; indeed, his constituents wired him not to bother to come home and then delivered him his credentials so that he never even had to leave Kragujevac, but others were not so lucky. Ranko Tajsić lost, as did Bogosavljević's close friend Milija Milovanović and, surprisingly, Pavle Vuković from Kragujevac. Even Jevrem Marković found it prudent to resign his seat and return to the border as an officer on active duty.

Bogosavljević and his allies continued their opposition during the reconvened session with undiminished vigor, but with lessened impact. Now more firmly in control than ever, Ristić easily passed a resolution approving all expenditures during the war, despite an admission by the minister of war that not all decisions had been cleared with the skupština committee as called for by law. Prodded by his minister of finance, Vladimir Jovanović, Ristić persuaded the skupština to take especially strong measures of fiscal austerity to help the country begin its recovery, to find ways to pay the war debt, and to assist the homeless. The strict economies included disbanding some military units, selling hospital supplies, and releasing officers from active duty. These measures managed to achieve balance in the regular budget. To finance the special budget, which included payments on the Russian loan and the wartime requisitions, the skupština approved an excise tax on beer and a special surtax of three dinars per tax head.[38]

The difference between the skupštinas of 1875 and 1877 was striking, even though their memberships were more or less the same. In 1875, reacting to strong pressure from the populist delegates and under the leadership of a sympathetic minister president, the skupština enacted the most radical set of laws passed by any Serbian skupština in the nineteenth century. Two years later the momentum of the Radical opposition, interrupted by the Red Banner Affair and sidetracked by the war, was broken when the Radicals resigned their seats, only to have some of their important members defeated in the by-elections. Under the new circumstances Ristić had little trouble pressuring Liberals who might have voted with the left in 1875 to fall in line behind the government.

In 1877 parliamentary life was little more than five years' old in Serbia. When the constitution of 1869 permitted relatively open political discussions in the skupština the three basic political groupings of Conservative, Liberal, and Radical existed in such a protean form that most delegates had only a fuzzy notion of where they stood.[39] The first realization of most skupština members was that two positions were possible—either for or against the government. On the government side Ristić had a vague idea of the importance of organizing his supporters, and he gathered a number of distinguished political figures around *Istok* into what he called the "National Liberal Party." On the other side the Radicals elected to the skupština in 1874 began coalescing as a distinct group when they saw each other opposing the bureaucracy and sympathizing with Svetozar Marković's ideas of self-administration. One cannot speak of a conservative parliamentary grouping as long as the older Conservatives such as Marinović led that faction, but when Milutin Garašanin entered the skupština in 1875 he sought out the help of others of like mind and a young Conservative group began to take shape. By the time the Eastern Crisis erupted, the three factions had achieved a modest level of self-consciousness. The Radicals grouped themselves around a nucleus in Kragujevac, the Liberals around *Istok*, and the young Conservatives around regular meetings they held in the Belgrade café, The King.

The first parliamentary fruit of this increased self-consciousness was the cooperation between Garašanin and Bogosavljević in 1875-76. In 1877, when the Conservatives and the Radicals became even closer, Ristić took the process leading toward the creation of true parties one step further by insisting for the first time on absolute discipline among the government's delegates. Serbia did not actually have a parliamentary government in 1877 because ministers were responsible to the prince and not to the skupština. But it had been clear since Marinović's resignation in 1874 that the smooth functioning of the state required the government and the prince to take the legislature into account. When Ristić wrote the constitution of 1869 he thought good relations would be maintained by a government leading and a skupština respectfully following. Now, pushed by the new organizational tactics of the opposition, he found another way to ensure harmony between the government and the skupština—party discipline. On the one hand, his innovation was an advance in the development of Serbia's political culture since party coherence is one of the important ingredients of a parliamentary system. On the other hand, since the Serbs were inexperienced with the sorts of compromises and accommodations that make a parliamentary system workable, the disciplined voting of the Liberals provoked the opposition to walk out, creating antagonisms that made parliamentary government more difficult.

Serbia's situation in 1877 was perilous. At the time of the 1877 skupština Serbia faced not only the problem of recovering from the devastating effects of the war of 1876, but also the necessity of preparing for the conflict that Russia's declaration of war against the Ottomans in the spring of 1877 made likely. Serbia rashly entered the first Ottoman war with no assurances of international support, except for a useless commitment from Montenegro. General Cherniaev's presence, along with hints from the Russian consul, had led Ristić to hope the Russians would come to Serbia's rescue, but that did not happen until the war was lost and an armistice was imposed. Now Ristić was keenly aware that a Russian victory would create a unique opportunity for Serbia. He had long since realized that Austria was poised to prevent realization of his and Prince Michael's main goal, Bosnia, but expansion to the south could not be ruled out, and de jure independence was certainly a possibility.

To achieve these goals, however, meant taking advantage of the Russian advance into Bulgaria by attacking a weakened Ottoman Empire once again. Ristić knew that Serbia was terribly weak also, but he believed that only bold action could turn potential into actual gains. He hoped to enter the war as an ally of the Russians, who would supply Serbia with the money it needed to arm and provision its troops. The Serbs would apply pressure to the Ottoman flank, which also happened to be in a region Serbia coveted, and in return at the end of the war Russia would ensure international recognition of an independent, enlarged Serbia.

At first Russia put off the leading questions Ristić posed about Serbia's possible role in the new fighting. The tsar did not wish to incur any obligations in return for the dubious help of an impotent fighting force. But as the war progressed and the Russian army became bogged down at Plevna, the added pressure even a weak and small Serbian force could apply to the Ottoman flank began to seem more and more desirable to the Russians. By fall serious negotiations were under way to bring Serbia into the war, and in November the Russians agreed to pay the Serbs a stipend for every soldier they put across the frontier against the Ottomans. On December 12, two days after the fall of Plevna and after several delays occasioned by Russian reluctance to finalize their financial bargain, Serbia declared war on the Ottoman Empire for the second time in eighteen months. The Serbs were somewhat better prepared financially by their agreement with Russia than in 1876, but Ristić was no more successful in obtaining guarantees about Serbia's future than he had been in 1876. This lack turned out to have fateful significance.

The Serbian army was much more successful in this war than in the first one for three basic reasons. The army had been reorganized in a way to minimize the weaknesses of the militia; the troops were led by capable Serbian officers; and Serbia faced far weaker forces than the first time. One of the best of the Serbian organizational minds was Sava Grujić, who became minister of war in 1876. Grujić realized that it was necessary to stiffen the back of the Serbian militia, so he split the standing army, which had seen little action during the first war, into thirty-two small units that acted as cadres for thirty-two large units of the militia. In 1876 Milan had kept the standing army out of combat, fearing to commit the troops he saw primarily as protection for his dynasty, but Grujić's reorganization turned that force into the backbone of a considerably improved Serbian fighting force. Serbia remained extremely short of officers (reserve battalions of eight hundred men had only one officer and two noncommissioned officers, for example), but at least in this war they were all Serbs. Just as in the first war, the untrained militia officers performed poorly, excelling in cursing and shouting more than in leading. But the professional officers performed very well. The best Serbian commanders, Djura Horvatović, Mihailo Lešjanin, and Jovan Belimarković, directed the army in the field, while Kosta Protić, one of the most successful officers from the 1876 war, became chief of staff. At the middle level many younger officers, including Jevrem Marković, proved both their heroism and their tactical ability. At all levels this was probably the most able military team put together by Serbia until 1912. The Ottomans, on the other hand, were weakened by their lengthy struggle with the Russians, who by this time were streaming through the Balkan passes toward Sofia. Defending Niš the Serbs found only four hundred regular troops and two thousand irregulars, which the Serbian force of fifteen thousand men was able to defeat.[40] After Niš the Serbs turned toward the southwest, and when the war ended only six weeks after it started Serbian troops had advanced well into Kosovo, revered by romantic nationalists as the seat of the medieval Serbian empire.[41]

Two imperfections marred the gloriousness of the Serbian victories. The first was the Treaty of San Stefano. Extremely disappointing, impossible to prevent, and of fundamental potential importance to the future of the Serbian state, San Stefano revealed to the Serbs that their Russian ally—the great Slav brother they counted on to support their claims and hopes—had betrayed them. Deciding that its interests demanded a large and strong Bulgaria, Russia told Serbia—whose aspirations for territory toward the southeast in the direction of Vranje and Pirot was thwarted by San Stefano—that it would have to be satisfied with territorial additions toward the southwest, in the direction of the Sandžak of Novi Pazar and perhaps Kosovo. Of course, as the Russians well knew from their agreements with the Habsburgs, expansion in that direction was not acceptable to the other Great Power directly involved, Austria. Victorious on the battlefield, Serbia found itself abandoned on the diplomatic front, supported by neither of the two Powers whose clientage was absolutely essential in the negotiations that followed the war.

The second imperfection was relatively minor, was dealt with quickly and ruthlessly, and did not fundamentally affect Serbia's future. But this second event, the Topola Mutiny, reverberated in the symbolic arena of Serbian politics for many years.[42] On December 6, 1877, six days before Serbia's second entry into war against the Ottomans, the national militia was mobilized for the march to the border. The next day peasants gathered throughout Serbia for swearing in. At the induction ceremony outside Kragujevac, as the swearing in of troops from that region began, one battalion and part of another started to shout, "We won't, we won't swear." When their commander could not quiet them and galloped off for help, about fifty of the soldiers, after failing to get support from the other battalions, marched off in the direction of Topola, the traditional home of the Karadjordjević dynasty, about thirty-five kilometers to the north. At first it seemed to the authorities that more than four hundred soldiers were missing from the ranks, but many were only wandering around confused and returned in time to be sworn in and sent to the frontier the next day. Late that night the mutineers and those they had gathered on the way, numbering around two hundred, arrived in Topola and attempted to create a military force that would overthrow Milan Obrenović and bring Peter Karadjordjević to the throne.

Unfortunately for the mutineers—and maybe for Serbia, since Peter was a much more open-minded man than Milan—the mutiny was neither well prepared nor well led. Its commander, a certain Milovan Živić, had been duped into believing he was part of a wider movement, which in fact did not exist. His peremptory commands to local kapetans to send troops or be executed produced no additions to his force. With his two hundred men he was able to withstand an attack on horseback by the forces of the local governmental agencies, but on December 11, only four days after the mutiny, a contingent of the standing army sent by forced march from Belgrade entered Topola without resistance. Within a few days all of the fleeing mutineers were rounded up.

The mutiny as such had very little impact. The rebels could not arouse the other battalions present when they initiated the revolt, let alone troops in other areas. The response they obtained even in an area noted for its sympathy to the Karadjordjevićes was slight, and the government's forces defeated them quickly without a fight. If anything, the Topola Mutiny demonstrated Milan's strength. Not that Milan was everywhere admired or even liked. But with the standing army at his side very few persons were willing to risk joining a revolt that had almost no chance for success. The Topola Mutiny underlined the lesson taught by the first Ottoman war that the day of peasant revolt was over. It was not the last peasant revolt in Serbia to be sure, but the message should have been clear. Serbia remained as socially undifferentiated as it was in 1804, but it was no longer the politically undifferentiated and militarily disorganized pashaluk that rose against the Janissaries and that established the rule of the Defenders of the Constitution in 1842 by peasant revolt.

It now had a political structure run by an increasingly self-interested and powerful political class that commanded a standing army not sympathetic to the peasantry.

Whereas today we can see that Milan was never in any danger of a mass revolt in favor of the Karadjordjević dynasty, this was not so clear in 1877 when word of the Topola Mutiny reached Belgrade. Peter Karadjordjević seemed to be a formidable pretender. Ten years older than Milan, he was a graduate of the French military academy, St. Cyr, and had fought honorably during the Franco-Prussian War as a member of a foreign legion serving with the French army. In 1875, with the outbreak of the Eastern Crisis, he entered Bosnia with a band of about two hundred men, where he fought under the pseudonym Peter Mrkonjić until May 1876.[43] All this evidence of personal courage and leadership ability contrasted sharply with Milan's taste for court politics and his lack of field experience. To make things worse, in the fall of 1877 Peter Karadjordjević published a declaration of intent to return to Serbia "soon," and in the spring of 1878 he actually crossed over into eastern Serbia with a small group of followers, although after spending two weeks lost in the Homolja mountains he was forced to return to Austria.[44]

As soon as he heard about the Topola affair, Milan, fearing the worst, jumped to the conclusion that a major Karadjordjevist plot must be behind it. Since it involved the mutiny of troops, Milan declared the participants subject to military justice and sent an extremely harsh commanding officer, Milutin Jovanović, to ensure no participant would escape lightly. Jovanović curtly rejected the many requests he received to moderate his roughshod investigation, even when they came from the minister of the interior himself. Nevertheless, Jovanović turned up very little of substance. Apparently two Karadjordjević supporters, a priest from Topola and a merchant from a village in the Smederevo region—themselves led into the plot by two merchants from Smederevo—had incited Živić to raise the standard of revolt, but no evidence of any further plot could be uncovered. A great many people who had cursed the ruler or the government, a common enough occurrence in Serbian taverns, found themselves caught in Jovanović's net, but neither these nor the main leaders of the mutiny constituted a particularly high-level plot.[45]

Interrogation of the two initiators of the plot, Djordje Golobočanin and Damjan Spasić of Smederevo, however, did hook some bigger fish. Golobočanin was a well-known Karadjordjevist, and as a stock trader who had known both boom and bust he had traveled extensively and made many acquaintances. Among them were Aćim Čumić, Milutin Garašanin, and an elderly, wealthy Karadjordjevist merchant from Belgrade named Ilija Kolarac. Golobočanin also knew Jevrem Marković and Vlada Ljotić, Peter Karadjordjević's secretary. It was said he had even met the pretender himself. Golobočanin claimed that he knew Čumić as a Karadjordjevist as early as 1872. Although he said he had broken off with Čumić for five years, Golobočanin maintained that early in 1877 Čumić was talking about unseating the prince at the Grand National Assembly of February 1877. As head of the Conservative Club that met at The King in Belgrade, Golobočanin recounted, Čumić had led the agitation for an uprising against Milan. Čumić had even met Peter Karadjordjević, according to Golobočanin, on a trip to Vienna in 1877. Golobočanin also accused Kolarac of providing the money for the plot and Garašanin of suggesting that a skupština get rid of Milan.

Spasić provided incriminating testimony against Jevrem Marković, backed up by an accusation by Golobočanin. Jevrem had given him, Spasić said, a letter to deliver to Vlada Ljotić asking Peter Karadjordjević for money. Spasić had done so, and Ljotić had responded that although there was no money Jevrem should meet him in Novi Sad. No copies of the letters remained, but Spasić claimed to remember the contents, which simply asked for money. A telegraphist, who probably was bribed for his testimony, confirmed Spasić's story.

None of this testimony, even if it were all true, connected any of these prominent men to the mutiny, and the court never found a single piece of evidence that did so. But Milan insisted there was a plot and so a plot had to be found. Milutin Garašanin escaped arrest because his family had served the Obrenovićes well for many years, but the other three men implicated were arrested, including the seventy-seven-year-old Kolarac. Čumić, one of the fieriest, if least effective, of Serbian politicians, admitted he had met with Vlada Ljotić once but never with Peter Karadjordjević. He stated that the Conservative Club in Belgrade was simply an informal group that gathered to play cards and discuss public affairs, nothing more sinister than that. And it was ridiculous, he pointed out, to suggest that he might have anything to do with the Radicals, who hated him and whom he had actually persecuted when he was minister of the interior. Even Golobočanin testified that when Čumić spoke of steps to be taken after the Grand National Assembly he talked in terms of organizing for the regular skupština, not in terms of rebellion. In his defense Čumić stressed his commitment to parliamentary practice. If one wanted to change policy, it was in the skupština that he had to muster the votes. "If the nation elected people who did not want war, if these representatives said they did not want war, if the skupština overturned the ministry that wanted war, and if it had not voted the sums necessary for war—the prince would not have been able to go to war."[46]

But Čumić's defense failed, and for a simple reason. Neither Milan nor Colonel Jovanović had any intention of bringing in an acquittal, no matter what the facts. Out of 195 persons brought to trial only 22 of the lowest-ranking and most peripheral persons were acquitted. Of the 70 persons considered the most important to the mutiny, 23 were condemned to death, including Čumić and Jevrem Marković, and 19 persons received sentences of 10 or more years in prison. Ilija Kolarac was sentenced to 5 years in prison. After serving several months the ill Kolarac passed away. The harshness with which Milan treated this respected old man who had no connection with the mutiny at all further damaged the prince's already tarnished reputation.

As soon as the convictions were announced, petitions began flooding into Milan for clemency, especially for Marković and Čumić, even from their political opponents. Eventually Čumić's sentence was reduced to imprisonment. In 1880, when his friends from the Conservative Club came to power, he was pardoned.

Jevrem Marković was not so lucky, The reason Marković was shot, along with six others, had little to do with any connections he may have had with the mutiny, which did not exist. Instead, Marković fell victim to Milan's fear and hatred of the Radicals, his abhorrence of political opposition in the officer corps, and his personal aversion to Marković. Jevrem Marković had been trained as an artillery officer in Prussia, where he participated as a Polish volunteer in the revolution of 1863. He returned to Belgrade to become an instructor at the artillery school and commander in 1868 of the Bulgarian Legion in Belgrade. In 1870 he resigned from the army to become a lumber merchant, in which capacity he became active in his brother's movement in the early 1870s. As we have seen, he was behind the organization of underground committees in Kragujevac and probably organized the demonstration of peasants at the 1873 skupština. For this reason Milan said he would consider a vote for Marković in the 1874 election as a personal insult. Nevertheless, Marković was elected and, although that election was voided, he was returned to the skupština in 1875. In that session he became president of the skrupština committee that was supposed to supervise the government's wartime expenditures. It is not clear whether he participated in the war of 1876, but in 1877 he resigned his skupština position to take up active duty with the army on the border as a major. Courageous and a good tactician, he distinguished himself in the battles for Bela Palanka and Pirot, for which he was decorated.

In his memoirs Avram Petrović describes Marković's feeling about the accusations against him. Early in 1878, while serving in Leskovac, Petrović was visiting the apartment of Nikola Pašić, who as an engineer attached to Colonel Djura Horvatović's army was serving there also, when Marković visited them. Jevrem scoffed at the rumors of his implication in the Topola affair, saying the Liberals were just trying to cook something up against him and that Milan would never allow it. Milan had "greeted him in the presence of many officers more than kindly, congratulated his personal heroism and even his leadership, and [even] took a medal from his [own] chest and put it on [Marković's]."[47]

Shortly after this encounter, Marković took leave because of poor health and visited Belgrade. There Jovan Avakumović, an old school friend of different political persuasion and a functionary who know from papers passing through his governmental office that Marković was about to be arrested, warned him to flee. But Marković refused. "I am certain," he said, "that no one in any form whatsoever can hold me responsible in any way for that affair."[48] The next day he was arrested, and a month later shot.

During his trial, which was held separately from that of the others because as an officer he had to be tried by a panel of higher officers, Marković denied all connection with the mutiny, and it is clear today that he knew nothing of it. The main piece of evidence which permitted the court to comply with Milan's wishes to convict Marković was the letter he was alleged to have sent to Peter Karadj-ordjević's secretary, Vlada Ljotić. Marković admitted to his friend Avakumović that he had maintained links in the past with Ljotić, but, he said, this was before going on active duty as an officer. As soon as he retook the military oath, he said, he broke off all relations with Ljotić.

There is no reason to doubt Marković's account, but it does bring up the interesting question of the relationship between the Radicals and the Karadjordjevists. In the days when political parties were just beginning to coalesce, when the skupština was beginning to be a forum for discussing change—but when experience with parliamentary government had not yet struck roots into the countryside—the main legitimating vehicle of protest for most Serbs remained dynastic. A new prince from the competing family was something everyone could understand, and there were areas, such as Smederevo and Topola, in which the Karadjordjevićes remained very popular. Furthermore, Peter Karadjordjević was noted as something of a liberal. In 1868 he published his own translation of John Stuart Mill's On Liberty. As he proved when he actually became king in 1903, he was committed to the creation of truly parliamentary government, a marked contrast to the erratic egotism of Milan. Another attractive side of the Karadjordjević movement was that the family had some money—less than everyone thought, but still enough to occasionally encourage political initiatives in their favor.

If the Radicals had objective reasons for maintaining contact with the Karadjordjevićes, they also had a vehicle for doing so through Vlada Ljotić. As the son of the secretary of Alexander

Karadjordjević, Ljotić had fled with his father when Prince Alexander went into exile in 1858. In 1865, at the age of nineteen, he returned to Belgrade, completed the gymnasium, and enrolled in the Velika škola, where he became a follower of the Omladina and of Svetozar Marković. Arrested and forced to leave the country in 1868, he took up study in Vienna, but when Svetozar Marković moved from St. Petersburg to Zürich, so did Ljotić. In Zürich, Ljotić became a socialist and a friend to not only Marković, but to Pašić, Todorović, Velimirović, and all the others. In 1872 Ljotić went to Novi Sad, where he established close relations with Svetozar Miletić, and with Milica and Anka Ninković. It was probably through the influence of Ljotić and Marković, who was in Novi Sad at the same time, that the two sisters decided to go to Zürich to study pedagogy and then to set up their woman's school in Kragujevac.[49]

Even though he was by principle a socialist, Ljotić remained a close family friend of the Karadjordjevićes. He often visited Vienna, where he discussed Marx and socialism with them. Alexander's wife was especially receptive to advanced ideas and helped radical causes from time to time. For example, it is likely she gave Vladimir Jovanović some of the money to start his paper, *Sloboda*, in Geneva when he was in exile in 1864 and it was she who enabled Dragiša Stanojević, a socialist, to publish his book, *La Republique*, in Paris later. Ljotić was particularly close to Peter Karadjordjević, who was almost exactly the same age as Ljotić, Marković, and the other young socialists.[50] After the war of 1876, the Karadjordjevićes set up headquarters in Temišvar, where Ljotić edited their newspaper, *Narodni prijatelj*. It was to this refuge that many leftist Serbs repaired after the Topola Mutiny, including such an important figure as Ljubomir Kaljević.[51]

Unfortunately, many of Vlada Ljotić's papers, including about one hundred letters between him and Svetozar Marković and many letters from Anka Ninković, were destroyed by fire in the great Serbian retreat of 1915. But one curious undated letter from Peter Karadjordjević to Ljotić, almost certainly from either 1874 or 1875, has survived. In this letter Peter asks Ljotić to find a reliable person to act as a propaganda agent "below" (this could mean Serbia or Bosnia).[52] Peter was also interested in the lay of the land, perhaps from a military or strategic viewpoint. He says that when he finishes the book he is working on, "I, you, and the engineer will travel through." The question is, of course, who is the engineer? Sofija Škorić, the most knowledgeable specialist on the young Pašić, believes there is little doubt that it can be only one of two persons, Pašić or Pera Velimirović.[53] As we know, Pašić did leave Kragujevac in the fall of 1875 to pursue propaganda work in Bosnia and, according to an undocumented comment by one authority, actually met Peter Karadjordjević in Bosnia in 1876. It is known that one of Peter Karadjordjević's first contacts in Bosnia when he arrived as Peter Mrkonjić in the summer of 1875 was Manoilo Hrvaćanin.[54] Hrvaćanin had been one of the closest supporters and friends of Bakunin among the Serbian students in Zürich during 1871–72 until controversies erupted between followers of Bakunin and the followers of Svetozar Marković; after which he remained in Marković's camp.[55] No concrete evidence links Pašić with Peter Karadjordjević during 1875–76, but it is highly unlikely that Pašić would have gone to Bosnia on behalf of the Radicals and not made contact with Hrvaćanin, who was active in attempting to turn the uprising to the use of the socialists. On balance, then, it does not seem unlikely that Pašić met with Peter Karadjordjević at that time.

Opponents of the Radicals accused them of being Karadjordjevists, both then and later; an accusation they either ignored or heatedly denied.[56] Clearly some of them did have connections to the opposing dynasty, and close ones at that. This is not to say they were primitive dynasts, like so many less sophisticated Serbs. Nor is it to say that they engaged in plots to overthrow Milan, at least violent plots. But most Radicals did believe, and correctly so, that Milan was poisoning Serbian politics with his erratic behavior and autocratic leanings. At heart the Radicals were republicans, but they realized that in the international climate of the 1870s a small state like Serbia could not realistically aspire to become a republic. In Peter Karadjordjević they had an attractive rival candidate for the throne and in Vlada Ljotić an intimate connection directly to that candidate. The Radicals hoped, as did Conservatives like Garašanin and Čumić, to call a Grand National Assembly some day that would rewrite the constitution. At that assembly it might be possible to call upon the people once again to cast off an undesireable ruler, as they had done in 1858. For that moment the Radicals were prepared. Milan may have been wrong in fearing a peasant revolt, but he probably was correct to fear a Grand National Assembly and to be apprehensive of the Radicals' political plans.

But Milan did not eliminate Jevrem Marković because he was a Karadjordjevist. Marković was shot because he was a potentially dangerous populist leader whose reputation as a brave and highly decorated officer undermined Milan in his strongest base of support, the professional army. Milan insisted that the officer corps be loyal to him personally. Surrounding himself with officers, he came to their defense even when he did not agree with them politically (as in the Belimarković case), and encouraged royalist and anti-democratic ideals in the officer corps. He favored officers schooled in the Prussian style of leadership, ones who would find, as he did, the ideals of the parliamentary parties abhorrent. The Radicals, on the other hand, were partisans of a popular army, the national militia. Before 1876 they considered the amateur officers of the militia, the notables from the people as they thought, a counterweight to the professional officer corps. After the failures of these amateur officers in the two Ottoman wars, however, when the consensus of opinion was beginning to turn toward creating a conscript army on the model of the other European states, a proven officer like Marković would have been an extremely valuable asset for the Radicals, especially since the wars did not shake his faith in the natural abilities of the peasantry. Unlike many of his fellow officers, Marković gave full credit for Serbia's victory to the ordinary soldiers who actually did the fighting. "Our peasant soldier [*narodni vojnik*] has so much courage and self-sacrifice that it redounds only to his glory and honor," he told Jovan Avakumović. "With such an army it was easy for us officers to go forward and achieve victories."[57] Marković's populist vision of the army's successes in 1877–78, which of course ignored the failures of 1876, was fully consistent with the Radicals' interpretation of Serbia's true needs, but it was an anathema to Milan. When the Topola Mutiny gave Milan a chance to rid himself of such an officer, he did not hesitate. After hinting time and again that he would spare Marković, he permitted him to be shot on May 31, 1878.

5 : FACING INDEPENDENCE

What freedom is to the individual, independence is to the state.
—Jovan Ristić

For the Great Powers the Serbian war efforts during the Eastern Crisis of 1875–78 were a ludicrous sidelight. The first war brought Serbia total defeat, salvaged only by Russian intervention; the second war seemed almost hyena-like, preying on the weakened and defeated Ottomans two days after the Russian breakthrough at Plevna. But for the Serbs who favored these wars they were not sidelights, but massive and costly efforts to rescue themselves from impotence and obscurity. The humiliation created by knowledge of one's own weakness in a world that valued autonomy and strength comes through in the private comments of Jovan Mišković, later minister of war in Ristić's postwar government, which he wrote in 1877:

> Is it possible for a small people to develop and to progress morally confined to one area; surrounded on all sides by enemies; not permitted either free trade or the right to regulate its own tariffs; now allowed to decide things even in its own country as it believes best; where foreigners without rights or diplomas are [treated like] nobility; whose citizens in foreign countries are subjected to tyranny; where to be connected with world trade or to build a railroad one has to depend on the mercy of a small-time Turkish official or of some kind of Hungarian [*očekuje milost jednog padišaha ili kakvog madžaror-*

saga]; where one has to constantly beg wherever one can for permission to receive arms; . . . where one must always await mercy at the hands of foreigners.

Is this life?

That is why we went to war, Mišković said—impotence. "We had to fight, even though in ten more years we would have been more ready." But impotence is not a justification for war to those who are powerful, and it was to the powerful that the Serbs had to justify themselves. To do so they used words and concepts invented and propagated by the Great Powers themselves, phrases that would make the Serbs recognizable to the civilization whose power was the mirror image of their own weakness. As Mišković again put it, "For us the war was—*a struggle for freedom and civilization* [original emphasis]." Through it Serbia "entered into the ranks of the world fighters for enlightenment and civilization, . . . into the first rank of the civilizing peoples." We created "sympathy and reputation in Europe . . . and placed a cornerstone in the edifice of civilization."[1]

In a limited sense Mišković was right. The Treaty of Berlin, signed on July 13, 1878, recognized the independence of Serbia and rewarded the Serbs with some 11,000 square kilometers of additional territory to the southeast, including the city of Niš and the towns of Vranje and Leskovac.[2] "The war for the liberation and independence of the nation," as the Liberals liked to refer to the second Serbo-Ottoman war, seemed to have achieved what the Liberals characterized as the goal of 500 years of Serbian history: independence, an increase in territory, and formal recognition by the Great Powers.[3] But Mišković's fundamental insight into Serbia's weaknesses remained even more valid. Small, poor, illiterate, undeveloped, deeply in debt from two wars that left as much as one-fifth of the population temporarily homeless, and abandoned by Russia—whom the Serbs, Mišković among them, had considered their great Slav brother—the newly independent state found its natural economic ties with the Ottoman Empire disrupted by new borders, its aspirations toward Bosnia and Hercegovina blocked by the Habsburgs, its statesmen under heavy pressure from Austria-

Hungary, and its reputation as an outpost of civilization nonexistent with the Great Powers. The Treaty of Berlin not only granted Serbia independence, it severely limited that independence as well. Serbia had to change its constitution to ensure the equality of all religions, which meant giving equal rights to Jews and permitting them to establish businesses in the interior; it was required to build a railroad and assume part of the Ottoman debt; it could not charge transit duties nor raise the low Ottoman import tariffs until it could make treaty arrangements with its individual trading partners; and it was directed to retain extraterritoriality for foreigners.

For all their rhetoric about the nation, few Serbian leaders grasped clearly what independence might actually mean; namely that it would require Serbia to face up to international obligations imposed by the Great Powers, that it would increase the pressure on them to align with one of the two Great Powers that were contesting the Eastern Question, that it would heighten their sense of weakness and desire to be modern, and that it would enormously increase the costs of government, and therefore taxation. No one was more aware of these negative potentials under which Serbia entered its formal existence as a state than Jovan Ristić, and no one was more determined to find ways to free Serbia from as many encumbrances as possible. Ristić's task was made very difficult by Austria's decision to use the crisis of 1875–78 to recover from the humiliations forced on it by Bismarck in 1866.[4] Excluded from influence in the Germanies for the first time since the thirteenth century by a strong Prussia, and suffering from both the economic crisis of 1873 and German protective tariffs of 1877, the Austrians and Hungarians chose the Ottoman Balkans as the place to demonstrate that the Dual Monarchy remained a Great Power. As early as January 1875 the basic decision to annex Bosnia and Hercegovina at an opportune moment was taken, and in January 1877 Russia agreed in principle.[5] Soon after the conclusion of the Treaty of San Stefano in February 1878 Vienna began applying pressure to the Serbs. San Stefano made it disappointingly clear to Serbia that the Russians had abandoned them to Austria, and Count Julius Andrássy, the Austrian foreign minister, made it discouragingly evident that Austria would step into the breech and support Serbian claims at Berlin only if Serbia agreed to build a railroad on Austrian terms and to sign a commercial agreement that would confirm Serbia's economic dependency on Austria. Ristić, certain that Serbia would get nothing at Berlin without the help of at least one major power, did his best to ensure that the arrangements to which he obligated Serbia were no more negative than his limited maneuvering room permitted, but he still had to agree that after the Congress of Berlin Serbia would work out a railroad convention and a trade protocol agreeable to Austria.[6] In return for these promises Andrássy successfully supported Serbia's territorial claims.[7]

During the war years internal politics in Serbia were muted, not because the Radicals approved of Ristić's conduct of the war or his internal policies, as the one regular skupština called during the period showed, but because wartime turned everyone's energies temporarily to the unfolding of dramatic events. Ristić contributed to the calm by keeping strict control over the press and did not follow the constitutional provision that called for a skupština session at least once each year. The session for 1876 actually took place in 1877, and the one scheduled for 1877 was not called until July 1878. Even Conservatives believed this was illegal, but, as Nikola Krstić put it, "Who among us today refers to the legal regulations?"[8]

The skupština that opened on July 6, 1878, was dominated by government Liberals. Within a week it adopted an address to the throne, noting with pleasure that the powers meeting in Berlin had decided to grant Serbia its independence. "Europe can not forget," the address stated hopefully but not too accurately, "that this is the same Serbian people that from time immemorial has stood on the side of Christian civilization against Asiatic barbarism."[9] Two weeks after the final act was signed in Berlin, Ristić laid Serbia's difficulties and accomplishments before the skupština. Serbia had hoped, he said, to enter into the critical moments allied with the other peoples of the Balkans (as Prince Michael and Ilija Garašanin had also hoped), but when the first war came only Montenegro stood by Serbia's side. "After these events . . . it was obvious that [the Balkan] peoples by themselves were not able to achieve a true political union" and there remained only the possibility of agreement with a Great Power. But such an agreement implied limitations, Ristić continued. Before going to war, Serbia agreed not to undertake any action on the Drina because Russia wanted Austria to remain neutral. Austria had also informed Ristić that it considered Bosnia and Hercegovina its sphere of influence. In this way the limits of Serbia's interest in the west were established. After the victory, Ristić pointed out, Russia agreed to assign territories in the other direction, toward the southeast, including Niš and other towns, to Bulgaria. After vigorous protests, Tsar Alexander assigned Niš to Serbia—privately Prince Milan had told the Russian commander that the Serbs would fight if they were asked to leave Niš—but Serbia went on to take the steps necessary to ensure success at Berlin by approaching Austria. Ristić acknowledged that there were those who were against the war, and some who believed independence was not as important as increasing Serbian territory, but he held that the final result of his efforts, independence, was no small achievement. "What freedom is to the individual, independence is to a state."[10]

The skupština, accepting Ristić's argument that independence was the basis of Serbia's future, approved the agreements he had made, accepted his recommendation to keep wartime measures in force, and put off consideration of touchy issues such as restoring Kaljević's press law until after the elections for the next skupština. Serbia was about to begin a new surge of political activity, but in the summer of 1878 the skupština's mood was one of acceptance of the less than dreamed of but more than anticipated results of the crisis of 1875–78.

In the countryside the mood was less sanguine. Three years of crisis had caused a marked deterioration in the Serbian economy and in the conditions of everyday life. To supply the army during the two wars the government had requisitioned supplies without payment, dragooned peasant carts, and confiscated cattle and horses. The peasants got receipts, but the feed, stock, and carts were, nevertheless, gone. Since a high proportion of the country's able bodied men had been mobilized to the frontier twice since 1875 the production of crops had suffered. In eastern and southeastern

Serbia—through which Ottoman troops swept in 1876—thousands of families remained without shelter, schools were not open, and even starvation was reported.[11] Newly drawn borders disrupted ancient trade relationships in the newly acquired areas, raiding groups of Albanians and Serbs taken to brigandage threatened public safety, and the economically skilled class of Muslims had fled or were under pressure to leave. On the Drina frontier the Austrian occupation of Bosnia and Hercegovina disrupted life, and commerce remained constrained throughout the country by the continuation of the wartime prohibition on grain exportation.

Surprisingly, however, the bad conditions did not produce a political reaction against the government. In October 1878 Milan set elections for November 10 and shortly thereafter Stevča Mihai-lović, nominal head of the wartime ministry, resigned to permit Ristić to assume leadership of the government in name as well as in fact. Ristić used the opportunity to create a coherent Liberal ministry. Vladimir Jovanović remained minister of finance, while his old mentor, Dimitrije Matić, became minister of justice and Alimpije Vasiljević switched to justice and church affairs. Ranko Alimpić, called "General Pasha" by Pera Todorović because of his alleged cowardice in 1876, took over the new ministry of public works, and Jovan Mišković became minister of war.[12] Opponents were less impressed with the coherence of the government than they were with the weakness of most of the ministers, whom they considered a band of Ristić's disciplined clerks.[13]

Naturally, Ristić's new government found ways to ensure that whatever discontent there might be did not find reflection in the electoral results. It called the election for two days before the end of the wartime regulations that gave even more leeway than usual to the local police.[14] Nonetheless, many oppositionists were elected, perhaps 30 out of the 172 members of the skupština, which had been enlarged to contain representatives from the newly annexed regions. The government did particularly well in those areas that had had no experience with elections and that were administered by governmental appointees, but it did poorly in the area most ravaged by war, the Timok region of eastern Serbia, and in places with a tradition of returning oppositionists, such as Ranko Tajsić's district.

The most important step Ristić took to create a docile and cooperative skupština, however, was to convene it not in Belgrade, and not even in Kragujevac, but in the newly acquired city of Niš. This decision had good ideological grounds. Since Niš was near the center of the peninsula some said it should be the new Serbian capital in order to offset the Bulgarian choice of Sofia and to act as an attraction to the yet-to-be liberated Christians. On the eve of the skupština Prince Milan, hoping to underline his success as the liberator of Balkan Christians, moved bag and baggage to Niš, where he lived for most of the next two years, buying the city's most important estate for a song and confiscating much of the best furniture and other household items from unfortunate Muslim merchants and landlords.[15] For the Liberals Niš symbolized the successful war for national liberation and independence, and they considered it, therefore, a good place to begin defining just what those grand words would mean in actual practice.

Holding the skupština in such an isolated city also had significant political advantages.[16] Niš and its surrounding area was completely untouched by prewar Serbian politics, indeed by Western style government of any sort; it was cut off from much of the country by terrible roads; and it was administered by special rules published just in time for the skupština that required everyone to have a passport to enter the city.[17] As if these obstacles to the opposition were not enough, mail service was disrupted, troops were called in, no one was permitted to enter the city just to visit the skupština, and press reports were restricted, even though at this point Serbia had only two papers, the official *Srpske novine* and Ristić's *Istok*. The English consul in Belgrade, Gerard Francis Gould, took a dim view of these preparations. "Under the cloak of a purely democratic and representative system of government," he complained, "there is hardly a country in the world where the people really have less control over their rulers than in Servia [sic]." The results of the election, he reported, "were known to a nicety long before hand."[18]

Gould's analysis was not entirely correct. Many of the results of the election could be predicted, but not all. To take care of those who slipped into the skupština despite all precautions, the government began to harass both its opponents and what Ristić called "unknown persons" the moment the skupština convened on December 3, 1878.[19] Thirteen delegates, some Radicals and some from the group that later became the Progressive Party, were denied their seats because of technicalities.[20] Adam Bogosavljević's election was annulled because the electoral officials left the voting table at 3 P.M. instead of 4 P.M., despite the certain knowledge that Bogosavljević's neighbors would elect him whatever electoral rules were used, and Nikola Pašić, able to run for election for the first time, was denied a seat because Pašić's opponent, who was also a member of the local electoral commission, refused to sign the official report until the day after the election. This invalidated Pašić's victory, since the report was supposed to be signed on the day of the voting. Despite these harassments, both Pašić and Bogosavljević were reelected in short order, as were all the others whose elections were contested.[21]

The address to the throne in the skupština of 1878 was only mildly controversial, occasioning none of the struggles that some of the prewar addresses had evoked. One of the most daring new oppositionists, Miloš Glišić, wanted to include a sentence about Bosnia, and the old nationalist Archimandrite Dučić gave a long speech about Serbia's historic right to Bosnia, Hercegovina, and Old Serbia (the Kosovo region), but it was an indication of the growing maturity of the Serbian legislature that the battles came over real rather than rhetorical issues. The government faced two overwhelming realities: the necessity of beginning negotiations with Austria for both a commercial treaty and a railroad convention, and the necessity to find a way to raise enough money to meet Serbia's debt obligations and maintain the expanded responsibilities of a sovereign state. The first of these had little impact at the skupština of 1878–79 because negotiations were just beginning. Ristić hoped to conclude the trade agreement first and then the railroad convention, because the Treaty of Berlin stipulated that "until the conclusion of new arrangements, nothing will change in Serbia from the current conditions in regard to the Principality's commercial relations with foreign countries."[22] In theory this meant that whereas Serbia could not raise its import duties beyond those allowed the Ottoman Empire (3 percent ad valorem), the

Dual Monarchy could set its import duties as it saw fit. In fact, the Serbs had managed to get around the defining agreement of 1862 by various special levies, so that imported coffee paid a 15 percent duty and sugar 25 percent, for example, but Ristić correctly understood—as did his Austrian counterparts—that until a commercial treaty was concluded, Serbia remained at Austria's economic mercy. Vienna showed convincingly what this might mean when during the skupština session it raised the duty on Serbian pigs from 1.05 florins in silver to 2 florins in gold, a devastating blow to the product that constituted 40 percent of Serbia's exports.

The skupština opposition was not impressed with the severe problems Ristić faced in his negotiations with the Austrians, and it was not moved by rhetoric about national liberation and unification. It agreed that economic prostration was an important issue, although, as we shall see, it did not agree with the government's solutions, but it contended that Serbia's main problem was the government's authoritarian style of rule. Debate on this subject took the form of a renewed struggle over the press law. Instead of reinstating Kaljević's suspended 1875 law, which would have been the technically correct step, the government proposed returning instead to the law Ristić had installed in 1870.

The issue remained as fundamental as it had been earlier in the decade: how to reconcile the need for order and the desire for freedom in a society trying to make itself European.[23] All the government's supporters said they favored liberty. "When we have a national representative body, we have freedom," said Panta Srećković. But, he continued, "freedom of the press is not a goal, it is a means, a condition for achieving the development of social life in all areas of human ability." As Minister of Internal Affairs Milojković suggested, "it is not freedom when some undertake to scold and make ugly remarks." Furthermore, the government's adherents claimed, Kaljević's law of 1875 had not worked. "The changes of 1875 . . . were ruinous for the people and for public morals," said Anta Pantić. "Its fruit was the appearance of the red banner in Kragujevac."

The oppositionists, on the other hand, saw the government's desire to return to the more restrictive law of 1870 as simply another in a long string of measures designed to retain its control over society. The most aggressive oppositionist on this question was Nikola Pašić, who, in his first speech in a Serbian skupština, gave notice that a new force had appeared on the scene.

> First of all I would like to say that I am delighted that the government has expressed its support of this proposal, which has been made by some illiterate people, that we turn backward eight to ten years. I am delighted because that clarifies something . . . that to this point has not been well understood. Until now we have believed that the people who are in power are liberals, which is what they call themselves and consider themselves. However, today we see that these people agree with a law, or a proposed law, by which our progress will be pushed backwards, and he who goes backward is called a reactionary.

As Pašić continued to make his point about Serbia moving backward, cries arose from the Liberal benches and Ristić himself had to intervene to restore order and to permit Pašić to continue. To call the Liberals reactionary was bad enough, but to suggest that Serbia was moving backward after the victorious war that had produced independence was too outrageous for some Liberals to bear. Pašić, unperturbed by the impression he was making, continued with the argument that all skupštinas since 1858 had sought greater freedom of the press and concluded with the basic point made by all advocates of freedom of the press that without it there is no way to call the government to account. If we do not keep the 1875 law, he finished, "then we lose all guarantees that we can correct a fallacious, or even duplicitous, governmental policy that is damaging the country. . . ."[24]

Ristić's rebuttal was a model of cool, confident, even condescending argument; clear, well organized, and for his supporters completely convincing. Far from being reactionaries, he began, we are the ones who brought constitutional life to Serbia, accepted ministerial responsibility, and introduced workable electoral laws. If our suggestions had been followed rather than those that actually were adopted by the 1875 skupština there would be more self-administration today in the opštinas than we got with the more radical bill. Something similar could be said for the press law of that year. It was a sudden and excited change, not one introduced with careful thought, and if we had not suspended it we would not be in Niš today. After the defeat of 1876 we would have degenerated into mutual recriminations that would have prevented us from acting in 1877. The question is not whether we want freedom, but the degree of freedom we want. Our principle is moderation, not convulsion. The provisions of the 1870 press law are similar to the analogous law in Prussia, "that leader in the world of progress. If there be anything to be desired for our homeland," Ristić said, "I would wish that it achieve that glory and culture that Prussia has achieved. If it is good enough for the land of Kant, Leibnitz, and Humboldt, it should be good enough for the place where . . . those communist papers from Kragujevac publish." We are not going backward, and in any event those who wish only to go forward are like the doctor who would rather keep treating the patient until he dies rather than let him regain his health without treatment. "I take on myself full responsibility before history for this step."[25]

Ristić got his way, and Kaljević's law was not reinstated. The press issue was an old one that the Liberals and oppositionists had debated for years. New for Serbia was the question of how to solve the fundamental economic problems posed by independence, which ranged from how to protect the country from being flooded with Austrian goods to how to meet the enormous new costs of government, including paying off the Russian loan from 1876. Ristić was doing his best in negotiations with Austria to protect Serbian mercantile interests, but in the skupština a narrower issue excited the well-to-do peasants and traders who made up a majority of the skupština membership. The parochial question of whether small peasant shops should be allowed to operate in remote villages was one of the few questions of Serbian politics of the 1870s and 1880s in which direct economic interests appeared in the skupština.[26] Merchants and craftsmen both in the skupština and outside it opposed what they considered the pretentions of the peasants who opened village shops with arguments that sounded very much like those voiced at approximately the same time in more developed countries by the bourgeoisie when it began feeling threatened by the working class. And yet, consistently with the general pattern of Serbian nondevelopment, the arguments are not that of an entrepreneurial bourgeoisie, but of a patriarchal stratum trying to keep Serbia traditional.

Even if they presented themselves as peasants or claimed to defend the interests of the peasantry, most skupština members came from the better-off peasantry or were town merchants. For this reason a committee report proposing that peasant entrepreneurs be prohibited from opening a shop in a place less than four hours' walk from a town and that, in any event, their merchandise be restricted to a specified list of necessities received considerable support. Advocates of this bill argued first that they sought to protect Serbian craftsmen from the flood of goods from "the west," but, in a theme picked up and echoed by the romantically inclined intelligentsia, they also argued that their bill would prevent the demoralization of the peasantry and preserve the patriarchal virtues of the peasant household.[27] In their view village shops tempted women and children to steal grain and spend it on luxuries like sugar. Years ago, they said, you could see peasant women wearing up to seven oka of gold and silver ornaments. Now they wear none and are happy with ready-made clothes. Why? Because of the peasant shops that have brought them foreign and luxurious goods. Peasants will not be able to throw away their money at village shops if they have to come to town to buy things, because if a major trip is needed to shop the male head of the household (domaćin) will be able to control the spending.

The argument is interesting not just because it is self-serving, but because it is an argument on behalf of a mercantile class in terms of a patriarchal peasant ethic, that is, an argument whose tendency is to idealize just that aspect of society that stood in the way of the kind of economic development that in the long run would greatly benefit the mercantile element. The argument is analogous to the one presented in 1873 on behalf of the Law on Six Days Plowing, which was designed to preserve the peasant household, even if this was not in the interest of development. In the case of the peasant shops the policy goal was to preserve patriarchal norms in the village, but for the purpose of protecting the interests of town merchants as well. In neither case was there any suggestion that Serbia might be strengthened by a more diverse economic network or that increased social complexity would in the long run profit those with resources to invest.[28] The undifferentiated class structure with which Serbia entered its era of development did not encourage a developmental mind-set among those with property. Embedded in a peasant society, even the merchants and craftsmen had no clear idea beyond short-term self-interest of what was needed in the economic sphere.

Some, but not all, opposition members spoke out against the proposed law. Peasant shops were not sinful, they said, and the desire for luxuries was not a peasant vice but an urban one. Peasant women and children were not like their counterparts in town who sat around without working and had time for shopping. Peasants worked. And it was not the little peasant shops but the well capitalized town stores that had got the peasants so deeply into debt that they could not pay it off. Despite these arguments, in the end the law was enacted, although it had little effect in preventing the actual spread of peasant shops.

Peasant delegates aired dozens of other complaints and suggestions concerning Serbia's economic condition at the 1878–79 skupština. The most well founded perhaps concerned the pitiable state of Serbia's highways, which even the minister of the interior admitted had received fifteen to twenty years of wear during the three years of the crisis, wear that could not be repaired since the able-bodied men were at the front.[29] Peasant members wanted the obligation to work on local roads abolished, but where would the money then come from to repair the roads? Many complaints about banditry showed that the roads, in any event, were none too secure. The rise of social violence since the beginning of the wars prompted many suggestions for making the punishments for crimes more severe, even exiling criminals and their families to a penal region after a second conviction.[30] Another subject that received attention was how to help the people burned out of their homes in 1876 and still unable to support themselves. It went almost without saying that the moratorium on the payment of debts would have to be continued, and it might be possible to help get schools restarted by transferring some funds from hospital accounts, but once again the question remained, where would the money come from?

The government was not unconcerned with these things, but it had even more serious money problems on its mind: how was the budget to be balanced, and, most importantly, how could Serbia begin paying off a war debt of over 30 million dinars, or about 1.5 times the regular annual budget?[31] Two-thirds of the debt was internal. The government had floated both a voluntary loan and a forced loan during the war. Both bonds were virtually worthless when the peace came, since prospects for their redemption seemed so poor. The receipts that had been issued promising repayment to those whose goods had been requisitioned for the war effort were a second major source of internal debt. And third, about 12 million dinars were owed to Russia. Disappointed though Serbia was with Russian lack of support in 1878, the debt had to be repaid none the less.

Adam Bogosavljević and some of his circle still naively believed that the answer to the money question was cutting the bureaucracy. They brought forward suggestion after suggestion for lowering the pay of state employees, cutting the wood allowance to officers, lessening the expense money of officials in the newly acquired lands, and recovering money they believed had been embezzled in the failure of the Serbian National Bank in 1873. During the budget debates they suggested cutting the funds allocated to almost every governmental activity, including the national skupština, pensions to retired state councillors, regular pensions, raises for state employees, credits for unforeseen expenses, and the budget for "exceptional needs"—all without success.

Most other observers, however, realized that Serbia could meet the obligations of independence only by finding new sources of income. The government's solution came from Vladimir Jovanović, the minister of finance, one of the few Serbian intellectuals who favored development and at the same time understood the structural needs of the Serbian economy. Jovanović had a comprehensive plan for dealing with Serbia's unfortunate financial situation that was at the same time a formula for development.[32] He had introduced Serbia's first indigenous money (small denomination copper coins) during the war years and now proposed to introduce gold and silver coins; he realized a national bank was essential for making cheaper credit available for business; he understood that Serbia would have to implement the metric system more quickly; and he even proposed building a packing plant so that Serbia would no longer have to export its main product, pigs, "as live animals, but as lard, ham, dried meat, and so forth."[33] Most of all, Jovanović knew that the only way to cover the enormous new costs of independence was to raise taxes. He advocated an entirely new tax, the official title for which was expressed in the "Law on the sources for retiring the state debt contracted in the war for liberation and independence of the nation." Unofficially the tax was called the "registration in business [upis u radnju]," but popularly it took on the derogatory name of the "patentarina."

The idea of a patent, or a fee for conducting one's trade, originated during the French Revolution both as a way to raise money and to further laissez-faire principles.[34] Under the ancien régime, when corporate bodies controlled entry into crafts, journeymen had to pay a large fee to the corporation (guild) upon becoming a master. The patente introduced by the French Constituent Assembly in 1791 did away with the corporations, and thus with this capital requirement; instead the Constituent Assembly decided to levy a fee on all who wished to enter a craft or profession. After April 1, 1791, a Frenchman could enter any profession that would "conform to his talents and be useful in his affairs" simply by announcing his intention to the local authorities and paying a tax amounting to 10 percent of the annual rental value of his home. The French chose this method of raising money rather than a tax on income to prevent investigations into the financial affairs of individuals, because "the insult to liberty of all domestic inquisitions should be rejected by all means."[35] Franz Joseph introduced the patent in the Habsburg Empire when he abolished guilds there in 1859.[36] In Serbia, however, Jovanović proposed a patent not as a social reform and not to liberate trade (since the Serbian guilds, although in decline, were not legally abolished until 1910), but solely to raise money.[37] Therefore, despite the unofficial title of the law—a "registration in business"—and despite overtones from the

French Revolution and from Austrian experience that gave the patent an aura of laissez-faire economics, for Jovanović the device was simply an annual tax by means of which he hoped to pay off Serbia's debt.

In fact, rather than being a proposal consistent with the liberal economics with which Jovanić's is identified, the patentarina was consistent with the general tendency of the state class in the nineteenth century to adhere to its bargain with the peasantry. Direct producers, which comprised the vast bulk of the peasantry, were not to pay the patentarina. Only trades considered economically nonessential were to pay. Thus the patentarina proposal specifically named moneylending, speculation, public baths, circuses, inns, tobacco shops, and playing-card sales as taxable.[38] Jovanović also proposed to tax the income of bureaucrats, monasteries, churches, and doctors. The most interesting inclusion on the taxable list were middlemen and factors, who apparently were not considered active producers of economic welfare but merely manipulators of goods produced by others. Excluded were all branches of agriculture, crafts and the skilled professions, literary work and bookselling, state enterprises, and performances at the state theater. Each person responsible for a named business or receiving income from a named source was to register with the local authorities and pay a tax on the gross income of his activities according to a tax table of twenty-one classes. A local committee was to review the income statement to make sure it was accurate. The most that could be paid in patentarina would be 4 percent on incomes over 50,000 dinars.

To give an idea of what this tax would mean to an individual we have the example of Nikola Pašić. In 1879 Pašić earned 2,526 dinars as a state-employed engineer and had to pay 20 dinars in patentarina.[39] This was not the only tax Pašić or any adult male would have to pay. The basic tax, called the *danak*, remained from Ottoman times and was paid twice a year. Originally a head tax on all heads of families, it had evolved by the late 1870s into a tax on adult males that included not only a basic tax but surcharges for schools, local government, road building, and war invalids.[40] Since Pašić's danak in 1877 amounted to approximately 80 dinars, his total tax burden in 1879 was probably about 100 dinars, or about 4 percent of his income.[41]

Jovanović's patentarina proposal came to the skupština one month into the session. Ristić had demonstrated his control over the proceedings with the passage of his press law and other governmental proposals, while the opposition remained poorly coordinated, in part because Adam Bogosavljević was ill and did not have the energy to work out the cooperative agreements he had fashioned in the 1877 skupština. But Ristić's crude efforts to harass the opposition kept them in a state of high moral dudgeon, which Ristić's supporters reciprocated with strong feelings of revulsion toward persons they considered threats to the stability of the crown and nation. In a legislative body without a tradition of loyal opposition and where the skills of accommodation and compromise had not yet had a chance to establish themselves, strong feelings on both sides led to intensely personal debates and attacks. The most notorious of these occurred when government supporter M. Trifunac jumped up at one point after Pašić had spoken and shouted "These men want to throw out our prince and our government as if it were 1848 when we all fled through the window." After a huge uproar Trifunac was expelled from the skupština for eight days.[42]

Less comic was Ristić's attack on Adam Bogosavljević. Early in the session Bogosavljević and some opposition colleagues, including Nikola Pašić, complained that the government was mistreating the citizenry of the newly acquired town of Prokuplje. Ristić's response was immediate. "Adam forgets that the war was not begun with his vote. . . . You contributed nothing to the liberation of our brothers here, and now you advise us how we ought to embrace them. . . . I reject that kind of advice from Mr. Adam."[43] Later, in debating the patentarina, Miloš Glišić, noting how Vladimir Jovanović had mentioned he had been in exile in Switzerland, said, "Fine, but that gives me the occasion to suggest . . . that perhaps even he himself will remember that 'Liberty,' [a journal] published by some sort of tobacco shop owner in Switzerland, which his proposal will now threaten. In terms of social science *[u nauci]* his proposal is nothing more than shoddy merchandise and garbage."[44] Jovanović answered this attack on the proudest moment of his life, his publication of an opposition paper entitled *Liberty* in Geneva while in exile from Prince Michael, by calling into question Glišić's courage during the wartime period. And finally, when Nikola Pašić proposed saving money in the budget by approving pay raises only for professors and telegraphists, Vladimir Jovanović responded by pointing out that in 1877 when Pašić was offered a position as professor of engineering at the Velika škola he turned it down because the rank offered was one level too low to suit him. Now Pašić was trying to deny others raises, Jovanović charged. Pašić retorted that he was willing to serve without pay if Jovanović was.

These emotional personal attacks created such an atmosphere of mistrust that by the time Jovanović introduced the patentarina the opposition was in no mood to see anything good about it. Jovanović presented the tax as one on luxuries, but several peasant delegates protested that this was a sophism, because whenever a merchant had to pay a tax he passed it on to the peasant anyway. Others feared this was only the opening wedge in a tax program that eventually would expand either to tax other items or to tax the peasantry directly. Today trade, tomorrow the peasant, was the warning by Ranko Tajsić.

Nikola Pašić gave the most realistic speech in opposition. Despite his congenital need to oppose anything proposed by the government, Pašić had some understanding of Serbia's developmental situation and recognized that its obligations were just beginning.[46] After a few sardonic comments about Jovanović's tendency to make corrections in his speeches before they appeared in the stenographic accounts, Pašić disputed the government's claim that the patentarina would help industry. He said that for industry to grow capital must be much cheaper than before and the government would have to introduce a protective tariff. "With this program we achieve almost nothing except making goods more expensive to consumers, wherever those goods are produced." Furthermore the government was wrong to say this was the only tax they would need. "In no way can we pay a debt of thirty million with this tax nor can we pay off that [portion of the Ottoman] debt we were obligated to accept by the Berlin agreement. And we have other debts to pay, much greater ones than any delegate can imagine at this time. This is only the beginning; we will have to introduce still other laws that will raise our income. Thus the only question is how to do it in a way that will not be damaging to the survival and progress of Serbia." What then was the best way to raise the money they needed? "I hold that tax is best which is assessed according to wealth *[po imućnosti]* and according to net income. . . . An indirect tax [like the patentarina] costs much more than direct taxes and by its regulations hinders the development of the state." However, having proved to his own satisfaction that the patentarina was unfair, immoral, expensive to administer, and damaging to business, Pašić had nothing better to suggest than putting the question off to the next skupština, an obviously unsatisfactory proposal.

The flaw in the opposition's complaints about the patentarina was that, except for Pašić's vague remarks about the desirability of a direct tax on incomes, it had no alternative program. One of the more demagogic Liberals, Panta Srećković, described the opposition's tax policy like this: "to call out the police, cavalry, swords, and revolvers, and whenever we meet up with a rich person say, 'Give, pay!' And if you have no money at least hand over your watch."[47] The Radicals complained that it was the Liberals who were proposing to hold up the peasant. Vladimir Jovanović, one of Serbia's most assiduous collectors of statistical data, rebutted this claim by presenting figures showing that in comparison with other countries Serbia was not heavily taxed.[48] Jovanović pointed out that the debt had to be paid in any event and this method was not only consistent with the best principles of Western administrative science, which for Jovanović was a strong point in its favor, but the fairest and least painful way that could be devised to undertake Serbia's obligations as a free and independent nation. Despite his reasoned arguments, the patentarina passed only 90 to 60, an ominous number of negative votes, about twice as high as the opposition could normally count on.

The skupština of 1878–79 passed a number of important laws concerning various aspects of Serbian life, but with the exception of the patentarina, it did not actually attack any of the serious problems Serbia faced. The overall direction of Serbia's economy and politics was not in the skupština's hands, since it depended in significant measure on what kind of lasting arrangement could be made with Austria-Hungary. In addition, few public figures grasped the enormous costs of becoming a European state, as all factions claimed they wished to do. In terms of Serbian political development the skupština of 1878—79 was significant, however, because it marked the appearance of Nikola Pašić on the public stage. Since no party organizations existed to coordinate positions after the November elections, and because Adam Bogosavljević was increasingly ineffective due to illness, the opposition in 1878—79 was less well organized than it had been in 1877. Because of Pašić, however, its future was considerably brighter. Pašić had three qualities that lifted him above the ordinary Serbian oppositionist. First, unlike Bogosavljević, he had a higher education, which not only gave him a broader vision of Serbia's position in the world, a modest understanding of European politics, and some technical expertise, but personal prestige equivalent to the numerous government ministers and representatives whom he opposed. Unlike Bogosavljević, Glišić, Tajsić, and others, he spoke the government's language. More significant were Pašić's personal qualities, two of which were central to his success. He had a keen appreciation of what was important and what was not, and he was an organizer. Pašić was quite willing to use any debating tricks, populist rhetoric, delaying tactic, or obstructionism that would hinder the government in completing its program. He was a consummate oppositionist; but he never confused these tactics with substance. "If in the practical struggle we attack this or that institution or even personality," he said in a letter to Miša Dimitrijević in 1876, "that is because the tactical struggle of the party demands it. The struggle for the lessening of the pay of bureaucrats is that sort of thing. One cannot deduce our positive program just from the fact that we attack."[49] And Pašić always was alert to what sort of organization would be needed to accomplish a goal. Oppositionists came to the 1878–79 skupština as individuals and, except for Adam Bogosavljević, without a leader. When they left, Pašić already had emerged as their man of the future.

The nine months that intervened from the closing of the 1878–

79 skupština on February 1, 1879, and the opening of the next skupština in November of the same year was a period of humiliating negotiations with Austria-Hungary externally and of outraged opposition to the patentarina internally. Ristić wanted to begin his negotiations with the Austrians with the commercial agreement. But when Serbia rejected out of hand an Austrian suggestion for a complete tariff union, Vienna demanded that the railroad negotiations proceed first. Then Ristić tried to insist that the negotiations be conducted with all four interested parties, Serbia, Austria-Hungary, Bulgaria, and the Ottoman Empire, on the two sensible grounds that the Treaty of Berlin called for such negotiations and that it was not reasonable for Serbia to build a railroad without assurance that it would connect with lines to the south. But Austria would not hear of bringing the other states into the negotiations until Serbia had agreed to its portion. In the meanwhile, to keep the pressure on Serbia, besides raising the tariff on pigs, Austria closed its border to beef cattle, claiming disease, and stopped its Danube River boats from calling at Belgrade.[50] Still, by the end of 1879 no agreement had yet been reached.

Inside Serbia the most emotional issue, and one the opposition seized upon with great vigor, was the implementation of the patentarina. Immediately after the new tax became law Vladimir Jovanović ordered local officials to levy it, even though the forms for gathering the necessary information were not ready yet.[51] By March the State Council approved the instructions for completing the registration, and on April two types of forms were distributed.[52] On the first, which was ordinary paper size, the individual stated his name and address, his type of business, and its location. He was also asked to indicate how much he had invested in his business and its gross income. The second form was a large register in which this information was entered and totals indicated. Questions immediately arose: did the law really mean gross income? (it did); did women pay the tax? (yes, if they owned income-producing property); was all income to be included? (yes, including income in kind, such as the wood supplied free of charge to teachers).[53]

From the beginning Vladimir Jovanović was impatient with such questions and with the results of the registration. By mid-May he already had determined that receipts were going to fall far short of what was needed. The reason was perfectly clear. The law on registration left the power of estimating the income of a business in the hands of local authorities. This meant that except for cases where vendettas were being pursued, the local business community conspired to keep everyone's tax as low as possible.

To overcome this difficulty, Jovanović took advantage of a provision in the law that permitted him to form commissions in the case of disputes and complaints. On May 20 he established "revision" commissions consisting mainly of bureaucrats loyal to the central government to look into reports of income.[54] In particular, the commissioners were instructed to look into the income of the members of the local evaluation boards and the wealthy persons of the towns, since, Jovanović believed, their estimates were the least accurate. And, lest the commissions be hindered in their work, Jovanović instructed local officials to assist them, even to the extent of allowing them to look at local court records and customs accounts.

The new commissions raised a storm of protest. The idea that the government should investigate a man's income in order to tax him was completely new and extremely unpopular, just as the French inventors of the *patente* in 1791 were certain it would be. Rumors spread among the peasantry that "the people would be ruined because now the tax was going to fall on land, on stock, on houses, on windows, and even on food."[55] Bureaucrats complained that merchants were not paying their fair share and reports from the countryside spoke of angry streetcorner discussions and threats against commissioners.[56] Even the foreign consuls complained, questioning whether the requirement that foreigners pay the tax was consistent with Serbia's commitments under the Treaty of Berlin.[57] The government could fob off foreigners by patriotically demanding in public that they pay while not actually forcing them to do so, as Milan Milićević cynically observed, but the Serbs themselves were not so easily handled.[58] Complaints poured into the local commissions, to the minister of finance, and to Ristić himself.[59] Some of these give an interesting insight into the social situation in the Serbian town. For example, one of the most dramatic cases concerned Aleksa Popović, the leading businessman of Užice, a member of the opposition, and later a Progressive president of the skupština.

Popović stated his income on the proper form on May 14, 1879. He indicated that he had 30,000 dinars invested in a trading company with a partner, Vučić Pavlović, and that the company had a cash flow of 30,000 dinars per year. He also received interest on 30,000 dinars in loans he had out. He lived rent-free in the house of his brother, Gavril, who was Prota of Užice, but also owned two houses, a small shop in Požega, some fields, his part of the family zadruga, and 2,000 dinars' worth of brandy. Against these was a debt of 7,800 dinars. From all this he claimed his income was 4,952 dinars, which would make him liable for a patentarina of 110 dinars.[60] On June 28, however, the treasurer of the local government, Mojsilo Nikolić, protested to Vladimir Jovanović that Popović had failed to mention 24,000 dinars in inventory, and that customs records showed he had imported another 32,000 dinars' worth of goods. Furthermore, Popović and a group of speculators had recently each made 16,000 ducats (192,000 dinars) supplying the Austrian army in Bosnia, which was never mentioned. Nikolić estimated that Popović earned approximately 50,000 dinars annually and owed 1,450 dinars in tax.[61]

The special commission Jovanović formed to investigate these allegations found that Popović and his partners were indeed more prosperous than the original declaration indicated because trade in Užice had boomed with the Austrian occupation of Bosnia. Even so, the commission thought it prudent to reach a compromise solution, perhaps erring on the low side. "If we were to register larger amounts," it reported, "the citizenry would be overloaded, which would be more likely to produce dissatisfaction because this is the first significant obligation with which they have been burdened and they will have to be accustomed to it gradually." The commission declared Popović's income to be 16,952 dinars a year, making him the richest man in Užice, and suggested he pay 290 dinars in tax, a recommendation that Vladimir Jovanović, and apparently Popović, accepted.[62]

Other incomes of interest shown on the registration forms

from Užice included that of the second richest man in town, Aleksa's brother Gavril, who earned 11,032 dinars a year; Milan Djurić, a priest under Gavril's supervision who was a member of the skupština and an ally of Aleksa, 2,510 dinars, mostly from his pay as a priest; Aleksa Popović's partner, Ilija Jokanović, 5,260 dinars.[63] Town incomes contrasted sharply with those of the rural areas. In nearby Požeski Srez, for example, Milan Žunjić, a member of the skupština opposition and president of his opština, earned 420 dinars.[64] Not much by the standards of Užice, it was enough to make him the third richest man in his rural opština. Returns from remoter regions show annual incomes of from 4 to 20 dinars to be not unusual at all, although it should be remembered that these are cash incomes from trade or speculation (moneylending) only, and do not include incomes from crafts excluded from the patentarina or direct agricultural production.

Despite the efforts of the revision commissions, which were successful in raising the amounts due from each local area, the actual receipts of the patentarina remained inadequate, and as the deadline for a payment on the Russian war debt approached Jovanović's exhortations became more and more urgent.[65] Typical was his secret memo of June 4 to one local official calling him to task for reporting that his okrug would produce only 9,068 dinars. "This figure does not correspond to the budget . . . and therefore the executors of the law have not met expectations, since the allotted payment does not amount to even a third of the amount anticipated." Jovanović ordered the načelnik (head man, kapetan) to report immediately how he carried out the registration and especially to explain "why such a relatively low annual payment was allotted." The načelnik got the message. By August 25 he reported that the revised amount would be 25,169 dinars. Jovanović replied that this was better but still not up to the budgeted amount of 30,000 dinars. By September 17 the desired figure had been reached.[66]

Everywhere, under the lash of the revision commissions and Jovanović's secret memoranda, the assessed amounts were brought up substantially. In one srez the commission increased its assessment from 2,164 dinars to 8,435; in another from 2,822 to 7,388;

and in a third from 1,662 to 4,640. Only one region, the Užički okrug exceeded its scheduled amount, but quite a few were unable to meet Jovanović's targets. The newly acquired and still devastated area of Vranje, for example, reported that it simply could not raise any more than 9,874 dinars out of its allotment of 35,000. But, in general, Jovanović's methods produced an assessment that at least approached the necessary amounts, although collections lagged from these figures considerably.

Jovanović's methods produced something else as well: the mobilization of the merchants and moneylenders of Serbia. If there was one thing that destroyed any possibility of widespread popular acceptance of Ristić's Liberal government in the towns and villages of Serbia after the achievement of independence it was the patentarina. The mood of crisis was heightened when a crop failure caused by a drought and a very cold fall caused the price of corn to triple and produced severe privation in the countryside.[67] By the time the second session of the skupština elected in 1878 convened in Niš on November 13, 1879, the dissatisfaction from much of the articulate population of the country presented Ristić with a serious political problem. The danger of the situation for the government was increased by an illness that kept Ristić in Belgrade far from the action. Only one day into the skupština, Todor Tucaković, president of the previous skupština and a government supporter, wired Ristić that unless Jovanović withdrew the patentarina the government was facing a vote of no confidence, despite its ostensible control of a majority of the delegates, and two days later Ristić's concerned ministers wired him that "the position of the skupština is very difficult. The committees probably will not be formed according to our desires. There is a strong current running against Vladimir and you, and even against the cabinet. With our approval Vladimir has offered his resignation. There is a strong movement as well for a free press and local self-administration."[68]

Prince Milan had spent most of the last year residing at his new estate in Niš. Out of touch with Ristić, he was not sure whether Ristić intended to accept Jovanović's resignation or fight it out with the skupština.[69] Ristić answered Milan's cabled question by saying that he did not intend to defend the patentarina, but not knowing the situation he could not give an opinion about Jovanović's resignation. Instead, he proposed announcing Jovanović's offer rather than an actual resignation and adjourning the skupština for a week.[70] Milan answered that it was too late. The legislative committees had already been elected and "any measures of postponement would have very unfortunate circumstances. I can accept your advice only if you insist."[71] Ristić, cool despite his illness, sent an interesting response. "I am for a postponement. I doubt that [my colleagues] have evaluated the situation correctly, but exaggerate. . . . You can determine best. . . . I will be leaving by the postal carriage on Wednesday."[72] Not concealing his low opinion of his cabinet's political nerve, Ristić wired them: "That there would be a movement against the minister of finance because of the patentarina could be foreseen. There is opposition in the skupština everywhere."[73]

It was true that the opposition was more formidable in 1879 than it had been in 1878. In the first postwar skupština the opposition had not had time to organize itself after the elections, but in 1879, in all likelihood because of spadework done by Nikola Pašić, opposition delegates came to the skupština with their own draft address to the throne already prepared and their candidates for skupština president already slated. Because Ristić remained in Belgrade, the government delegates were not as well prepared, and in the election of skupština officers and committees many Liberals voted for whomever they wished, rather than a government slate. Accordingly, several oppositionists, including Dimitrije Katić and Milan Djurić, received enough votes to be placed on the list of six persons from whom Milan selected the president of the skupština, and the oppositionists managed to gain control of the finance committee. Among the members of that committee was Nikola Pašić, who squeezed in by a close vote as the last member selected.[74] This is the show of strength that so alarmed Ristić's colleagues.

When Ristić arrived in Niš to take stock of the situation, he realized that the government had to regain the initiative. The historian Slobodan Jovanović suggests that only Ristić had the confidence, factual preparation, and authority to bring the skupština to heel, the delegates listening to him as if they were schoolchildren.[75]

Nikola Pašić claimed Ristić's methods were less savory, including opening the delegates' mail, offering to help delegates from the new territories who might be facing legal problems, and even threatening others.[76] At the political level Ristić advised the prince to accept Vladimir Jovanović's resignation, which he did on November 14.[77]

But neither the stick nor the carrot calmed the oppositionists. On November 20 they presented a proposal signed by sixty-six delegates, about half the normal attendance of the skupština, that the patentarina be suspended. Pašić and others claimed that Jovanović had broken the law by overcharging, and they ridiculed him as the "secret" minister for his confidential memoranda ordering local officials to produce results.[78] The opposition wanted their proposal declared urgent and sent to the finance committee, which they controlled, but Ristić got his majority in the skupština to refer the proposal to an ad hoc committee created especially for this purpose by combining all three parliamentary committees into one large body, thus assuring himself the majority he would not have in the finance committee. A few days later this expanded committee reported that new revision commissions would be established and that all complaints would be heard, a solution the skupština adopted.[79] In other words the patentarina would not be dropped. The opposition was outraged. They read into the record the report about Aleksa Popović's high unreported income, and Dimitrije Katić went so far as to call Vladimir Jovanović a tyrant. When the issue refused to die, Ristić finally succumbed. In January 1880 he presented a proposal to scrap the patentarina entirely and replace it with the alternative that had been used time and again when tax reform proved unpopular, a surcharge on the semiannual danak (head tax).[80] Pašić and the opposition were again very much opposed to this solution, claiming that it would be unfair to the poorer regions and that the only equitable tax would be one on income. Pašić even proposed selling state land or printing paper money as alternative solutions, but he was the only member of the Finance Committee to oppose the bill, and the surcharge on the danak passed. Not until 1884 did it prove possible to restructure the Serbian tax system from its traditional Ottoman form into one more suitable for the European country that Serbia was trying to become.

As Nikola Pašić recognized, the patentarina issue was an ominous one because it hinted at the enormous costs and even sacrifices that Serbs were about to be called upon to make as part of their struggle to enter into the ranks of the civilized nations. Who would be making the sacrifices and who would be benefiting? How could Serbia preserve peasant society, as it appeared so many wished to do, and at the same time become more European? Two issues brought before the skupština of 1879–80 hinted at what the answer would be. The first of these was public health, and the second the question of how to integrate the newly acquired territories into Serbia. In the case of public health, a problem that affected every Serbian peasant, the skupština refused to take any action, despite a clear demonstration of an overwhelming need, while in the case of the new territories it took action aimed at maintaining the undifferentiated social structure that had characterized Serbia since 1830. The two cases illuminate tendencies that intensified as the century neared a close. The first was to minimize the resources put toward the direct benefit of the peasantry even while extolling the virtues of peasant society, and the second was to use the powers of the state for the benefit of those who administered or controlled it—such as the Liberal carpetbaggers who rushed into the newly acquired lands after 1878—always, however, with the justification of introducing sound principles of government based on those of the emulated European cultures. Both confirm the fact already made clear by the Law on Six Days Plowing and the debate on peasant shops that the skupština favored proposals that maintained peasant life without change and suspected those that would lead to development.

As one might expect in an almost completely peasant society, Serbian public health was very poor. Not only had there been a serious outbreak of typhus in the newly acquired territories, but the low standards of everyday life left ordinary Serbs prone to disease. Dr. Vladan Djordjević, founder of the Serbian Medical Society and the Serbian Red Cross, as well as chief of the Serbian medical corps during the Ottoman wars, delivered a depressing report to the skupština that is worth quoting at length for the insight it provides into the state of national health and sanitation.[81] "Public health is public wealth," Djordjević said, purposely quoting Benjamin Franklin, "but [in this regard] Serbia today still stands at the first beginnings of civilization."[82] Ancient customs create the most serious health problems. For example, Djordjević said,

> I know of cases . . . where mothers, when the hour of sublime but terrible trial arrives, . . . have to go out from the warm room into the winter to the furthest recess of the garden to experience on snow and ice that terrible hour when they oscillate between life and death. And why? Because the father and head of household [domaćin] is in the room, and it is [considered] a tremendous shame if he should hear even one scream of that most holy pain. Shame!

There are heads of households among us, Djordjević continued, "that when they send their children to school scream as if they were being put on forced labor [kuluk]. Not rarely does one hear 'What more do you want of me? I gave a soldier and I gave a student. I can't do any more.'" And the schools—he described them as wretched, with scarcely enough air to breathe. Often the child would go off for a whole week taking his food with him, sleeping in the filthy, lousy school. And what did the peasant eat anyway? "Dry corn bread or corn gruel, onion, peppers, cabbage, beans, and sometimes a white fig," only rarely eating some fat and old lamb, almost never beef. What about clothing? Only the wealthy peasants (gazde) would have wool trousers and shoes for the winter—everyone else would be freezing. Now houses:

> In a huge courtyard you have a building which is called a house. Closely set around it [there are] as many small outbuildings for sleeping quarters [vajata] as there are married members of the zadruga in the family, a few corn cribs, a vat for figs, a well in the middle of everything, and that is usually all. Pigs and animals wander everywhere in the courtyard. . . . [The house] is built of logs supposedly lying one on the other, but in many places I have been able to put my fist through

these so-called walls of logs. The building is covered by a roof
of cornstalks but in the middle of that not even primitive roof
there is a hole that makes duty as a chimney, but often very
badly, because almost everywhere when a fire is burning in a
house there is so much smoke that throughout the villages
there is a constant occurrence of inflamed eyes. That fire burns
in the middle of a house not only on bare, but often very damp
ground, which acts as a floor. Over this "hearth" hangs a pot
of water on metal legs, near the fire is a pot of beans or cabbage,
and in the ashes cooks the cornbread [*proja*]. . . . The smoke is
so terrible and the darkness so great . . . that very often even
in the winter it is necessary to open the door.

Finally, Djordjević said, sanitation was dreadful, even in the
army, where from 1835 to 1875 there were over 100,000 cases of
serious illness, enough so that each soldier had to enter the hospital
at least once a year, and some of them many times. And the recruit-
ing statistics shows that the youth were undersized to begin with.
Djordjević believed that the Serbian army was the least healthy in
Europe.

Djordjević's lengthy report heralded a new kind of consciousness among educated Serbs. Health had always been bad among
the Balkan peasantry, but government officials had not seen it as
a matter for state concern, let alone action, nor realized that Serbia
could not be civilized until it undertook to improve peasant health
both physically and morally. But this concept was directly at odds
with the general view that Serbian peasant life was a superior one.
Therefore, whereas the government proposal to create a national
health fund (*narodni sanitetski fond*) was difficult to oppose with
vigor, since it spoke of bringing civilization to Serbia—in theory a
goal accepted by all—the idea found little actual support because
it required a new tax, a surcharge on the danak for setting up
health agencies in every okrug. "Rather than giving money to
hospitals," said Nikola Pašić, "it would be better and more to the
point to give loans to the people, . . . because in the hospitals it will
help only a few people and what are we going to do with the hungry
people?"[83] "Vladan's proposal is a good one in principle, but the

times are such that we have to satisfy more pressing needs."[84] With the opposition's mood similar to that of the rest of the skupština, no money was provided and the government was forced to postpone the project.

If the resolution of the national health fund issue suggests that the "edifice of civilization," as Mišković called it, did not include peasant health, the integration of the newly acquired lands into Serbia gives a hint of what some thought the positive content of that phrase might be. Prior to 1878 social relations in the newly acquired areas, which had been an integral part of the Ottoman Empire, can be described with justice as feudal.[85] With the exception of Niš, which was a sizable town of almost twenty thousand, and two or three other small towns, the territory was overwhelmingly agricultural. Ownership, as it was understood in the West, was not a strong concept, although the Muslim landlords had accumulated important use rights and depended on the labor of their peasants, most, but not all, of whom were Serbs. A sizable number of Albanians also inhabited the region, usually as peasant sharecroppers or shepherds.

With the advance of the Serbian armies into the Niš region late in 1877 most of the Muslims—landlords, peasants, Albanians, and townspeople—fled.[86] According to a report by Augustus Baker, British vice-counsul, when the Serbian army took Niš the Muslim population retired to the fortress, whereupon their houses were plundered. After the surrender most of the movable property of the Muslims disappeared, even including the valuables of the Mufti, and the Albanian bazaar was razed. Twelve of fifteen mosques were torn down, as were 1,300 of the town's 4,000 houses. Serbian troops used the wooden houses of the Muslim section for firewood and the remaining Muslim houses were sold at less than 10 percent of their previous value. General Djura Horvatović, for example, purchased a fine fifty-acre estate for only 500 ducats.[87] The Serbian justification for these acts was simple and had a certain justice to it. When the Ottomans passed through eastern Serbia in 1876 they had razed the countryside leaving some 200,000 people homeless—now they felt it was their turn.[88] Furthermore, Albanian raiding parties continually crossed the border from Ottoman terri-

tory, giving the government an ongoing excuse to treat them ruthlessly and leaving the border area "a perfect wilderness," as Consul
Gould put it.[89] Still, Ristić considered the first prefect of Niš so
arbitrary that he was shot. The next prefect, Kosta S. Pavlović, was
more benign, but as Baker put it, "he arrived poor and left rich."[90]

Revenge was not the sole nor even the main justification for
reorganizing the new territories. That justification was the introduction, as Prince Milan put it, of "civic culture, state order, and
national enlightenment." With independence most articulate Serbs
had come to see themselves as the propagators of the advanced
norms of Europe against the backward forces of Asia. Very quickly
after taking Niš they began a modernization program, widening
the streets by tearing down buildings owned by Muslims, Jews, and
even recalcitrant Christians. Central to the civilizing process in their
view was the introduction of Western legal precepts, which the
Liberals in particular believed stressed equity and fairness, equality
and justice. They contrasted this with what they considered the
underlying principle of the Ottoman system, hierarchy, or privilege
for the Muslims and servitude for the Christians (Serbs). Given the
different social setting of the new territories, however, the judges
who were sent to the region on the heels of the army were told to
use neither the Serbian law code nor the Ottoman regulations, but
to judge by "conscience, conviction, and their knowledge of justice
and the customs of the people."[91] A story told by Avram Petrović,
who was appointed clerk to the new court in Vranje, indicates how
that idea worked in practice and what liberation actually meant to
ordinary Serbs:

> A peasant brought a complaint against a chorbadji [prosperous
> merchant] from Vranje. Both answered the invitation to come
> to the office. The peasant took off his cap and placed it under
> his belt, crossed his hands over his belt, and stood near the
> doorway. The chorbadji came directly toward us and the table,
> took a chair, and sat down. I told him that by Serbian law the
> parties to a suit had to stand together before the court and I
> told him to rise. He said "I am not a peasant [rajatin] that I
> have to stand next to this donkey." I said to him that before

our laws all were equal and ordered him to stand. He got up angry and grumbling and stood by the table. I invited the peasant to approach nearer. The peasant began to cross himself and said, "Thank the Lord I have lived to see a chorbadji equal beside me." The chorbadji was insulted by these words and went to the door to leave. I shouted to him to stay and I began the trial.[92]

If the local peasantry was pleased by the Serbian principle of equality before the law, it was less so with the Liberals' defense of property rights that went with it. The Serbian government essentially accepted the legality of the property rights of Muslims, even if they had fled. "We must, gentleman," said Minister of Justice Stojan Veljković to the skupština, "respect private rights, which belong to individuals."[93] The occupying army, while waiting for these rights to be adjudicated, even tried to force the peasants to continue paying their rents for the support of the military occupation. The peasants, not pleased with this concept of liberation, often refused to make their payments, believing that this would prove they were the lawful owners of the land, since real owners did not pay exactions to landlords. In some instances their resistance had to be put down by force.[94] Meanwhile, Serbs from prewar Serbia, often Liberal bureaucrats, were buying up small parcels of land at depressed prices from departed Muslims—who realized they were unlikely ever to get full value for their holdings—while the local peasants, who had very few resources, complained that the land should by rights be theirs.

The full integration of the new lands into the Serbian legal system, which supported the carpetbaggers with the entire panoply of property protections that were part of the Serbian civil code, took place with remarkable rapidity, being completed by 1883, only about five years after the conquest. But at the skupština of 1879–80 one of the main questions of debate became how rapidly this process should proceed and whom it should benefit.[95] The Liberals wanted the process to be gradual in part because they dominated the political and economic processes there. The oppositionists, on the other hand, wanted the laws and regulations in the newly acquired areas to become the same as Serbia's immediately and sought at the same time to change those laws so that they would benefit the peasants (a less centralized opština organization, for example).

Finally, after vigorous debate, the skupština reluctantly passed the Agrarian Law of February 3, 1880.[96] This proved to be a workable compromise that permitted a high proportion of the Serbian peasants in the newly acquired area to obtain title to their land, while at the same time minimally satisfying the foreign powers who ostensibly were protecting Ottoman interests and enforcing the Treaty of Berlin. On one category of property peasants received title to land they had tilled for at least ten years, or if a shorter time than that the right either to buy the land or to settle for a pauper's plot without making any payments. But on the majority of the land, to obtain title the peasant had to reimburse the Muslim landlord over a seven- or eight-year period. Since payments could be made in kind, and since peasants had not made any rent payments for two years at the time the bill was passed, it seemed unlikely the departed landlords would receive much in the way of compensation. For this reason the Ottoman government formally protested the arrangement.[97] British Consul Gould advised his government to counsel restraint on the part of the Ottomans, for otherwise it was unlikely the former landlords would get anything at all.[98] After two years of controversy the Serbian government was able to secure a loan abroad by which it paid off the Muslim landowners, in return for which the peasants who got their plots were to repay the government over a fifteen- to twenty-five-year period.[99] In this way the newly annexed territories acquired a social structure of relatively undifferentiated independent peasant landowners matching that of Serbia itself. This success helped greatly in quickly integrating the new territories into the nondevelopmental mainstream of the country and it ensured that the only culturally and economically powerful institution in the region, just as in Serbia proper, would be the state.[100]

The skupština of 1879–80 was a long one, lasting three months, and it accomplished a good deal. As had been the case since an opposition had first appeared early in the 1870s, however, each issue, whether it was major or minor, produced a vigorous debate in which the now relatively coherent oppositionists railed against the government's proposals almost as a matter of routine. Still, Ristić was able to settle some of the unresolved issues hanging on since 1875 in his own way. When the oppositionists tried once again to lessen centralized control over local government, Ristić was able to retain the rules of 1878 by which the opštinas remained under the administrative supervision of the minister of the interior. He beat back renewed efforts to restore the liberal press law of 1875, and he ensured the passage of the law on agrarian lands in the new territories.

When the skupština of 1879–80 closed its doors in February 1880, therefore, it had confronted many problems of importance to the new Serbia. But it remained unable to even discuss, let alone solve, the most difficult problem the country faced, its relationship with Austria. Just what independence was going to mean to Serbia depended on what kind of agreements the government could work out with the Habsburgs. Six weeks after the skupština closed Ristić concluded the first of the agreements that would answer that question by fixing the conditions under which Serbia would build the railroad that was forced on it by the Treaty of Berlin. In the north, the Serbian line was to connect with a new line the Hungarian railroad system proposed to build from Budapest to Zemun (across the river from Belgrade), whereas in Serbia it was to run from Belgrade to Niš.[101] At first the Austrians had insisted that the Serbs continue the line from Niš to Vranje, but since the Serbs had no agreements with either Bulgaria or the Ottomans concerning where, or even if, their line would be able to connect with Serbia's in the south, Ristić refused to make that commitment. "And what can you do?" he asked the Austrians. "You can occupy Serbia. That would be a political misfortune for us, but if we sign a clause that will bring about our financial collapse we will call down on the country an even greater economic misfortune."[102] When Milan supported Ristić, the Austrians backed down, and an agreement to build the railroad was reached.

Since the next regular meeting of the skupština was not scheduled until November, Ristić was forced to call a special session to
ratify the railroad convention. It opened on May 23, 1880, not in
Niš, but in Kragujevac. After electing its officers, the skupština sent
the convention to the joint committee of twenty-seven persons
rather than to the nine-member Ways and Means Committee (zako-
nodavni obdor) to which laws were normally sent for consideration.
As in the last skupština Ristić used this device to lessen the ability
of the oppositionists to produce a negative report. Just before the
committee was ready to report, however, thirty-seven members
of the opposition surprised the government by proposing not to
consider the railroad convention at all but to call a Grand National
Assembly to do so, a move that would require a special election. As
an alternative, the oppositionists called for all members of the
skupština to resign so that new elections could be held to test the
will of the people on the matter. "The representative system," the
oppositionists self-righteously intoned, "is at its most developed
when the people can choose on each individual question."[103] The
oppositionists knew, of course, that Ristić had no intention of calling a Grand National Assembly that would risk an electoral defeat
and would have to meet in volatile Belgrade, since it contained the
only building in the country large enough to hold the more than
six hundred delegates, the National Theater. For the same reason
they were quite sure he would not call another regular election.
They were simply trying to buttress the authenticity of their political voice in contrast to that of the government by suggesting that
the latter was not in touch with the people and was unwilling to go
to them for guidance.

Both the government and the skupština quickly rejected the
oppositionists' ploy, and the ad hoc committee reported back 26 to
1 in favor of the convention. One of the main reasons it did so was
the fear that Austria intended to wage economic war on Serbia if
the convention was not accepted. Since Serbia was a land-locked
country having no borders with any other European state, most
observers believed such an economic war would be a disaster. The
ad hoc committee presented figures showing that the amount of
trade in pigs with Austria had dropped about 50 percent from the

years 1875 to 1879, due largely to the increase in Austrian tariffs and temporary border closings for disease. To break with Austria would be a disaster, Ristić said, and that is why the convention was signed.

The opposition did not agree, of course, and as an engineer who had been trained in railroad design, Nikola Pašić was in a position to raise hard questions about the technical and financial feasibility of the proposed line, preliminary surveying for which he had done in 1873. Ranko Alimpić, minister of public works, reported for the government that a great deal of work had already been done, starting with investigations as early as 1865. The route surveyed in 1873 was reviewed again in 1879 and found adequate and a general plan, therefore, existed. Still, Alimpić was not able to say how much the railroad would cost or where the money would come from, since these would be matters for negotiation, nor could he predict how profitable it would be, although Alimpić hopefully suggested there were railroads elsewhere in Europe whose business had proven to be ten times what the original estimates had been. The minister ended his plea for the convention by suggesting the railroad would be competitive with anything the Austrians might build in Bosnia, because it would be 160 kilometers shorter from Vienna to Salonica through Serbia.

Pašić did not have much trouble criticizing this report. The 1873 analysis was useless, he said, since its purpose was only to estimate the costs of a line and the committee of specialists was divided at that time on whether a railroad could be profitable in Serbia. In any event, the work in the newly acquired areas was poorly done and would have to be redone. Profitability in fact could be calculated in advance, "because in the industrial world there are well known rules and methods how one can come to a reliable estimate of railroad profits," and these included taking into account population, industry, import/export figures and similar data.[104] Finally, Pašić suggested the length of the line had been miscalculated and was only sixty-three kilometers shorter than a Bosnian route would be, and therefore not likely to be more profitable.

Pašić's arguments were of much less moment in the skupština than the debate over whether the railroad's main terminus would be in Belgrade or Zemun. Naturally the government wanted it in Belgrade, and the convention agreed that it would be placed there. This meant, however, according to international rules, that Austrian railroad regulations would be in effect until a southbound train got into the Belgrade station, just across the border that ran through the middle of the Sava River. Even though this was inevitable in any railroad agreement, some oppositionists jumped on this miniscule extension of Austrian regulations as a lessening of Serbian sovereignty. Ristić answered by noting that Sardinia (the House of Savoy) had a similar agreement with Austria in 1856. "You know what is Sardinia. You know what Sardinia was and what it is now. . . . Sardinia unfurled the flag of liberty and unification of Italy. We do not want to be cleverer or more patriotic than those glorious men who led the fate of Sardinia then."[105] Ristić ended his speech by pointing out that Serbia's future lay only in the direction of Salonica, her potential outlet to the sea, and this railroad was the first step in that direction. "Salonica," he ended. "To Salonica!"[106] Enthused by these nationalistic encouragements, and controlled in any event by Ristić, the skupština passed the railroad convention 122 to 40, with 3 abstentions.

During the skupština debate over the railroad convention, Ristić had ridiculed Pašić's unwillingness to accept the agreement, since Ristić believed such a rejection would mean an undesirable economic war between Serbia and Austria. "And I am confident," Ristić declared, "that Mr. Pašić, who belongs to that circle of people who said that their fields would not be larger if war with the Ottomans was started [that is, who voted against war in 1875], will surely vote for economic war with Austria-Hungary."[107] In this instance Ristić's sarcasm was unfortunate because before long he himself chose to advocate economic war with Austria. In many ways Ristić was a realist, an able politician who knew how to achieve power and how to make as much as possible out of the limited diplomatic opportunities offered to his small and weak country. But Ristić's cold demeanor and his reputation for calculation hid a streak of aggressiveness that at certain critical occasions boiled to the surface. His push for war in 1876 was such a moment. He calculated the likelihood of defeat as well as anyone, but his intuition told him that an historic moment had been reached and it was time to throw the dice. In his view victory in 1878 confirmed the worth of the risks he took in 1876. In 1880 he once again came to a point at which he felt he had to throw the dice of Serbia's future, this time in the direction of Austria-Hungary.

When Austria forced Serbia to postpone discussing the commercial treaty called for by the Treaty of Berlin until after the railroad convention was approved, Ristić tried to assert Serbia's commercial independence by concluding temporary—and primarily symbolic—trade agreements with England, Italy, Russia, Switzerland, and Belgium. Then early in 1880 he signed a permanent agreement with England, whose trade with Serbia was modest to the extreme. His hope was to send a message to Austria that Serbia was indeed independent, but his effort backfired when in mid-June Baron Herbert informed Serbia that since Austria had most-favored-nation status, and since the Treaty of Berlin stated that nothing should change the status quo, Austria had the right to choose whether it wished to continue the old tariff arrangement from 1862 or the one outlined in the Anglo-Serbian Treaty.[108] Because the latter treaty embodied the principle of free trade, Herbert's demarche meant that Serbia would be prohibited from establishing any protective tariffs whatsoever on Austrian goods. Ristić could not accept the Austrian interpretation, not so much because he feared that Austrian goods would flood the country and prevent Serbia from developing its own industries—he did not think in developmental terms—but because it would doom the Serbs to a position of permanent subservience and thereby vitiate the one claim they had to European dignity, their independence. In his reply to Herbert he suggested a Serbian delegation come to Vienna to discuss the matter.

When the Austrians not only agreed, but insisted that a Serbian delegation appear in Vienna by July 22, 1880, the Council of Ministers instructed its negotiators that the basic Serbian policy must be one of equal treatment, not overwhelming advantage for Austria and subservience for Serbia. If independence was going to mean anything, it had to mean reciprocal agreements among sovereign states, not demeaning submission of the weak to the strong. But the Austrians remained adamant in their insistence on a treaty that heavily favored their products. By mid-August the negotiators were back in Belgrade empty-handed. On August 21 the Council of Ministers wrote Milan that "we cannot accept, and we dare not accept, Austrian demands."[109]

Milan had been working on his own agenda during the summer. Late in June he left for Vienna, whence he visited Ems. There he met Emperor William I of Germany, with whom Milan believed he achieved a great personal success.[110] The historian Milan Živanović is convinced that this meeting had an enormous effect on Milan, whose most fervent desire was to find acceptance among the crowned heads of Europe, especially the emperors of Germany and Austria-Hungary. For Živanović, the courtesies shown Milan by William at Ems were the crucial element that convinced Milan, who had spent almost two years of isolation in Niš, that he could find the imperial acceptance he craved by attaching Serbia to Austria.[111] Milan informed Ristić that since the Ottoman Empire was disintegrating he thought it politic to stay on good terms with those who could, if they were unfriendly, prevent Serbia from taking advantage of the situation. Still, he averred, we must not do anything "inimical or incompatible with our dignity or our national independence."[112] By the middle of August, however, Milan's determination not to compromise Serbia's dignity, never a strong emotion with him, was wavering. He could not find time to bring up the reciprocity question in an audience with Franz Joseph because, as he put it, "my time was very taken up with the honors they were showing me." Dazzled by his courtly successes, he was becoming convinced that any sort of agreement was better than the status quo. An agreement with Austria, he thought, could be "like some sort of California for Serbia, while an economic war with her I consider our economic and political ruin."[113]

In September, undoubtedly encouraged by the success they were having with Milan, the Austrians increased the pressure by threatening to close their borders. By this time Ristić had concluded that Serbia stood at a fundamental turning point on the road toward respectability. Either Serbia would succumb to Austria and remain in reality a colonial province as it had under the Ottomans, or it would stand for its rights as a sovereign nation and achieve real independence. Therefore, instead of giving in, he tried to play a card later used by his successors from time to time, the creation of a tariff union with Bulgaria.[114] Prince Alexander of Battenberg visited Belgrade officially in October to discuss the possibilities.[115] The cabinet stood firm behind their minister president. They backed Ristić's insistence on reciprocity with Austria. But Milan did not. At the end of September, having just returned from Austria, he declared his dissatisfaction with the Anglo-Serbian treaty and a week later Ristić admitted to his ministers that whereas they were agreed, Milan was not. "For that reason," he said, "there is a prospect of a change of ministries."[116] On October 14 Ristić wrote Vienna that Austria's refusal to agree to reciprocity in the trade agreement was absolutely unacceptable. One week later he outlined the situation to the prince. If we make a concession, he said, will it be the last? Certainly not. "The appetite of the neighboring monarchy toward the east is growing. . . . It is time to say 'We do not surrender. We defend ourselves!' "[117] When the prince did not agree, Ristić and his government could only resign.[118] Milan called a group of Young Conservative oppositionists under the leadership of Milan Piroćanac and Milutin Garašanin to form a new government.

Ristić's departure ended an era, an era he dominated. Whatever concessions he had been forced to make to the realities of Serbia's weakness, he held to his belief that if his country was to be a state like other states it must retain as much independence as possible. His call for a tariff war in 1880 failed, not only because of the opposition of the prince, but because he was unable to call out public opinion on his side, as he had in 1876. But his belief that Serbia would be better served by a tariff war than by obsequiousness toward Austria, even though it was based on political judgments rather than economic ones, and even though it flew in the face of obviously superior Austrian power, may well have been a sound judgment. For the next twenty-three years Serbia stagnated economically as a client of Austria. No fresh challenges broke through the stable system of smallholders in direct contact with their means of production. Only after a new dynasty came to the throne in 1903 did the Serbs, starting once again with a customs union with

Bulgaria, accept the gauntlet thrown down by Austria. Only then could it be said that Serbia began its true entry into the economic world of Europe.

Politically, however, Serbia's development did not come to a halt with Ristić's resignation. Quite the contrary. Ristić remained the leader of the Liberals and returned to politics at the end of the 1880s as a senior statesman, but his primary role ended in 1880. Serbia did not respond to his call for a tariff war in 1880 and, therefore, more or less retained its traditional economic and social structure; but Ristić's introduction of an operating parliamentary system set Serbia on a path of political development that proceeded forward, despite relative economic and social immobility. By creating a parliamentary system he could in many ways control, Ristić at the same time laid the groundwork for losing that control. The dynamic of elections, parliamentary debates, and political publicity created its own pressure for moving on. When Ristić stepped down his successors, who came to be called the Progressives, took the logic of political development one step further by permitting the formation of real political parties.

6 : PARTIES AND THE NEW LEVEL
OF DISCOURSE

Fireworks that do not warm and that leave nothing after them, but
which for the moment sizzle, throw off brilliant sparks, and glow—
and the world likes it, runs over, and looks.—Pera Todorović describing his writing in *Samouprava*

Within two months of Piroćanac's assumption of office, Serbia's
first partisan political clubs with independent organizations formed
out of the three main groupings that had been in a process of
development for many years. During the 1870s the most coherent
of these groupings had been the Liberals. Ristić's tutorial and
authoritarian style of leadership matched the undeveloped political
consciousness of the peasant society he administered as well as the
fearful apprehensions of the prince he served. Many Serbs believed
that any sort of concerted political activity not sanctioned by the
government was revolutionary and potentially traitorous. But the
idea the Liberals used to justify their role contributed significantly
to the erosion of this ethic.

From the time of the First Serbian Uprising, and even before,
the only legitimate popular authority—as opposed to the authority
exercised by the Ottomans through right of conquest—was the
traditional right of leadership granted the head of the extended
family and, in the case of civil affairs, the patriarchal leader writ
large, the prince. Princes of both the Obrenović and Karadjordjević
families claimed further that their leadership during the First and
Second Uprisings gave them an additional justification for ruling.
The uniqueness of the prince's legitimacy was eroded during the

1840s by the Defenders of the Constitution, who made their claim that an oligarchy of strong men could administer the realm, but it was only during the 1860s that agitation by liberal oppositionists, although not by Ristić himself, successfully established that the people were also an authentic source of legitimate power. Ristić called his adherents in 1873 not the "Liberal Party," but the "National [*Narodna*—from *narod,* the people] Liberal Party," adopting the new view that the Liberals were the spokesmen of the Serbian nation.

Despite the Liberals' claim that they represented the people, the persecution that some Liberals experienced during the 1860s fostered in them the belief that their devotion to the national cause had been so thoroughly demonstrated that they had little further obligation to consult the people. Their appeal to the people was rhetorical, not actual; a form of political discourse, not a program. Confident that they understood the needs of the nation better than the nation itself, they used the state bureaucracy to impose their policies and to ensure that Ristić's government would remain in power. Not incidentally, this created the conditions for their own social ascendancy. As early as the St. Andrew's skupština of 1858 even the most democratic Liberals proved that they would take a back seat to no one in their eagerness to fill government positions with their friends and allies. Beneath the ideology, getting and keeping power was a fundamental practical concern for the Liberals, and indeed, for each group that followed them. In an economy as undifferentiated as Serbia's, there were few places except state service for the educated and the trained. Therefore, once the Liberals established the principle that power should be exercised on behalf of the people, it was only a matter of time before others came forward to make the claim that they too represented the people, indeed more truly than the Liberals, and, therefore, had a right to participate in the political struggle over who was going to control the richest and most modern institution in Serbia, the state. The demands for self-administration and other reforms in 1875–76 were the first efforts of the Radicals to put forward just such claims. But the war years gave Ristić the opportunity, justified in a way, to limit, indeed almost to eliminate, any chances for an opposition to get its views into print or to organize politically and mobilize support. He was able to maintain control of the situation for more than a year after the end of the wars, but by the time the skupština of 1879 convened, signs that the government party could not continue to control either political activity or legitimating discourse began to appear. Besides the unrest in the skupština itself, foremost among these signs was the appearance of an opposition newspaper, the first since the demise of Kaljević's *Srbija* in 1875.

Two oppositional tendencies were apparent in the skupština of 1879, the Radicals, organized primarily by Nikola Pašić, and the Young Conservatives, whose pedigree ran through Jovan Marinović back to Ilija Garašanin.[1] Milan Piroćanac was one of the most prominent of the Young Conservatives. Not himself a member of the skupština, Piroćanac was a judge on the Court of Cassation (Appeals) who had trained for the law in Paris.[2] In the month preceding the opening of the 1879 skupština he and his friends, one of whom mentions in his diary that they already "felt like" a party, began discussing the possibility of starting a political newspaper.[3] Piroćanac's rival and antagonist in the difficult negotiations that followed was Milutin Garašanin, son of Ilija. Whereas Piroćanac could rightly be called an intellectual because of his capacity for political theorizing, Garašanin was simply the son of a great man—handsome, strong of voice, a man "with the dark secret look of a young pretender," as Slobodan Jovanović put it—but lacking both insight and foresight.[4] In mid-December Piroćanac and twelve other persons (not including Garašanin) agreed to begin their paper, which they decided to call *Videlo* (Daylight).[5] Financial support was forthcoming from the wealthy Conservative Sabac merchant Djordje Topuzović and from Serbs in Hungary, so that the paper began with a sizable war chest of about 4,000 ducats.[6] Piroćanac and Milan Kujundžić agreed to write the paper's program, a step tantamount to writing the political program of the Young Conservative party. Even though no permanent editor had been found by the day of first publication, and though Garašanin still coyly refused to join the editorial group, on January 14, 1880, the first issue of *Videlo* appeared.[7]

The leaders of the Young Conservatives constituted the flower of the Serbian intelligentsia. Of the ten readily identifiable persons who attended the organizational meeting of *Videlo* only two had not been educated abroad, and they were Stojan Nova-ković, Serbia's leading philologist, one of the country's best historians, and a vigorous educational reformer, and Milan Dj. Milićević, a self-educated peasant's son who was an encyclopedic writer about the details of nineteenth-century Serbian life. Of the other eight, four were prominent legal scholars and judges, two others had each translated one of the great authors of English positivistic history, Henry Thomas Buckle and John William Draper, another was head of the teachers' school, and the last was a noted philosopher. At least three had been vigorous liberals in the 1860s, followers of Vladimir Jovanović and participants in the Omladina, but by 1879 all of them believed that Ristić was not lifting Serbia up to the level of civilization promised by the advances of Western political culture. Slobodan Jovanović's ironic description of how they contrasted in tempera-ment and aspiration with the older generation of liberals is worth quoting at length:

> [In the 1850s and 1860s] the liberal intelligentsia brought back from western universities the cult of science and political freedom; for Western customs, especially urban life, they were unenthusiastic. In their way of life, the Liberals re-mained half patriarchal. They did not know either luxury or comfort. A younger generation with an already over-refined sensibility, the [Young Conservatives] accepted from the West not only its science and its free thinking, but its way of life. They felt the pleasure of the material culture of the West and admired the dignity and comfortable life of its upper classes. They happily traveled through Europe and many used French words in their speech. They denigrated Serbian domestic conditions, tried to form a higher social circle, and had in their manners and carriage some of the arrogant pretentions [*odnarodjenost*] of the Wallachian boyars of the nineteenth century. But they lacked the estates [*spahi-*

luci] of the boyars, and without great wealth they were hard pressed to live an elevated life. They asserted that liberal constitutionalism was false; the same could be said of their bourgeois airs [*gospodstvo*].[8]

By "false constitutionalism" the Young Conservatives meant that the Liberals had mistakenly distorted Western constitutionalism to accommodate the patriarchal traditions of peasant Serbia, particularly by creating a unicameral skupština, three-quarters of which was elected popularly. They did not agree that ancient traditions of democracy and love for freedom prepared the Serbian peasant for integration into Western political institutions. They held the view that Serbian peasant life could not possibly be the basis of a modern society because the experience of Western Europe showed that only science, philosophy, and knowledge or, in short, only educated expertise (*znanje*) could promote progress. By rejecting the idea that the peasant was the true source of Serbian political principles, the Young Conservatives relieved themselves of the fundamental contradiction inherent in the Liberal and the Radical views. How was it possible to seek modernity through nationalism when that nationalism placed its faith in a decidedly unmodern peasantry? The answer for the Liberals, of course, had been to concentrate on politics and not to worry about social or economic modernization, creating a constitution, a legislature, and a bureaucracy, and in external affairs achieving de jure independence.

The Radicals were more of two minds, Svetozar Marković emphasizing political reforms and Nikola Pašić emphasizing Serbia's economic needs; but even the Radicals could not easily reconcile their faith in the peasantry with their hope that Serbia would somehow become modern. The Young Conservatives did not have this problem. They rejected the premises that peasant traditions were potentially progressive and that they needed to be preserved. For them the constitutional system of classical liberalism, the central point of which was to respect the autonomous individual and protect his rights and freedoms, was the most advanced political philosophy yet achieved. "Pure constitutionalism" meant introducing civil liberties and raising Serbian political culture from its patriarchal level to the more advanced level of true civilization that, they believed, was achieved not in the social or economic spheres, but in politics.

In the first issue of *Videlo* Pirocanac and his colleagues laid out their ideas on how to achieve this "pure constitutionalism." Truly representative government cannot exist without political parties, they pointed out, and yet Serbia had none.[9] Instead, groups of politicians followed individuals. Serbia needed parties based on principle, on programs for moving the nation forward, not merely on personal loyalties and patronage. At the top of the list of policies that would permit the appearance of such parties were free speech—particularly in newspapers—and freedom of assembly and organization. In order that personal security might be protected and commerce encouraged, the courts should be independent from political interference and public officials must be held responsible for their acts. Finally, and significantly for the Young Conservatives, intelligent and educated persons must be permitted to stand for election to the skupština, even if they held government positions as professors or teachers. Without this change the skupština would continue to be made up primarily of representatives of the traditional culture, rather than the educated adherents of the new and more progressive standards of the West.

Videlo's program reveals the resemblance of the Young Conservatives to the English and French liberals of the 1830s and 1840s.[10] Like their Western predecessors, the Young Conservatives believed in representative government, not democracy. But an important difference separated them from the British and French liberals. For the Young Conservatives the protection of property, which formed the centerpiece of liberal theory, involved not real property, but intellectual property. The purpose of the state for *Videlo* was not so much to protect real property or to enforce business law—although the Young Conservatives certainly were in favor of that—as it was to protect the freedom of individuals to enjoy the fruits of their education, which usually meant to be employed in a school, court, or ministry. The Young Conservatives, therefore, had no intention of dismantling the state apparatus in the way populists like Adam Bogosavljević demanded. They had no reason to object to a state that paid for their education and offered them secure and honored employment. But by limiting some of the arbitrariness of the state toward the educated class, by permitting judges to work without political interference, and by allowing newspapers to publish without censorship, they hoped to increase this class's opportunities to live a cultured life and rise fully to its natural position of leadership.

The skupština of 1879–80 was still in session when *Videlo* appeared. The new paper began following the events in Niš, embarrassing Ristić's government when possible. For example, Ristić had invalidated the election of Djordje Topuzović, ostensibly because proper electoral notice had not been published, but probably because Ristić knew Topuzović was financing *Videlo*. When Topuzović was reelected, a *Videlo* correspondent reported from Šabac that "about five hundred citizens, with women and even children, each with two lighted candles in their hands, gathered to the accompaniment of music in front of Topuzović's house." The writer was at a loss for words to describe the dancing in the streets. "Šabac has never experienced such a day until now," he rhapsodized.[11] More significant was a critical article by Milutin Garašanin, who eventually had been coaxed into participating in the newspaper, on the railroad issue. "Beautiful contents," enthused Milan Milićević, "this is the child of Ilija's in a new and enlarged format."[12] Ristić took notice of the paper by confiscating several issues in the first two months of publication. "No patriotic Serb would permit this article," he said on one occasion, and he followed up his observation by forcing the author of the offending piece, Milan Milićević, out of his government job.[13]

But *Videlo's* pages were not limited to the Young Conservatives' efforts to publicize their views and to harass Ristić. *Videlo* also became a vehicle for the Radicals, whom the Young Conservatives considered their allies in opposition.[14] This collaboration became especially important after the tragic death of Adam Bogosavljević in March 1880. Bogosavljević's populist opposition had always angered Jovan Ristić, who took particular pains to make life difficult for Bogosavljević and his relatives. Even though Bogosavljević voted for war credits in 1876, Ristić brought up again and again the fact that he and some of his colleagues had voted in 1875 against a resolution stating that war was desirable. And Ristić held a trump card. In 1876, when the Ottomans overran southeast Serbia, Bogosavljević, like many of the people of his region, burned his house to the ground and fled the invaders.[15] When he and his villagers had consumed what they had taken with them, Bogosavljević returned to the territory occupied by the Ottomans and found an intact village grain supply at Dubočane, which was less than ten kilometers from his home village. In the presence of a witness from Dubočane, at whom he allegedly pointed a weapon, Bogosavljević and his uncle took three hundred okas of corn for his own villagers. Later that year someone from Dubočane swore out a complaint against him for stealing these publicly owned goods, but local officials never did anything about it. When Bogosavljević returned to his village at the conclusion of the war he rebuilt his house, not in the same location but at the edge of his property, at the point farthest removed from Koprivnica, his native village, a decision later to have decidedly negative consequences for him.

Ristić did not take any action against Bogosavljević during the war, but during the skupština of 1879–80 he raised the accusation that Bogosavljević had stolen community goods. At the same time local officials near where Bogosavljević lived took advantage of the changed location of his homesite to declare him now a citizen of a different opština, not the one where he had been elected kmet and skupština representative by heavy margins since 1872.[16] As soon as the 1879–80 skupština was over, Ristić moved to arrest Bogosavljević on the 1876 charges. In order to minimize the likelihood of a popular outburst the authorities brought him not to Negotin, but south to Zaječar, where on March 29, 1880, Bogosavljević was placed in the local jail. Already ill when he entered prison, and with a history of lung disease, within hours Bogosavljević took a turn for the worse and on the next day had to be transferred to the Zaječar hospital. One day after that, March 31, he died of double pneumonia.[17]

Bogosavljević's sudden death only two days after being taken into custody on what was clearly a vindictive charge made it look as if the Liberals had killed him, perhaps by poison, certainly by mistreatment. In 1875 Bogosavljević's internment in Negotin had brought sixty horsemen to the seat of local authority to rescue him. This time Nikola Pašić, with the full support of *Videlo*, orchestrated a more modern response. First, despite an autopsy that proved Bogosavljević died of pneumonia, Pašić succeeded in creating suspicion that Bogosavljević was poisoned.[18] The minister of internal affairs ordered the autopsy as soon as he heard that Bogosavljević had died in captivity. When Pašić protested that the three doctors who made up the autopsy team were partial and should be changed to include a representative of the family and a representative of Bogosavljević's political colleagues, the minister obligingly permitted two more doctors to attend the commission's work.[19] Their finding of April 5, in which all five doctors concurred, was that Bogosavljević died of natural causes. But just in case, the two Radical doctors asked that a chemical analysis be made of various internal organs. Accordingly, the appropriate bodily parts were packed up and sent to Belgrade. Having successfully met all of Pašić's demands and having demonstrated that Bogosavljević was not killed in prison, the minister of internal affairs at this point made a mistake. Accepting the findings of the doctors as overwhelming, which they were, he not only declined to undertake the chemical analysis, but told Pašić that he was free to have one made at his own expense if he wished. This put the power of doubt in Pašić's hands. As long as the Radicals did not analyse Bogosavljević's organs they could continue to claim that it had not been proven that Bogosavljević had not been poisoned. They never undertook the analysis and continued to hint at the government's guilt for several years.[20]

But Pašić's second move was even more astute and important in the long run. He found a way to use Bogosavljević's death to establish a network of local committees of Radicals throughout the country. Bogosavljević's death brought forth a genuine outpouring of sympathy and grief because of his reputation as a defender of the peasantry and opponent of the bureaucracy. Requiems were said in many towns. *Videlo* published lists of persons who attended, as well as reported on incidents in which people were punished for attending or even for putting up notices that a requiem would be held.[21] On April 4, only four days after Bogosavljević's death, Pašić and two friends created in Požarevac a "Fund for educating and supporting Adam's family." Three days later their announcement in *Videlo* called upon "all friends to turn their thoughts in their area to the creating of a committee that will gather contributions for Adam's family."[22] Later in April Pašić announced the definitive creation of an executive committee of the Adam Fund, of which he was the chairman, and appealed to all patriots to form Adam committees in their towns. He listed thirty places, including most of the main towns, where there was either already an Adam committee or where Pašić called on specific individuals to form one.[23]

The special skupština that considered the railroad convention with Austria took place only seven weeks after Bogosavljević's death. Far from deflecting Pašić from his organizational purposes, the skupština gave him an opportunity to make the Adam Fund committees into something more than an eleemosynary organization. Shortly before the skupština convened Pašić published a lengthy statement on the views of what he styled, following Ristić's earlier example, the "National Radical Party."[24] Starting with a detailed complaint about poverty, high state expenses, debt, and the obligations of the Treaty of Berlin, he went on to state what amounted to a political platform. Besides agreeing with Piroćanac and all previous oppositionist groups that freedom of the press should be widened and civil liberties enhanced, and besides making a gesture at increasing the self-administration of the opštinas, Pašić called for a Grand National Assembly to do away with the State Council, promised to make the entry of Jews into the Serbian countryside more difficult, supported putting off further talks on railroad-building until Austria-Hungary would agree to a commercial treaty, proposed a trade agreement with the Ottomans, called for improved education, and argued that the army should be organized around the national militia rather than around a standing army of professionals.

This hodgepodge contained foreign policy elements from Ristić and civil liberties proposals from the Young Conservatives, as well as several obviously emotional appeals based on the fact that this was also the moment when Pašić was organizing committees throughout Serbia to memorialize Adam Bogosavljević. This suggests that Pašić was not putting forward just another pre-skupština proposal, but had in mind using the Adam committees as a rough-edged framework for a national political party. On the very day that *Videlo* published the list of thirty-seven oppositionists who proposed resigning in order to force an election on the railroad issue, it also published the "Rules for Adam's Fund," which now undertook to publish a "Life and Works of Adam," as well as to send his children to school.[25] Of the thirty-seven protesting legislators, eighteen had been on the list of persons to whom Pašić appealed in April to form local committees. Although many of these would turn out in the next year to be Progressives rather than Radicals, in a state that prohibited the organization of political movements Pašić had succeeded in creating the preliminary organizational basis for the Radical Party that was to come.

Pašić's activities and the success of *Videlo* motivated the Liberals to begin talking about how they might organize as well. Already in January 1880 the editor of *Istok*, noting the appearance of the well-financed *Videlo,* had asked Ristić for secret help, observing prophetically that the Liberals "stood only one step from a struggle of huge dimensions, the like of which until now we have not even dreamed."[26] Early in July the government discussed Ristić's suggestion that a literary society named "Kolo" be formed to act as a quasi-political club.[27] Two weeks later Ristić suggested establishing a newspaper that could be more openly partisan, although *Istok* clearly represented that government view. Alimpije Vasiljević and Radivoje Milojković believed that the best way to proceed was simply to hold private meetings with important individuals to draw them into the Liberal camp, whereas Vladimir Jovanović urged the creation of a regular society with statutes and mass meetings. Even though Jovanović won over his two colleagues, Ristić would not agree to an organization so foreign to his tutorial instincts. Therefore, as the crisis with Austria moved into high gear at the end of the summer of 1880, the Liberals did not take the steps that would prove necessary to match those of their rivals.

Instead, Ristić used the methods that had served him well in the past, punishing opponents as his authority permitted. The most exciting case was the firing of Mita Rakić, one of the founders of *Videlo* who worked as an administrator for the ministry of finance, to which Vladimir Jovanović had returned as minister on June 17. Within a month after returning Jovanović got into an argument with Rakić over whether *Istok* was a government paper; Rakić claiming that it was, Jovanović that it was not. The cabinet decided to fire Rakić, but *Videlo* struck back, not only printing Rakić's angry account of his dismissal, but reprinting several of Vladimir Jovanović's most liberal articles from the 1860s. Much to the delight of the oppositionists the government seized the papers with Jovanović's articles in them, thus placing itself in the position of suppressing its own minister's pleas for civil freedoms.[28] The result of these controversies, of course, was to solidify the opposition. According to Stojan Novaković it did not matter that the Liberals controlled the government and had a majority in the skupština. The educated people (*svet*) were now informed. "That is why we founded *Videlo*. . . . And when we are ministers we will support one another, and none of us will deviate from our program, because that would bring us into ridicule from all those who stand with us."[29] The chance to become a minister came to Novaković sooner than he expected.

The fundamental policy on which Milan refused to compromise with the Liberals was accommodation with Austria.[30] In the Serbian system as it had evolved up to 1880 the only way to defeat the prince in a matter of this importance was to rally public opinion. Ristić could rally the skupština, or at least a majority of it, and perhaps he could call a Grand National Assembly to consider the issue. But to gird the country for the rigors of a tariff war he needed the kind of extensive support that he had not been willing to organize. Events of the next two years showed that significant anti-Austrian feeling could be brought to the surface, but the Liberal style made it impossible for the Liberals to tap this potential for political purposes. Ristić may have had an inkling of the problem. Just before his government formally resigned he told a private meeting of his supporters that a resignation was not enough, that a further written explanation would be needed.[31] But it was too late for explanations. With little support in the countryside, no fully partisan newspaper, and faced with opponents eager to trade peace with Austria for internal reforms, Ristić, backed into a corner of his own making, simply left.

It took Milan a few days to put together a new government. His first instinct was to turn, as usual, to the old conservatives in the person of Jovan Marinović, despite Marinović's lack of support either in the skupština or among the people. But not only did the worldly Marinović have no intention of giving up his post as Serbian ambassador to Paris, and not only did he believe that the government should go to the Videlovci, as the Young Conservatives were called after their newspaper, but worse, he also did not agree with Milan that a tariff war with Austria was out of the question.[32] With Marinović out of the running, the prince would probably have preferred Milutin Garašanin, whose bluff manners had earned him access to the court without the necessity of making formal appointments; but the prickly Piroćanac, whose presence in the government all agreed was essential, insisted he would participate only as minister president.[33] Finally, Garašanin agreed to Piroćanac's demands, but since the fundamental condition Milan put to them was that an accommodation had to be reached with Austria, they agreed on a third party, the former Liberal Čedomil Mijatović, as foreign minister. Piroćanac took the ministry of justice and Garašanin became minister of the interior. Not only would this arrangement deflect any possible onus of an agreement with Austria away from the head of the government onto the newcomer to the Progressive ranks, Mijatović, but more important to Milan it put a man in the foreign office who was his close personal friend and who had the reputation of never refusing anyone anything.

The coming of the Videlovci to power was not just a case of a younger group of the Serbian elite changing places with an older one, new claimants to the resources of the state gratifying the prince in order to edge up to the trough; although the Young Conservatives did in fact prove unmerciful in purging the bureaucracy to make way for their adherents. The new people differed from the Liberals who dominated the 1860s in two fundamental ways. First, as we have seen, they did not believe in the whig theory of Serbian history by which Serbia became a candidate for modernity through the democratic traditions of its patriarchal past. The Young Conservatives believed that Serbia had to be lifted up to European civilization, and this most certainly did not mean relying on traditions from the Serbian countryside. Second, and related to this, they emphasized internal freedoms rather than foreign autonomy for Serbia. Their fundamental criticism of the Liberals was that they placed foreign affairs first. "But every healthy Serbian consciousness knows," *Videlo* said shortly after the Young Conservatives assumed power, "that the country's policy must be based on its internal policy of freedom first."[34] Just as in 1875, when Milan had been willing to bring the left-Liberals to power in order to avoid war, in 1880 he was willing to give the Young Conservatives wider latitude in domestic policy than his inclinations would normally permit because he had decided to reach an agreement with Austria. The Young Conservatives showed their willingness to do this only days after they took power when they accepted the Ottoman tariff convention of 1862, which the Austrians had set as a precondition for discussions of a trade agreement and which Ristić had steadfastly refused to recognize.

Personal reasons, as always with Milan, were involved in the prince's decision to accept Austrian protection. He had hopes of remedying his chronically precarious financial situation with Austrian resources, and the flattery he received on his trip to the baths in late summer of 1879 had convinced him that his full stature as ruler, possibly even elevation to the rank of king, could only be satisfied in Central Europe. But there were sound geopolitical reasons for making a commitment to Austria as well. Russia had abandoned Serbia in 1878 and Austria was occupying Bosnia and Hercegovina. What possibilities were left? The only one, except defiance, was to ally Serbia with Austria in return for its help in expanding into Macedonia. This was the reasoning, along with Milan's ambition to become a king, that lay behind the notorious secret convention of June 1881 by which Milan agreed to restrain Serbia from any agitation concerning Bosnia and Hercegovina and the Sanjak of Novi Pazar in return for an Austrian promise to support possible future Serbian initiatives into Macedonia.[35] Austria agreed to recognize the elevation of Serbia to a kingdom if and when Milan decided to do it, and Milan agreed not to conclude any treaties with other states without consulting Austria. This last stipulation almost caused Piroćanac and Garašanin to resign, but in the lawyerly fashion that typified his way of thinking Piroćanac was able to get a rewording from the Austrians that permitted him to believe Serbian sovereignty was salvaged, although Milan undermined even this concession by promising Vienna orally that he would follow the original agreement.

Milan's reputation suffered enormously when his secret concession finally leaked out more than ten years later. In 1881, only Mijatović knew about it at first, with his colleagues Piroćanac and Garašanin finding out only later by accident. By giving up claims to Bosnia and Hercegovina, nationalists charged, Milan had demonstrated a lack of belief in the Serbian national mission. The more realistic assessment of historian Slobodan Jovanović is that Milan gave up what was surely lost in the not unfounded hope of future gain. It was Russia, not Serbia, that gave Austria the right to annex Bosnia and Hercegovina. The Three Emperors' League (*Dreikaiserbund*) was signed only ten days before Milan signed the secret convention. Needing a period of peace and quiet to consolidate its position in Bosnia and Hercegovina before annexing it, Austria offered Serbia a future possibility in Macedonia in return for not agitating in Bosnia. Milan accepted. The other possibility was to defy Austria, not only in trade terms but by nationalist agitation that would hinder Bosnian pacification. Benjamin Kállay suggested what that might mean when he told Milan that Austria's alternative to friendship with Serbia was occupation.

Having relaxed Serbian policy toward Austria to satisfy Milan, the Young Conservatives turned to their end of the bargain. Within a few days of assuming power they prorogued the skupština and called for new elections. Prince Milan pardoned those who had been convicted of political crimes under Ristić, so that Radicals such as Pera Todorović and Pera Velimirović, who had been in exile in Paris and Bulgaria respectively, and left-Liberals such as Ljubomir Kaljević, who had been in exile in Hungary, could return. The Young Conservatives realized this would heat up Serbian

political life, but Milutin Garašanin's initial message to local bureaucrats was to tell them not to worry if there were a more lively
political struggle than they had felt comfortable with under Ristić.
Such activity was actually a sign of maturity, he said. "The country
is in a full process of political development. . . . This struggle is a
sign of life and political health, not in any way a demonstration of
the decline of the people. All political thoughts are equal before
the law as long as they do not interfere with public order and legal
regulations. All have the right to enter into public confrontation
[*borba*] and to propose themselves to the people. Therefore, all
have the right to move within the law and not to be limited or
hindered."[36] Garašanin followed this remarkable statement with
orders to his local načelnici that "elections of popular representatives [to the skupština] are to be completed without any influence
from the authorities."[37] To put some teeth into this rule, the government let it be known that meetings and associations of persons
should be freely permitted, since they would allow people to know
what the candidates stood for.[38] The Young Conservatives believed
that these changes would permit political parties to come into being,
the next step, in their view, on the road to raising Serbian public
life to a European level.

The Radicals applauded these changes, but it did not take
them long to stake out their own contrasting position. Two weeks
before the election for the new skupština, which took place on
December 12, 1880, Nikola Pašić and four other "like-minded
persons" who had "hastily" gathered in Belgrade, published their
views, which they called a proclamation (*proglas*).[39] After going
over all of Ristić's evil doings and emphasizing the struggle of
the opposition for everything positive and good, Pašić and his
companions hedged their support for the new government. The
government had proposed a program of freedoms that they too
had stood for, they said, and "until now we have worked only for
these freedoms and national well-being. But let no one think we
are lending our name to the new government" before we see how
it behaves, they added. "Only acts can attract our sympathy and
our support."

Ristić and the Liberals were quick to exploit the potential split

between the Radicals and the Young Conservatives this pronouncement seemed to reveal. In a cleverly conceived and biting attack
Istok suggested that the Videlovci were simply manipulating the
Radicals, as demonstrated by the lack of a Radical in the cabinet.
This was only natural, *Istok* continued, since it was obvious that
nowhere in Europe were radicals competent to rule. They were
only critics, without a positive program, and furthermore their
ranks were filled with uneducated persons whose ability to govern
was suspect. *Istok* attacked Pašić personally as someone who, in the
case of Pašić's abortive appointment to the Velika škola in 1878,
had said he was willing to give up his principles if he could enter
state service. Pašić answered in kind, pointing that if, for example,
Paja Vuković, the Radical from Kragujevac, was someone "without
a calling" (*bez zanimanja*) as Ristić claimed, then what was Ristić,
since it was Paja's father who supported Ristić's family when Ristić's
father was working as an itinerant salesman wandering through
the Serbian countryside? And as for the Velika škola job, Pašić
pointed out, it was precisely because of his principles that he did
not get the job.[40]

The personal level of these mutual attacks was not new in
Serbian politics, but the intensity of the antagonism between Ristić
and Pašić reminds us that we are not observing only abstractions
of state construction, discourse modulations, or class relations, but
real life charged with emotion. Although Pašić was calculating even
as a young man and was known later as an enigmatic and cool
politician, in 1880 his exterior demeanor—which later hid the deep
feelings that political struggle released in him—had not yet been
deadened by decades of experience in public life. He let his anger
show in public during that year. One of the bitterest letters he ever
wrote, and one of the most revealing, came when someone listed
in Pašić's call to form Adam committees turned around and condemned Adam and the committees. Pašić responded with a heavy-
handed warning to the author "that there will come a time when
you will regret your letter."[41] He closed by saying that "for me and
my comrades it is sufficient that in the future we will not even
burden you with a glance." In the heat of the irritation that moved
him to write this letter Pašić revealed what some might feel was his

true political credo. "Politics is measured only by the yardstick of success (*da se politika meri samo merom uspeha*)," he said, a motto one should keep close at hand when analyzing Serbian radicalism. It was an uncharacteristic revelation, because Pašić, unlike many of his colleagues who found it impossible to stand aside from the emotional struggles they were involved in, usually remained able to separate the emotional from the functional. That was one of the talents, or perhaps others would call it a curse, that pushed him to the center of Serbian politics.

Presumably Pašić worked through the Adam committees in an effort to elect Radicals in the 1880 election called by the new government. Data is not available. The efforts of the Young Conservatives are easier to follow. Unlike its predecessors, the new government did not take the tried and true method of using local officials to make the elections for it, but the Young Conservatives did make an effort to draw up slates of candidates and to generate support through *Videlo*.[42] In Belgrade they held a caucus of "200 fine citizens" to select their candidate. *Videlo* called this the "first demonstration of the ability of our citizens to be usefully served by freedom of association and agreement. It is significant as the first example and proof that our honest co-citizens know how to use that right within the borders of order and courtesy."[43] In actuality, the meeting was not as orderly as *Videlo* made out. The honest citizens had a great deal of difficulty picking the second of two candidates, and in the resultant struggle both candidates for the second slot resigned, "so that there will not be any misunderstanding," they said.

The Liberals, now out of power, had few such excitements. As soon as the government resigned they had agreed to form a "liberal party" and through *Istok* to keep a watch on the new government and the Radicals.[44] But as we have seen this did not mean creating any special organization, nor holding any electoral gatherings. Ristić did not expect the Liberals to win a majority in the election, but he did anticipate a significant number of Liberal victories and thought that the Liberals would surely win Belgrade.[45] The actual results of the election, which was perhaps the freest held in nineteenth-century Serbia, came as a great surprise.[46] Unable to use the power of the state to make the election, unpopular because of the patentarina and the difficult economic situation, and without real links to the countryside, the Liberals won only 7 seats out of 128 positions, none of them in Belgrade. It was a shocking defeat. *Videlo* rubbed it in by printing both pre- and post-election comments by *Istok,* including its absurd allegation that Liberals did not vote because their opponents were only the dregs of society and they did not want to dirty themselves at the polling places.[47] Perhaps a bit stunned, the Liberals remained passive until the gathering of the skupština. In contrast, both the Radicals and the new government moved aggressively to take advantage of their sudden political good fortune.[48]

During the month that intervened between the election and the convening of the skupština the Young Conservatives began preparing for reform. They organized a committee to rewrite the opština law, began to draft new laws on judges and on the right of association, and attempted to professionalize the organization of local governmental bodies by requiring stricter bookkeeping and quicker disposition of routine business.[49] They did not ask the Radicals to participate in the new government nor to help in working out their proposals, but the two factions of the former opposition apparently remained on good terms, despite the overtones of Pašić's earlier pronouncement. For example, when Pera Todorović returned from exile in Paris, he immediately visited Milan Milićević, who took him to visit Milutin Garašanin, with whom Pera had a long conversation.[50]

The skupština itself opened uneventfully on January 11 and was marred by few of the interminable wrangles over electoral results and seating of members that plagued skupštinas under Ristić. In the election for president the Young Conservative Aleksa D. Popović received the most votes (141), and Nikola Pašić was second (134). Prince Milan, however, fearing—among other things—what he thought might be a hidden republicanism among the Radicals, passed over Pašić for the vice presidency and appointed the former Liberal but now Young Conservative, Milan Kujundžić.[51] A special committee consisting of nine Young Conservatives and six Radicals wrote the address to the throne, and the skupština obligingly adopted it unanimously.[52] If the Young Conservatives dominated the Ways and Means Committee by a 7 to 2 margin, the Radicals dominated the Finance Committee by the same margin.[53] On the surface, it appeared the two former opposition parties were operating well in harness, even if they did not agree on everything.

The political shock was electrifying, therefore, when, unexpectedly and dramatically, on January 20 a new newspaper appeared on the streets of Belgrade. *Samouprava* (Self-Administration) announced itself as the official organ of "The National [or 'Popular' or 'People's'] Radical Party" (*narodna radikalna stranka*) and presented a political program signed by thirty-eight skupština members and endorsed by thirty-eight more. The program for internal reforms was consistent with earlier Serbian radicalism and with the fundamental themes expressed by Svetozar Marković in the last year of his life.[54] Naturally, as its title stated, it called for self-administration and the freeing of opštinas and srezes from state interference. The Radicals could not call for a republic directly, but they did want to overbalance the prince and the State Council by making the skupština, where they could hope to dominate, supreme. In other regards, too, their program retained the populist-democratic tone adopted in the 1870s and which Pera Todorović propagated at his defense in the Red Banner Affair. The national militia, despite its discreditable showing a few years earlier, remained the basis of national defense for the Radicals, who still rejected the idea of a professional standing army. They modified their insistence on electing judges by proposing a mixed system of elected and permanent judges. New demands, but still consistent with radical populism, included a call for a direct, progressive tax on incomes and property, a more urgent proposal since the patentarina controversy, and the creation of a national bank with local branches charged with helping agriculturalists and artisans. Naturally, the new party called for the implementation of all the ordinary civil liberties.

Had this been the extent of the new program of the Radicals, it could not have been considered exceptional. Far more dramatic, both in content and in presentation, was their nationalist policy for external expansion, which was just the area in which the Young Conservatives had agreed to remain passive. Pašić himself agreed later that the internal reforms that he and his colleagues put forward in 1881 were actually secondary to a larger goal, which was "to prepare the conditions and circumstances that would help bring to fruition the great and holy idea of Serbian liberation and unification."[55] "We were always nationalists," said Radical Jovan Žujović in his old age.[56] The wording of the program itself was cautious but clear. *Samouprava* urged harmony with "all brotherly neighboring peoples," a formulation that left out Austria-Hungary as a state but included its Serbian and Croatian subjects, and proposed that Serbia "organize cultural help for the dispersed and yet-to-be freed portions of Serbdom, [assist in] the lively awakening of a consciousness about our national unity in the separated Serbian areas that are subjugated to foreign elements, and with our own products clear the old [trade routes] and open new routes and markets." In this tortuous prose the Radicals turned from an emphasis on popular uprising to create a federation of Balkan peoples—which had been Svetozar Marković's ideal—to a new goal, the creation of a Greater Serbia, although they did not use that term. The program did mention the necessity for agreements with Bulgaria and Montenegro, but the emphasis on Balkan federation was weakened. In its place the future ideal of a Greater Serbia can be seen breaking through to the surface.

Advocating Serbian expansion in itself was not new. Prince Michael had dreamed of a Balkan Federation under Serbian leadership, and Jovan Ristić's Liberals took great pride in the success of the "war of liberation and unification." The significance of the Radical program lay less in the policy itself than in the way the Radicals presented it. Prince Michael pursued foreign policy for the good of Serbia as he understood it, but without making the slightest attempt to mobilize popular support on its behalf. Ristić understood the need for at least some public support for governmental policies, but thought of that support as coming from the right-thinking members of the Belgrade public and the state bureaucracy when it was controlled by the Liberals. At first the Young Conservatives did not even realize the necessity of mobilizing public support—at least outside of the intelligentsia—since they were intent on raising Serbia up from its peasant past, not immersing themselves in it. Now the Radicals came along to claim that they understood the true national mission better then any of their opponents, and to make that claim in a way calculated to enthuse the widest range of the Serbian public. They proposed not just a foreign policy, but a mobilization of the Serbian masses.

Samouprava declared:

> This is not a *theoretical* program which will be realized only in the distant future, but a program of *practical reforms* that the party brings forward in the firm hope that it can *immediately* turn to their realization in the *shortest possible time*. This program has not been invented in some clerk's office. It has been built by people from the nation, members of the national skupština. It has taken into account every kind of thought, and has approached the peasant in his traditional jacket and sandals [*u gunjcu i opancima*], the local [*narodni*] priest, the merchant, and the professor. . . . The demands that are put forward in this program are not cited from books nor brought in from abroad. They are taken from the lips and the spirit and the heart of the people. . . . This is not a program of some undisciplined mob [*gomilice*] but of the entire people, a program of all those who wish that this our beautiful land will flower in liberty and in progress, that it will be everywhere renowned and glorious, that our people will be rich, happy, and satisfied, that they will sing joyfully in their homes in their freedom, and will be their own selves in our bloody and tear-washed but nonetheless dear to us homeland.[57]

This extravagent statement was the work of Pera Todorović, who had been back from exile only a few days before the first issue of *Samouprava* appeared. Moving in immediately with Nikola Pašić, Todorović took up where he had left off as Serbia's first great journalist. "I felt like the old cavalry horse who has not participated in a battle for a long time and suddenly hears a trumpet sounding charge," he said.[58] Several scholars have suggested that because Pera spent a year or so in exile in Paris the program of the Radical

Party was heavily influenced by French radicalism. Todorović was in Paris from 1879 to 1880, during the period of the creation of the Third Republic. He was reputed to have been an admirer of Leon Gambetta and especially of the debating ability of the French delegates he often heard when he attended the Chamber of Deputies. Todorović was also welcome in socialist circles and was a personal acquaintance of Petr Lavrov. His wife Milica, who late in 1879 returned to Zürich for study, used an introduction from Lavrov to meet Karl Kautsky and Eduard Bernstein, on whom she made a great impression.[59] When Todorović returned to Belgrade, therefore, he was well prepared with ideas from Western radicalism and socialism.

But Todorović's contribution lay not in the program itself, which actually had its roots in Serbian radicalism of the 1870s rather than in French radicalism, and which was in any event probably the work of Nikola Pašić. Todorović's contribution was the style and rhetoric with which he clothed that program. Todorović took pride in painting Radical aspirations in the most emotional phrases possible in order to attract attention and draw people to the party. "Fireworks," he called such phrases, "that do not warm and that leave nothing after them, but which for the moment sizzle, throw off brilliant sparks, and glow—and the world likes it, runs over, and looks."[60] In his discussion and justification of the otherwise rather blandly written Radical program, he distanced the Radicals from their erstwhile allies by suggesting that the Young Conservative program was merely theoretical, a swipe at Milan Piroćanac, who was an able theorizer but whose practical political intelligence was open to doubt, and stole the main legitimating principle of the Liberals by emphasizing the nationalist character of the Radical program. These were clever and successful tactics, but they were secondary to the language itself, the vigorous, emotional, gutsy words and phrases, the fireworks, that made Pera Todorović the greatest innovator of Serbian political rhetoric. No one had put their politics so strikingly, in a way so calculated to inflame emotions. Todorović's exaggerated, earthy style moved nationalism from the arcane level of a legitimating notion to the more dangerous level of an emotional plea for expansion, based on the righteous principle that bloody and tear-washed Serbia deserved renown and glory. Eventually all political parties would have to claim not only that they represented the true interests of the people better than their opponents, but that they were more resolute in bringing Serbia the respect that nationalists seem always to find receding just out of reach.

The upping of the ante of political debate represented by this first article in *Samouprava* was inevitable after the idea took hold that authenticity could be achieved by calling on the people as the legitimating force. Once the nation was accepted as the natural underlying fundament of sovereignty by the Serbian intelligentsia, those who sought power always had the option of claiming that they were more legitimate representatives of that nation than their opponents. This could lead in two directions, the programmatic and the rhetorical, both of which the Radicals took. First, they began moving toward a policy of Greater Serbia, attempting to present themselves as more thoroughgoing nationalists than their opponents. And second, they raised the emotional pitch of their appeal in order to encourage the nation that everyone rhapsodized about to rally to their support politically, to turn the abstraction into a living, breathing political force. The Liberals took the first option also through their expansionist foreign policy in 1876 and Ristić's defiance of Austria in 1880, but they could not take the second option because they believed that the policies themselves were the important thing, not the mobilizing rhetoric that described or justified them. The Young Conservatives did not understand the necessity to control the rhetoric, both because they agreed with the Liberals that the policy itself was the main thing, and because they relied on "the preponderance of mind over raw numbers," not populist reform. Only the Radicals realized that in socially undifferentiated Serbia politics were what François Furet has called in a different context a "competition of discourses for the appropriation of legitimacy."[61]

Serbian political parties did not represent economic interests or classes. They were cohorts of educated men who rallied around individual politicians and certain basic principles that were probably related to the decade of their education. The goal of all of them was to achieve control over Serbia's one great asset: the state, the richest and strongest element in society, while at the same time making that state an expression of Serbia's aspiration to modernity. As the necessities of independence increased the size and complexity of the Serbian state, pressure to find a more potent method of justifying the right to control the system became ever greater. Todorović's way of responding to that pressure implied pushing the Radicals further from consideration of socioeconomic change into the political realm where emotion could have a practical function. He bid to appropriate for the Radicals the underlying source of authenticity of the post-French Revolutionary system, the people. Accepting the early Liberal position that putative representatives of the nation had the right to participate in the dance of power, the Radicals now claimed that there was really only one correct vision of the national interest, expansion, and one effective voice, populism. In the battle for control of the discourse, the Radicals moved suddenly ahead.

The difference between the Radicals, the Liberals, and the Young Conservatives at this initial moment of differentiation was social and generational as well as ideological. A comparison of the ages of ten leading figures from the three groupings shows that in 1881 the Liberals averaged 50 years of age (including Jovan Mišković, who was 37—without him the average is 51.4), the Young Conservatives 41.1 years of age, and the Radicals 31.5, an almost perfect correlation of chronological age and political generation. This indicates, perhaps, the narrowness of the political parties still in 1881, when they remained closely knit coteries of like-minded individuals following in adult life the differing traditions in which they were socialized and educated. The Liberals tended to reach political maturity in the 1860s under Prince Michael and were part of the first generation of Serbs to be educated abroad. They remembered Bach's Central Europe, the unifications of Italy and Germany, and Michael's autocratic manner. The Young Conservatives tended to be much more highly educated than the Liberals, many in the queen of the political sciences, the law. The cream of the Serbian intelligentsia of the 1870s, they reached political maturity under Ristić, who, in their view, limited their wholly justified right to political preeminence. They objected to the whiggish nationalism of the Liberals, and wanted instead to create an elevated political culture that their educational attributes would allow them to dominate. In comparison with both the Liberals and the Young Conservatives, the Radicals, who were just coming to political maturity, were an intellectual proletariat. Educated in technical subjects rather than law and political economy, born in small towns and villages rather than larger cities—as the Young Conservatives tended to be—committed to a tradition they liked to call socialist, and younger by a decade than the Young Conservatives, they were not satisfied with drawing-room politics and not willing to wait their turn. The wanted to bring their "practical reform" into effect "in the shortest possible time," and preferably through their own efforts, not through any sort of coalition. They were impatient, sure they were right, enthusiastic about organizing, and not abashed about embarrassing or undermining the new government.

For all these reasons, then, the Radical intitiative in publishing a newspaper and in signing up skupština members behind a program was a great shock to the Young Conservatives, who felt they had been working well with the Radicals since coming to power. They had hired the socialist Mita Cenić to work as an editor for *Videlo,* for example, and got Pera Todorović and Milutin Garašanin together.[62] Raša Milošević, a Radical from Aleksinac, was from time to time a guest at the home of Milan Milićević. They even appointed Kosta Taušanović, the Radical tobacco merchant, as one of the government's representatives to the skupština.[63] But Pašić's statement in December, immediately after Piroćanac's assumption of power, indicated that the Radicals were not likely to be won over by half measures. Pašić claimed later that the Radicals and the Young Conservatives had a verbal agreement to run a joint electoral list and to consult with each other.[64] But when the Young Conservatives did not appoint a Radical minister to their government or attempt to convince a reluctant Prince Milan to appoint Pašić as vice president of the skupština—as the number of votes he received entitled him—the Radicals realized that they would never be equal partners with their former oppositionist allies. Knowing also that their political program differed substantially from the classical liberalism of the Young Conservatives, the Radicals plunged ahead.[65]

The Young Conservatives had been only dimly aware of the depth of the Radicals' discontent. When *Samouprava* appeared with its aggressive program they were not only surprised, they were outraged. "That is how our brother Radicals show how much honesty and courtesy they have," complained Milan Milićević.[66] "Without agreement with us, ignoring our program, they are going to take responsibility for their own program." "You've set [the government's] pants on fire," was the more colorful way Aćim Čumić expressed it to Pera Todorović.[67] The question went beyond hurt feelings, however, since it appeared that, with seventy-six adherents, the Radicals would have a majority in the skupština, and Piroćanac let it be known immediately that without a government majority he would resign, raising the spectre of the return of Jovan Ristić. Panicked, the Young Conservatives called a hurried meeting at their regular meeting place, Joca Krstić's tavern, to work out a response.[68] They quickly concluded that they too would have to form a party. Within five days of the appearance of *Samouprava* the Young Conservatives adopted a set of bylaws, and on January 30 *Videlo* reported the formation of the "Club [*zbor*] of the Progressive Party" with a program based on the principles the paper published in its first issue in December 1879 and the prince's speech from the throne of 1881.[69] By choosing to designate their organization with the Serbian term *zbor*, rather than the international word *klub*, which would have been a reasonable Central European choice for a grouping of parliamentary representatives and which they had already been using, the Progressives suggested the pressure they were beginning to feel from the Radicals' nationalism.[70]

The formation of the Progressive Club left the Radicals with a decision to make. Should they forbid signatories to their program from signing the Progressive program, thereby perhaps causing the government to fall? Pera Todorović argued that that was exactly what they should do. He urged the party to inform the government that "[we] will be true and faithful allies and helpers, but together and with joint control, and that the government can count on [our] support as long as it seriously and faithfully works for the introduction of true constitutionalism in the country."[71] Pera said that if that was not enough for them, let them do what they wanted, and the Radicals would go their own way.[72] But Nikola Pašić's contrary view prevailed. Pašić not only feared that Ristić might return if the government did not have a majority, but he was also concerned that taking a hard line would alienate the moderate elements the party needed and would make the Radicals appear inexperienced and churlish. With Pašić's approval, 103 members of the skupština signed the Progressive program, many of them having signed the Radical program only a few days earlier.

Despite his willingness to let Radical signatories sign the Progressive program, Pašić must still have been surprised when the president of the Progressive Club turned out to be Miloš Glišić. Not only had Glišić been one of the four signatories of the hurried statement Pašić put out in December, but he had participated in the working out of the Radical program up to the last minute.[73] Even the secretary of the Progressives was a former Radical, Nikola Krupežević.[74] Glišić's and Krupežević's turnaround suggested that, at first, neither of the two new parties differentiated themselves publicly as fully as their antagonistic political and rhetorical positions implied. They still remembered Ristić, and they still had many common planks in their programs. The Progressive Club suggested in its first article that it was not to be thought of as an opponent to the Radicals.[75] In fact, the Radical program was much closer to the Progressive Party's than to the traditional forms of European radicalism, *Videlo* claimed, since it recognized the position of the Orthodox Church and did not advocate a republic. The Radicals too tried to play down the disruptive significance of the formation of their party. Naturally they wanted to achieve "that level of culture to which all peoples who have a future in history must attain," *Samouprava* said.[76] Every society contains many tendencies. Therefore, it was only natural in a representative system that parties emerged on the basis of "aspirations and inclination among the simple people and on the basis of principle among the intelligentsia." For three years the opposition worked for certain principles, the Radical paper continued a few days later, and they favored the coming to power of the Videlovci because they held principles similar to the Radicals. They felt it was a mistake for *Istok* to suggest, as it did as soon as the Radical program appeared, that the government did not have a majority. It did, and the Radicals were part of it, but they simply felt they should reserve the right to be independent.[77]

But these initial protestations of mutual regard could not hide the hostility rapidly developing between the two camps. The overt breakdown came in March when the government presented its proposal for a large loan to build the Belgrade to Niš railroad; but well before that the normal day-to-day activities of the skupština provided ample opportunity for smaller controversies. If we do not count the normal interpellations by the peasant wing of the Radical Party—such as Ranko Tajsić's queries about the per diem expenses of local officials and Raša Milošević's demand that expense account abuses in the newly acquired areas be investigated; or traditional suggestions, like abolishing peasant shops and forcing the army to buy its supplies in Serbia—the first major issue that the two parties confronted was the government's proposal for a regularization of the position of judges in the Serbian court system.[78] As one could predict on the basis of their composition and interests, the Progressives put the highest priority on this bill, the purpose of which was to increase the prestige of judges by requiring them to have legal training and by raising their salaries to impressive levels. Since written law was essential to a modern country, and since only highly trained persons could interpret it, the best guarantee of justice, Milutin Garašanin wrote in *Videlo*, was a well-paid, well-educated judiciary.[79] Furthermore, judges themselves were to nominate replacements and new colleagues to the minister of justice, who would send them to the prince for appointment. The idea was to professionalize the courts not only in terms of the quality of the services they provided, but in terms of the collegial responsibility of the judges. By nominating the candidates for judicial positions, the judges would obtain a good deal of that self-control of entry that is an important aspect of professional status.

The Liberals, never ones to advocate too great a mixing of the people in the affairs of state, showed their opportunism by declaring the Progressive proposal would not work because it did not provide for any checks on the judiciary except that of the minister of justice, who, as they knew well from their own experience, would not be inclined to overturn his own judges.[80] *Samouprava's* populist view was that the problem was not that judges were poorly paid or that they were insecure, but rather that legal processes were so formal and complex that they were difficult to understand.[81] What Serbia needed, it said, was simpler laws and judges who were closer to the people—that is, judges who were popularly elected, not self-appointed judges who were going to be paid astronomical salaries.[82] It was on this last point that the members of the skupština became excited, not only on the floor, but in the Progressive Club too, where negotiations took place between Radical attendees and the Progressives. The solution finally adopted was that if the Progressives would lower the salaries of the top judges, the skupština would pass the bill.[83] When on February 11 it did so, including even 100,000 dinars to pension off the untrained judges who would have to be replaced, the strength of the government, which had been placed in doubt because of uncertainties about who stood where in the Radical/Progressive split, received "a most striking demonstration."[84]

Two further impressive victories for the government were a new press law and a law that permitted the establishment of political organizations. The first of these changed the long-standing rule, broken only briefly by Kaljević's changes in 1875, that forced papers to present a proof-copy to the police an hour before publication. The new law provided that the police were to receive a copy all right, but they could only proceed with prosecution after publication, and could prosecute only for defaming the prince and proposing revolution.[85] A more important law, the one on public societies and meetings, was not as popular with the Radicals, although they favored it in principle. It stated that anyone wanting to establish a political organization could do so upon presenting a statement to the government, which was obliged to approve it unless the society's purpose was illegal. A government representative had the right to attend public meetings, which had to be announced to the police at least one day in advance.[86] The Radicals thought the guarantees were "illusory" because of many loopholes that would permit intervention of the police "in the interests of public order," but, nevertheless, this significant law, the first in Serbian history that permitted political organizations to work openly and publicly, eventually passed by the end of the skupština session.[87] It was the basic innovation that made organized political parties possible.

These successes, while solidifying Piroćanac's government, did not bring the Radicals and Progressives closer together, as the bitter debate over the huge loan proposed to finance the Serbian railroad demonstrated. After approval of the railroad convention in 1880, which obligated Serbia to begin construction by the end of that year, Ristić was not able to attract a reasonable offer from abroad to do so.[88] The Progressives who inherited the problem did not ask for public bids, but sought to find a suitable financier through, for example, their diplomatic representatives. Their problem is a familiar one today. A poor country with few resources and no industry seeks significant foreign investment to undertake a large construction project. How does it get it? There are two basic ways, one through political clientage, the other by paying a price on the world capital markets that is commensurate with the risk of investment in an uncertain economy. In 1881 the Serbs did both. The only really serious bid came from Eugène Bontoux, who had made a reputation in Austria as a railroad builder but, in fact, was a French speculator. In 1878 Bontoux left his position as head of Südbahn in Austria to found General Union (*Union Général*) in Paris, the purpose of which was to promote foreign railroad bonds on the French securities markets. Realizing that the Treaty of Berlin meant the likelihood of Balkan railroad building and that Austrian support would be important in the new situation, late in 1880 he founded the Österreichische Länderbank in Vienna with a capital of 100 million francs.[89] The emperor himself appointed the head of this bank, which the Austrian government welcomed because it promised to improve its international credit, help Habsburg trade and industry, and provide—in the narrow-minded conception of the Habsburg court—greater security than could be provided by the Jewish banking institutions of Vienna.[90] Bontoux was in Vienna organizing the Länderbank when the Austrians put him onto the Serbian need for a broker to finance their railroad.[91] Hurrying to Belgrade immediately, despite the harshness of the winter that made travel on the rivers hazardous, Bontoux began passing out bribes through the journalist Michael Rozen and agitating for acceptance of General Union as the financier, builder, and operator of the proposed railroad.[92]

The deal Bontoux sold to the Progressive government provided for a fifty-year loan of 100 million francs (71,400,000 effective) at 5 percent (7 percent effective) that Bontoux would place on the French capital market over time as the railroad was being constructed.[93] His company would take the funds thus generated and construct the railroad for 198,000 francs per kilometer, not including building the Sava Bridge or buying the necessary land. To provide the funds for that purpose, and to pay off both the war debt to Russia and the internal debt still outstanding for the requisitions carried out during the two Ottoman wars, General Union floated a fifty-year lottery loan of 33 million francs (24,585,000 effective) at 5 percent (6 percent effective).[94] This would be placed immediately and the cash used to start construction and to retire the requisition debt. The single-track line would be state property with rates and schedules set by the Serbian government, but General Union would operate it for twenty-five years for a fixed fee.

The agreement with Bontoux came before the skupština on March 16, 1881, and the debate that ensued lasted more than a week. The Radicals produced a number of good arguments in opposition to the railroad. They argued that the 198,000 franc-per-kilometer construction cost was high by 38,000 francs per kilometer, according to the cost estimates of a survey conducted by an engineering committee a few years earlier. Bontoux himself later admitted that he expected about a profit of 45,000 francs per kilometer. They observed that the Serbian government made all the guarantees whereas Bontoux made no concessions and provided no guarantees. The only change the Serbian negotiators had been able to get out of Bontoux from his original proposal had been to lower the cost per kilometer from 200,000 francs to 198,000 francs, not exactly a major victory. Otherwise, all the provisions for financing the project were very favorable to General Union, which Bontoux estimated privately would make about 30 million francs on the entire operation. The Radicals pointed out that no time limit was placed on Bontoux for constructing the railroad, that twenty-five years was a long guaranteed operating contract, and that, in comparison with past Serbian economic experience, the addition of 6 million dinars (one dinar equaled one franc) to the annual state budget was an overwhelming burden that would fall on the back of the ordinary taxpayers.[95]

The Progressives did not really dispute these points. They simply pointed out that Serbia was required by the Treaty of Berlin and by agreement with Austria to build a railroad, that this was the best offer they had received, and that the economic benefits of a railroad were so certain that there would be no problem in repaying the debt once the railroad was in operation.[96] On the basis of these arguments, and on the basis of the solidarity of the government party, the Bontoux agreement passed the skupština by a vote of 97 to 57, with 5 abstentions, on March 24.[97]

Despite the government's victory, two aspects of the debate made it particularly bitter. The first harked back to the law already passed on judges and was related as well to skupština rules concerning a quorum. One way the Radicals thought they might defeat the railroad loan was to resign their positions, thus preventing the three-quarters attendance necessary to conduct business. But they did not have quite enough supporters to do that.[98] On their side, the Progressives believed the Radicals were stringing out the debate on the railroad loan because the new law on judges was to come into effect on March 20, in the middle of the debate, and when it did some Progressives who were newly appointed judges would have to leave the skupština, increasing the chances of disruption through a quorum call.[99] Concerned about this, the Progressives decided to act. Twenty-four hours before the old law on judges ran out, Piroćanac pensioned twenty-five judges and dismissed four others, most of them Liberals, and replaced them with Progressives, so that when the new law that provided for the irremovability of judges came into effect, the judiciary would be dominated by Progressives. Nine of the new judges were members of the skupština, but they managed to get in their votes for the railroad loan only two hours before being sworn into their new positions.[100] Clearly, the Progressives, in the tradition of the Liberals of 1858 and of Jovan Ristić, intended to treat their accession to power as a property right.

The irritation and frustration Progressive maneuvering produced on the Radical side was matched by the anger the Progressives felt at the nationalistic tenor of the Radicals' arguments. The Radical attacks raised the pitch of excitement in the skupština and in the public to levels not previously experienced. On the first day of debate large crowds gathered outside the skupština, and for the first time in Serbian parliamentary history the president of the skupština had to prohibit expressions of partisanship from the gallery. On the third day of debate, after a door in the hallway of the building had been broken down, guards had to be placed outside the building.[101] In one of the popular Radical speeches Ranko Tajsić broadly hinted that the Progressives were being bribed by reading a report about railroad corruption in Wisconsin, the implication being that no agreement so against the national interest could be passed without chicanery. But the most talked about speech was given by Radical Svetozar Nikolajević. After giving a tendentious historical survey of Serbia's development in the nineteenth century that praised the "revolution" of 1858 and Prince Michael's "holding high the flag of a national policy abroad," Nikolajević accused Ristić of undermining Serbia's economic position—which he ingenuously claimed the Radicals considered the most important basis of Serbian progress in the future—and blamed the Progressives for giving over the "national flag" to Austria. "It is my firm conviction," he continued, "that by adopting this convention we are digging the grave of our political freedom and of our state. . . . We are what no Serb wants to be—traitors to the Balkan peoples."[102] When Nikolajević uttered the word "traitors" the skupština burst into an uproar. Progressives tried to attack the speaker while Radicals jumped to defend him. More ominously, the crowds that had gathered from the beginning of the debate outside the building where the skupština was being held suddenly raged out of control. At this point the stenographic record of the skupština read as follows:

Outside, struggle of the police with the public. . . . From the street terrible noises and the police striking the public. . . . There must be a terrific spectacle. Representatives get up from their places and look out the windows. Some police take out their revolvers, for what reason is not seen. Mićić, commander of the police, forbids them to use arms. Rocks land on the police. The mayor of the city and the clerks intervene.[103]

Eventually order was restored, but the impact of Nikolajević's speech on the crowds was not lost on the Radicals. The excitement provoked by an agreement that could be represented as favoring Austria showed how nationalist rhetoric could have a mobilizing effect on the Belgrade public and, by extension, on the Serbian public in general.[104] Everyone knew that Bontoux was the founder of Länderbank, so the Radicals argued against the agreement because it was Austrian. They never inquired whether such a connection would be good or bad for Serbia in the post-1878 international situation, but simply castigated it as inconsistent with the dream of uniting the Balkan lands under Serbian leadership. "Gentlemen," Nikolajević said, "Serbia, which is called to be and which we all wish to be the Piedmont of the Balkans; Serbia, which must spend on its army and culture; that Serbia, dare it pawn what it must live from as a state?"[105] The Progressives, too, suspected that Bontoux must have an Austrian connection, although Bontoux kept secret from both them and the Radicals the 30 percent interest that Länderbank actually held in the loan deal; but they believed that only with Austrian diplomatic support could Serbia exist. Still, provoked by the Radicals, they had to deny that they would contemplate signing the agreement if there were a direct Austrian participation. By inciting the crowd and putting the Progressives on the defensive, Nikolajević's speech showed the Radicals that Austria-baiting could be a powerful weapon. They did not wait long to use it again.

With the passage of the railroad loan, the next step was to work out a way to pay for it. Two years earlier Vladimir Jovanović had come to grief trying to pay off a war debt of 30 million dinars, only 9 million of which was owed abroad. Now, in theory, that debt was covered by the 33 million in lottery bonds, but Serbia was

Table 1. Serbian State Debt as of 1883 (in dinars)

Internal debt

War loans and requisitions	13,487,000		
Accumulated budget deficits	16,534,000		
Total	30,021,000		

External debt

	nominal	*effective (%)*	*annuity*
1876 Russian war loan	6,965,000	5,488,000 (78.8)	400,000
*1881 Railroad loan	90,000,000	64,260,000 (71.4)	7,050,000
1881 Lottery loan	33,000,000	24,585,000 (74.5)	1,630,000
1882 Anglo-Austrian agricultural loan	8,403,000	5,997,600 (71.4)	500,000
Total	138,368,000	100,331,000 (72.5)	9,580,000

Average Serbian annual budget 1880–82:

Expenditures:	24,154,000
Income:	20,659,000

All figures are approximate.

* Originally 100 million dinars, the railroad loan was reduced by 10 million dinars by applying 11 million dinars of the lottery loan of 1881 (the residue was General Union's fee).
Sources: Vladimir Jovanović, "Statističan pregled," GSUD, 52 (1883): 117–33; Vladimir Jovanović, "Novi statistični pregled financijskog stanja Srbije u god. 1880., 1881., 1882.," GSUD, 68 (1889): 7–11; John R. Lampe, "Financial Structure and the Economic Development of Serbia, 1878–1912," PhD. diss., University of Wisconsin, 1971, p. 142; and VMO, 2:387–92 (note: the pages at this point are misnumbered— the reference is to the second page 387).

obligated for an annual interest and principle payments of about 6 million dinars. (For a summary of Serbian debts as of 1883, see table 1.) How could it be done? The Progressives proposed to find the money with three new taxes on tobacco, alcoholic beverages, and on shops. For the latter a sliding scale established that the smallest urban shop would pay 5 dinars per year, the largest 300 (a rate approximating 2 percent or less). In the villages the tax was proportionally higher; 25 dinars a year no matter what the volume of business, unless soft goods (candles, fabric) were sold, in which case the tax would be 100 dinars. "In this entire law," the Radical Milan Djurić said, "I see nothing other than the old patentarina," while another complained, "I fear that Vladimir Jovanović's patent-arina is coming [back]." Pašić restated the Radicals' position: "In general I am against every tax that is not based equitably on prop-erty and net income."[106] Because of this opposition, the government modified its proposal in order to tax the first 5,000 dinars of turnover at a rate of 4 dinars per thousand and everything above that at 5 dinars per thousand, the amount of taxable turnover to be decided by local opština committees. By means of this tax and the two others the government optimistically hoped to raise some-thing like 10 million dinars a year, and Pašić, as chairman of the Finance Committee, was able to present a balanced budget to the skupština.[107] The relative lack of controversy provoked by these new taxes reflected a sort of resignation once the railroad loan had passed. Just as Pašić had predicted the previous year, Serbian obligations were beginning to grow at a pace never before imagined.

One final step remained to fulfill the commitments Ristić was forced to make at Berlin—to complete the commercial agreement with Austria. In order to provide time to work out the final text of the agreement, the government recessed the skupština, recalling it after one month. Dissatisfaction with the railroad loan and negative rumors about the commercial agreement made it difficult to achieve a quorum when the skupština reassembled, but when one was achieved the new agreement became the major item of busi-ness.[108] The main thrust of the convention was to open Serbia to cheap imports of manufactured goods from Austria at the low end of the technological scale, such as beer, kerosene, matches, sugar, and paper, while at the same time giving Serbian agricultural goods preference in the Austrian market.[109] Austria's obvious intention was to cultivate Serbia as an agricultural resource for the Habsburg Empire and to hinder its possibilities for starting small-scale indus-tries that might compete with Austrian counterparts.

Austria's challenge presented one of the few occasions in the nineteenth century when Serbs debated the fundamental question of developmental policy directly. Despite the Radicals' increasing concentration on organizing the peasantry for political purposes, and despite their continued glorification of the natural qualities of the Serbian people, Nikola Pašić based his criticism of the commercial agreement not on Svetozar Marković or on populist rhetoric, but on the ideas of Mihailo Vujić, Professor of National Economy and Finance at the Velika škola. Vujić, Serbia's greatest nineteenth-century economist and later a leader of the Radical Party, believed that even the advancement of agriculture required industrial development, and for industry protective tariffs were essential to a poor country. Following Friedrich List closely, Vujić held that all the main industrial powers, from mercantilist England to contemporary America, protected their industries in their early days and, therefore, prospered, whereas weak regions such as South America and India followed free trade and were poor. Serbia had all the qualities it needed to be industrial—mines, geographical position, rivers, and social equality. The route to modernity, therefore, was to develop national industries through state help and to introduce a protective tariff. Talking about agriculture was not sufficient. "We want to play the role of Piedmont," he said, but in order to do that Serbia had to take care of its own industry.[110]

On the other side, the Progressive Čedomil Mijatović, a noted economist in his own right, vigorously defended the agreement.[111] Serbia was an agricultural country, he pointed out, not an industrial one, and what this agreement did was to ensure the prosperity of the Serbian peasant. In his view the argument Pašić presented was doctrinaire and politically impossible. The Radicals wanted an open market for Serbian agricultural goods exported to Austria, but high tariffs on manufactured goods imported from Austria. Mijatović argued that they could not have it both ways. Either the government aided agriculture or protected industry, but it could not do both. Since Serbia was an agricultural country, and since the latter choice meant economic war, Mijatović felt Serbia should choose an agreement with Austria. Mijatović's argument easily prevailed, and the commercial agreement passed by a vote of 122 to 22, with 6 abstentions.

Mijatović's argument on behalf of the commercial agreement was consistent with the earlier discussion of the Law on Six Days Plowing and the previous debate on restricting peasant shops. The pattern seems to lie in an implicit arrangement between the Serbian political class and the peasantry. If the state class would not insist that the peasantry change its mode of life, the peasantry would permit the state class to dominate politics. The Radicals may have presented the other side of the argument in this latest case, but in general they too sought a deal that would permit them someday to exercise power. Since they were not yet in power, they sought it by mobilizing the peasantry rather than by bribing them.[112] The question at issue was not so much whether the traditional social structure of the Serbian countryside would be preserved—it would be. The question was which faction of the state class would prevail.

Slobodan Jovanović has suggested that the Radical argument against the commercial agreement was contradictory in at least two senses. First, it conflicted directly with Radical claims to be the representatives of the people and especially the peasantry. As in the case of the peasant shops, where they stood on the side of the town merchant, the Radicals took a stand that favored Serbia's nonexistent industry against the immediate economic interests of the peasantry. Second, Pašić earlier severely criticized Ristić for bringing Serbia to the brink of economic war with Austria. Now the Radicals defended a policy that would have produced a tariff war with Austria. Raša Milošević even argued that Austrian factories would be hurt more by closing the Serbian market than would Serbian agriculture, which could survive such a struggle on its own.[113] Having accused Ristić of giving in to Austria when in fact he refused to do so, the Radicals opposed Mijatović's policy of subordinating Serbia's trade to Austria on much the same grounds that Ristić did. On the surface this clearly appears to be opportunism, opposition for the sake of opposition; which is exactly what Ristić accused the Radicals of. And in a sense the Liberals were right. The Radicals were opportunists as well as oppositionists. If the party in power proposed something, they opposed it, a tactic Pašić defended as early as 1875. The common thread in their argument, however, is that they opposed both Ristić and the Progressives using nationalistic, anti-Austrian rhetoric. In other words, in the day-to-day struggles over this and that issue the Radicals were groping toward their most powerful political tool, domination of the idea of the nation. They did not defend the peasantry's immediate interests in the case of the commercial agreement with Austria, turning instead to ideas of development and protectionism that were part of their intellectual equipment. And yet the party soon became recognized by a large portion of the peasantry as their true defender. The explanation for this anomaly cannot lie in any sort of class analysis, but only in the ability of the Radicals to secure a firm hold on the legitimating discourse.

7 : ORGANIZATION, CONFRONTATION, AND MOBILIZATION

> Struggle is a sign of life and political health, not in any way a demonstration of the decline of a people.—Milutin Garašanin

The Progressives made political parties possible in Serbia by the law of April 13, 1881, which legalized public organizations. Before this innovation, political parties of the modern type would have been considered illegal conspiracies, but now, in the summer and fall of 1881, all political groupings knew they could legally expand their parliamentary clubs, which they already loosely called parties, into organizations with local branches, dues, conventions, and all the other attributes of the modern political party. By the end of the year all three had done so. But before they could turn to this basic task, each political group faced disruptive and contentious issues that distracted their attention.

As the party in power, the Progressives were the ones who had to administer the country. This involved one serious crisis and one bitter dispute. The crisis can be disposed of quickly—it was Milan's secret agreement with Austria, which has already been discussed. The second issue, however, the dismissal of Metropolitan Mihajlo of Belgrade, head of the Serbian Orthodox Church, inspired a lengthy and acrimonious struggle.[1] As in other Orthodox lands, the Serbian church was not tied administratively to the ecumenical Patriarch of Constantinople in Istanbul. The Hatti-sherif of 1830 established its autonomy, and the Patriarch recognized its complete independence in 1879. Inside Serbia, however, the church was closely linked to the state. Regular priests received a small salary from a tithe levied by the state on every taxpayer, monks were sustained by the income of their monasteries, and Serbia's four bishops and one Metropolitan were paid directly by the state.[2] Despite this cozy relationship, the church thought of itself as being self-regulating and independent. For this reason, when the skupština of 1881 imposed a tax on appointments to the priesthood and to higher church offices, Metropolitan Mihajlo immediately protested that the tax had not been approved by the bishop's council and was contrary to canon law. Austria had already indicated to Milan that they were not happy with the activities of Metropolitan Mihajlo, who was a Russophile and a close political associate of Jovan Ristić.[3] In July 1881, therefore, the minister of education and church affairs, Stojan Novaković, answered Mihajlo's protest with a cold and pedantic letter that pointed out that the issue had been discussed at length by the skupština, which had refused proposals to modify the taxes. "It is a lamentable but undeniable fact," Novaković said, "that it is necessary to find the reason for this refusal in a weakening, in a quasi-annihilation, of the prestige of the church and its servitors among the people, owing to those too frequent controversies in which the clergy opposes the popular sense of morals, and in the visible absence of a strong discipline and solid preparation for the ecclesiastical vocation."[4] Novaković did not mention the more likely reasons for the government's irritation: that Mihajlo was one of Jovan Ristić's closest Liberal allies, and that the Metropolitan was an outspoken opponent of Milan's pro-Austrian policy.

The Metropolitan responded to Novaković's insulting letter by getting the council of bishops to vote early in November that the church would not enforce the new tax, on the principle that the state had no right to tax the church. By taking this stand, Mihajlo gave Milan just the chance he had been looking for to get rid of an impediment to his Austrophile policy. A week after the synod's vote, Milan removed Mihajlo from office. Had Stojan Novaković been a bit more diplomatic and had he cultivated the individual bishops more adroitly, Mihajlo's removal might have been accomplished smoothly. Instead, the bishops objected strongly, and a lengthy struggle ensued. In the end Milan and his Progressive government had to remove not only Mihajlo, but the other four bishops as well; moreover, they had to rewrite the rules governing church elections, and to consecrate their new Metropolitan in Karlovci, outside the Serbian border. This last act could be done only with the permission of the Hungarian government, which gave the unmistakable impression that Austria-Hungary, after having imposed a railroad concession and a trade convention, was now imposing its will on the Serbian church. Actually, Austria did not take much interest in Serbian church affairs, especially after Mihajlo's removal, but Milan's intransigent opposition to Mihajlo forced him from one difficult decision to another until he succeeded in gaining control over the church, only at the cost of confirming the Progressives' reputation of being pro-Austrian, which was to say, antinational.

Metropolitan Mihajlo's removal was only the most egregious of the purges the Progressives undertook to get control of the apparatus of state they inherited from the Liberals: the appointment of a large number of new judges one day before the new law on judges came into effect was another notable case in point. Živan Živanović (a Liberal sympathizer) compiled figures to show that in their first year the Progressives pensioned off sixty-five persons and removed twenty-six others from service, whereas in over nine years of power during the regency and the war years Ristić had pensioned off only fourteen and removed from service only two.[5] Naturally the Liberals fought back, attacking the Progressives on both religious and national grounds. Since the former would, as Mousset puts it, "only moderately agitate Serbian opinion," they concentrated on nationalist rhetoric. Most of their arguments were reminiscent of the ineffective whig historicism typical of the 1860s. "A New Kosovo" is what the Liberal paper *Srpska nezavisnost* called Mihajlo's defeat. "The history of the Christian church will inscribe the name of Stojan Novaković after those of the frenzied Nero and the horrible Caligula," it intoned later. "That which no vizier had ever dared to hazard to the Ottoman Sultan; that which the passionate Calvinist Hungarian, Koloman Tisza, has never dared to propose to his Catholic Emperor and apostolic King Franz Josef; that which the Russian tsars, heads of the Russian church have never accomplished with their lack of respect and brutality, the minister of education and church affairs has the audacity to propose."[6]

The Liberals also had to meet the challenge of the Radicals' newly emotional nationalism. In one of the best examples of this effort, an anonymous Liberal calling himself "A Monk" and writing in the Liberal party newspaper *Srpska nezavisnost* in 1882, established his right to contest Milan's action against Mihajlo and the bishops with these words:

> I am a Serb. My father, grandfather, and great grandfather all were true and pure Serbs. All my ancestors, as people from the nation, lived among the people and participated with them in every good and bad fortune, every good and evil. . . . And thus the blood of my forefathers was spilled at Čačak, Ljubić, and Mišar, and their bones are scattered on all the battlefields on which Serbian freedom, Serbian literature, and the Serbian kingdom, for which I fought in 1876 and 1878, were established. I am thus a true Serb, body and soul, and today I live as a Serb and will remain so for the rest of my life. . . . I love my nation, it seems to me, much, much more truly than many others who are called "patriots" and who are always shouting "For the People; For the People," but in fact stand only for themselves and their own rule.[7]

The argument is petulant, but is also revealing. "A Monk" does not use religious values to argue that contemplation, piety, charity, and service to God are ordained by the divine traditions of almost two thousand years of Christian belief and, therefore, have a moral value that transcends the mundane concerns of political expediency. Instead, he argues in effect that there is a new moral basis of society, one based on the natural law that makes each individual of the nation equivalent, and that even monks partake of the power inherent in that now widely accepted principle. Nothing could indicate more clearly how deeply the new standard of legitimacy had penetrated into the consciousness of literate Serbs. At the same time the defensive, almost whining, tone of the argument shows how difficult it was for the Liberals to find a voice to match the fireworks of Pera Todorovič.

The Radicals were not particularly interested in the debate over the fate of the Serbian church. In the summer of 1881 they had a more serious challenge to face, the accusation that they were not the heirs of Svetozar Marković. Just as the Liberals of the 1870s took pride in the activities of the Omladina one decade earlier, so the Radicals of the 1880s considered their movement sanctified by Marković's death and by the persecution most of them had undergone in Kragujevac in 1876. "That group of people, which for the first time appeared in *Radnik* (sic) in 1871–72, has never stopped living like a principled party whole," Steva Milićević said in April 1881. "After *ten years* of work, persecution, and much bitter experience, here it is today strengthened and confirmed by people from the nation."[8]

The occasion for Milićević's outburst was the appearance in mid-March 1881 of a newspaper edited by Mita Cenić and Djura Ljočić whose title itself, *Radnik,* indicated what its editors thought of the Radicals' claim to be the true heirs of the socialist movement of the early and mid-1870s.[9] Both editors had been collaborators of Marković on the original *Radenik,* and of the two Cenić became the Radicals' harshest critic. He had studied medicine in Russia and worked with Marković, but spent most of the 1870s in prison, first a short stint in France, and subsequently seven years in irons in Serbia. After his release in 1880 he worked briefly on *Videlo* as editor of the political events column, but when the opposition split into two parties he decided that he agreed with neither.

Cenić attacked the Radicals for concentrating too much on politics and not enough on the material basis of society, an argument which, as we have seen, had a good deal of merit. "Reforms that the bourgeois politicians propose today deal exclusively with political relations," he wrote in July, "but we consider that the true basis of legal status is economic fact, and that therefore the institution of justice is a consequence of economic relations. Reforms of civil society do not deal with the basis of that society, private property."[10] For Cenić the state was a class agent; socialism would come only through revolutionary means, and only two sorts of parties existed: those that believed existing social arrangements were final, like the Radicals, and those that did not, like the socialists, that is, like Cenić. What the Radicals had done, Cenić said, was to call "sophistically" on Marx to claim that since Serbia was industrially undeveloped, the conditions for the victory of socialism did not exist and, therefore, they were justified in turning to bourgeois political reform. However, due in good measure to Cenić's lack of familiarity with socialist literature because of his long time in jail, he could not come up with any better solutions than the Radicals. In the end he was reduced to calling merely for equal attention to the economic, political, and moral factors, since "these three factors taken together create the moral revolution, and only a new morality can raise up and sustain a new social order."[11]

The Radical reply, strung out over more than six weeks, was detailed, erudite, and forceful, but it did not entirely vitiate Cenić's critique. Lazar Paču, a young doctor and a member of *Samouprava*'s editorial board, provided the defense in a lengthy serialized article entitled "Civil Society and its Socio-political Party." Thoroughly versed in European socialism, including Marx and Engels, Paču reviewed the development of society in Western Europe from a socialist viewpoint. It is fruitless to ask whether there should or should not have been oppression, he wrote, or whether society could have developed otherwise than from Ancient (slave) to Feudal (serf) to Bourgeois (liberal). The fact is that it happened. The French Revolution abolished feudal and monopolistic rights, and the Declaration of the Rights of Man established equality before the law, but this did not establish true equality because it did not help the worker, whose surplus value continues to be appropriated. "The living conditions in which man finds himself, which until now have lorded it over man, will come under the governance and supervision of man, and thus for the first time he will become the conscious lord of nature. . . . The association of people . . . will become their own free act, from which time all objective forces that until then ruled in history will fall under the supervision of the people themselves. . . . That is the leap of humanity from the realm of necessity to the realm of freedom."[12]

Having made this principled statement, however, Paču went on essentially to admit Cenić's fundamental point—that the Radicals, however much they talked like socialists, in fact were not. "Our society," Paču concluded, "is a primitive society; our production is still completely undeveloped, at the level, so to speak, of Asiatic culture." Serbia does not have a class society, but simply a difference between the state and its people. "Thus socialism here cannot be considered a reaction to social contradictions, as it is in the West." We cannot, therefore, pursue the kind of revolutionary class policy that is appropriate to the West. We need to develop "production, but without class contradictions, as the basis of material independence and as the broad democratic basis for the state."[13]

Cenić remained, after seven years in prison, the angry young man, the unreconstructed revolutionary socialist to whom principle was more important than practical politics. The Radicals, on the other hand, while insisting on the clarity of their theoretical position and the authenticity of their links with Svetozar Marković, had arrived at a political program they believed had practical potential for Serbia. Cenić's insistence on the separation of church and state seemed to the Radicals simply inapplicable to Serbian circumstances, and probably damaging to their efforts to recruit young and better-educated priests into the party. They found Cenić's sarcasm, personal attacks, insults, and accusations difficult to bear. Cenić ridiculed the Radicals as donkeys in lion's clothing, excoriated their practical socialism as "prostituted socialism," and harped on points of personal criticism, such as accusing Nikola Pašić of acting in a way disloyal to Svetozar Marković in 1875. "Sometimes *Radnik* angers me so much with its malice and slander," wrote Pašić in the fall of 1881, "that I reach the point of giving everything up, of going into the wilderness [*u šumu*], into a foreign world, or of withdrawing somewhere into some barren Albanian village to flee human meanness and malice."[14]

But, of course, the Radicals were no more kind to Cenić than he was to them. Their most damaging accusation was that Cenić was an agent of the Progressives. And, in fact, *Radnik* did not attack the Progressives to the extent it did the Liberals and especially the Radicals. Seemingly in return, the ministry of the interior looked with unusual tolerance on some of Cenić's more inflammatory editions. Slobodan Jovanović thinks it likely that Cenić accepted support from the Progressives on the revolutionary principle that if the cause is just the source of the material resources to pursue it matters little.[15] In fact, financial support seems to have come from Cenić's partner, Djura Ljočić, who thought the paper might lose 2,400 dinars a year.[16] By October, however, after six months of publication six days a week, *Radnik* was 7,000 dinars in debt and had to drop down to appearing three days a week. In December, when Ljočić refused to inject any more money, it closed completely. Cenić had calculated that he could succeed if he got 1,500 subscribers, but at their peak subscriptions reached only 1,060, half of which were cut-rate student subscriptions.[17]

Vast readership was not what kept the other newspapers in Serbia afloat either. None of them achieved the 1,500 subscriptions that it took to be profitable. What saved them was the backing of a party organization. If each of the political groupings had their problems as 1881 wore on—the Progressives purging Mihajlo and the church, the Liberals struggling to find a voice to match the Radicals, and the Radicals fighting to preserve the authenticity of their past—they all realized that the law of April 13, 1881, offered them an unprecedented opportunity to expand their parliamentary clubs into broad political organizations.

First among the parties in terms of seniority were the Liberals, who could look back to the St. Andrew's skupština in the 1850s, the Omladina in the 1860s, and the "war for national liberation and unification" in the 1870s.[18] If the Radicals could draw authenticity from a decade of opposition, the Liberals could draw it, or try to, from a decade of leading Serbia through the sacrifices and successes of war, when, as they put it, the people and the ruler with one spirit achieved independence.[19] But the inability of the Liberal leaders to dirty their hands with actual solicitation of support from the Serbian peasantry, whether from lack of inclination or simply from advancing years, prevented them from taking full advantage of their agitational possibilities. Liberal impractibility is nowhere better illustrated than in the way they went about taking advantage of the law on associations. Instead of translating the term "National-Liberal Party," which Ristić used as early as 1873, into organizational reality directly, the Liberals formed instead something called "The Society for the Support of Serbian Literature." Already in

July 1881 the government approved the bylaws of this organization, and on September 29 seventy-four Liberals, all of them friends
and associates of long standing, met in the Belgrade Reading Room
to found the new society.[20] It goes without saying that Jovan Ristić
became its president.

Despite its title, the obvious intent of the society was political.
Its main purpose was to publish a newspaper that would bring the
Liberal message to the Serbian public. The wherewithal for this task
was to come from selling memberships, which could be obtained by
buying 1 or more of the 500 shares originally offered and/or by
paying dues of 6 dinars per year. By the time of the first public
meeting of the society at the end of November 1881 all 500 shares
had been sold to 190 persons, and since many of those paying dues
paid more than 6 dinars (many paid less also), 6,816 dinars had
been raised.[21] By the end of the year 1,138 persons throughout
Serbia had pledged their 6 dinars for membership, and 518 had
actually paid.[22] The new newspaper, entitled *Srpska nezavisnost* (Serbian Independence), brought together into one publication the old
Istok, which the Liberals had always unconvincingly claimed was an
independent paper, and *Novi vek* (New Era), a short-lived paper
reflecting the somewhat more aggressive liberalism of Vladimir
Jovanović and Stojan Bošković.[23] The lead article in its first issue,
which appeared on October 13, 1881, far from being a discussion
of how to encourage Serbian literature, was a "Program of the
National-Liberal Party," the main goal of which was "to unite
our scattered parts and lands on the Balkan peninsula within
natural ethnographic borders and in the form of their ancient
historic glory and power, both in the political and church
spheres," preferably through a confederation of the Balkan
nations.[24]

This goal differed from the similar Radical one only in its
mention of the Orthodox Church.[25] The main differences lay in
how the Liberals propagated their goal and who responded to it.
Successful though the figures on membership may appear, the
Society, in fact, mounted no broad membership drive and attracted
only those who were already committed to liberalism. In Belgrade
this meant, according to an Austrian agent, "the more well-to-do

merchants of Belgrade" who tended to meet together, sometimes
with the Russian consul, to console one another now that they were
out of power.[26] The Liberals' method of self-reinforcement rather
than extension outward is illustrated by a dinner they held in
Belgrade at the Golden Cross restaurant on Terazije on the evening
of December 12, 1881, following the first public meeting of the
society. At midnight, as the date changed to December 13, a toast
was offered to the fourth anniversary of the beginning of the "war
of liberation," for which those present took credit. The toast made
"a most pleasant impression," according to its author, but from the
rock that was thrown through a window during the dinner one can
estimate how isolated the Liberals actually were.[27] According to the
memoirs of Avram Petrović, the society tended to attract only
pensioned Liberal bureaucrats, older merchants, older priests and
teachers, and very few peasants.[28] In Vranje, an area that had
previously known no public political life, where the Liberals had
been able to dominate political life since the occupation of 1878,
the society had forty-four members by the end of 1882, but one-
half of these were bureaucrats, former bureaucrats, or priests. Only
two were peasants and one of those was a kmet.[29] In the changed
circumstances of the early 1880s this sort of support was of little
political use. As Ristić himself put it in his report to the second
annual meeting of the society late in October 1882, "it is not possible
to deny that our communications have not had their impact on
public opinion."[30]

Both the Radicals and the Progressives were more aggressive
than the Liberals, and both were more successful. Surprisingly,
since the Radicals are often thought of as the first party to organize
on a mass basis in Serbia, it was the Progressives who got off
the mark first. Presumably after discussing the project over the
summer, on September 15, 1881, leaders of the Progressive Club
met at The King, the traditional café of the Young Conservatives,
and decided not only to register their party with the government,
but also to create a joint-stock company, the Progressive Printing
Society. A few days later 50 Belgrade Progressives gathered and
approved the bylaws of both the party and the printing company.[31]
The former was to have branches in as many towns and places as

possible, while the latter was to be capitalized at 60,000 dinars through the sale to party loyalists of 1,200 shares at 50 dinars each, of which only 25 dinars had to be paid in a first installment and the rest "as needed." On September 30 the bylaws of the 2 proposed organizations were submitted to the government, and by October 8 some 110 persons had bought 540 shares of the Progressive Printing Society, creating an initial capital of 13,500 dinars.[32] This amount already exceeded the highest figure for cumulative receipts of the Society for the Support of Serbian Literature of which there is a record, 12,880 dinars.[33] When on October 12 the minister of finance approved the rules of the printing enterprise and the minister of the interior approved the party statutes, the Progressives became the first grouping in Serbia to be legally recognized as a political party.

The Progressives had better success in local organization than the Liberals, and not entirely because they were the party in power. In most of the main towns Progressive representatives, which often meant minor government officials, invited those they considered illustrious citizens to join the "great circle of people who are working for the progress of the country."[34] By the end of the year *Videlo* announced the formation of at least seventeen such local Progressive clubs, while a document in the papers of Milutin Garašanin entitled "Temporary Committees of the Progressive Party, 1881," lists ninety-eight persons in twenty-eight places, with a penciled-in addition of twenty-eight more persons in twenty-one places.[35] In contrast to the Liberal Party, which attracted a high proportion of government or former government employees, the largest single group on Garašanin's list were merchants (*trgovci*). Forty-five of the ninety-eight persons listed fall into this category, whereas only fifteen were government employees. The list included ten priests, four lawyers, only one teacher, and no peasants. According to Avram Petrović, in general the party attracted the new bureaucrats and merchants (*liferanti*), and a few priests, teachers, and peasants.[36]

The party also selected a new leadership, but a peculiarly unimpressive one. Apparently it was felt that government ministers should not at the same time be among the officers of the party, because at their first meeting on October 13, 1881, the Belgrade Progressives elected a curious central committee. For president the meeting elected the old bugbear of Serbian politics, Aćim Čumić. Ljubomir Kaljević and Milan Kujundžić, both left-Liberals in the 1870s, were elected vice presidents, and Mita Rakić, reformed socialist, was elected one of the secretaries. This slate caused such a flurry of irritation from both Garašanin and Piroćanac that eventually Čumić declined the presidency, which then went to Mihailo Pavlović, an otherwise undistinguished figure.[37] Questionable formal leadership of the party did not seem to present a great problem to the Progressives, however, since they controlled the government, the traditional "party" of Serbian politics.[38]

And, finally, the Radicals organized. The Radicals had several advantages over both the Liberals and the Progressives. For one, they were not in power and never had been. Perceived as a disadvantage by most Serbian politicians, the sense of being outsiders, in fact, not only inspired the Radicals almost to the point of religious fervor, but forced them to organize a party that could stand alone, without the government crutch. The Radicals were also younger than their competitors, ten years younger on average than the Progressives, and twenty years younger than the Liberals. They pursued their organization with a vigor the other two parties could not match. And the Radical style of leadership was vastly superior for the newly open political conditions of the 1880s. Ristić was too coolly removed to take advantage of them; Novaković and Piroćanac had peculiar gifts for antagonizing people; Mijatović flitted from one project to another; and Garašanin was lazy. But the Radicals had Pašić, a quiet genius of political infighting, and Todorović, who wielded Serbia's most daring pen.

In a way Nikola Pašić began the Radical campaign when, at the conclusion of the skupština meeting in June 1881, he returned to the town he represented, Zaječar, and reported to his constituents. As obvious a step as this may seem to bring political events home to the provincial Serb, Pašić's report was an innovation. In a forty-minute speech he laid out how the Radicals had come into being, why they had gone into opposition, and what they hoped to do at the next skupština.[39] Other Radicals did the same, including

Ranko Tajsić and Raša Milošević.[40] During the summer plans were made for organizing in the fall. Pera Todorović, in Austria to take the baths for his painful rheumatism and liver ailments, composed a draft of the party statutes.[41]

The controversy with *Radnik* that summer preoccupied the Radicals. Cenić's accusations produced a vigorous debate at *Samouprava*, with Todorović wanting to take the Radicals in a more socialist direction and Pašić holding out for a more practical approach.[42] Their compromise was not to change the direction of *Samouprava*, but to let Todorović resuscitate *Rad* as a continuation of his earlier journals *Rad* (1874–75), and *Straža* (1878–79). The new journal would complement *Samouprava*'s practical political writings with some more obviously socialist articles. Todorović could not only indulge his leftist inclinations, but he might also be able to win back to Radicalism some of the significant number of Belgrade students attracted by Cenić's socialism.[43] This latter aim was clear from the composition of the editorial board, which consisted mostly of Belgrade academics, who, the leadership hoped, would have an impact on the young intelligentsia.[44] The new journal proved useful to Pašić also, permitting him an outlet for views to the left of those he felt able to take in *Samouprava*. For example, in discussing the case of Metropolitan Mihajlo, Pašić, while criticizing the government, commented that he was not defending the church. "To us, who are led exclusively by the principle of national sovereignty, this example is welcome . . . [because] it shows that the national will is larger and stronger than any old, outdated laws that were tailored [*krojeni*] for completely other circumstances and for other times." Just as the state had taken the education of children away from the priests, Pašić continued, so the state should not force adults to follow a faith against their consciences, although whoever sought to separate church from state must also teach his fellow citizens to respect one another.[45] There is little doubt that this statement, which is as close to anticlericalism as the Radicals ever got, was produced to combat Cenić's accusations that the Radicals were insufficiently radical, particularly on the issue of the separation of church and state.

But the indefatigable Todorović was not satisfied, as the Liberals were, with simply starting a new journal. He wanted to bring the new politics directly to the people. In September he set out on a tour of Serbia to nurture the seeds of local party organizations that had been planted by Adam Bogosavljević and others years earlier and had been revived by Pašić's Adam committees in 1880. For six weeks he visited one town or village a day, and when he returned to Belgrade he had to remain in bed for two weeks to recover.[46] As for the Adam committees themselves, whereas they unquestionably served their purpose as a forerunner of the party organization, they suffered from a lack of sustained purpose that overt political activity might have given them. Pašić gave his final report on the activities of the committees late in October 1881. The central committee by then had collected something over 1,946 dinars from more than 250 contributors and had spent a little more than 714 dinars, 600 of which went for Bogosavljević's autopsy. Many who later became Progressives had contributed to the fund. Even the original treasurer, Sava Obradović, had gone over to the Progressives and was demanding his contribution of 120 dinars back. They had done their best, Pašić complained with a curiously flat and tired tone, "but it seems to me that many, even too many, did not do what they could have and what it was their duty to do."[47]

Dispirited though Pašić appears to have been in the fall of 1881 (it was about the time of the report on the Adam Fund that he wrote Tajsić saying he felt like retreating to an isolated Albanian village), he was not one to miss political opportunities or to ignore political necessities. The other parties were organizing, so the Radicals had to organize also. In October Pašić invited those that Todorović had contacted, as well as other known Radicals from throughout Serbia, to Belgrade for a meeting to discuss and adopt a party statute.[48]

A day before the meeting, which was to be held on November 20 and was not publicly announced, *Samouprava* gave notice not only that the Radicals too were organizing, but that their challenge was going to extend far beyond the cafés of Belgrade. Their notice confirmed their superior insight into a new realm too, the realm of pathos as ideology. The article in *Samouprava* continued along the following lines. First there were the Liberals. And what was their program? "Ristić, Ristić, and again Ristić." Then there were the remnants of Marinović and company, plus the lower bureaucrats who make up the Progressives. What have they produced? Bontoux and Austria. And then there were the Radicals. "What does our party want? What is on our banner? Ten years of its life, work, and struggle answer that question."[49]

> We have neither leaders nor chiefs. . . . Our command is our fraternal compact and agreement. And our army? All those who suffer and endure. . . . Our inexhaustible reserve is the entire impoverished Serbian nation, all those who wear the peasant jacket and sandals, all those poor on whom the rich impose the danak and onto whom the rich transfer the burdens of the state from themselves, all those thirsting for justice and enlightenment, all the humiliated and fleeced. Before the eyes of this isolated mass still hangs the black veil of night and ignorance, but we will tear it off, and they will be with us.[50]

It is not known how many attended this first meeting of what became the Radical Party's central committee, but one week later *Samouprava* published the statutes the meeting had adopted, and on December 13 the government granted the party its necessary approval.[51] The statutes provided for the formation of local party units, membership in which would confer membership in the party as a whole, but the central committee (*glavni odbor*) had the authority to set party policy and carry it out.[52] Candidates for the skupština, for example, could be chosen by local committees, but the central committee had to approve them. Members were to pay six dinars a year in two equal instalments, the receipt for which became a party membership card. The local committee could retain one-third of these dues and one-half of any other monies raised, but the remainder went to the central committee for general uses. These included not only publishing *Samouprava* and *Rad*—although these were supposed to be self-sustaining—but also maintaining reading rooms and libraries, publishing other materials, holding public meetings, lectures, and cultural evenings, and assisting the organization of producers' cooperatives. The central committee, and local executive committees as well, was supposed to meet at least once a month and each year report to a general meeting of the whole party.

Now that the Radicals were registered as a legal party organization, scores of enthusiastic volunteers set to work putting together local committees throughout Serbia and especially in the countryside. At first the peasants were skeptical. Was this three dinars every six months not some sort of tax laid on by the Belgrade gentlemen to bleed the peasants in a new way? What about the future, when opinions changed? Would not membership in the party open them to retribution? And what about the Radicals' opposition viewpoint? Everyone knew governments did not tolerate opposition. But the Radicals persevered. They showed the peasants copies of the statutes with the stamp of the minister of the interior. Many peasants got the impression that the Radicals had "extracted" from the government the right to sign up peasants like shopowners had "extracted" the right to open a country store, or tavernkeepers to sell alcohol.[53] The membership card, in the form of a receipt, also made a big impression.[54] To the illiterate peasant, possession of such an elegant proof of partnership with the "gospodi" was a powerful incentive, even if it was expensive. "The masses want the [membership] card and it has a great influence on them," reported an organizer in Boljevac early in 1883. "However," he continued, "the people don't have any money. Our members are the real *reaya* [cattle], poor people who endure the greatest hardship."[55] No one had asked the peasants to participate in such a widespread movement in a formal way before, and once a few signed up and found they were not put in prison, more and more did so, even when they had no money to pay, until soon a great wave of enthusiasm began to spread across Serbia for the Radical Party. Early in 1882 the pages of *Samouprava* were full of the notices of local executive committees being formed, of meetings, of speeches, of receptions, of success. By the time of the party's first annual meeting in the summer of 1882, at least fifty local executive committees were functioning, many of them in the main towns but more than half of them in very small towns and even villages.[56] For the first time an independent political group was rallying Serbia's only real social class—the peasantry.

Organizational success in the countryside was not matched in urban Belgrade. Legalization of the Radical Party meant, as it did elsewhere, the formation of a local Belgrade party committee, which took place on December 16.[57] The immediate task the committee faced was the election of a new representative to the skupština from Belgrade. By-elections were held in several places in Serbia on December 25, 1881 [not Christmas in Serbia due to the differences in the Orthodox calendar], for positions vacated by the protest resignations that had followed approval of the railroad and trade conventions at the previous skupština. The coming skupština, in which these new members would take their seats along with the remaining representatives elected in 1880, was scheduled to convene on January 19, 1882.[58] The new Radical committee for Belgrade selected Tasa Banković, a Belgrade merchant and member of the central committee, to run in the capital city. It was a curious choice, since Banković had at one time written for *Istok* and Belgrade contained many noted Radicals, but after his selection Banković held daily meetings trying to bring out the vote, making such favorite populist suggestions as cutting officers' pay supplements, closing all diplomatic offices abroad, eliminating four of the five bishophrics, and abolishing the State Council.[59] Such arguments were suited for rural areas, not for the city, and Banković's candidacy was doomed from the start. The decision of Mita Cenić to run for the skupština did not help. Three days before the election, when Pera Todorović was speaking to a meeting of two hundred citizens, one of Cenić's supporters spoke out on behalf of the Radicals' rival, and a day later heckling from Cenić's young student supporters broke up a Radical meeting. When the police went around the cafés taking the names of those who had indicated they were for Banković, it confirmed in the Radicals' minds the link between Cenić and the Progressives.[60] In the election the Progressive candidate won the Belgrade seat handily. Both Cenić and the Liberal candidate outpolled Banković, who came in last.[61]

By the time the skupština convened on January 22, 1882, all three political groupings had organized themselves into operating political parties. Now that the political dividing lines were drawn with unprecedented clarity, the stage was set for a dramatic confrontation, especially between the two strongest parties, the Progressives, who held about ninety seats, and the Radicals, who held about forty seats (the Liberals held fewer than ten). The Progressives, convinced that the Radicals were incapable of running the government, and Prince Milan, who feared that the Radicals were alienating the affections of the peasantry from him, agreed that the government should exclude the Radicals from any meaningful participation in skupština life. Taking advantage of heavy snows that prevented the timely arrival of opposition delegates from the hinterlands, the government convinced the Progressive Club of delegates to vote only for approved candidates to the committee that was to write the address to the throne, and subsequently to exclude all Radicals from the three standing committees.[62] While neither unprecedented nor illegal, this narrow partisan policy surpassed the normal, if modest, practice of accommodation that had developed over Serbia's ten years of parliamentary experience. The previous year, for example, the Radicals dominated the Finance Committee, and this had not hindered the government in passing its budget. Other signs showed that a reasonable working agreement had existed among the parties up to this point. Early in December 1881, when Milan pointed out that Serbia was "almost without roads," the government appointed a commission to recommend the best way to improve Serbia's roads and it had included as members the Radical Pašić and the Liberal Mišković.[63] Later in the same month sixty members of all parties met at the Progressive Club to establish a Serbian gymnastic society.[64] But once the skupština started, the Progressives became impressed with their estimate that the Radicals had only 30 to 40 votes in the skupština (out of a total of about 150). Lacking leadership with the tact or foresight to grasp the potentially serious consequences of their act and unable to resist using the power their majority position gave them, they decided to embark on a policy of confrontation. In less than two years this policy brought on armed rebellion.

Once again, therefore, as in the early 1870s, the writing of the address to the throne provoked a tumultuous debate. When, on January 27, the proposed address was read before the skupština Pašić rose and declared that in as much as the Radicals represented half the country and had had no say in preparing the address they would present their own. Their draft was thoroughly respectful toward Milan but highly critical of the government. After three days of acrimonious debate, the government draft passed 99 to 50.[65] When the president of the skupština left a copy of the address on the front desk of the skupština for all the members of the skupština to sign, as was the custom, the Radicals did not sign.[66] Furthermore, they announced they would not take part in the traditional visit to Milan to present the address, and in fact they did not do so. Since Milan would not receive them separately to hear their version of the address, they printed it in *Samouprava*. Ranko Tajsić lectured the skupština that the fifty members of the opposition were not school children "but full grown adults who do not need any lessons . . . from whatever source."[67] This kind of intransigence could only further alienate Milan, who complained publicly that the Radicals were taking the country toward ruin and that he had no intention of permitting "rubbish from the gutter" to tell him what to do.[68] Milan had never been drawn toward the Radicals, whose socialist background, underground republicanism, and Karadjordjevist leanings he rightly feared. Their unwillingness to follow the polite formality of visiting court with the 1882 address to the throne turned him violently against them. His vigorous participation in the Progressive policy of confrontation was critical to its unfortunate outcome.

This heated argument was interrupted by shocking news from Paris. As *Samouprava* put it in a bulletin that appeared on January 18, 1882, the day before the skupština opened: "Crash in Paris. Bontoux's bank [i.e., General Union] falls from 3,400 to 1,100 dinars; Länderbank from 1,300 to 500 dinars."[69] By January 30 it was revealed that General Union was bankrupt.[70] Serbia's railroad building program seemed to have collapsed under a mountain of debt. In the second half of 1881 France had experienced a speculative boom. When a correction expected in the fall did not materialize, shares skyrocketed. But at the end of the year a drop in prices on the Lyons bourse caught some speculators short, and when they tried to unload a large number of shares in Paris, the market burst. Ambassador Jovan Marinović sent reports from Paris beginning on January 10 that General Union did not seem in danger, but in fact when the bust came General Union lost half of its 160 million-franc capital in only four hours of feverish activity. On January 18 the Länderbank, the secret partner whose role was unknown to the Serbian government but suspected by the Radicals, refused to back General Union further, and Bontoux's enterprise failed. The Progressives were concerned but they did not panic because, whereas the Serbian obligations had been printed and deposited with General Union, they were good only when countersigned, and this was to be done in stages as the railroad was actually being constructed. Unfortunately, however, without the knowledge of his colleagues, although with Milan's approval, Minister of Finance Mijatović had signed 40,000 bonds in July and another 40,000 in October, and also had traded 110,000 negotiable lottery bonds for 20,000 unsigned railroad bonds.[71] Thus Serbia was already obligated for 35,600,000 dinars. When the definitive news of General Union's fall arrived in Belgrade on January 30, Mijatović took off for Paris so precipitously that he only had time to leave Pirócanac a note saying that he would pay with his head if Serbia suffered a loss. In actuality he was contemplating fleeing to America. Receiving sympathy and vague promises of support en route to Vienna, Mijatović spent ten days in Paris confronting the worst possible news. Since General Union was linked with Orleanist opposition to the republic, the French government was not displeased at its demise, and the court-appointed administrator informed Mijatović that Serbia would have to wait its turn like every other creditor, which would take from a year to a year and a half. As the crisis wore on into February, Milan informed the Austrians that either they would have to find a way to save Serbia or the government would resign, Ristić would be restored to power, and Milan would abdicate. Two days later Garašanin and Pirócanac decided to resign. Apparently this was enough to catalyze the Austrians, since suddenly in Paris a firm called Comptoir National d'Escompte approached Mijatović with a proposal that cut Serbia's losses to about 12 million dinars and gave hope that even that loss could be made up from the assets of the bankrupt General Union. In addition, the building of the railroad could continue. Relieved, not to say overjoyed, Mijatović agreed.

The railroad agreement had been completed in May 1881, and already by June three hundred men had begun work on the short spur from Belgrade to Topčider. Early in July Milan had broken ground for the Belgrade to Niš main line.[72] Construction brought a number of foreign workers into Serbia, many of them Catholic, and they were not well received. In August a crowd of hostile Serbs jeered and threw rocks outside the performance of a French singing society, and in September *Samouprava* complained that Germans were taking all the good railroad jobs.[73] Despite Serbia's huge debt, money for the project even before the crash seemed scarce and Radical engineers like Pašić criticized the construction as "slow and poor."[74] The peasants must have been mystified by the railroad as well. *Samouprava* described an incident in which a construction crew had cut a ditch for the railroad through the road peasants normally took to deliver their crops from Železnik to Belgrade without announcing it or providing another way around, provoking enormous jams of carts and some serious cursing.[75]

To compound the government's problems caused by these dissatisfactions, in 1881 a revolt broke out against the Austrians in the Bay of Kotor, on the Adriatic Coast, and early in 1882 it spread into Hercegovina.[76] Many Serbs, especially Liberals, frustrated by the Austrian occupation of Bosnia only three years earlier, felt a great deal of sympathy toward the rebels. *Srpska nezavisnost* constantly reminded its readers of Serbia's potential destiny in Bosnia. But since Prince Milan had agreed to prevent any agitation in Serbia over Bosnia, while the Austrians subdued the revolt by force during the late winter and spring, the government forbade all forms of support for it. This included prohibiting contributions for those in need in Bosnia, even though Catholic nuns from Austria were permitted to raise funds in Belgrade for the same purpose.[77] Once again Milan and the Progressives could be portrayed as agents of Austria rather than defenders of Serbia's national interests.

Frustration over the Progressives' pro-Austrian policy and the social problems caused by railroad construction, the crash of General Union, the election of only Progressives to the skupština committees, and the acrimonious debate over the address to the throne all combined to reinforce Radical self-righteousness. Nonetheless, before attacking the government over the railroad debacle Nikola Pašić and Svetozar Nikolajević, the latter a member of the skupština and the Radical central committee, approached the Progressives to see if a compromise could be worked out. Milićević reports that Piroćanac, not Serbia's most gifted politician, simply laughed.[78] The Progressives interpreted the Radicals' unwillingness to participate in the presentation of the address to the throne as almost a revolutionary act. So instead of working out an agreement with their opponents, they sent the adopted address and the prince's criticisms of the Radicals, which hinted that the opposition really wanted revolt, to every local official with instructions to inform the public of the Radicals' pernicious policies and the prince's irritation.[79] At the same time they made it difficult for the Radicals to spread their version of the situation by not letting them use the telegraph service to send details of the General Union collapse to their committees in the interior.

In this situation, the Bontoux affair gave the Radicals a perfect issue, a "bugle call to open fire on all sides and move to the attack," as Pera Todorović put it.[80] On February 7, 1882, three days after their unsuccessful overture to the Progressives, the Radicals presented a formal interpellation in the skupština asking the government for an explanation. "The opposition is undoubtedly in an excited state of mind," reported the British consul, "and shows no symptom of having been daunted by the Message of the Prince."[81] The Progressives were reduced to confusion and hesitation, and they did not answer the interpellation. Indeed, they could not, since Mijatović was having trouble salvaging the situation in Paris. Still, they managed to conduct a relatively normal parliamentary life for almost six weeks after the arrival of the initial news and the Radical's first interpellation about it. The government presented a bill to create elementary schools for agricultural training and a bill to reorganize opštinas. Meanwhile, Piroćanac scrambled to find a saving ploy.

One of the provisions of Milan's secret agreement of the previous year with Austria was that the Austrian government would support the declaration of Serbia as a kingdom when the Serbs decided to take that step. The elevation of Carol of Romania to kingship early in 1881 made it seem imperative to Milan to achieve the higher rank as soon as possible, and both Garašanin and Piroća-nac had favored the move before Milan signed the secret agreement.[82] Even Ristić was promoting the possibility.[83] By the opening of the skupština the preliminary diplomatic work had been completed and no foreign opposition existed.[84] The Bontoux crisis and the rumors that the Radicals were preparing to boycott the skupština convinced the Progressives that they needed a success of sufficient magnitude to take the initiative away from the opposition. Milan agreed that the time was right, but, as usual, saw another benefit as well. He demanded and got a raise in his civil list from 700,000 dinars a year to 1,200,000 dinars, a sum he needed to recoup from the heavy losses he had suffered speculating in General Union stock. Accordingly, just after the initial news arrived in Belgrade that Mijatović had found Comptoir National d'Escompte, on March 6, 1881, the president of the skupština proposed "to the astonished assembly" to make Milan king. "The progressists rose to the feet with the cry 'We will,' " British Consul Locock reported. "The opposition, taken by surprise and feeling the project so often discussed was now an accomplished fact, hesitatingly followed their example."[85]

Declaration of the kingdom passed international muster quickly, and was greeted with cannonades, flags, dancing, and even a dinner at court during which the Radicals toasted the king.[86] All the superficial joyful proprieties were observed. Milan even permitted the town of Karanovac to change its name to Kraljevo (from the Serbian word for king, *kralj*).[87] If the Progressives expected these distractions would save their situation, they were wrong. The Radicals continued to meet "uninterruptedly night by night at the Radical Club" until they finally decided, as they put it, that their "cup of patience had overflowed."[88] After many unsuccessful attempts to get an answer from the government on the extent of Serbia's losses or on the new agreement with Comptoire National d'Escompte, on March 15 Pašić declared that if the government did not respond in twenty-four hours the Radicals would resign their seats, making continuation of the work of the skupština impossible. The following day Piroćanac answered, but by letter, not in person, that that was not the way to elicit a response, and the government would answer when it was ready, not before. Pašić pointed out that the skupština bylaws stated that after a committee concludes a question is in order, which it had long ago, the government must either respond or say when it will respond.[89] Nevertheless, the government refused. When the skupština opened the following day, with a large crowd in attendance in the galleries, the Radical seats were empty except for that of Ranko Tajsić.[90] The president refused to let Tajsić read the text of the resignations into the record, but did permit him to read the names of those who had resigned, which Tajsić did. Fifty-one legislators were on the list.[91] Complaining that the conduct of the Radicals was unworthy and illegal, the Progressives, nevertheless, were forced to adjourn the skupština until elections could reconstitute a body that could meet the quorum requirement.

Elections to fill the seats of the delegates who had resigned were set for May 27, almost two months off. The Progressives hoped that the delay would give time for the tension that had marked the last few weeks of the skupština to abate and to enable the newly crowned king to make a celebratory tour of the country. The Radicals, on the other hand, were beginning to reap the benefits of their organizational efforts and were confident that a delay would only help them, especially given the widespread dissatisfaction over the crushing of the Bosnian revolt and the Bontoux disaster.

The Radicals' first step was to take home reports of what had happened. In some places crowds as large as four hundred persons showed up to hear the Radical legislators explain why they had resigned, whereas in other localities the načelnik prevented the Radicals from gathering.[92] The citizens of Zaječar greeted Pašić with fireworks and a party at which La Marseillaise was sung. A bit daringly Samouprava suggested that the descendants of Hajduk-Veljko, a famous rebel from the times of the First Serbian Uprising, knew how to honor a friend.[93] The jumpy Milan, who had already been warned by the president of the skupština, Aleksa Popović, that the Radicals were determined on revolution, could not have failed to catch the ominous allusion.

The Progressives' response to these Radical initiatives was typical of Serbian governmental reactions to opposition since Ilija Garašanin, to punish all those it could find in the government's service who might not be loyal. *Srpska nezavisnost* reported that between October 1880 and December 1881 the Progressives relocated, pensioned off, or fired 849 persons, most of them teachers who were Radicals.[94] In 1882 they intensified this campaign. About half of the regional načelniks were replaced, as well as many opština kmets.[95] In February Stojan Novaković directed all schools to "carefully watch student discipline and the execution of each teacher's duties" so that the teachers will not be "running around the villages undertaking political agitation."[96] By April many teachers were being transferred, even though it was only two months before the end of the school term, which meant that the teacher could neither take up his new duties effectively nor examine the students in the school from which he had departed, even when an opština might offer to pay the teacher with its own money.[97] Arrests were made too, many of them duly reported in *Samouprava*.

Whereas the government's efforts to intimidate and harass the Radicals were not new in Serbian politics, the fact that the government now faced an organized party to oppose these tactics was. Concerned about the arrests and transfers, on March 29 the central committee of the Radical Party called on its local committees to forward the names of any persons transferred or arrested so that their names and circumstances could be printed in *Samouprava*, and to start collecting contributions to help them. Any amount is useful, the central committee said: "A cake is made grain by grain, and a palace stone by stone."[98]

As the second prong of the government's campaign, King Milan undertook late in April a monthlong ceremonial tour of Serbia, but with mixed success. In Čačak he was extremely irritated to find Ranko Tajsić among the citizens elected by the local communities to greet him, and Milan refused to accept Tajsić's greetings. After visiting Čačak he set out for Užice, where he was able to receive an Austrian general from Bosnia in the name of Emperor Franz Joseph. En route he met with a ragged group of peasants, encouraged by the Radicals to turn out in poor clothing to give an impression of how badly they were doing under the Progressives.

When the Radical priest Novak Milošević began giving a flowery speech of welcome, Milan interrupted him with great irritation and turned to the gathered public:

> If you come to meet me as the heads of your households, then you should listen to your own head of household, and the house will prosper. And now listen to my word as the head of your household: the source of the fact that you pay and get no use from it, that you have no roads and no schools, is that you listen to priests and teachers and that you send me in the skupština representatives who do not know how to and do not want to tell me your will, that you send me representatives who abandon the skupština like women, like cowards. Don't choose such representatives for me, but elect those people who know how to tell me your needs and desires. . . . Priests and teachers will return you only bad things. My grandfather did not liberate this land with priests and teachers, but with the people and the army, and I did not achieve independence with priests and teachers nor anyone else, but with the national peasant and my officers. Listen to me, when I come to you.[99]

Unlike Miloš Obrenović and Pera Todorović, Milan did not speak the peasants' language, either literally or figuratively. He blustered at them. No amount of elegant uniforms, festive arches, and religious panoply could overcome this fault. When his listeners to this dressing-down shouted "We want Father Novak," the rest of the assembled group took up the shout.[100] Greatly angered, Milan canceled his visit to Užice, which was just as well, since further embarrassments cooked up by the Radicals awaited him there.[101] Milan's utter inability to create a folk mythology around his person made it a good deal easier for the Radicals to attract peasants with their own version of the national myth than it might have been if Milan had been a more charismatic person.

Other problems besides the king's difficulty with his subjects intensified an already tense situation in the weeks before the election. In Belgrade students armed with three hundred whistles and noisemakers disrupted a play critical of Radicalism, shouting "Down with Garašanin." The gendarmes, called by Garašanin him-

self, entered the National Theater and opened fire with their revolvers, injuring several people, bringing on a riot that took the
mounted police two hours to quiet and resulted in twenty people
in jail.[102] Elsewhere, a small caravan of arms for the Bosnian rebels
escorted by sixty Montenegrins with valid Russian passports was
intercepted while heading from Bulgaria to Bosnia. The Progressives, claiming not only that they were neutral in the Hercegovinian
conflict but that the Russians were trying to influence the forthcoming election through bribery, confiscated the arms, once again
calling their pro-Austrian policy forcibly to the attention of the
electorate.[103]

When the day of the long-awaited by-election to fill the vacated
positions finally arrived, Garašanin abandoned all the pretenses of
fairness that had characterized his initial instructions upon taking
office. In Ranko Tajsić's district, for example, the authorities went
around in the days before the election telling the villagers that "the
king has ordered you not to vote for Tajsić. If he is selected the
Austrian army will immediately occupy our country and will take
your maize for three groš an oka for the insult."[104] If the voters of
an opština, nonetheless, selected an elector favorable to Tajsić, the
authorities simply repeated the election after jailing the person
originally selected. Local officials felt confident that these methods
had assured that Tajsić would get no more than between 28 and
32 votes from the 160 electors. When the public voting for Tajsić's
position began in the square in Užice, however, a large crowd of
ordinary peasants, mobilized by the Radicals, entered the square
and stood around the electors. Under this pressure from their
peers, who were overwhelmingly for Ranko, the vote turned out
115 to 45 in his favor. Scenes similar to this were repeated around
Serbia, and as a result the Radicals won forty-five of the fifty seats
contested in this election, with the Liberals winning two others.
The Progressives won only three seats. Since twelve more delegates
needed to participate in the skupština to achieve a quorum, the
government still found itself unable to convene the skupština without help from the Radicals.[105]

For the Progressives, this result was "a heavy blow" and "a
painful surprise."[106] Without independent sources of information

in the countryside, they depended on the government's tried and true ears, the state bureaucracy, which often provided information calculated to fit the prejudices of its leaders. For example, only five days before the election Pirocanac, after returning from a visit to Pašić's home town with the king's entourage, told a friend that "there is not a sound about the Radicals among the people. Only two questions interest them: in old Serbia peasant shops and in the new territories distribution of land formerly held by the Ottomans [agrarni odnosi]."[107] The Progressives did not think they were pursuing an antinational policy, as the Radicals and Liberals charged; quite the contrary, they believed that conditions for healthy democratic debate had never been greater in Serbia. "From many sides our friends complain how the Radicals are upsetting them," Milan Milićević wrote in his diary. "They do not understand that this is a consequence of freedom and blame us that we do not use the state administration to stop them. No! That we will not do! When there is freedom, let it be freedom with all its good and bad points!"[108] And what did Milićević say when one of those bad points turned out the next day to be a complete Radical victory? Well, he said, either the Radicals had the confidence of the people, or some sinister forces were at work, such as Russian bribery. And sure enough, within a few days chastened local bureaucrats began to report extensive bribery as the real cause of the Radical victory.[109] But not even the Austrian consul believed these allegations.[110] The facts were all too clear: the Radicals were finding enormous support throughout Serbia.

The new skupština was set to open June 2, 1882, but it was not certain whether the opposition representatives would attend so that a quorum could be reached. When none of them appeared on the appointed day Pirocanac recommended that his government resign.[111] Garašanin, in return, proposed simply calling a Grand National Assembly to rewrite the constitution, and getting the whole thing over with. Milan Kujundžić was resolutely opposed to resignation because he knew it would bring Ristić back to power and, since he was a deserter from the Liberal camp, he feared he would have to go into exile.

The Radicals too were debating their moves. On the day the

skupština was due to open the party central committee asked all its local committees to send in their opinions as to whether the Radicals should stick to the policy of boycott or whether they should compromise.[112] Two days later the Radical priest Milan Djurić appeared at the meeting of the Progressive Club held at The King café and suggested a joint ministry; then on the next day Pašić, Djurić, and two others met with King Milan to see if he would permit them to share power.[113] Finally, on June 7 a delegation of five Progressives headed by Aleksa Popović, president of the skupština, met with a delegation of five Radicals headed by Pašić for a final try at compromise. At this three-hour meeting it was the Radicals' turn to be stubborn and to choose a policy of confrontation. For in the negotiations of the previous few days the Progressives had expressed a willingness to permit oppositionists to join skupština committees, perhaps even to choose a Radical as vice president of the skupština, or to offer the Radicals one or two seats in the government.[114] The Radicals refused these offers. One reason almost certainly was the firmly negative reactions to compromise that were coming in from the local committees, which recommended that the Radical delegates not attend the skupština.[115] Or perhaps Pašić simply had his eye on the main goal, achieving power himself, because the Radical delegation insisted that the only way to achieve a stable situation was to call a new general election and that all members of the skupština should resign to bring that about. The Progressive Club not only rejected this "solution," but became so irritated at the Radicals' insistence on calling a general election that it forbade Radicals from attending its meetings, something the Radicals had been doing freely since the club's formation.[116] With negotiations at a complete impasse, the events of a few weeks earlier repeated themselves. Thirty-nine opposition members of the skupština once again resigned. This discouraging outcome led Piročanac to submit his government's resignation, but Milan refused to let the Progressives step down. Finally, at a "tumultuous" meeting at which the Progressive Club condemned Piročanac's resignation, the Progressives decided to call yet another election to fill the newly vacated spots. Milan initially wanted to wait three months, but in order to get things moving he agreed to set the election for five days later, June 12.

Surprised at the call for hurried new elections, the opposition still swept the field, winning all the contested seats.[117] Again Piroća-nac tried to resign, but the man who had become, in effect, the leader of the government party over the party few months, King Milan, strongly supported by the Austrian consul, absolutely refused to hear of it.[118] He informed the ministers that he would abdicate before yielding to the demands of the opposition.[119] By his firmness Milan prevented the return of Ristić, but at the same time he exacerbated the situation, for the electorate had clearly spoken against the government. To achieve a quorum in the skupš-tina, Piroćanac declared ex post facto that all those who had resigned their seats a second time had been ineligible for the election and directed the local načelniks to certify those who came in second to them as the true representatives. In nine districts the opposition-ist had been elected unanimously, but in the other twenty-eight districts there were losing candidates, some of whom had received as few as two votes. For this reason, the Radicals quickly dubbed all the government's "successful" candidates from the second election "two-voters," a derogatory nickname that stuck. Local electoral boards, following the electoral rules, gave credentials to the victori-ous oppositionists, but the local načelniks followed orders and certified the "two-voters" as the official representatives. Both sets of delegates headed for Belgrade.[120]

Even at this late date, the Progressives sought out the Radicals for one more try at a solution. The day before the second election Ranko Tajsić met until nine in the evening with Milutin Garašanin, and three days after the election a delegation headed by Pašić made an offer of conciliation to Aleksa Popović.[121] On the very day the skupština finally resumed, Kosta Taušanović reported that Piroća-nac had suggested that, at the very least, the two parties agree to reduce the harshness of their rhetoric.[122] But it was too late for compromises. Despite the ridicule that the two-voters received as they passed through the countryside en route to Belgrade, the government went ahead with its plan, expelling the opposition representatives from Belgrade. On June 20 the skupština reopened with its newly created quorum.

Having held power by the slimmest of margins, now in control of a complaisant skupština, and in the full fury that weakness sometimes calls forth, the Progressives pushed through restrictive new regulations they hoped would make it impossible for oppositionists to disrupt skupštinas in the same way again. A fine of 1,000 dinars, an absurdly large amount, was established for any elected representative who refused to attend the skupština or who resigned in an effort to hinder its work.[123] Next, to curb the ability of the opposition press to heap scorn on the government in the manner of Pera Todorović, they changed the press law specifically to forbid the appearance of expressions of what they termed "nihilism" and "communism" in newspapers.[124] The Progressives explicitly instructed local officials that criticism of the government was permitted, but the new rule gave the authorities much wider latitude for harassing the opposition press than had the press law of a year earlier, a latitude they began using immediately. On July 6, the first blank space appeared in *Samouprava*, indicating the deletion of a column deemed offensive by the Belgrade authorities.[125] As an additional restriction, if in correcting an error brought to a paper's attention by the authorities the editors added anything that they could not prove was true, the fine was to be 500 dinars or 6 months in jail. Most important in the eyes of contemporaries, the entire section on defaming the state, libeling individuals, and committing lèse-majesté was removed from the civil code and placed under the criminal code. In another measure, for the first time in Serbian experience, the skupština established a domestic police force "in order to guard the borders, jail hajduks, and in general to secure fuller security for property."[126] Until this point enforcement of the law or apprehension of wrongdoers was undertaken by kmets or načelniks, who gathered around them such force as particular occasions might call for, and border patrols were undertaken by the tiny standing army, perhaps supplemented by temporary mobilization of a few members of the national militia.

Not only the Radicals found these measures excessive. A significant number of Progressives, including many of whom had switched over from the Radicals in 1881, voted against passage of the press law, and when Garašanin introduced some of the harsher clauses to the skupština without discussion Dimitrije Katić told him that "with these [clauses] we will bury our name, both as human beings and as a party."[127] Milan Milićević agreed, and did not even want to go to the skupština the day the law passed. "Those small, wretched souls who when they are alone and no one can hear them laugh and run down empires . . . shout and complain against the press as if it alone was the source of this excited state."[128] Naturally, Pera Todorović found ways to ridicule the government's steps, the best example of which was to dub the new internal security force *sejmeni* (sing: *sejmenin*), which was the name for the mounted armed men that had accompanied the janissaries early in the century and who had a reputation for committing atrocities against the Serbs. The term, which was derogatory not only because of its connection with the Ottomans but also because the sejmeni had been riffraff, took hold among the people and became one of the Radicals' most successful propaganda points.

It is highly likely that the Progressives believed that by excluding the Radicals from the skupština they had prevented their opponents from effective political action. After all, in the Serbian political system that had developed since 1869 exclusion from the skupština had meant exclusion from influence: the debates in the skupština provided the best opportunity to express political views, put forward policy proposals, and attack the government, all of which had provided the grist for the mills of the opposition newspapers. But the Progressives' assessment was wrong. The Radicals now found a new and effective forum for reaching out to ordinary Serbs, the annual party meeting. As soon as it became clear that the Radicals were not going to participate in the June skupština, Nikola Pašić, Kosta Taušanović, and Stojan Protić, the young editor of *Samouprava*, left Belgrade to visit local committees and make arrangements for convening Serbia's first national political convention.[129]

The first congress of the National Radical Party, held in Kragujevac, August 7–9, 1882, was an unprecedented event in peacetime Serbia. According to the committee on credentials, 574 members of the party attended, along with perhaps 100 visitors. At least 60 percent of the attendees were peasants.[130] Local party organizations from every part of the country sent

delegates, and their meeting, held at a spring outside of Kragujevac, was not just a formal political function, but a great
festive gathering that peasants throughout Serbia talked about.
Naturally, the government was very nervous about a gathering
of so many peasants for a political function not directed by the
state.[131] At first the local načelnik had refused permission for the
congress to meet and requested a decision from Minister of the
Interior Garašanin.[132] In due course Garašanin approved the
gathering, but he sent his personal representative to attend, and
the minister of war found this a convenient time to inspect the
Kragujevac munitions plant.[133] King Milan, no doubt recalling
Kragujevac as the home of Serbian socialism and of the Red
Banner Affair, postponed his departure for a European tour
until the congress was over. *Srpska nezavisnost* and *Borba,* hostile
Liberal and socialist papers, swallowed their pride and asked for
press credentials so that their reporters could cover the event.[134]

In one sense the government's fears proved to be unfounded.
There were no disorders. The congress proceeded with great
enthusiasm but almost formal precision. At the initial meeting
the delegates elected Nikola Pašić chairman and provided for
two vice presidents, four secretaries, and nine members of a
credentials committee. Later in the day, at the second session,
the congress elected ten members and six alternates to the party's
central committee, with Pašić once again at the head, and chose
Belgrade as the regular meeting site of the central committee.
But after these formalities, the real innovation of the conference
became manifest in the speech with which Nikola Pašić ended
the first day's session. Pašić provided a review of the history of
the party from the time of Svetozar Marković until the recent
resignation of the Radical delegates, a presentation that was not
too dissimilar from the report he gave to his constituents in
Zaječar a year earlier. But he began his talk with a striking appeal
that suggests that the real purpose of the conference was less to
tap the views of the delegates than it was to excite them, persuade
them that the Radicals were their true representatives, and, in a
larger sense, link radicalism in their minds with the nation itself.
Pašić began as follows:

In Europe there is not a people that deserves to be the unlimited sovereign in its state more than the Serbian people, because in Europe there is not a single state created by the ordinary people themselves.

Gunjac and opanak liberated this land from the powerful Turkish rule![135]

Gunjac and opanak sprinkled this land with its blood so that freedom, justice, and equality could sprout!

Gunjac and opanak traversed mountains and valleys, rivers and fields, hurrying tirelessly from one battle to another, subduing the Turkish agas and spahis that had swarmed over the land!

Gunjac and opanak worked tirelessly, whether in the hottest sun, or in the rain, snow, and dark, to fill the cribs with fodder, the barn with grain, the stables with stock, the larder with wine and brandy!

Gunjac and opanak left the mouths he was responsible to feed and in a hungry and barren year let the judges dispense justice to him, let the army teach him the military arts and to arm himself with better weapons, let the cultured people [prosveta] train the young in knowledge, respect, work, and patriotism, let the police defend his property and protect him from attack and insult!

Gunjac and opanak—that is the Serbian nation that created this state by blood, maintains it by sweat and work, protects it by life and property, and moves it forward by knowledge and experience!

Gunjac and opanak . . . is the Serbian nation that built and created this state, and by right and reason, through work and sacrifice, [it] ought to be the supreme ruler in its own land![136]

Pašić's litany of gunjac and opanak struck an unprecedented chord of response in the Serbian countryside. For years afterward the common terms "gunjac i opanak" were associated with the Radicals and with Pašić, who fortified his already strong reputation with the ordinary peasant. Forty-five years later at the time of his death the peasants of eastern Serbia still believed that "Baja knows what he is doing."[137] Pašić's speech was part and parcel of the Radical effort to replace the pallid and academic whig theory of Serbian history made popular among the educated by the Liberals of the 1860s with a juicier, earthier, and more emotional form of nationalism.

The greatest practitioner of this kind of rhetoric, of course, was Pera Todorović, and on the second day of the congress delegates heard him review the party's program.[138] Since the basic thrust of this program was to change the constitution and create a democratic and responsible government, it necessarily dealt in abstractions not always familiar to the ordinary Serb. Todorović translated these abstractions into earthy, everyday metaphors in a tone and with a vocabulary that made it sound as if he was a plain man speaking of things everyone knew, rather than a sophisticated journalist from the capital city.[139] For example, in opposing the Progressive proposal that a senate be added to the skupština, Todorović explained that an upper house was a "gentlemen's skupština" that arose in Western Europe where the "spahis" were of the same blood and religion as the people. In Serbia the people had "dispersed all the foreign bloodsuckers by sword and fire, returning their land to themselves from the spahis and taking all authority onto themselves." The Europeans had not been able to do this. The best they could do was to establish a skupština (lower house), and their own blood stayed in that skupština. "As you see, therefore, the gentleman's skupština [senate, upper house] is nothing other than an upper crust [velikaška] body by which the rulers want to keep the people in a mess [škripu] and to keep them from making the laws they want [shouts: 'Don't let them; is that what they want?']. Now that I have told you what a danger to national rights the gentleman's skupština represents, I would like to tell you who are the people who have grown most fond [prirasla za srce] of that gentleman's skupština [Shout: Hey—tell us who they are!]. They are our Progressives [Shout: Ah! Neće im vala upaliti!]."[140]

In describing the Radical plank that all adult males should have the right to vote (only those who paid the danak had that right at this time), Todorović said this:

This is an important thing, brothers. You know how we elect a kmet. They find the man who pays the full danak, the head tax—and then he can elect the kmet. I have heard from Gara-šanin's own mouth that he would be happy to make it that way for deputies too. And not only Garašanin thinks like that. Both here and elsewhere there are people who measure human rights by the purse. The larger your wallet, the greater your rights. Whoever has no property has no rights. But duties, you see, there are. When it comes time to go to the border, they do not say "you are an ordinary poor man, you don't enjoy any kind of rights in the opština, you don't dare show up at the voting place, therefore now sit at home—you don't have to go to war." No! Rich or poor: march! And the poor people in the first line, the rich ones behind, if they even show up [Shout: That's it, by God]. . . . Participation in state affairs cannot be measured by the depth of one's pocket. . . . The Radical Party doesn't want that. The Radical Party says: Just *because* I am poor I have a three times greater right and desire to participate in state affairs, exactly because I am poor and my spine is thin I feel more heavily every state burden and injustice, which I support by my naked and lean shoulders. And when they pinch me and hurt me [here Todorović slapped himself on the back of his head] I have the right to seek a remedy for my pain and misery.[141]

No other Serbs could match Pera Todorović in finding a voice appropriate to an occasion. His listeners, most of them attending their very first public political rally, did not see his speech as condescending, although ordinarily Todorović neither spoke nor wrote in this country style. Instead, they heard a Belgrade intellectual talking to them in their own language, telling them things they could understand and believe, convincing them that in the new political arena they were the real people, and that the Radicals were part of them.

Others spoke too, and if not in so impassioned or homey a manner, at least they provided the delegates with some food for thought. Jovan Djaja, for example, gave an exposition of the weaknesses of Serbian foreign policy when faced with the imperialism of the great powers.[142] The Progressives, he said, think of Serbia as weak and Austria as strong; but this was a formula for disaster. Look how England and France took over Egypt. "This is the modern way of conquest. Draw some nation into your sphere of influence, entangle it with debts, economically ruin it, and then defend your interests with guns." Instead Djaja concluded, Serbia had to defend its own interests in alliance with the other peoples of the Balkans, especially with Bulgaria and Montenegro. In another area, Raša Milošević criticized the government's taxation policies and severely condemned the sale of the salt monopoly to a Hungarian enterprise.[143] The way to raise money is by an income tax fairly distributed, he said, not by loading up the peasant with expensive salt. Finally, Ranko Tajsić proposed that party membership dues be lowered from six dinars a year to three, given all the talk about the poor.[144] Adopting all these statements with enthusiasm, the delegates dispersed peacefully back to their homes. The disturbances the government feared had not occurred.

Relieved, King Milan left for Europe. The Progressives chuckled a bit. The peasants had gathered and peacefully gone home. The Austrian consul, seeing that the congress proceeded in good order and that revolution had not come, wrote to his government that the congress was a fiasco. But they were all wrong. In fact the Radical Party Congress of 1882 was an enormous success. The delegates not only liked what they heard, they liked the way they heard it. Their enthusiasm for the populist policies of the Radicals and their growing sense that the Radicals literally spoke their language undermined the authority of the king, the government, and Austria in the most damaging kind of way: by word of mouth, both in the sense that the rhetoric used by the speakers attracted the peasant listeners and in the sense that those listeners went home to talk about their party, not only to their friends and neighbors, but even to peasants they met along the road en route. The Kragujevac congress intensified the hold of the Radical Party on the Serbian peasantry, a hold that was to last sixty years into World War II. It also undermined the legitimacy of the king and the Progressives and contributed to the confrontation between them and the Radicals, helping to bring about their dramatic clash in 1883.

If the Serbian peasant understood the Radical message and accepted the Radical Party as his own, this does not mean that the party congress had been a consultation of the party leaders with the people. It actually was a skillfully managed plebiscite. All the officers of the congress and the party, as well as all the reports, were elected or adopted unanimously, with little leeway for comments or amendments from the floor. One delegate tried to change a provision in the program concerning how long the party was to recommend a recruit should serve in the army. He was ruled "out of order," and the program was adopted unanimously.[145] Another delegate complained about giving money to *Čosa*, a humorous magazine that supported the Radicals. Pašić said that it was more or less a party paper and anyway the loan technically had been made before the party was legally registered.[146] A third delegate asked if there was any truth to the rumor that the party had entered into an agreement with the Liberals. Pašić answered that there was not, and that if any such alliance should be proposed the local committees would have a chance to comment. "Besides," Pašić continued, "the Radical Party does not need an alliance with any party, because it is a strictly principled party." If that is so, the delegate suggested slyly, why not strike out that portion of the statute that says we can make alliances? "Well it's not really necessary to change the statutes just for that," Pašić replied lamely, and they were not changed.[147]

When the central committee returned to Belgrade it continued to demonstrate the kind of organizational skill evidenced at the Kragujevac congress. The central committee assigned Pašić, Nikolajević, and Andrija Nikolić to write rebuttals to attacks and charged all members of the editorial committee of *Samouprava*, along with several others, with producing at least two articles a month.[148] As president, Pašić formed committees to write a draft constitution and an opština law, as well as to consider matters of finance, education, and even administration.[149] In addition, the central committee began an intensive effort to get local committees interested in national affairs. To make its last task easier, the leadership decided "not to reject poor members because they cannot pay the entire dues, but to consider them as debtors," a change from the policy of six months earlier, when the central committee had told the local committees that when a poor person could not pay "the better-off members of the party [should] take on themselves the patriotic party sacrifice and pay the dues of their very poor comrades."[150] At first, the leadership had seen dues as a sign of commitment, but now, when they realized the possibilities of truly mass membership, they began to relent.

In September the central committee wrote to each local committee to find out who was being persecuted for their politics, to ask each committee to select a person to represent it when the constitutional draft would be discussed, to ask whether the Radicals should organize a joint-stock printing company as the Progressives had done, and, finally, to encourage the local committees to work harder.[151] Pašić tried to infuse the local committees with the same energy that he himself brought to organizational matters. They were not too busy now, he said, but the time would come when they would need to organize in every srez. All the members needed to think about this now "when it is quiet and when other work is not building up. An army perfects its training and supplies itself during peacetime so that it can respond to the demands of war. If a party wants to win and put into effect its demands, it must prepare everything necessary to secure its victory."[152]

Prodded, local committees began to respond. A committee from near Negotin reported signing up thirty-nine persons, despite the načelnik's efforts to hinder their meeting and despite their feeling that the dues were "a new burden on the *vilajet* [the old Ottoman name for a county]."[153] Valjevo reported similar difficulties with the authorities, as well as with unrest due to hajduks [bandits], but objected to a joint-stock printing company because it feared that the shares would "pass into capitalist hands."[154] Valjevo's answer reflected the relatively high level of sophistication that often appeared in replies from the towns, but many of the answers from the villages and srezes revealed that, although local committees were loyally attempting to organize, questions concerning joint-stock companies and constitutions were only dimly understood.[155] Smaller towns in Šumadija complained that they did not understand the questions too well, and even the local committee from Niš, the main city in the newly acquired territory, where the government party was working hard and successfully, said it could not transmit its views on legal subjects like a constitution since it had no experts on such things.[156] Newly introduced into the mysteries of party life in a constitutional state, most peasants still relied on the intelligentsia in Belgrade for their views of abstract matters. On their side, many of the leaders believed that they had to teach the people what was needed, even to direct them a bit when necessary. The central committee instructed local committees "when forming a new committee always to include one or two [educated] persons to interpret our program and our work."[157] The relatively sophisticated Kragujevac committee suggested that all questions from the central committee be sent first to the larger urban committees, because "the ordinary people in the srezes . . . [have] little intelligence."[158]

The contrast between the oratorical style of the Kragujevac congress and the precision with which it was conducted, as well as between the relatively sophisticated political and organizational goals of the central committee and the lack of understanding of these goals in the countryside, suggest the depth of the gulf that urban populists like the Radicals had to span to mobilize support. But it was precisely the rhetorical and organizational effort to bridge this gulf that constitutes the originality of the Radicals and differentiates them from the other parties, as well as from the king. Excluded temporarily from the skupština and rejected by Milan, the Radicals went directly to the people. In this they were simply extending the methods the Liberals themselves had introduced in the 1860s. The Liberals had outflanked the prince, who monopolized the sources of legitimacy, by introducing a new legitimizing concept, the nation. The Radicals outflanked the Liberals, as well as the Progressives and the king, by actually seeking out the people who constituted this nation. In so doing they not only helped their own cause by building electoral support, but they also educated their supporters in the elements of modern public life, both ideologically, by creating in them a feeling of nationality, and technically, by introducing them to the rudiments of organization. The greatest educator in the modern world has been the state, which establishes and inculcates the norms of national behavior through its educational system. But in Serbia the Radical efforts to mobilize the people they spoke for occurred before the Serbian educational system had been able to teach the peasant in what ways he belonged to the nation. Therefore, many peasants learned their sense of what it meant to be a Serb from the Radicals. This association of nationalism and radicalism in the minds of many peasants gave the Radical Party a primacy in Serbian politics it never relinquished.

8 : THE TIMOK REBELLION

Politics is measured by the yardstick of success.—Nikola Pašić

The support the Radicals were building in the electorate by their rhetorical and organizational measures in the summer of 1882 could not do them much immediate good. The government did not have to call another election until late in 1883 when the three-year mandate of the skupština ran out. In the meantime the Progressives, with Milan's stiff backbone holding them up, would be in control. During the summer lull, however, one emotional issue did arise that the Radicals used to good effect: a scandal over paying off the requisitions from the war of 1876.[1] Since most peasants who had receipts for requisitions had long since despaired of any payment for them, a lively speculative market had developed in which some operators had accumulated a very large number of receipts. These were now presented for payment from the resources generated by the foreign loan contracted for the purpose. One of the speculators, Periš Savić, presented a bill for 4,400,000 groš from a poor area near Užice in which the government calculated it had dispensed only 111,000 groš in receipts.[2] When Savić and his partners were arrested for falsification they implicated Aleksa Popović, president of the skupština and a good friend of King Milan—the same Aleksa Popović accused in 1879 of falsifying his patentarina statement. At his trial Popović claimed that he had broken his partnership with the accused in 1881, remained only nominally associated with them, and did not know what was going on. Savić was convicted of fraud and sentenced to two years in prison and Popović's erstwhile partners received sentences of four years each. Popović himself was acquitted "for lack of evidence," even though a judge said privately that "Aleksa is guilty. Perhaps the judges freed him for lack of evidence, but he is guilty."[3] Naturally, the Radicals did not waste any time drawing the link between the apparent fraud by the president of the Progressive skupština and the disastrous Bontoux loan. With the exception of the requisitions affair, however, after the end of the Radical Party Congress in Kragujevac Serbian political life fell back into its normal state of backbiting and petty sniping. When the calm broke, however, it broke suddenly and furiously, in fact, with a bang.

King Milan spent August and September of 1882 abroad, as was his custom, visiting Vienna, Germany, and various spas.[4] As was also his custom, he spent far too much money, losing a fortune at the Jockey Club in Vienna. But Milan tended to put his trips to serious uses also, and this trip was no exception. Milan Piroćanac never had fully agreed with Milan's position that Serbia's future lay in Macedonia rather than Bosnia, and to push his point Piroćanac inspired articles in the German press that perhaps Austria could win the complete loyalty of Serbia if Vienna would grant it Bosnia. Milan realized what lay behind these articles and, obtaining confirmation from the Austrians that they had no intention of giving up Bosnia, informed Piroćanac of that fact. Piroćanac once again began to talk about resigning.

Milan arrived back in Belgrade on the morning of October 23 at about 9:30 A.M. and repaired immediately to the Orthodox Cathedral (saborna crkva) of St. Mark to give thanks for his safe return. Just after he entered the vestibule and kissed the sacred relics a woman suddenly stepped out from behind a pillar and fired a shot.[5] Milan did not react immediately, because he was looking the other way and because the bullet missed him, but when the assassin, who was only a few steps from Milan, raised her pistol to fire again an adjutant grabbed her arm and spirited her off to prison before the angered crowd had a chance to injure her. Milan, at his best in moments of stress, showed himself around the capital, returned to the church in a splendid dress uniform for services of thanksgiving, and graciously received the respects of his people at court later in the day.

Unfortunately for the Radicals, the would-be assassin was Jelena Marković, widow of Jevrem Marković. Jelena, who was known by her nickname Ilka (thus the common name for the event, *Ilkin atentat,* or Ilka's assassination attempt), was a well educated woman from a well-to-do family in the Vojvodina. After her husband had been shot in 1878 she became increasingly obsessed with his death. Taking an apartment near St. Mark's, she went into deep mourning, visiting the church every day. Earlier in 1882 she had received permission from Garašanin to have her husband's remains returned to Jagodina, but she remained in Belgrade pursuing her morbid fantasies. Two months before the assassination attempt she told Raša Milošević, then an assistant to the director of the Craft and Trade School in Pirot and the Radical representative from that town, that she wanted to kill Milan. Milošević did not tell the police, but wrote Ilka a letter in which he laid out the reasons against such an act. When the police searched Ilka's apartment they found a copy of the letter, but transcribed in Ilka's own hand and without personal information that would allow identification of the author.

Suspecting that the assassination attempt may have been a Radical plot, the authorities brought in Milošević for questioning, along with Pera Todorović.[6] During the interrogation the authorities read Raša's letter to the two Radicals asking if they knew anything about it. They said they did not, and since Ilka staunchly maintained that her sole motive was revenge against Milan and kept all her relations with the Radicals secret, it was not until forty years later that the true author of the letter became known.

A strange incident recounted later by Milošević indicates the anxiety this incident created among the Radicals, and gives an insight as well into the intensity of Nikola Pašić's character. It is highly likely that Radicals other than Milošević knew of Ilka's desire. They did not enter into an active plot to kill Milan, but having heard that Ilka would try to kill the king at the church on his next visit, and knowing from custom when that would be, the Radicals did nothing. Like the Liberals of 1868 who knew of plots against Michael, the Radicals, while not entirely guilty, were not entirely innocent either.[7] Therefore, they had every reason to fear the authorities' interest in Milošević and Todorović. After the two were released from their interrogation, they repaired to Raša's apartment for lunch. Pašić, concerned that Pera had not come back to his apartment after visiting the police, came over to find out what had happened. Milošević described Pašić's uncharacteristic reaction when he found them: Pašić "came into the dining room and opened the door. His jaw dropped. He became infuriated, turned around, and slammed the door behind him. I will never forget Pašić's angry face. We had difficult moments, but he always knew how to control himself. He would show happiness, or diligence, but bitterness and anger he knew skillfully how to hide. Later the same day we found Pašić and talked with him about why he had become so agitated. 'Let that be a lesson not to write such a letter, and even less to save it, even in a transcription.' "[8] Pašić's obsession with following his own advice has made the task of those who wish to penetrate behind the public, and eventually even private, mask he created for himself a difficult one.

Knowing they were in trouble, the Radicals did everything they could to limit the damage. The day after the assassination attempt *Samouprava* printed a glowing article of joyful thanksgiving that the king and royal family had been spared, and the central committee notified local committees that they should deny vigorously any suggestions that the Radicals were to blame.[9] Both the Liberals and the Progressives, burning with the appropriate amount of righteous indignation, moved to the attack. *Srpska nezavisnost* claimed that Jelena got her ideas from Svetozar Marković, who trained in the school of Nechaev and nihilism, but the most vicious attack was an article in *Videlo* by Milan Kujundžić entitled, "The Markovićers" *(Markovićevci)*.[10] Kujundžić described the young Svetozar Marković as follows: "The suffocating stench of [Ristić's] regency was smothering every free spirit, when into the Serbian political ring entered a sleazy horse trader [*džambas*] on a state-owned horse who began to wave his arms around in all directions, dragging behind him, through all the prominent ranks of society distraught with painful concern, a mob of happy-go-lucky and spoiled children." Kujundžić concluded, "Down with the Markovićers."

The impact of the new, emotional rhetorical style is clear in this article, as is the Progressive's bitterness as they tried to undermine one of the most important aspects of Radical legitimacy, the legacy of Svetozar Marković. The Radicals fought back, entitling their article "Down with the Progressives," by pointing out how many Karadjordjević supporters there were among the Progressives. *Videlo* countered by accusing Todorović and Paču of writing for a Karadjordjević paper while in exile. *Samouprava*'s response was to ask *Videlo* to prove it and, meanwhile, to list all their current contributors who wrote for the same paper.[11] And so it went, the debate degenerating into petty bickering. Milan Milićević for one found the spectacle offensive. Speaking with Garašanin at a meeting of the Progressive Club, he suggested that the Progressives think over the harshness of their rhetoric, since perhaps they were also a little at fault. But the other members of the club, who had won against the Radicals earlier in the year by not conceding anything, met his suggestion coldly.[12] On their side, the Radicals finally decided that the bitter verbal struggle was detracting from real issues. They agreed to stop any further responses to *Videlo,* and the debate, if not the anger, subsided.[13]

Meanwhile, the actual crisis continued. When the king continued to pressure the government to arrest the Radicals for involvement in the plot, evidence or not, and started to sound out Austria on the advisability of a coup d'état, the Progressives decided, for the umpteenth time, to resign, prompted as well, no doubt, by Pirocanac's disagreement with Milan's Bosnian policy, or rather his lack of one. Four days after the assassination attempt Milan turned momentarily to Ristić.[14] By chance, the Society for the Support of Serbian Literature, the Liberal Party front, was holding its annual congress at just that time. This gave Ristić a chance to arrange a special visit of all the three hundred delegates to the palace, where the king praised them as the party of order.[15] Two days later, on November 1, Milan, already disabused by Austria of his thoughts about a coup, asked Radivoje Milojković to look into forming a new coalition government with Garašanin and Mijatović as ministers of the interior and foreign affairs respectively. The Radicals had to move fast to combat this alarming alliance, by which the Liberals and Progressives would combine against them. On November 4 Pašić offered to cooperate with the Liberals on the conditions that the present constitution be respected, that a new constitution eventually be written, and that the Liberals keep the present laws on freedom of the press and public meetings. The Radicals feared that the crisis might easily lead to a coup d'état followed by a period of reaction that could be very dangerous to them.[16] Milojković accepted their offer, and it appeared that a reasonable coalition that included all three of the contending parties might emerge. But the effort failed, because, in fact, neither Ristić nor Piroćanac, both equally prickly about rank and seniority, really wanted it; the former because he would not accept Milan's views on foreign policy, and the latter because he did not want either Ristić or Mijatović to become superior to him in any new government. Slobodan Jovanović says that under these circumstances Milojković withdrew his offer, while the story told around Belgrade was that Milan handed the government's resignation back to Piroćanac with the words: "there is no need for you to tender your resignation. When I judge it opportune for you to retire I will take care to tell you."[17]

Having retained power and survived the assassination attempt, the Progressives now turned their attention to convening a skupština late in 1882. This was not as easy as they hoped, even with the threat of a 1,000 dinar fine hanging over the head of anyone who was absent without good reason.[18] By-elections were needed in twenty places to replace excluded Radicals, members who had resigned, and delegates from districts in which no election had been held because of disorders. But even after these were held, further resignations, including some by Progressives who were embarrassed to be a part of the two-voter skupština, delayed the opening almost ten days. Typical of the lack of enthusiasm for the session was the case of one disgruntled delegate who refused a free ride to the skupština in a government mail coach and insisted on driving his own peasant cart. "I understand he is still on the road," Locock remarked laconically one week after the skupština was supposed to open.[19] Finally, on December 15, 1882 the skupština opened, even though it was eight persons short of a quorum.

Purged of its oppositional elements, the skupština worked with the sort of calm subservience that marked Ristić's skupštinas a decade earlier. "My God," *Samouprava* remarked, "how beautiful is a skupština without opposition—as peaceful as a plump young woman."[20] Accordingly, it was a most fruitful session. The skupština made grammar school education compulsory, created a National Bank, and established a ministry of the national economy. The most important piece of legislation, at least from the point of view of the events of the next year, was a new army law. The Ottoman wars had demonstrated clearly the deficiencies of a national militia that depended on a self-armed and untrained peasantry. After the great Prussian victories of the 1860s, the European ideal for military organization became the relatively small but highly professional standing army, buttressed by a large reserve force trained over time through conscription. Under Prince Milan's urgings, this skupština introduced the conscription system to Serbia. In theory, all able-bodied men were to serve two years as recruits and then return to private life to make up the active reserve until they were thirty years of age.[21] Reservists were to provide their own clothing and transportation, but the state would continue to provide, as it had in the past, the weapons. The national militia was abolished, and the ministry of war was reorganized to begin what was envisioned as a ten-year program of training to bring the reserve force up to its expected level of proficiency.

When the successful skupština ended its work, the Progressives may have felt that they had the political situation under control and that they could look forward to a peaceful and successful 1883. In fact, 1883 turned out to be one of the most tumultuous years in modern Serbian history. By the end of the year not only had the Progressives fallen from power, but the Radical leadership had been driven into prison and exile, disgraced by the failure of the last great Serbian peasant revolt. The first unrest that presaged this revolt resulted from a convention between Austria and Serbia regulating the health of beef cattle. Austria sought to protect itself from the numerous livestock diseases prevalent in the Ottoman regions of the Balkans by forcing the Serbs to close their trade in beef cattle with Romania, Bulgaria, and the Ottoman Empire, none of which had agreed to the veterinary rules established by Vienna.[22]

Serbia also had to conduct a census of cattle located within thirty-seven kilometers of the borders with those lands and to brand local cattle to distinguish them from potentially diseased foreign animals.

When the authorities went out in the winter of 1882–83 to begin the census and branding, peasants in the border regions of eastern Serbia, a Radical stronghold, reacted strongly. In particular, the citizens of Golubinje, a small village on the Danube near Donji Milanovac, refused to have their stock branded. In response, Garašanin authorized local officials to use the newly created "guardians of public security" if necessary. The result, according to *Samouprava* at least, was rape and sword-slashing by the gendarmes. This was the point at which Pera Todorović took to calling the gendarmes *sejmeni*, after the notorious mounted enforcers of janissary rule during the Ottoman period.[23] The gendarmes had been used for the first time early in January in the town of Salaš in the Krajina region southwest of Negotin, and in the Timok River village of Grljan a confrontation led to the arrest of eight men who were marched the seven kilometers into Zaječar under armed guard.[24] In an incident reminiscent of similar efforts to free Adam Bogosavljević eight years earlier, the entire village of Grljan, including women and children, descended on Zaječar and successfully demanded the release of their men.[25]

By far the most serious incident in these continuing instances of government heavy-handedness—which were, to be sure, designed to control serious diseases—occurred near Gamzigrad, a hill village of 150 illiterate Vlachs and 2.5 hours' walk from Zaječar.[26] The government officials charged with conducting the branding in Gamzigrad did not announce they were coming and did not explain to the peasants why they were insisting on registering and branding the local cattle.[27] Not understanding what was happening and fearing some oppressive new tax or confiscation, the Gamzigradians refused to participate, even when the local officials brought along a few gendarmes; instead, the peasants insisted on sending Milan a petition asking the branding be put off until fall. Milan responded by ordering two battalions of the standing army from Niš, rather far to the south, to head for Zaječar.[28] While local officials were awaiting the troops they tried to enter the village with a force of sixty-two gendarmes, but when the peasants fired on them they had to retire. Milan appointed the relentless old conservative Nikola Hristić to visit the area and report, but before the army could arrive Gamzigrad gave up. Fifty-five persons were arrested, including the author of the peasants' petition, a Radical priest from Boljevac named Marinko Ivković, better known as Pop Marinko. Eventually Pop Marinko received an eight-month jail sentence and seventeen others received sentences ranging from two and one-half years in light chains down to a few months for the three least responsible participants. After this massive show of force the branding was completed without further incident.

The Progressives suspected that the Radicals were behind resistance to the registration of cattle, but in fact the Radicals were only reacting to and taking advantage of real frustration in the countryside. Ever since the assassination attempt on King Milan the Radicals feared that they were facing the possibility of a coup d'état by the king—which would mean the suspension of the constitution, the imposition of martial law, and the disbanding of their party by force—so they tried to stay within the law as much as possible. Taking as their official position the principle that "the law was the highest authority," they urged those among the peasantry who turned to the party for advice to acquiesce in the branding of stock, because to do otherwise would be to break the law.[29] "Inform your villagers to be peaceful," Pop Marinko told the Gamzigrad peasants as he forwarded their petition for a delay to the government. "If the Minister says that you have to accomplish the registration at once, then do not oppose it."[30] But at the same time the Radicals knew that the anger of the peasants was real. In February the Krajina Radical committee reported that it had a "great deal of difficulty dissuading the people from taking steps that would bring about even greater excitement and perhaps even disorder."[31] It was precisely this sense of wrong among the peasants that made the Radicals strong in eastern Serbia. Not only had the two wars with the Ottomans left the area severely damaged, but trade that once had been relatively easy with Bulgaria and areas to the south had become difficult because of the drawing in 1878 of a new international border.[32] So it was not just the registration of cattle that produced an antigovernment feeling in eastern Serbia and turned the countryside toward the Radicals, but also a strong sense that pro-Austrian policies had led the government to ignore the area's needs. At the same time the growth in Radical strength that this situation created made it easy for both Milan and the Progressives to reverse the order of causality and to believe that the government's problems in eastern Serbia did not result from their own policies, but rather from Radical agitation.

Milan also feared that the Radicals were actually pro-Russian, Karadjordjević supporters. Milan always had a tendency to see Russian influence behind untoward events. The seizure of Russian arms headed for Bosnia and the assassination attempt were only the most recent incidents in which Milan saw a Russian hand. Therefore, when news arrived in January 1883 from Montenegro that Peter Karadjordjević had become engaged to Prince Nikola's eldest daughter Zorka, it seemed perfectly clear to Milan that such a marriage must be yet another Russian intrigue, since Montenegro was a Russian client. In fact, as Charles Jelavich has shown, the match was arranged by Nikola and Peter on their own to embarrass Milan, which it did.[33] But, spurred on by the engagement, Milan concluded that the events in eastern Serbia were due not only to Radical agitation, but were perhaps a Russian-sponsored Karadjordjević plot as well. The Radicals' well-known Russophilism helped confirm in his mind the Karadjordjević link he had always suspected. When Raša Milošević had come to present the congratulations of Pirot to Milan in 1882 on the occasion of the proclamation of the kingdom, for example, Milan dressed him down for being a Karadjordjević supporter who wanted to give Pirot to Russia's ally, Bulgaria.[34] As if in response to these worries, reports from the interior began to arrive making the appropriate link. Typical was a report from near Kragujevac that the local Radical leader there was telling the peasants that if they elected Radicals to the next Grand National Assembly this body would get rid of Milan, bring in Peter, and cut out the danak for five years.[35] By July, the month of Peter's wedding, Milan's secret logbook was filled with this kind of report. To combat it, Garašanin told all local officials to characterize the wedding—when it finally took place—as "an unfriendly act toward Serbia and the king, and a traitorous act against Serbdom. And do not spare Russia," he added.[36]

While Milan worried about the future of his throne, the Radicals pursued two main lines of activity, investigating the possibility of an alliance with the Liberals and drafting a new constitution. Ristić had never been in favor of a coalition with the Radicals, whose ideas of self-administration went counter to all his political instincts, but he did not prevent other party members from talking with them, particularly about electoral alliances in specific places to make sure that the two opposition parties did not split the vote and thereby permit the Progressives to win all the seats.[37] The Radicals were willing to think about electoral collaboration, but they also feared that Milan or his government might turn to exceptional measures, such as suspending the constitution; in which case the opposition parties would have to put up a united front in order to survive. In February 1883 the central committee reported to local committees that since the assassination attempt private talks had worked out some areas of agreement between the two parties. These included the necessity of upholding the present constitution while seeking through legal means to introduce a better one. The circular letter asked what the leadership should do. Could it, in principle, make an agreement with the Liberal party and, if so, under what circumstances? If uncertain, would the local committees authorize the central committee to use its best judgment? "This is a very serious and important matter. Please give it your most serious attention and make your decision exclusively according to the interests of the country and the nation, suppressing any personal feelings toward this or that personality."[38]

Rather quickly the local committees began to respond. Some were vigorously opposed. "We know the Liberals," said the Zaječar committee. "A wolf can change its appearance, but never its nature. The people no longer wants a tutor. It wants to take care of its own business; not only wants to, but is convinced it can. Therefore the people are against any agreement."[39] But a majority of those who answered, 16 to 9, said that an agreement would be all right, at

least in case of dire need, but the central committee felt this was
not strong enough support and informed the local committees that
at this time no formal alliance would be concluded with the Liberals,
although if a serious situation should arise they would ask again.[40]
Despite this announcement to the local committees, it appears that
the leadership did maintain its contacts with the Liberals.[41]

The second issue was writing a draft constitution. When Ristić
fell in 1880, one of the first promises the Progressives had made
was that they would change the constitution. The skupštinas of
1881 and 1882 passed the enabling legislation that the constitution
required for calling a Grand National Assembly for constitutional
revision, and late in 1881 Piroćanac appointed a committee headed
by Nikola Krstić, senior judge of the highest appeals court in the
country, to head a committee charged with making proposals on
how to reorganize the government.[42] Piroćanac had already been
collecting criticisms of the 1869 constitution, reading Benjamin
Constant and John Stuart Mill, studying foreign constitutions, like
those of France, Württemberg, Portugal, and Greece, and even
writing his own constitutional proposals. By 1883 the Progressives
were well along in the process of producing a constitutional draft
that reflected their view that those with *znanje* (knowledge that
comes as the result of education) should run Serbia.[43] Their draft
proposed to establish a three-tier system of voting based on tax
payments to increase the influence of those with a stake in society,
and to create a senate that would limit the willfulness, as they
considered it, of the peasant skupština. The Progressive view is
clearly seen in the suggestion that the faculty of the Velika škola
be able, as a corporate unit, to elect one senator.[44] Otherwise, the
Progressives would maintain a system of civil rights rather similar to
the one they had already put into effect. Despite the conservatizing
thrust of these proposals, especially in comparison with the populist
demands of the Radicals, Milan was upset. When he saw what they
were proposing he said, as the English consul put it, that he would
rather die than accept the constitutional reforms posed by his
cabinet.[45] Piroćanac's resignation seemed likely again, but as usual
Milan refused to listen.

A new constitution was important to the Progressives, since

many of them felt they were honor bound to bring about the changes they had long sought; for the Radicals, however, a new constitution was vital. Only if their ideas of national sovereignty were put into law, the Radicals thought, could the excesses of both the king and the government be brought under control. If anything, the Radicals put too much hope in a new constitution, coming to see it as a panacea for Serbia's problems. The Radicals of the time, Pera Todorović said later, "came to exhibit all the signs of religious fanatics," and their dogma was a new constitution.[46]

The central committee of the Radical Party made a serious effort to involve local committees in the creation of a constitutional draft, although perhaps it did so as much for practical political reasons as for the principle of participatory democracy. After the Kragujevac gathering in 1882 a split had developed between the urban and rural factions of the party over the question of what role the monarch should play in the reformed state.[47] Some of the more extreme party members in Belgrade favored a republic, but the overwhelming majority of the peasantry could not envision a state without a king. The practical minded politician par excellence, Nikola Pašić, feared that the republican views of Pera Todorović, Svetozar Nikolajević, and Kosta Taušanović would place the party in an isolated position, both in relation to Milan and in relation to the peasantry that constituted the party's main support. In addition, Pašić realized that a constitution calling for a republic would outrage both Serbia's current protector, Austria, and the great power he placed his hopes in, Russia. It is likely, therefore, that the invitation to all local committees to send delegates to Belgrade in mid-April to discuss the constitutional draft resulted, in significant measure, from Pašić's desire to increase the impact of the peasant elements that favored retaining the monarchy.

In preparation for this meeting the Belgrade leadership hammered out its draft in two weeks of nightly discussions.[48] As befitted their populist and democratic leanings, most of the discussion centered on how to express the sovereignty of the people, which is to say what role the king would play, and what the rights and duties of each Serb would be. By the time the eighteen delegates from around the country arrived for the April 14 meeting, a draft was ready. After initial difficulties with the authorities who insisted, unsuccessfully, on their right to attend, the gathering took place on April 17. Pašić set the tone when he opened the discussion with the following words: "According to our program the dynasty and religion remain. On these questions there can be no discussion. They stay unchanged. Our concern will be to assert them even more strongly."[49]

Two months later the final draft was ready. The Radicals knew that, despite their protestations of loyalty to the dynasty, King Milan would find their draft objectionable. Not only did it expressly state that the people were sovereign and establish direct elections to a unicameral skupština, but it provided that the army take its oath of allegiance to the constitution, not to the king, and that the constitution come into effect when passed by the Grand National Assembly and not when signed by the king. Therefore, to make sure a premature disclosure of the proposal did not ruin the chances of convening a Grand National Assembly when the central committee produced thirty-five copies of the draft and sent them to local committees by special messengers early in July, it numbered each one and declared them to be "our greatest party secret."[50] Each recipient was to sign for his copy, and further copying was forbidden. "Anyone who does so will be considered a traitor to the party."[51] The plan was that each local committee should discuss the project by August 6, after which another gathering in Belgrade would be held to approve the final draft on August 18. Public announcement of the Radical draft would come at a full party conference to be held just before the convening of the Grand National Assembly.

Having produced a draft, however, the Radicals needed a Grand National Assembly at which to realize it. Since the previous two regular skupštinas had passed the necessary formal initiatives, Serbian law required the Progressives to call a constitutional convention before convening the next regular skupština, which itself had to meet before the end of 1883. The necessity for the government to make a decision became even more pressing when Milan announced his intention to leave the country to attend maneuvers in Germany in mid-August.[52] Caught in a time bind of their own making, the Progressives hesitated to go ahead with a Grand National Assembly because it required a general election that they might lose. Many Progressives felt morally committed to calling a Grand National Assembly, but Milan, becoming more and more hostile to the Radicals and fearing not only for his government but for his throne, opposed it.[53] In June Stojan Novaković tried to smoke out Radical and Liberal intentions by getting a friendly German correspondent to publish reports in German newspapers that the government had definitely decided to hold the election for a Grand National Assembly in July, but, in fact, the government could not make up its mind.[54]

Eventually, only a few days before Milan was to depart in mid-August, the government implemented a compromise election plan based on the final agreement for linking up the Serbian railroads to the south that had been signed by Serbia, Austria, Bulgaria, and the Ottoman Empire on May 21.[55] The terms of the agreement required that ratification be accomplished by October 1. Using this pretext, which some thought the Progressives had included in the Vienna agreement precisely for this purpose, Milan and the government decided to call neither a regular skupština nor a Grand National Assembly, but rather a "special" skupština for the sole purpose of ratifying the Vienna convention. But the letter in which the government forwarded this suggestion and which Milan accepted also committed both him and the government to calling a Grand National Assembly before the end of the year.[56] Nevertheless, since the three-year mandate of the old skupština elected in 1880 had expired, new elections still had to be held for the "special" session. These were set for September 19. Both Milan and the Progressives hoped the election would permit them to assess how the voters felt without risking loss of control over either the regular skupštinas for the next three years or the constitution-writing process. But by calling any sort of election the Progressives dropped the fat in the fire. Milan Dj. Milićević knew it. "This is the end of our government [party]," he predicted.[57]

The ensuing campaign evoked enormous excitement. "Travelers say that in places where earlier the government had to force the citizens to come to the polls, now they are holding meetings of

200 to 300 people where they discuss questions of state and opština interests," Milićević noted.[58] The Radicals threw themselves into the struggle with what Pera Todorović called "feverish zeal. Day and night they worked with terrible energy." As one Progressive put it, "They [the Radicals] prepared themselves as if tomorrow was Kosovo. They spoke of the elections as if they would decide the life and death of either us or them."[59] *Samouprava* printed the relevant portions of the electoral laws, pointing out that not every opština had a copy of the laws and that officials tended to be legalistic literalists when government candidates were defeated, and Raša Milošević produced a lengthy article providing detailed instructions on how voters could legally combat the various tactics the government might use to influence or even steal the election.[60] On their side the Progressives adopted the position that the "opposition was evil beyond any measure" and would "do anything to disrupt the elections or to create disturbances." According to them the Radicals had a newspaper run "by an expelled student, and their chiefs are an uncertified professor and a competitor hungry for building contracts," whereas the Liberal paper was run by "a fired secretary and a whole band of fallen monks, ministers, officials, contractors and disease carriers."[61] More seriously, the Progressives accused the Radicals of fomenting revolution and calling the people to arms.[62] "If the country should experience any serious unrest either before or after the elections," *Videlo* said, "you [Radicals] are the main guilty parties."[63] The Radicals fought back. "The Progressives have had three years to win," *Samouprava* advised the voters. "Now you have one day to judge."[64] Pushing the anti-Austrian rhetoric that had become part and parcel of the Radical seizure of nationalist discourse, *Samouprava* asked "Who's for Austria?" "Now we'll see who wants, who will dare, to vote for Franz Joseph."[65]

Both sides awaited election day "with beating hearts," as Pera Todorović put it. Five days before the election the Progressives held a party meeting in Belgrade on the model of the Radical meetings, but it was only a moderate success. Milićević marveled at the strange situation. "No real source for dissatisfaction, but so many unsatisfied!"[66] Todorović, fearing government intervention, was not hopeful that the voters would be able to hold to their views. He describes how the Radical leadership sat nervously around a table in the Golden Cross café on September 19, election day, awaiting news. They knew that the Progressive candidates in Belgrade were piling up a big majority. "Just before noon the first report arrived from Zaječar: 'To this point Pašić 144, the Liberals 5 votes.' . . . We drank to Nikola's health, and our worried faces turned to serenity and satisfaction."[67] Todorović took a walk in town. When a Progressive acquaintance asked him about the big government victory in Belgrade, Pera answered, "'Perhaps the election in Belgrade—that is simply a list of cops, clerks, bread pushers, barkeeps, and Jews, and we don't count on them. But, my dear boy, tell me what song you hear from the interior.' 'The interior! What can you expect from the interior?! Perhaps that fur hat from Imolj or those peasant trousers from Užice know something. If you win there, it will only be another proof that it's easy to fool the simple people.' "[68]

It turned out that the fur hats and peasant trousers did know something, at least how to overcome the pervasive government efforts to prevent a Radical victory, since the opposition, of which the Radicals were the strongest element, soundly defeated the government. The exact count of party mandates differs in the various sources, but when the skupština convened on September 27 at least 72 of the 146 persons present registered themselves at the Radical Club, which, when added to the dozen or so Liberals elected, gave the opposition a small but effective majority.[69] The exact count was not so important. The main result, clear to all, was that the government had suffered a grievous defeat and the Radicals had shown themselves to be the strongest party in the country.

In a truly parliamentary state, a coalition cabinet dominated by the Radicals would have assumed power after an election like this, at least had the election not been for a special skupština. The Radicals hoped that their strong showing would convince the king that they were the logical choice to head up the next government. Most of their opponents, however, did not believe the Radicals were capable of forming a government, since the Radicals had neither the higher educations nor the social graces considered necessary for high government officials. As possible cabinets were rumored around Belgrade, the Progressives made fun of the less cultured Radicals, amused at the story that Kosta Taušanović had suddenly decided to learn French, and Giga Geršić to take mazurka lessons.[70] More important questions were posed too. If the Radicals came to power, would they "make only the richest pay by means of a direct tax on income? Would they give the poor money from the state treasury?" Would they cut the pay of state employees and reduce them to poverty?[71] Worse: would they persecute and imprison the Progressive leaders?

Because Milan was in Germany, answers had to wait. Milan, in a measure that some considered illegal but also a strong sign of his confidence in the Progressives, had turned over most aspects of his sovereignty, except control of the military and a few symbolic functions, to the government for the duration of his absence, but the Progressives still did not dare to act.[72] Before the election Piroćanac said the government would resign if the Progressives lost, but after the election Milan telegrammed Piroćanac saying that he should go ahead and start the skupština in the king's absence, despite the election loss, since the skupština was only for the purpose of ratifying the Vienna agreement.[73] Meanwhile, Piroćanac was meeting almost every day with Queen Natalija, who had not accompanied Milan to Europe. The queen, who was as clever as her husband if not more so and had begun to take an interest in politics since the time the Progressives had come to power, was so irritated at the Radical victory that she burst into tears of fury when discussing it.[74]

In the meantime the Radicals, elated by their victory, called their second annual party convention to meet in Belgrade on September 25, two days before the opening of the special skupština. In its aggressive announcement *Samouprava* said that the election proved that the Serbian people knew how to use their freedoms, that the Radicals were not the creators of the current tensions, and that any effort to stop this national movement by force "would be an incomprehensible, dangerous and unsuccessful rejection of the national will, which must inevitably be satisfied."[75] The convention itself was considerably calmer than this strong statement implied it would be. The central committee decided that with Milan out of the country and no decision yet announced on the Grand National Assembly, it was not the correct moment to make their constitutional draft public. To make fuller consultation with the local committees possible, the central committee alleged, that subject was stricken from the meeting's agenda.[76]

Pašić opened the convention with a speech deploring both the attack on the king and the efforts of the Progressives to hinder the party, reported that the party now had about sixty local organizations, and proposed various policies the Radicals would undertake if they assumed power, like lessening national expenditures, improving the law on meetings and on the opština, and building the railroad with Serbian funds.[77] Most of the convention was as thoroughly routine as this speech. Membership fees were lowered; it was decided to hire a paid secretary; a review of finances showed that almost 5,000 dinars had been dispensed to needy and persecuted party members during the past year; and a central committee that excluded one of the party's few educated leaders, Svetozar Nikolajević, was elected. Held on the eve of the opening of the first skupština that the Radicals controlled, the second annual convention of the party had none of the dramatic rhetoric or satisfied enthusiasm of the 1882 Kragujevac meeting. The clock was ticking and everyone had at least one ear tuned to it.

The second Radical convention did resemble the meeting in Kragujevac in one important way, however, and that was in how little importance it had in the actual decisions the party leadership was making. It appears that the Radical leaders had made two basic decisions concerning the possibility that they might be asked to form a government. The first, which they undoubtedly saw as essential to gain Milan's confidence, was to assure the king a completely free hand in the choosing of a minister of war and in military affairs in general, despite the party's programmatic opposition to the reserve army created by the recent law. But second, remaining true to the main thrust of their campaign for a new constitution, they insisted that they would not take power unless the king agreed to calling a Grand National Assembly to change the constitution.[78]

Another strategic decision—clearly made before the election, and without the promised polling of the local committees—was to cooperate with the Liberals both in the election and in the skupština. And this they would have to do; for, despite their significant electoral victory, the Radicals did not have an absolute majority without Liberal support. If the twelve Liberal votes went over to the government, the Radicals would once again be in the minority.[79] It became obvious when the skupština convened on September 27 that the two parties had worked out an agreement. The first skupština vote was on the composition of the credentials committee, which ended up containing seven Radicals, two Liberals, and no Progressives. Unfortunately for the stability of the system, the Radicals and the Liberals now gave to the Progressives the same medicine of exclusion that the Progressives had fed them in the last skupština. Worse for the Progressives, when the credentials committee reported back it found that the government had interfered in some way in almost every election in the county. The committee rejected some fifty complaints received on behalf of Progressive candidates as being simply the efforts of local officials to present an excuse for not having fulfilled their duty of bringing home a winner for the government, and instead declared most of the Progressive credentials out of order owing to various irregularities.[80]

Meanwhile, King Milan was making his way home. At first he considered a delay in Vienna, but the Austrians convinced him he had to go home and deal with the "disorder" there. He telegraphed Natalija that he was on his way and that he "could not give in to the element of unrest."[81] Pirocanac and Natalija met his ship up the Danube on September 30 and traveled the last few hours with him to Belgrade. Constitutionally, Milan told Pirocanac, the Radicals should come to power, but if they did "Serbia would be in the same international situation that it was when Marinović was in power," that is, Serbia would lose the support of Austria. Of the Liberals, he said, there can be no question, since they have no more than twelve votes, but at least Pirocanac could take satisfaction in their defeat. But next, when Milan asked Pirocanac his view, Pirocanac said nothing. In a display of weakness and political indecisiveness that was characteristic of his leadership, the minister president said that it was not his place to give his king advice.[82] Perhaps Pirи́канас knew that Milan had long since made up his mind and was just playing with his minister president. At Homburg, where Milan had witnessed German maneuvers, Emperor William I had shown the Serbian king the honor of meeting him at the train. William is supposed to have asked Milan if he would be able to restore order "down there."[83] In Vienna Milan had met the king of Spain and was much impressed with the way he dealt with his subjects. The martial mood these visits created in his mind, and his desire to appear strong to the emperors whose approval constituted the only authentication and legitimacy he valued, made up Milan's mind. In Prussia he had "put on his boots," as Pera Todorović put it, and in Vienna he decided that "the moment had arrived to throw away glove and slipper and to rule . . . with boot and whip."[84]

Milan docked at the Sava quay at 3:30 P.M., October 1, 1883. His decision was clear at once. Completely ignoring the delegation of Radical delegates who greeted him with cheers of "Long live the king," he warmly greeted the Progressive ministers and departed. "Already we saw what time it was," Pera Todorović said.[85] From this moment events moved rapidly. That evening Milan accepted the resignation of the Progressive government, which it had decided to give a week earlier, and to the surprise of everyone appointed a government of nonparty persons led by the tough old police administrator Nikola Hristić. Equally to the Radicals' surprise, two days later *Videlo* published the Radical's draft constitution. Despite the extensive efforts to maintain the confidentiality of the draft, laxity on the part of the local committee in Arandjelovac had allowed a copy to fall into the hands of the government two weeks earlier.[86] The initial reactions to the draft of everyone except the Radicals were extremely negative. Pirи́канас claimed such a constitution would mean the ruin of the country because, he said with strange logic, the king would not have even as much authority as he would in a republic. The even-handed British consul, Sidney Locock, who later defended the draft as being well within the bounds of European constitutional practice, reacted initially by calling it "utterly subversive of the most elementary principles of Constitutional Monarchy."[87]

In this heated atmosphere the skupština continued its organizational work. Two days after Milan's arrival it voted a list of candidates for president.[88] The Radicals continued to believe that their majority would allow them to press for a Grand National Assembly and even perhaps for the place in government that they believed their electoral victory should have assured them. On the other hand, they made it as difficult as possible for their opponents to give in. Strongly believing in the rightness of their cause and heedless of the overtones of the situation, they prepared motions of no confidence, impeachment of former government members, and further investigations into the Bontoux deal, and they made clear their intention to prosecute and imprison Progressives, just as Milan had said they would.

The next session, held on October 4, began normally enough. From the list of candidates for president selected the previous day the government announced Milan's choice of Radicals Sima Nestorović and Arsa Drenovac as president and vice president, and the skupština went on to elect four secretaries, as was its custom. Next on the agenda was the address from the throne. At this point Hristić's new minister of justice rose and in the space of less than five minutes read two decrees one right after the other. The first, completely formal in its content and very short, officially opened the skupština, as Milan would have done in his address, and the second, equally formal and brief, closed it. "Profoundly astonished," as the British assistant, Mr. Mason, put it, the delegates were "so disconcerted they seemed to have lost the power of speech."[89] Dazed after this "five-minute skupština," as they called it, the delegates wandered about Terazije for a while, and the next day went home.[90] Before they did so, however, a delegation, including Radicals, visited the king, as was the custom, to bid farewell to the king. When he chided them for their draft constitution, they responded that they were not revolutionaries, but they had no confidence either in the last government nor the present one. They concluded ominously that if things continued in the way they were now going, "it would be impossible for them to answer for the consequences."[91]

What did the Radicals mean that they would not be responsible for the consequences? Right after the abrupt ending of the skup-ština, the worried Radical leadership hurriedly gathered at Kosta Taušanović's apartment to discuss the situation.[92] According to an account published many years later, Pašić opened the meeting with a plea for secrecy, since the king had obviously opted for a strategy of "me or the Radicals," and a very serious confrontation seemed imminent. Todorović spoke about the need for organization and, though not advocating an uprising, he pointed out that the party was unprepared for the use of force by the king.[93] In the circum-stances the best defense against a coup in which Milan abrogated the constitution, they decided after spirited discussion, was to de-fend Ristić's constitution as best they could, even if this meant taking up arms as a last resort. At the same time they decided to convene meetings of every local committee on November 13 for the purpose of getting signatures on a petition asking the king to change the constitution. Having been once again excluded from skupština politics, the Radicals turned, as they did in 1882, to organizing the countryside. Pledging to save constitutionalism as a principle, they hoped their petition would present the government and the prince with irrefutable evidence that a change in the consti-tution itself was needed.

For the next ten days misleading calm descended over Serbian political life. *Videlo* spent a few issues complaining about the Radical draft constitution without actually going into any detailed explica-tion and without publishing its own version, and *Samouprava* re-turned vituperation for vituperation.[94] But other than that, all seemed quiet. The British consul reported that Hristić's govern-ment was carrying out a moderate program of even-handed justice, that the press remained free, and that public meetings were undis-turbed.[95] Pera Todorović visited Vienna for a biopsy of his diseased liver; when he returned it seemed to him that "the new government was turning all its attention to economic progress, and that it had never been more peaceful in the country."[96] Todorović was refer-ring to the successful sale of the initial shares of the Serbian Na-tional Bank, which the two-voter skupština had authorized. Seeing the bank as a key institution for the development of Serbia's economy and hoping to be able to have as much influence as possible over this development, the Radical Party leadership concentrated during this month on encouraging Radicals to purchase the shares.[97] Partially as a result of this campaign, the bank's offering was greatly over-subscribed, and each purchaser had to be limited to five shares.[98]

Beneath this calm of apparently normal activity, however, a climactic confrontation was brewing. The catalyst was the decision by the government to exchange the old and obsolete weapons of the national militia for new Mauser rifles, among the best in the world at that time. The decision to buy these rifles had been made in 1881, well before the military reform of 1882 (though the law actually is dated January 1883), and it was in part because of the impending arrival of these weapons that military reorganization had become pressing.[99] In the past, when the government obtained weapons for the national militia, it had distributed them to the peasants, who then were responsible for bringing them to the front when they were mobilized. But no responsible officer could dream of putting the expensive new Mausers in the hands of peasants who, they claimed, might stack them in their pigsties and clean them irregularly if at all, or who, they feared, might turn them on the king's regular troops. Therefore, when General Tihomilj Nikolić, Progressive minister of war until the government's fall, directed his commanders to go into the field and register all eligible adult males into the new reserve army, he ordered them also to "exchange" any old military equipment, by which he meant primarily the old rifles in peasant possession, for the new rifles; but the new rifles, instead of being given directly to the peasants, would be stored in state military magazines. The order appeared in the official *Military Gazette (Vojni list)* on July 7, 1883.[100]

As far as the peasant was concerned, of course, General Nikolić's "exchange" was not an exchange at all—it was confiscation of his rifle. Under the Ottomans the Serbs could not bear arms as a rule, so when the First and Second Uprisings expelled the Ottomans the ordinary Serbian male overcompensated, coming to feel by 1850 that a man was undressed in public if he did not appear with a weapon. The widespread distribution of arms during the

Ottoman wars did nothing to lessen the sense that the rifle was a man's true support. And, in mountainous regions full of hajduks, it was. The Radicals, well attuned to this feeling on the part of the peasantry, reacted strongly to Nikolić's order. Within a month Pašić published what came to be a famous article entitled "Disarming the National Militia." Its tone is a particularly good illustration of what Radical appropriation of the discourse of nationalism actually meant in 1883.

> What a rifle means to a Serb—that we all know. It is the greatest weapon a Serb has; it is as dear to him as his wife, brother, or sister; a Serb would rather part with his head and his soul than with his arms. Without a rifle and arms there is no freedom. If you would like to eliminate the freedom of a people, if you would like to lead them into slavery, then take away their arms. . . .
>
> The Turks always were willing to promise much if only the Serbs would pass over their weapons, and the Serb always refused, always was ready to die of torture rather than give up his weapons. He knew that without weapons there is neither life nor freedom. . . .
>
> Think how the Serb will feel when his rifle is taken from his wall, the rifle with which he has found luck and misfortune in war, the rifle that was his comrade in camp, the rifle with which he felled his enemies, the rifle that saved his life, the rifle with which he defended his children, clan, and homeland, the rifle which every soldier intends to leave to his descendents as a memento, a charge, and a pledge from two difficult and bloody wars!
>
> And why [are they going to be confiscated]? . . . To sell them to Jews who will trade with them. To sell them for a dinar or two to those who laugh and make fun of the Serbian name, Serbian heroes, Serbian freedom. . . .
>
> There is only one reason for this. You fear the people, who have arms in their hands. . . . That is the only reason, . . . to

make Turkish raja out of soldiers and heroes, *which the Turks tried many times in vain.* . . .

And you, the people of our nation, if you are not so fortunate as to save your wartime memento, your weapon, give it up, but do not leave your home without it because you will destroy the oath of your forefathers, trample the pledge of those fighters who fell for our freedom, leaving your family, your clan, and your homeland a wasteland which can ruin and destroy everything. Watch out for yourself, when those who are given the task of watching out for you do not do so.[101]

Although the rhetoric of this article gave some the impression that it was written by Pera Todorović, its ambiguous style was definitely that of Nikola Pašić. For example, what could it mean to say, "if you are not so fortunate as to save your weapon, give it up, but do not leave home without it?" One of Pašić's most characteristic traits was to speak or act in such a way that listeners or observers could leave with a variety of opinions as to what he had said. On occasion, people left meetings with Pašić holding completely contrary views of what had been decided. In meetings Pašić's own view was usually very difficult to discern beneath his nods, grunts, and cryptic statements. The debate over this crucial article, therefore, centered on the question of just what Pašić was proposing. The Progressives thought they knew—*Videlo* said it was a call to revolt; and the government agreed—it confiscated the papers in which the article appeared, although this did not stop the Radicals from distributing copies privately.[102] But whether the article was a call to resist, or simply a spirited comment on the new law, in either case it is an example of the emotional rhetoric that was a fundamental part of the Radicals' appeal.

For about three months the army took no action on Nikolić's order to exchange arms, but on October 7, ten days after the close of the five-minute skupština, members of the registration commission appeared in the mountainous district of Boljevac, not far from Zaječar, to begin registering the peasants in the new regular army and to collect their old weapons. Eastern Serbia, which is drained by the Timok River, was a Radical bastion. Not only did many party leaders come from the area, but the region had a history of rebelliousness and independence typical of a border area. It was the home of daring national heroes, like Hajduk Veljko of the First Serbian Uprising, but had been added to Serbia only in 1833. The Timočani had suffered a great deal during the wars with the Ottomans, and the region's main towns of Zaječar and Knjaževac had both been burned to the ground. The peasants of this economically backward area were proud of their fighting traditions and convinced that the government had not helped them sufficiently after the Ottoman wars; used to hearing criticisms of the government from Radical politicians, they resisted the order to give up their arms. The Timok Rebellion *(Timočka buna)*, the last major lashing out of peasant rage in Serbia, resulted from that resistance.

The first few small collections of arms in eastern Serbia went smoothly, but soon peasants began to object, first as individuals and then as entire villages.[103] Near Banja, which adjoins the Timok regions, the same objections surfaced, and soon the local exchange commissions were ordered to arrest the leaders of any village that refused to give up arms, a policy resembling the way disturbances over branding had been handled in the same region. By October 23 several prominent village men had been jailed in Boljevac. Peasant reaction to the imprisonment of their leaders followed the traditional path. A hundred or more villagers converged on Boljevac. When they could get no satisfaction, they broke into the jail and made off with their leaders.

Whereas previously the government had backed down when peasants gathered to free imprisoned notables, this time Milan was eager for a confrontation. At the time the first refusals to hand over weapons occurred, Milan confided his determination to the British consul. "If I lose my throne, it shall not be because I have given way before the people in the street; if I must fall I prefer it should be after I have done my best to put them down; and it will in all probability come to this: they will not be quiet; they will not be long before they give me an occasion for interfering with them, and when it comes I shall not hold my hand."[104] The occasion had come. Milan dispatched a group of sejmeni (gendarmes) and a squadron of cavalry to the offending area, backing them up by mobilizing the standing army unit in Kragujevac.

On their side the Boljevac peasants organized as well. They sent out messengers to neighboring villages, and when the local bugler sounded the call to arms on November 1, about five hundred peasants answered; they surrounded the government force that had appeared in Boljevac and persuaded the calvary colonel in charge to disarm the sejmeni. The peasants were thrilled by what they believed was a demonstration of strength. The government, on the other hand, interpreted the event as an act of rebellion. On November 3 Nikola Hristić, suspending the law on association and the law on the press, declared martial law in the Boljevac region. By this decree anyone who broke the public peace could be condemned to death, the sentence to be carried out without appeal within twenty-four hours. The next day Milan put the army on alert, doubled the pay of all military personnel who took part in putting down the revolt, and made any resisting area responsible for meeting the costs brought about by its resistance.[105]

In the first few days of November the aroused peasants retained their hold on the village of Boljevac, but they were so disorganized and unprepared for the step they had taken that a local government official was able to slip out of town on November 1 with the Boljevac treasury, and it was not until November 5 that the peasants decided to look through his papers and to send some militiamen to guard the passes into the area. At the same time the leader of the Boljevac peasants, Pop Marinko Ivković, who had advised the Gamzigrad peasants during the branding crisis earlier in the year, sent a relative to nearby Banja to enlist the support there of Ljubomir Didić, the town's best-known Radical. After further consultation with another Radical leader, Aca Stanojević of Knjaževac, Didić had the drum and bugle of revolt sounded in Banje and was able to imprison the local government officials without difficulty on November 6. The next day, November 7, when a large number of armed peasants, irritated and frustrated by the government's efforts to confiscate their arms, appeared in Knjaževac, they easily took over the administration of the town under the leadership of Stanojević. They quickly elected an executive committee, proclaimed their loyalty to the crown, and began to consider how to aid their peasant allies in the nearby regions.

Meanwhile, in Belgrade the public knew very little about what was happening.[106] Nikola Hristić was so concerned to repress news of the uprising that he personally received and decoded all reports from the affected area himself, often in the presence of King Milan, who spent most of the crucial days at the telegraph office. Only one major piece of news appeared in public, a lengthy report on events in Banja and Boljevac that *Samouprava* managed to publish on November 1, before the press law was suspended.[107] The next day Pašić, instead of staying in town as he usually did, took the precaution of staying overnight at the quarry outside of town where he was mining rock under a contract for constructing the Sava railroad bridge, and on November 4, the day martial law was introduced, he called Pera Todorović and some others to visit him at the mine. Todorović found an "anxious and unhappy" Pašić tired from lack of sleep. "Do the people want to fight?" he asked. Todorović said he thought the affair was a government plot to trap the Radicals, but Pašić was not so sure; the government would not pick that region to try such a thing. Maybe so, Todorović responded, but there was little chance for peasant success. There were no plans, no agreements. He thought an initial failure would break the people's spirit and, furthermore, the Radical leadership in Belgrade was certain to be arrested soon. Pašić inquired which was better then, to stay put and be jailed or to go to the people? Obviously the answer was to go to the people, even if this meant risking death. "Well, let us die. We've lived enough," Todorović reports Pašić as saying. "He said these words in a dejected tone," Pera wrote, "but decisively, in the voice of a completely persuaded man. And really, Pašić seemed to me at that moment as a man who had decided to die."[108]

Todorović's description of this meeting was written later and has some of the qualities of self-justification that mark accounts of important moments. There is also room for legitimate doubt that Pašić expressed himself in such an openly emotional way. But there is no doubt that Todorović's account captures the Radicals' almost impossible situation. Faced with a king determined to thwart them and a government hostile to their hopes, they now had to decide whether or not to join a peasant uprising of their most loyal supporters that was almost certain to fail. In the final analysis, they had very little choice. If they held back they would risk losing the confidence of the people and Milan would probably hold them responsible for the uprising anyway. The necessity of their decision did not make it any less nerve-racking. Pašić and Todorović decided that most of the central committee was not cut out for revolt, but the four most committed leaders should leave for the interior: Pašić to the Timok region through Hungary, Romania, and Bulgaria; Pera to Rudnik in Šumadija; Kosta Taušanović to Aleksinac on the edge of the area of unrest; and Raša Milošević to Pirot, his home constituency far to the south near the Bulgarian border.[109]

On November 5, in order to quiet rumors that the Radicals were leaving to lead the revolt, Pašić stayed overnight in Belgrade. Through Raša Milošević he sought protection for the central committee from the Russian consul, Persiani. But Persiani had received orders from his government to keep out of the turmoil and was, in any event, out of favor with Hristić's pro-Austrian government; so he could offer them little assistance.[110] At a final meeting held at the editorial offices of *Samouprava* on November 6 the committed members of the central committee affirmed their agreement to set out for the interior. Even at the time, Pera Todorović said later, he noticed that Pašić's route would allow him a safe journey and permit him to see when he got to Vidin whether the uprising was succeeding or not. Supporters of Pašić later saw this as just another proof of Pašić's political acumen, but opponents saw it differently— as a cowardly way of saving himself while his colleagues were risking all in the interior. Friends urged Milošević to travel by this route too, but he declined. In any event, the die was cast. The four shook hands and said "God be with you" (*zbogom*), which in Serbian has a finality to it not conveyed by the normal phrase for "Goodbye" (*do vidjenja*—until we see each other again). "I won't [say *zbogom*]," Pašić said. "In ten days or so we will all greet each other again, meeting just like this in Vračar or on Topčider."[111]

It was relatively easy for Pašić to leave. As a contractor on the Sava bridge he simply took out the boat he used to inspect the work and continued over to the other side. By November 10 he was in Vidin. But he was the only one among the central committee who actually left Belgrade. When the moment came, none of the others could take the decisive step, even though they were certain they were about to be arrested. On November 6 they simply sat in their homes or in the cafés of Belgrade until the evening when the authorities came and got them. Pera Todorović entered prison with gloves and a cane, Jovan Djaja wore a top hat, and Giga Geršić was picked up in his favorite café.

At the time the Radical leadership was arrested the uprising was not yet suppressed. The day they went to prison Ljuba Didić led the seizure of Banja by the rebels. The next day, November 7, a confrontation between the standing army and a peasant force moving out from Boljevac resulted in a crushing defeat of the disorganized and poorly armed insurgents, but at the same time this was the day when Aca Stanojević established a provisional government in Knjaževac. Stanojević was more experienced in administrative affairs than either Pop Marinko or Ljuba Didić, and he ordered each locale to set up a committee and report to an executive committee in Knjaževac. He secured the town's money box, urged the insurgents not to loot, and treated the local officials with consideration. As Slobodan Jovanović put it, Stanojević, familiar with the procedures of the bureaucracy, "conducted the revolt according to all the rules of state administration."[112]

The day that Knjaževac revolted, November 7, the British consul expressed concern to his government. "Should the troops meet with a check, should there be much bloodshed, should the insurrection spread to other districts, or should there be a sign of disaffection among the troops, there would probably be an outburst of feeling which would prove dangerous indeed to his majesty."[113] The Belgrade officer corps was uneasy too. On November 4 Milan had summoned them and pointed out how much their position would be diminished under the proposed Radical constitution. The king expressed his confidence in his officers, an indication in itself of his doubts, and called upon their loyalty, which they expressed. But General Mišković, who was present, found the entire incident troubling. "No good result can come of this," he worried.[114] Locock reported that the Belgrade officers were disgusted at being called on to put down peasants, and that Belgrade was pervaded with "general uneasiness and fear."[115]

Given the outcome of the Timok Uprising, it is important to remember this moment of fear and foreboding in Belgrade between November 4 and November 7. It was not impossible that the uprising would spread across the country, at least in the mountainous regions, and cause very serious complications, nor was it certain in the officer's minds that their troops would fire on their countrymen. But on the next day, November 8, the weakened peasant force from Boljevac, still in the field, failed to take its main objective, Zaječar, and lost a final battle at Stolica almost without struggle. Unaware of these defeats, villagers were still appearing hoping to join the insurgents, but spirits were declining. Finally, on the eleventh, after a decisive seven-hour battle at Vratarnica, the rebels were finished. The next day the army occupied Knjaževac and the revolt was over, with one exception. The very day that Knjaževac fell, the town of Aleksinac rose up under the leadership of Radical Serafim Negotinac, but it was a week too late. Had Aleksinac revolted the day after Knjaževac, and had the Radical leaders actually gone into the countryside and tried to raise the peasants in their own districts, there is a real possibility that the Timok Uprising might have become a full-fledged peasant war led by the Radicals. But it did not. The peasant members of the regular army did not refuse to fire on the insurgents, and the uprising, confined to eastern Serbia, was put down quickly and relatively easily.

Some of the leaders of the rebellion escaped. Aca Stanojević made it to Bulgaria, where he joined Pašić. The two of them stayed there in vigorous opposition for the next six years. But most were captured. Milan's court-martial operated with what Dimitrije Djordjević has called "staggering expediency."[116] "The Court met four times a day and sentenced 29 people daily on the average." The total number brought to trial was 809, of whom 94 were sentenced to death and 640 to various terms of imprisonment. Only 75 were declared innocent. Included in the 20 who eventually were shot after Milan granted clemency were the main leaders in the field, Pop Marinko, Ljuba Didić, and Serafim Negotinac. The Belgrade leadership escaped this fate. Five of the ten members of the central committee were found innocent, while Taušanović and Mihailović were sentenced to eight and five years of hard labor respectively. Milošević and Todorović were sentenced to death, but their sentences called forth what Dimitrije Djordjević calls "some good political theater." The Belgrade community of government and intellectual leaders implored the king for mercy for individuals whom they saw as part of their own state class—perverse, wrong-headed, and irritating perhaps, but still privileged in their rights as players of the political game. The convicted pleaded with the king as well. A few days after his imprisonment, and before the outcome of the revolt could have been known to him, Pera Todorović wrote to Milan asking for mercy. This time there would be no dramatic defense, no play to the populace, as there had been in the Red Banner Affair. His life was at stake. Milan did not grant dispensation at once, and permitted the Radical leaders to be shipped off to Zaječar in chains. When their convictions were announced shortly thereafter Milošević and Todorović wrote to the king immediately. Milan, stretching the tension to the limit, and in order to make sure he had time to receive the pleas, directed the twenty-four-hour deadline for the execution of the convicted to be extended. "Mercy our sublime Ruler! Mercy our noble King, Mercy!" begged Todorović and Milošević. At the last minute, Milan accepted the humiliation of these two most caustic of his opponents, and commuted their sentences to ten years in prison.[117] The Timok Rebellion was over; the Radicals were crushed; Milan was triumphant. The heroic phase of creating political parties in Serbia was over.

CONCLUSION

The players on stage at the time of the Timok Rebellion remained there for the next twenty years. Milutin Garašanin and Vladan Djordjević led the Progressive Party until its demise at the end of the century; Jovan Ristić headed his second regency when Milan abdicated in 1889 and stayed politically active until his death in 1899; Nikola Pašić spent the next forty years at the head of his party; and King Milan bedevilled Serbian politics until his death at the age of 46 in 1901. Even Nikola Hristić returned for a third ministry in 1889.

The crushing of the Timok Rebellion led to a forced respite in Serbian political life, a two-year period in which Milan and his army ruled the country. Milan permitted the Progressives to return to the government again early in 1884 under Garašanin, and they were able to continue enacting their program of modest reforms, including an important revision of the Serbian taxation system; but Milan remained the main political actor. In 1885 he attempted to put into effect his belief that Serbia's hopes for future expansion lay toward the south by attacking what he thought was a weakened Bulgaria. His countrymen neither understood nor supported the war, especially since many Serbian intellectuals believed that the Bulgars, Serbia's south Slavic brothers, were potential allies and associates. Rather than leading to the glorious expansion that Milan hoped to achieve, the adventure ended in a crushing defeat in which the Bulgars would have occupied Serbia had Austria not intervened. Humiliated, Milan decided to abdicate, although it took him four years actually to put his intention into effect. Milan's decision set off a train of events that for the next twenty years turned Serbian politics into the laughing stock of Europe. The central problem in this mad sequence was not Macedonia, Serbian backwardness, relations with Austria, nor any question of real import, but rather the personal quarrels between King Milan and Queen Natalija, especially over who would exercise the dominant influence over their son, Alexander, who succeeded Milan in 1889. Their arguments were played out in one farcical and emotional public squabble after another.

During these twenty years of turmoil each of the three political parties had its day in the sun, including the Radicals, whom Milan pardoned (except for those still in exile) as early as January 1886. Two years later, in order to achieve a divorce from Natalija and favorable financial terms for his abdication, Milan offered the Radicals the new constitution they had been seeking for a decade. In 1888 a committee chaired by the leaders of all three parties wrote a constitution that established a good many of the Radicals' goals, including a more powerful skupština and more autonomy at the local level. The two-year government of the Radical Sava Grujić (1889–91) was the first to operate under this new fundamental law.

In the sickly atmosphere created by the quarrels of Milan and Natalija, as well as by the youthful and ill-considered attempts to assert personal authority by the ill-equipped King Alexander, neither the Radicals nor anyone else were able to establish an effective government for very long. Crude and shortsighted exercises of raw power alternated with desperate efforts to avoid personal disgrace. Milan abdicated, came back, then left, then came back, then left again. Natalija did much the same. Pašić returned from exile and headed up the skupština, only to be imprisoned and threatened with execution over a plot to bring Peter Karadjordjević to the throne. Milutin Garašanin had to spend a year in exile. King Alexander married a considerably older woman who was allegedly a former prostitute and who then faked a pregnancy in an effort to get public sympathy. And so it went, to the amusement and, eventually—with the brutal assassinations of Alexander and his wife in 1903—to the horror of the rest of Europe.

Was the process then that created the Serbian parliamentary

system from 1869 to 1883 merely the prelude to the twenty-year spectacle of passion and revenge that succeeded it? Such a conclusion would be easy to make and, insofar as politics in fact *is* in significant measure a spectacle of lust and revenge, correct. But it would be a significant error to let it go at that. In the first place, observers from large countries tend to forget the similar spectacles in their own histories when they smile indulgently at the passions of the small and weak. Seventeenth-century England is the locus classicus of the battle for supremacy between parliament and king; the "glorious revolution" is the model for all future analogous battles, including the one between Milan and his skupština in the years 1870 to 1883. A close examination of the day-to-day events of early modern England, however, reveals a constant and bitter struggle for personal advantage and power in which the winners subjected the losers to exile, incarceration, or even, in the sixteenth century, disembowelment. Recent histories of this era of English history suggest that constitutional theory occupied the mind of almost none of the participants in what we think of as a grand and significant event. Instead, short-term advantage was the meat and drink of these complex events.[1] Even in the nineteenth century, when we assume British parliamentarianism was well established, William IV acted more as King Milan did than as a constitutional monarch. "In his short reign of seven years, he [William IV] thrice dismissed a ministry; twice dissolved Parliament for political purposes before its time; three times made formal proposals to his ministers for a coalition with their political opponents; and on one celebrated occasion allowed his name to be used, independently of his political advisers, to influence a crucial vote in the House of Lords."[2]

After contemplating the politics of seventeenth-century England, Anthony Fletcher concluded that "great events do not necessarily have great causes."[3] The obverse may well also be true: the pettiness of the events does not necessarily imply they are without meaning. The Serbian case provides an excellent example of how the idea of popular sovereignty, first essayed in England but later made actual in the European mind by the French Revolution, eats away at static political structures. As Benedict Anderson has pointed out, the French Revolution has accumulated such an over-whelming written memory in literate cultures that, whereas its meaning remains the subject of endless debate, its "it-ness," so to speak, is beyond question.[4] Once human beings learned, as they did after 1791, that a written code could establish certain individual or civil rights, the possibility always existed to argue that existing political or social arrangements, whatever they are, inadequately carry out the "true" implications of popular sovereignty (or whatever other principle of equity its advocates propose). A strong regime can repress such criticism, but not eliminate it permanently. Whenever states in the post-French revolutionary world permit a bit more openness, voices emerge to claim what many people have come to understand as their rights. Such criticisms are never innocuous, because they contain the possibility of rallying a faction that will support challengers for power. There is, that is to say, an inevitable pressure toward pluralism and political competition in the very premise that a constitution can be written, or that the nation is sovereign, or that civil rights exist, and this pressure is not related to any particular social condition.

Once begun, the process of political development in nineteenth-century Serbia engendered its own intrinsic momentum. The starting point, if we discount the St. Andrew's skupština of 1858 as premature, was Ristić's constitution of 1869. Had Prince Michael lived as long as his father (that is, until 1903), Serbian political development would surely have been different. The experiences of Bulgaria and Romania suggest that a strong-willed ruler like Michael could have derailed progress toward a pluralist system in the Balkans. But in Serbia, Ristić's effort to introduce a *Rechtsstaat* on the Prussian model during the youth of a less than resolute prince inevitably produced public discussion, then an inchoate opposition, and finally organized party opposition.

The path to a party system looks smoother in retrospect than it seemed at the time. When Ristić departed in 1880, the stability provided by his strong leadership evaporated, as did the solidarity his strength had called forth among the opposition. Offered an opportunity at power, the two opposition groups were unable to find a way to cooperate, or even to tolerate one another. Taking control of the government, the Progressives immediately made it clear to the Radicals that they did not intend to share power with their former allies in opposition. Failure to include a Radical in their government was only the first step in an almost day-to-day worsening of relations that led to the exclusion of Radicals from skupština committees and the nearly complete breakdown of relations between the two parties.

The fault was not completely on the side of the Progressives. From early in his career Pašić made it clear that the basic Radical political strategy was to attack. After Ristić's resignation Pašić withheld his endorsement of the new Progressive government. When he realized that the Progressives were not going to offer the Radicals any concessions he prevented the skupština from making a quorum by having the Radicals resign. Parliamentary obstructionism was not unusual in the nineteenth century, but the intransigence of the Progressives, who refused Radical participation, and the tactics of the Radicals, who refused to permit government to go on without them, destroyed any chance of establishing the Serbian equivalent of a loyal opposition.[5]

And, in fact, the Radicals were not too loyal. Some of their most important leaders not only had links with the Karadjordjevićes, but underneath their public protestations of support for the monarchy many of the urban intellectuals favored a republic over rule by their young and erratic king. Milan has been rightly characterized as a vacillating spendthrift, a quick-witted but unstable leader unable to place his country's interests before his own mania for squandering money. But without Milan it is doubtful that Serbia would have developed a bona fide party system.[6] Milan was an Austrophile not only because the Habsburg court successfully flattered and wooed him, but because he believed that small and weak Serbia faced destruction should Austria ever turn against it. When Austrian patronage was at stake, therefore, Milan was willing to deal with almost anyone. In 1875, knowing that Austria would not permit Serbian interference in Bosnia, he brought Kaljević to power, certain that reforms of which he did not approve would result. In 1880 he brought the Progressives to power and let them introduce reforms he did not like because he did not think Serbia could face a tariff war. His marriage and his personal finances were factors in these decisions, since Milan's political schemes were never far from his personal ones, but Milan was quite willing to deal with politically distasteful bedfellows whenever a clear-cut policy or personal goal forced him to do so. His rapprochement with the Radicals after 1885 in order to smooth the way to abdication was just such a deal. This is why the Radicals faced such difficulties between 1880 and 1883—no obvious political need pressured the king to seek their support. Quite the opposite was the case. The Radicals were Russophile and plebian. Milan was Austrophile and doted on the honors granted him by emperors. Therefore, Milan simply would not replace the Progressives until they proved in the election of 1883 that they were totally incapable of quieting the Radical groundswell.

Whatever battles the Liberals, Progressives, and Radicals found themselves in with Milan or with each other, all parties advocated adopting the institutional forms that were the visible political manifestations of the developed West. After the 1840s, when the first Serbian students began to study in Europe, the eyes of educated Serbs were constantly focused on Europe. Ristić took satisfaction at his reception in Vienna in 1873 because he experienced as much respect as if he were a member of the English government. The skupština, when abolishing corporal punishment in 1873, hoped this would place Serbia in the "ranks of the rest of the cultivated European states." General Mišković saw the war of 1877–78 as creating "sympathy and reputation in Europe," and the Serbian victory as placing a "cornerstone in the edifice of civilization." Serbs believed their task in 1878 was to bring European civilization to the lands it had acquired.

When Serbian public figures spoke of themselves as aspiring to civilization, or perhaps spreading it, they referred to European political and legal structures. The remarkable but quite usual aspect of this fascination with foreign political forms, which is common in every country facing the challenge of the West, is the admission that foreign ways are better, even though one of the effects of adopting those ways is to increase the sense of national pride. The paradoxical problem that faced all the Serbian politicians of the nineteenth century after Ilija Garašanin, who denounced "forms brought in from foreign lands," was how to make the changes they believed were necessary to achieve progress and enlightenment, while at the same time creating pride in the uniqueness of national selfhood, which was in itself one of the norms being adopted. Put more simply, in a situation of admitted subordination and imitation, how does one maintain self-esteem?

The Liberals of the 1860s were the ones who found the basic solution to this problem. They introduced the Western idea that the people are the source of political power in the modern world (this contrasts with the Ottoman idea—and the Orthodox one— that God is the source of all power and the sultan the temporal source of authority); they then coupled it with an analysis of why the Serbian people, in spite of all appearances to the contrary, were capable of exercising power. Far from being unsuited to the Western political style, the Liberals argued, Serbs were uniquely suited to it by their history and customs, and, in fact, Serbs had long stood on the ramparts of Christian civilization against Asiatic barbarism. There is something analogous in this argument to the efforts of some historians in Yugoslavia after World War II to find a bourgeoisie among the peasants of nineteenth-century Serbia. The Liberals simply stated that, all appearances to the contrary, the Serbian peasant was really a liberal nationalist.

Jovan Ristić believed that the Prussian-style government he preferred did have to provide for some popular representation, but only as a forum for "venting hot air." He hoped that the traditional Serbian skupština would docilely support his bureaucratic administration. This, in his view, would be an advance over the system of Ilija Garašanin and Prince Michael, which left out the nativist element and relied solely on an Austrian-style bureaucracy presided over by an autocrat.

If, as the Liberals contended, the Serbs were suited by their history to become a modern state, politicians had no need to make any special effort to mobilize popular support. The nation might consist of the people, but it was an abstract nation and a distant people. Least of all did the arrogant Ristić feel a need to consult the nation. He knew how to bend a skupština to his will, but he did it without conceding in the slightest that anyone in the hall might be his equal. Cool, logical, energetic, and authoritative, Ristić did not speak of a tear-stained, blood-soaked Serbia, but rather of Serbia as Piedmont and of Salonica as an historic Serbian goal. This schoolmasterish argument, understood best by the educated and accepted by the peasant delegates on authority, contrasted with Ristić's very powerful sense of Serbian national aspirations. No Serbian statesman has exceeded Ristić in his desire to carve out a truly independent position for Serbia. But, confident of his own authority, Ristić could not imagine it might be necessary to instruct people as to what their nation was and what it might mean to be a member of it.

The Progressives understood the difficulty of basing the construction of a modern state on a theory of nation when the nation itself was a backward peasantry. The party leadership, which consisted almost entirely of intellectuals trained in the law at foreign universities, found the idea that the common Serb was trained by his past and his culture to enter into the modern political world little short of ridiculous. For Serbia to achieve stature with Europe and to enjoy a smoothly functioning state the best educated would have to rule, and this meant professionalizing the judiciary, improving education, and creating a senate that would be able to keep a bridle on the peasant skupština. This did not mean abandoning the idea of nation, of course, because once it was introduced no party could afford to be seen as antinational. But the idea remained for the Progressives just as abstract as it did for the Liberals— useful but not visceral.

For both the Liberals and the Progressives, therefore, Serbian progress was to be played out in the realm of politics. Ristić considered Serbia's international situation of primary importance and needed a state apparatus to enhance it, whereas the Progressives sought to create a state apparatus appropriate to their own educated interests. Neither had a vital interest in reforms that would lead to the economic development of the countryside. Even Ristić's advocacy of economic war in 1880 was based on his desire to keep Serbia independent rather than on any strong economic sense, and the Progressives in the same year accommodated themselves to

Austria in part to maintain the traditional peasant economy. But what the Progressives and Liberals failed to grasp, or were irritated at when they did grasp, was that by 1880 the Liberal idea of the sovereign nation and the Progressive logic of national interest had spawned an unwanted child—emotional nationalism on a popular level. The Progressives outmaneuvered and out-argued the liberals, both in terms of their program and the way they presented it, only to find themselves attacked in a new way by the Radicals.

The Radicals found an opening for their attack because national elections inevitably forced every politician to appeal for votes, even though in Serbia's transitional stage of political development getting the votes did not always mean coming to power. The favored method of mobilizing the electorate was for the government to coerce the voters. Ristić proved more effective at this in the 1870s than the Progressives did in 1882 and 1883; but every group that took power in Serbia sooner or later did its best to "make" elections, however dedicated to the principles of fairness it may have been in opposition, or whatever its original intentions. The method had a high probability of success, but also the serious disadvantage of not building underlying support, as Ristić discovered as soon as he was unable to pull the bureaucratic strings in 1880.

The government's rather large stick of coercion was not quite balanced by its small carrot of symbolic attraction, which took the form of trying to inspire loyalty to the prince. The usual device was to have Milan tour the country, speaking with the peasants. The prince made a serious effort to surround himself with all the accoutrements of grandeur—a military guard, elegant uniforms, festive arches, and religious panoply. When he had to act on the spur of the moment, as after the assassination attempt, he could be positively regal. But Milan did not speak the peasants' language, either literally or figuratively. He blustered at them, told them to obey him as head of their national household, and resorted to force when they did not. As a result, no folk mythology grew up about him, as it had with Prince Miloš, and his trips to the countryside proved more a liability than an asset. The peasantry believed Serbia had to have a king, but Milan had neither the humor, the patience, nor the spirit to translate that belief into support for the politicians he favored. Milan's office sustained him, but a mythology of kingship did not.

A much more important forum of symbolic interchange was the press. All the political groups used their newspapers to make their cases, although these could have little immediate impact on the illiterate peasant voter. The vicious and petty harangues that filled the Belgrade press remained the avocation of a relatively small group. The Liberals and the Progressives knew this, but since they considered it appropriate that those with learning should be the ones concerned with political affairs, they saw little need to push the rhetoric of legitimacy beyond what would appeal to the educated and informed.

The Radicals, however, seized the opportunity provided by the theory of popular sovereignty. If the Liberals outflanked Prince Michael by claiming a new basis for legitimacy, the Radicals outflanked the Liberals and Progressives by pushing their own arguments one step further and actually getting the nation to participate in politics, both through organization and through going to the people. Svetozar Marković pinpointed the peasant as the potential source of power in Serbia. Pera Todorović's appearance in the papers Marković edited and the strong response to the extensive reporting on the work and persecution of Adam Bogosavljević gave an indication in 1875 of the power an appeal to the countryside might have. Todorović's new voice also inspired those who heard his defense at the Red Banner trial. But not until the appearance of *Samouprava* in 1881 did the Radicals hit their rhetorical and organizational stride. The stylistic fireworks introduced in the first issue of that paper changed public debate in the direction of increasingly emotional arguments. The designation of Serbia as our "bloody and tear-washed homeland," the appeal to gunjac and opanak, and the emphasis on anti-Austrian rhetoric were three elements in this new style. But the ordinary Serb was not able to read the newspapers in which such arguments appeared. The true originality of the Radicals was to seek out these ordinary peasants through a national political organization. By reporting to constituents, organizing local party committees, collecting party dues, and holding annual conventions, the Radicals created the first political organization in the Balkans to give the term popular sovereignty a practical, visceral meaning.

If the Radicals transformed the style with which nationalism was presented, they changed its content as well. Like the Liberals, the Radicals appealed to history and custom to demonstrate that the Serbian peasant was ready for self-rule, but the thrust of their argument was quite different. Whereas the Liberals turned to the distant past and to the concept of social harmony, the Radicals tended to emphasize what they considered the self-directive role of the peasant in the Serbian uprisings and the communal tradition of the zadruga. Never mind that the peasants of western Bosnia did not rise in 1875–76 as expected, and never mind that the Radical constitution was almost incomprehensible to the peasantry. The Radicals succeeded in fixing the myth firmly in the public mind that the Serbian peasant wanted and understood democracy. Hating oppression, he had risen, shaken off the Ottoman yoke, and seized the land for himself, creating by this spontaneous and heroic effort the firm basis of true democracy, which the bureaucratic state had ever since been stifling.

This interpretation fit well with the foreign political model that the Radicals favored—the populist socialism which they had learned in Zürich and which they kept alive with ritualistic references to Svetozar Marković. This socialism had more in common with Lassalle than Marx, and was closer to French radicalism than to the First International, but it still pointed the Radicals in the direction of the Serbian peasantry. In the absence of a working class, the Radicals made Serbia's producers, the peasants, the class basis of their program, and in the absence of a bourgeoisie, they turned their criticism on the state bureaucracy, which they considered the dominant class in Serbia. By introducing local self-administration and a sovereign skupština, and by supporting the retention of the national militia, they proposed to break the ability of the state to control the local political life of the peasantry and in that way to construct a Serbian democracy.

Two paradoxical elements marked the Radical program, however, both of them similar to the ones that the other parties faced.

The first was the contrast between the backwardness of the peasantry they championed and their desire for a modern society, and
the second was the necessity of achieving power if they were to
have any hope of putting their ideas into effect. In the first area
the Radicals were more conflicted than either the Liberals or the
Progressives. Nikola Pašić wrote early in his career about the inevitable coming of industry to Serbia. He knew the Serbs had to do
something about the economic forces encroaching on Serbia, and
he later spoke about the need for a progressive income tax and
even a protective tariff to help Serbia develop economically. But
the kind of economic development that such policies were designed
to encourage would threaten the traditional life-style of the Serbian
smallholder, who was the main supporter of the Radicals. For this
reason the Radicals usually tended to avoid economic issues, and
stuck to relatively safe political appeals that praised the natural
rights and abilities of the peasants. In other words, the logic of
appealing to the nation pushed the Radicals, just as it did the
Liberals and the Progressives, in the direction of purely political
programs and reforms and away from confrontation with Serbia's
economic backwardness.

The second paradox was that if the Radicals were to have any
hope of making the changes they sought, they had to join the class
of intellectuals and politicians who dominated public life, and they
had to achieve power, either by dominating the skupština or by
being appointed to cabinet positions. In other words, they had to
take control of the very state they saw as the cause of Serbia's
problems. In the period covered by this study they made a good
start in entering into the state class, but they utterly failed to achieve
power. Their efforts brought prison and exile, not power, although
in a curious way, in the long run the state's persecution of them
only enhanced the view in the peasant mind that to be a real
Serb, a rebel on behalf of the people, meant to be a Radical.
Imprisonment and harassment by the state simply proved the gen-
uineness of their claim to authenticity.

And yet, despite their program and their favoritism toward
the peasantry when they finally did achieve power, the Radicals
were not really a peasant party. With a few exceptions who never

found their way to the inner circle (for example, Ranko Tajsić), the Radical leaders were urban intellectuals. Todorović sometimes may have spoken like a man of the people rather than the sophisticated journalist from Belgrade, but he was really the latter, not the former. Pašić may have praised gunjac and opanak for building the country, but he was an engineer, not a plowboy. Jovan Djaja, Lazar Paču, Svetozar Nikolajević, Stojan Protić—all were educated abroad and found Belgrade the only place in Serbia suitable for their expanded vision. In the final analysis Radicals were bona fide members of the state class, just as were the Liberals and the Progressives. When they eventually came to power, their minds naturally focused on issues similar to those faced by any government—should relations with Russia improve, what action should be taken in Macedonia, where should loans for the military or for railroad-building be raised, and so forth. The Radicals could no more make good on their promises to rid the peasantry of the ever-growing Serbian state than they could resurrect Svetozar Marković. Instead, with power they became more and more similar to their opponents; members of the state class who competed for the favor of the king, for seats in the skupština, and for ministerial portfolios.

That the Radical leaders used organization and ideology to impress their vision on the peasantry and yet clearly remained members of the state class does not mean they were cynical manipulators. True, Nikola Pašić always kept his eye on the main chance and understood that what was really at stake was power. "Politics is measured by the yardstick of success," he said in 1880. And Todorović, after he broke with the Radicals following the Timok Rebellion, never again spoke to the peasant masses in the way he did at Kragujevac in 1882. But cynicism and calculation is the behavior of those who either have never believed in anything or have believed too much. The Radicals were as much the captives of their ideology as they were its propagators. They thought the sympathetic chord they struck with the peasants proved that they were advocating what the people really wanted. They did not look on their program as a method of gaining power, but gaining power as a method of achieving their program.[7] The Radicals had many opportunities before 1883 to take up full membership in the state class on the same terms that their predecessors had accepted. Both Ristić and the Progressives offered them the chance. But the Radicals refused. In these early years they were motivated by a strong sense of the rightness of their program, and they believed that to implement it they had to achieve power on their own, not through someone else's government. Eventually, however, they had no choice but to become members of the state class. To achieve their goals the Radicals would have to take power. If this had the result of tarnishing their principles and tempering their criticism of the state and its bureaucracy, that was a chance everyone who hopes to have an impact on public life must take.

Because of Serbia's economic backwardness, the only sphere of public life that could attract the ambitious and the able was state service. With a traditional agricultural economy, an ineffectual church, no aristocracy, a miniscule army, an undersized bureaucracy, and a weak royal apparatus, Serbian politics held out more promise to the ambitious for achieving scope, importance, and power than any other sphere of endeavor. This was already true in the 1850s and 1860s, when education provided a route to high social status in the state bureaucracy. It became even more true after the introduction of the Ristić constitution, which opened up the possibility of entering the state class through political competition. Independence raised the stakes of this competition. The small Serbian state felt it had to expand to encompass the country's new dignity, and it was forced to take on heavy obligations by the Great Powers. Serbia established and maintained embassies, built a railroad, reformed and equipped an army, concluded loans, built schools, and administered new territories.

Ballooning of the state into the overwhelmingly dominant institution in Serbian society was possible because through the course of the nineteenth century the intellectuals, bureaucrats, and other members of the educated elite of the country—which I have termed the state class—worked out a bargain with Serbia's single real social class. The state would impinge on the peasants' traditional life as little as possible, and the peasants would not object to the construction of a powerful centralized state. Neither side was able always to keep the bargain. The "exchange" of the national militia's weapons in 1883 was the most striking instance of a direct violation of the agreement, and it resulted in rebellion. But on balance, the Serbian state in the nineteenth century took few steps to disturb the traditional style of peasant life and many to preserve it. During the period discussed in this study the Law on Six Days Plowing kept farm holdings small and secure; laws slowed down the proliferation of shops in the countryside; local authorities winked when peasants broke the laws against cutting forests; speeches by Belgrade intellectuals about improving the health of the peasants by changing the way they lived were not supported by skupština action; the Progressives aligned with Austria to preserve peasant agriculture rather than face what would be a developmentally stimulating tariff war; and the administration of the new territories ensured that smallholdings would be the dominant form of land ownership in them. Even the Radicals did not favor change in the countryside. Svetozar Marković's plans to organize Serbia around the smallholding peasantry implied preserving the old ways, and in the early 1880s Radical views on economic development were not permitted to deflect the party's efforts to mobilize the peasantry. Whether the Radicals understood that the economic policies they sometimes espoused in the skupština might transform the economy in a way that would harm the smallholder and create hostility toward their party is unlikely. In any event they did not seek direct change in the countryside. They even opposed the secret ballot at the end of the 1880's because they thought it would break down the solidarity of the peasant community.

Having assured themselves of a relatively acquiescent countryside, the state class was able to construct institutions that increased its scope without having to concern itself with fundamental social change. The railroad provides a good example. Expensive, at the forefront of nineteenth-century technology, international in its implications, requiring an entirely new level of administrative sophistication, and impressively massive, the railroad brought little immediate benefit either to the Serbian peasant or to the national economy.[8] But it did force Serbia into its first large foreign loan, it did require a new bureaucracy to run it, and it did demand constant attention from the state. Not long after the line was finished, the government took over operation of the railroad from the original concessionaire and ran it as a great national project. The army was a similar institution. Expensive, requiring an extensive bureaucracy, along with the railroad technologically the most advanced segment of the Serbian economy, as the army grew it provided scope for ambitions unmatched in the rest of Serbian society.

Since the socioeconomic fact of smallholding established a framework that inhibited economic development in nineteenth-century Serbia, educated Serbs found their rewards in a sphere in which development toward modernity could take place—politics. The European-style state, which seemed to reflect Serbian socioeconomic relations so poorly, could come into being precisely because of the advantages it gave to the state class. In a way the Serbian state took the form it did, not in spite of Serbian lack of development but because of it. The willingness of the state class to leave the peasantry undeveloped left an open field for expanding the state and for finding scope and power in its service. Political struggle took place in the competition over control of the rhetoric of legitimacy, which the participants correctly perceived as being directly related to power in a system that was static socially but fluid politically. What changes did occur, such as building the railroad and creating an army, were carried out by the state for purposes of enhancing its own power and authority, thereby benefiting the state class that conducted political affairs without changing socioeconomic structures. In nineteenth-century Serbia the fundamental sphere of modernizing development was not social or economic, but political.

NOTES

NOTES TO INTRODUCTION

1. B. R. Mitchell, *European Historical Statistics, 1750–1975*, 2d revised ed. (London: Macmillan, 1981), p. 612; and Sergije Dimitrijević, *Socialistički radnički pokret u Srbiji 1870–1918* (Belgrade: Nolit, 1982), p. 21.
2. Dimitrijević, *Socialistički radnički pokret*, pp. 16–17; and Jozo Tomasevich, *Peasants, Politics, and Economic Change in Yugoslavia* (Stanford, Calif.: Stanford University Press, 1955), pp. 204–6. The Serbian situation may be contrasted with that in Hungary, for example, where in 1914 a handful of estates over 10,000 hectares constituted almost 20 percent of the land (Scott M. Eddie, "The Changing Pattern of Landownership in Hungary, 1869–1914," *The Economic History Review* 20 [1967]: 302–3), and with Croatia-Slavonia, where in 1895 the 209 largest latifundia (those above approximately 600 hectares) controlled 22.5 percent of the landed area, although their owners constituted only 0.05 percent of the rural population.
3. *Državopis Srbije* (Serbian Almanac) for 1889. The overall literacy rate was about 9 percent.
4. Gale Stokes, *Legitimacy through Liberalism: Vladimir Jovanović and the Transformation of Serbian Politics* (Seattle: University of Washington Press, 1975).
5. Using these criteria, Karl Kaser argues that the Radical Party was the only fully realized Balkan political party in the nineteenth century ("Typologie der politischen Parteien Südosteuropas im neunzehnten Jahrhundert," *Österreichische Osthefte*, 1985, pp. 331–65).
6. Serbia proclaimed itself a kingdom in 1882.

NOTES TO CHAPTER 1

1. Peter Sugar, *Southeastern Europe under Ottoman Rule, 1354–1804* (Seattle: University of Washington Press, 1977), p. 3.
2. Michael B. Petrovich, *A History of Modern Serbia* (New York: Harcourt Brace Jovanovich, 1976), 1:271.
3. For a disjointed but sympathetic sketch of Ristić see Živan Živanović, *Politička istorija Srbije u drugoj polovini devetnaestog veka* (Belgrade: Geca Kon, 1923) 4:140–88.
4. For a more detailed discussion of the quality of Ristić's liberalism and the left-Liberals' whig theory of history see Gale Stokes, *Legitimacy through Liberalism: Vladimir Jovanović and the Transformation of Serbian Politics* (Seattle: University of Washington Press, 1975).
5. David MacKenzie has called Ilija Garašanin a Balkan Bismarck, even though he shows that Garašanin never aspired to the same kind of manipulative power over his sovereign as did the Prussian original. See MacKenzie, *Ilija Garašanin: Balkan Bismarck* (Boulder, Colo.: East European Quarterly Press, 1985). In my opinion it was Ristić, not Garašanin, who aspired to that kind of control but neither was ever able to achieve it.
6. This was not accidental. Under Ristić's prodding local officials prevented the election of intellectuals, particularly left-Liberals who might advocate a constitution in which the skupština would be the main locus of power. For some specific examples of the lengths to which the government went, see Stokes, *Legitimacy through Liberalism*, pp. 158–59.
7. "The Prince is the head of the state, and as such has all the rights of state authority, which he executes according to the provisions of the constitution," read the third paragraph of the constitution *(Zbornik zakona* 22 [1869]: 31).
8. Mihailo Bjelića, "Borba za slobodu štampe u Kneževini Srbiji," *Istorijski časopis* 24 (1977): 203, cites Grgur Milovanović, *O slobodnoj štampi uopšte* (Belgrade, 1901), as his authority for the statement that the 1870 press law was based on the Austrian law of 17 Dec 62. However, the papers of Nikola Krstić, who apparently drafted the Serbian law, show that he was relying on a Prussian model (Zaostavština Nikole Krstića, SANU, 7966, "Projekt zakona o pečatnji"). Nevertheless, the main provision of the law did come from Austria, but from Bach's restrictive rules of 1851 rather than from the more liberal law of 1862. On the Prussian law see Eberhard Naujoks, *Die parlamentarische Entstehung des Reichspressegesetzes in der Bismarckzeit (1848/74)* (Düsseldorf: Droste Verlag, 1975), and for the Aus-

trian laws see Marianne Lunzer, *Der Versuch einer Presselenkung in Öster-reich 1848–1870* (Vienna, 1954).

9. This example suggests that the similarly thoroughgoing laws of press responsibility in the socialist countries of Southeastern Europe after 1945, and by extension perhaps other failings of civil liberties as well, cannot be laid exclusively at the door of Leninism.

10. "[The law] has enough guarantees [to maintain] order," Ristić commented laconically in J. Ristić to F. Hristić, 10/22 Nov 70, *Pisma Jovana Ristića Filipu Hristiću* (Belgrade: SKA, 1931), p. 5.

11. Živanović, *Politička istorija Srbije*, 1:248.

12. Jaša M. Prodanović, *Istorija političkih stranaka i struja u Srbiji* (Belgrade: Prosveta, 1947), p. 254.

13. Ibid., p. 339. Ristić dominated the regency period, but a caretaker government composed of his allies and friends, the closest of which was Milojković, ran the ordinary affairs of state.

14. Six weeks before the trip an agent of Benjamin Kállay, the Austrian consul in Belgrade, reported that Blaznavac had said he "was watching every step of Ristić carefully, and as soon as he decided to treat with the Russians, he [Blaznavac] was prepared to put Ristić in jail" *(Dnevnik Kalaja*, 5 Sep 71, p. 401). Blaznavac spent most of the next year trying to explain to Kállay why, in that case, the trip actually occurred.

15. Prodanović, *Istorija političkih stranaka*, p. 346.

16. Despite his dominance, Ristić was always careful to keep his relationship with Blaznavac on a formal level of complete equality. See his letter to Filip Hristić of 28 Aug/9 Sep 73, which describes also the preparations among Blaznavac, Ristić, and Milojković for the prince's majority *(Pisma Ristića Hristiću*, pp. 146–48).

17. Blaznavac died from what Slobodan Jovanović calls *angina Ludewighii*, a condition from which an operation even then could have saved him. His conservative doctor, whose name was Mašin, either did not know the procedure or was afraid to operate. Dr. Mašin was also physician to Prince Milan, who immediately fired him *(Dnevnik Kalaja*, 6 Apr 73, p. 526). Vladan Djordjević was the first physician in Serbia to use up-to-date surgical techniques (VMO, 1:284–85).

18. Garašanin to Marinović, 3/15, 5/17 Apr 73, *Pisma Ilije Garašanina Jovanu Marinoviću*, 2 (Belgrade: SKA, 1931): 321, 322; and *Dnevnik Kalaja*, 13 Apr 73, p. 528.

19. Živanović, *Politička istorija Srbije*, 1:273.

20. Kállay reported that Ristić included Grujić on his first list of cabinet members, but that the prince, in front of an "ashen" Ristić, tore the list

up *(Dnevnik Kalaja,* p. 785). Jovan Milićević accepts Živanović's version that Grujić turned the offer down (Jovan Milićević, *Jevrem Grujić: Istorijat svetoandrejskog liberalizma* [Belgrade: Nolit, 1964], p. 205; and Živanović, *Politička istorija Srbije,* 1:274).

21. Živanović, *Politička istorija Srbije,* 1:275; and J. Ristić to F. Hristić, 26 Apr/ 8 May 73, *Pisma Ristića Hristiću,* p. 220. Garašanin believed Ristić just wanted to be surrounded by people he could order around (Garašanin to Marinović, 11/23 Apr 73, *Pisma Garašanina Marinoviću,* 2:327).

22. See Gale Stokes, "Prince Milan and the Serbian Army before World War I," in Béla Király and Nándor F. Dreisziger eds., *East Central European Society in World War I* (Boulder, Colo.: East European Quarterly Press; New York: distributed by Columbia University Press, War and Society in East Central Europe, vol. 19, 1985), pp. 555–68.

23. Ristić to Hristić, 25 Jan/6 Feb 73, *Pisma Ristića Hristiću,* p. 193; and VMO, 1:290–92.

24. Živanović, *Politička istorija Srbije,* 1:275. His disgust must have been tempered by the success of his overtures and by the cordiality of Andrássy, who Ristić said received him with as much attentiveness as if he had been a member of the English government (Ristić to Hristić, 26 Apr/8 May 73, *Pisma Ristića Hristiću,* p. 221). For Kállay's analysis, see *Dnevnik Kalaja,* 17 Apr 73, pp. 529–30.

25. John Lampe, "Serbia 1878–1912," in Rondo Cameron, ed., *Banking and Economic Development: Some Lessons of History* (New York: Oxford University Press, 1972), p. 136. On banking in Serbia see Lampe's doctoral dissertation, "Financial Structure and the Economic Development of Serbia, 1878–1912" (University of Wisconsin, 1971).

26. "I'd like to ask you a favor," Ristić wrote Hristić on 28 Aug/9 Sep 73, "and that is not to give us advice over personal questions that have no connections with your work. You are far away, and one should not entrust everything to paper." On 26 Apr/8 May 73, he wrote, "Observing from afar you have proposed this and that, as if you had never lived in Serbia. You wanted some sort of coalition, but you are forgetting that that is the weakest government, and you forget that here no one will give first position to anyone else" *(Pisma Ristića Hristiću,* pp. 148, 220).

27. When Hristić returned he sent his brother-in-law a nice pair of boots as a gift. But Ristić, aware of Hristić's double-dealing, returned them with the comment that they were too well shod to accept. A Serbian proverb, "Potkovati nekome opanke" (to nail horseshoes to somebody's sandals), means to plot against someone (Živanović, *Politička istorija Srbije,* 1:277).

28. Milan's first impulse, apparently, was to write a letter similar to the one

Prince Michael supposedly wrote to Ristić in 1867 when he called Ristić "obstinate and hateful." Ristić's opponents published this letter in 1874, but he always denied its authenticity. Marinović claimed to have seen the letter the day Ristić received it, but its provenance remains uncertain since the original apparently is not extant. For a copy of the letter see *Dnevnik Kalaja*, p. 794. See also ibid., pp. 579–80.

29. *Pisma Garašanina Marinoviću*, 1:xvi–xviii.

30. VMO, 1:313.

31. Ristić thought very highly of Mijatović. In 1872, when Mijatović was in England, Ristić wrote that he would already be minister of education if he were not abroad (Ristić to F. Hristić, 26 Nov/7 Dec 72, *Pisma Ristića Hristiću*, pp. 163–64). Therefore, Ristić was not amused when Mijatović, alleging that Marinović's line would closely follow Ristić's and that duty to the prince's call obliged him to accept, took the cabinet position (AJR, I/30 1/125, Mijatović to Ristić, undated, but 1873).

32. On Čumić see VMO, 1:91, 222–24, 312–15, 332–34, 382–83, 519–23.

33. Ristić said that "only a few professors, such as Čumić, Pavlović and people around Kaljević, want members of the senate to be elected by the people, but they do not constitute a party" *(Dnevnik Kalaja, 29 Dec 69, p. 135)*. Even Čumić later said he would support the government, however (ibid., 31 Dec 69, p. 137).

34. The vote was overwhelming, according to Kállay's information *(Dnevnik Kalaja, 5 Jan 71, p. 353)*.

35. See Ristić to Hristić, 23 Feb/7 Mar 71, 9/21 Mar 71, 26 Apr/8 May 71, *Pisma Ristića Hristiću*, pp. 32–34, 48.

36. Paja Mihailović's diaries, book 11, AJR. The proposal appears also in *Oslobodjenje*, 31 Jan/12 Feb 75. It was signed by Djoka Vlajković, Aćim Čumić, Pavle K. (Paja) Mihailović, Jevrem Marković, and on some copies, Vaso Pelagić.

37. Čumić ran in four cities. In Belgrade the government brought in ringers, such as night guards, to vote, and counted votes given for "Aćim" as being for the government's candidate Jovan Aćimović (VMO, 1:140).

38. On his contempt citation, see letter of 28 Sep/9 Oct 72, AJR, 3/1497 III/ 23. On Kállay's affair with Čumić's wife, see *Dnevik Kalaja*, pp. 369, 373, 427, 481, 503, as well as other pages cited in the index. Through all of 1872 Kállay rented a small house where he and Čumićka could meet.

39. Prodanović, *Istorija političkih stranaka*, pp. 353–54.

40. *Protokoli*, pp. 9–12. Milan said that he was happy to entrust the government to persons "whose loyalty toward the Obrenović dynasty is for me beyond any doubt" (Prodanović, *Istorija političkih stranaka*, p. 351).

Obviously, the prince did not always have such confidence in his previous minister, Jovan Ristić.

41. *Protokoli,* p. 45.

42. *Protokoli,* pp. 36–51.

43. *Protokoli,* p. 713.

44. Prodanović, *Istorija političkih stranaka,* p. 358.

45. Krstić, who was the author of the original press law of 1870, took considerable satisfaction in Kaljević's defeat, for which he took credit (Bjelića, "Borba za slobodu štampe," p. 206).

46. Živanović, *Politička istorija Srbije,* 1:286.

47. VMO, 1:317.

48. *Zbornik zakona* 26 (1874): 60–63.

49. See the discussion in *Istok* a year later, 22 Dec 74/3 Jan 75. Ljubomir Kaljević also favored an import tax *(Dnevnik Kalaja,* p. 804).

50. For traditional Serbian measures in metric equivalents see *Zbornik zakona* 26 (1874): 19–20.

51. *Dnevnik Kalaja,* 27 Mar 74, p. 581.

52. Michael R. Palairet, "Farming in Serbia c. 1830–1875: Impoverishment Without the Help of Malthus," forthcoming from the East European Program of the Woodrow Wilson Center, Washington, D.C.

53. Complaints that "the rich always win, the poor always lose," brought Čumić into the debate for one of the few times in this session, even though Marinović had brought him into the government in part to speak for the government on the floor of the assembly. Using the full weight of his booming voice, Čumić told the legislators, among other things, that if they interfered in the independence of the courts, they would be no better than Janissaries. "But we have no other place to express ourselves," responded one delegate, "except here in the national skupština." Čumić, having scared the delegates more than convincing them, apologized *(Protokoli,* pp. 233–48).

54. The skupština presented a list of 6 candidates, consisting of those who received the most votes in a skupština ballot, from whom the prince chose the presiding officer.

55. Krstić's diary, 13/25 Dec 74.

56. See, e.g., Kállay's comments of 4 Apr, 21 May, 26 Jun, 4 Sep 74 *(Dnevnik Kalaja,* pp. 585, 797, 799–800, 604).

57. Mali Zvornik was a small enclave on the eastern side of the Drina that the sultan so far had refused to cede to Serbia.

58. Slobodan Jovanović, "Carigradski put Kneza Milana," *Srpski književni glasnik,* n.s., 16 (1925): 44–49.

59. In one of his efforts to undermine Marinović, Ristić had his agents spread rumors that he and the prince had agreed that Ristić should take some time off to rest in order to show the people that others could not run the government as well as Ristić. Kállay believed rumors like this had an effect on the peasants, to whom such plotting seemed plausible, and who, therefore, hesitated to support Marinović *(Dnevnik Kalaja, 27 Mar 74, p. 581)*. Kállay reported also that Ristić seemed very well informed on what went on in Istanbul, and shortly after the prince's return had already formed a shadow group of Liberals who would work with him in any new government. These included Jevrem Grujić, Stevča Mihailović (a Liberal war-horse from 1858 and a Karadjordjević supporter), and Radivoje Milojković *(Dnevnik Kalaja, 13 Jun 74, p. 590)*.

60. Živanović, *Politička istorija Srbije*, 1:293.

61. Milan was not a rich man for royalty, in part because he had not inherited Prince Michael's fortune, but he did have a personal income of about 14,000 dukats a year, and his civil list was 40,000 dukats annually. But Milan had a passion, indeed an illness, for spending money. By 1874 he was only twenty years old, but he had already gone through all of his capital and was starting a lifelong habit of extensive borrowing. His insatiable need for money made the question of his marriage important from the financial as well as the political point of view *(Dnevnik Kalaja, pp. 795–97)*.

62. Report of Kállay to Andrássy, *Dnevnik Kalaja*, p. 796.

63. Ristić is supposed to have commented, "Religious people are beginning to fear that they will wake up one morning to find the Belgrade Cathedral *(saborna crkva)* opened as a tavern *(mehana)* first class" (VMO, 1:368).

64. N. Krstić to K. Cukić, 30 Jul/11 Aug 74, SANU 7966. Krstić was a staunch conservative (as was Cukić, Serbia's new representative in Vienna), but he deplored Čumić's heavy-handed frame-up, and thought he should resign. See also Krstić to Čumić, 26 Aug/7 Sep 74, SANV 7966.

65. *Istok* began publication in 1871 in Vršac (Austria-Hungary), but quickly came to Belgrade, almost certainly with a subsidy from Ristić *(Staro oslobodjenje, 10/22 Dec 75)*. Under the regency it supported the government, but when Marinović was in power Ristić turned it into a rallying point for his Liberals. *Budućnost* (The Future), edited by Uroš Knežević, was another Liberal paper.

66. *Istok*, 27 Jun/9 Jul 74. For a discussion of Serbia's role as Piedmont see also 17/29 Nov 74, 5/17 Jan 75.

67. Kállay reported that Milan's extravagances on this trip had surpassed all bounds. Obsessed with uniforms, Milan had spent 25,000 francs in Paris

on clothing alone, even though in the previous 17 months he had paid his Vienna tailor 17,000 forints for uniforms. After he wore a uniform once or twice he would send the "used" outfit to a relative in Austria who made a handsome living reselling the splendid castoffs. When he visited Victor Emmanuel II on this trip, Milan and his staff dressed in their most elaborate uniforms, only to be kept waiting a half hour by the frugal king. Victor Emmanuel eventually appeared in a sweater and coolly informed Milan he wished the Serbian prince had done the same. "The prince will not grasp the seriousness of the situation," commented Kállay *(Dnevnik Kalaja,* 27 Oct 74, p. 612).

68. "In significant measure, he himself brought on the inflamed party passions in the elections of 1874 by his personal involvement," said Slobodan Jovanović (VMO, 1:371).

69. See, e.g., *Istok,* 21 Nov/2 Dec 74. The Liberals believed there should be organized parties, *Istok* reported, and that is how they went to the polls—based on principles. "Political societies without a program and without political leaders are without significance," said Nikola Krstić (Krstić to Cukić, 7/19 Feb 75, SANU, 1966).

70. Two who did not agree were the French consul, who reported that Marinović was stronger than ever *(Dnevnik Kalaja,* 5 Dec 74, p. 619), and Čumić himself, who seemed to think initially that only government people were elected ("Memoari Alimpije Vasiljevića, AS:PO-102-136, p. 49).

71. *Istok,* 26 Oct/7 Nov 74.

72. This report came to Kállay from the none too reliable journalist, Dr. Mihailo Rosen, who was on close terms with the Conservatives *(Dnevnik Kalaja,* 11 Nov 74, p. 615).

73. Krstić's diary, 30 Oct/11 Nov 74.

74. Slobodan Jovanović calls Topuzović a Conservative, but *Istok* listed him among the 18 victorious Liberal candidates. Krsmanović was not listed (VMO, 1:373).

75. *Protokoli,* p. 15. The skupština greeted the prince with cheers, but his speech with silence, because it was "quite cold, without any elaborated phrases" (Krstić's diary, 10/22 Nov 74).

76. Krstić's diary, 10/22 Nov 74.

77. The four were Milan Kujundžić, Uroš Knežević, an excitable journalist, and two men who quickly became identified as populists, Milija Milićević and Adam Bogosavljević *(Srpske novine,* 13/25 Nov 74). Milan Dj. Milićević, a moderate journalist, was elected at first, but had to decline because of poor health (Milićević's diary, 9/21 Nov 74, SANU, 9327/6).

78. Krstić's diary, 11 Nov 74, p. 615; and *Protokoli*, pp. 14–15.
79. SB, 1874, p. 59; *Dnevnik Kalaja*, p. 617; and Krstić's diary, 14/26 Nov 74.
80. The committee, which was elected directly by the skupština, contained several prominent opposition members, such as Glišić, Kujundžić, Knežević, and Sima Nestorović, but only a few prominent Conservatives (*Protokoli*, pp. 27–30).
81. Ironically, Kujundžić was one of the government's own appointees who had been left on the prince's list through Čumić's incompetence (Krstić's diary, 24 Nov/6 Dec 74).
82. *Istok*, 24 Nov/5 Dec 74.
83. SB, 1874, p. 89.
84. Even Nikola Krstić, who spoke vigorously in favor of the government in the skupština, believed that its position was "strange" (N. Krstić to K. Cukić, 22 Dec 74/3 Jan 75, SANU, 7966).
85. SB, 1874, pp. 92–93. *Istok* often interpreted events in the light of its goal of parliamentary government. When several Liberals were among Milan's appointees to the skupština, for example, it piously (as well as inaccurately) exclaimed that they showed the "strictly constitutional . . . conviction of our ruler, who showed his readiness thereby to [make Serbia] . . . a purely parliamentary land," and reported that with the choice of Topuzović and Grujić as president and vice president "the skupština has legitimized itself as the true agent of the national current in Serbia" (14/26 Nov 74).
86. SB, 1874, pp. 103–4.
87. SB, 1874, pp. 105–12. To the Conservatives this outburst confirmed the danger of permitting open discussions in the skupština. They feared that a runaway skupština would overthrow the prince, as it had in 1858 (see, e.g., Milićević's diary, 22 Nov/3 Dec 74, SANU, 9327/6). "Such are the motives that rule the majority," clucked Krstić (Krstić's diary, 21 Nov/3 Dec 74).
88. Of the 61 votes for the government, 28 were from its appointed delegates. Only 3 of the appointees voted for the opposition (Krstić's diary, 22 Nov/4 Dec 74).
89. "Marinović really was inclined to continue his work," Nikola Krstić wrote to Kosta Cukić later. Krstić was working on changes in the press law for Marinović (N. Krstić to K. Cukić, 7/19 Nov 74, and "Sveti Jovan," 1875, SANU, 7966).
90. Marinović was convinced Čumić had plotted against him (Krstić's diary, 26 Nov/8 Dec 74; and *Dnevnik Kalaja*, 9 Dec 74).
91. Milan to Marinović, 23 Nov/5 Dec 74, SANU, 8814/22.

92. Krstić wrote to Cukić that there were no consultations with Marinović's or Čumić's supporters concerning either the resignations or the appointment of the new government. Krstić felt that Marinović did not do all he could have to ensure his government's success (letter of 22 Dec 74/3 Jan 75, SANU, 7966).

93. On 17 Nov 74 Dr. Rosen reported to Kállay that Čumić had said he could stay in the government only if the address from the throne included promises of a free press, imprisonment only on court judgment, greater autonomy for opštinas, and other similar demands, as well as the firing of Filip Hristić, minister of education and church affairs (*Dnevnik Kalaja*, p. 616). These ideas were very similar to the ones expressed in the socialist manifesto Čumić signed in 1871, as well as to the promises he made to the skupština when he became minister president.

94. Milićević's diary, 25 Nov/6 Dec, 18/30 Dec 74; *Dnevnik Kalaja,* 7 Dec 74, p. 620; and Krstić's diary, 25 Nov/7 Dec 74.

95. Marinović's friends found Kaljević's inclusion a particularly bitter pill to swallow, not only because of Čumić's earlier complaints about Marinović's "fusionism," but because they believed Kaljević to have been implicated in the plot to assassinate Prince Michael (Krstić's diary, 26 Nov/8 Dec 74). Concerning this possibility, which is not at all farfetched, see Stokes, *Legitimacy through Liberalism,* pp. 141–45.

NOTES TO CHAPTER 2

1. Svetozar's father, Radoje, was a clerk to the načelnik of the srez (chief administrator of the region) in which Zaječar was the main city. He married the načelnik's daughter, and had six children with her. When both his mother and father died, Svetozar (age six) and the others were sent to a foster home in Jagodina, where they grew up. By the standards of his day Radoje Marković was moderately wealthy by reason of his government job. In 1858 a listing of his estate showed a worth of 18,860 groš on assets of a house, two small shops on the market square in Zaječar, and two small fields, one near Zaječar and one near Gamzigrad. See Svetislav Prvanović, *Timok i Timočani* (Zaječar: Razvitak, 1963), pp. 49–62.

2. The literature on Svetozar Marković, who is almost a national hero in Serbia, has become enormous. Still standard are Jovan Skerlić, *Svetozar Marković, njegov život, rad i ideje* (Belgrade: Prosveta, 1966, orig. pub. 1910); Slobodan Jovanović, "Svetozar Marković," *"Političke i pravne rasprave,* 1 (Belgrade: Geca Kon, 1932, orig. pub. 1903): 61–298; and

Woodford McClellan, *Svetozar Marković and the Origins of Balkan Socialism* (Princeton, N.J.: Princeton University Press, 1964). The most accessible collection of Marković's writings is *Sabrani spisi*, vol. 1, ed. Najdan Pašić (Belgrade: Kultura, 1960), and vols. 2–4, ed. Radovan Blagojević (Belgrade: Prosveta, 1965). An interesting illustrated edition containing many rare photographs is Djordje Mitrović and Savo Andrić, *Svetozar Marković i njegovo doba* (Belgrade: Rad, 1978).

3. On Marković's stay in Russia see Gale Stokes, "Svetozar Marković in Russia," *Slavic Review* 31 (1972): 611–25.

4. McClellan, *Svetozar Marković*, pp. 77, 119, 188, 200, 212, 215.

5. *Sabrani spisi*, 1:153–86.

6. Djura Ljočić was the first Serbian student at the Zürich Polytechnicum, where he studied railroad engineering. He entered private practice in Belgrade, quitting *Radnik* before it was banned to concentrate on his work. He became a wealthy man, but eventually squandered his fortune in pursuit of younger women after he turned fifty. See the fascinating Jeremija D. Mitrović, "Djura Ljočić," *Zbornik Istorijskog muzeja Srbije* 13–14 (1977): 105–128.

7. Pera Velimirović was also an engineering student. Convicted of political agitation in 1875, he lived in exile until 1880, when he returned as one of the founding members of the Radical Party. In 1883 he fled again into exile but later in the decade he returned to become perhaps Serbia's most able minister of public works of the nineteenth century.

8. Skerlić, *Svetozar Marković*, p. 43.

9. Marković, *Sabrani spisi*, 2:126–27.

10. On Marković and the Omladina, see Stokes, *Legitimacy through Liberalism*, pp. 180–215, and Dušan Nedeljković, ed., *Svetozar Marković, Omladina i Marksizam* (Belgrade: SANU, Naučni skupovi knj. 14, Odeljenje društvenih nauka knj. 4, 1982); and Andrija Radenić, "Svetozar Marković i Ujedinjena omladina," in Živan Milisavac, ed., *Ujedinjena omladina srpska: zbornik radova* (Novi Sad and Belgrade: Matica srpska and Istorijski institut, 1968), pp. 105–32.

11. Marković was close to the student society *Pobratimstvo* (Blood Brotherhood), which was banned in the spring of 1872 because of the same disturbance mentioned in chapter 1 involving the replacement of Čumić (when he became kmet of Belgrade) with a professor who did not have the approval of the faculty senate.

12. McClellan, *Svetozar Marković*, pp. 105–19; and *Sabrani spisi*, 1:225–361.

13. McClellan, *Svetozar Marković*, p. 107; and *Sabrani spisi*, 1:284.

14. For an excellent discussion of morality as the basis for the thought of Mar-

ković and other Radicals in the 1860s and 1870s see Ellen Claire Hadidian, "A Comparison of the Thought of Early Bulgarian and Serbian Radicals, 1867–1876," Ph.D. diss. (University of Wisconsin at Madison, 1980).

15. *Sabrani spisi,* 3:123–221. Published in 1872, this work was an extended treatment of the ideas presented to the Omladina congress in 1870.

16. The opština was actually only the name for the smallest unit of administration and in Serbia had no implications concerning ownership. Marković was probably thinking of the Russian *mir,* with which he was familiar through Russian populism. See the discussion of the opština in chapter 3.

17. Marković always had a far too rosy notion of the actual role of the Sovjet in the First Serbian Uprising. The most contemporary interpretation of the First Serbian Uprising is Wayne S. Vucinich, ed., *The First Serbian Uprising, 1804–1813* (Boulder, Colo.: Social Science Monographs; New York: distributed by Columbia University Press, War and Society in East Central Europe, vol. 8, 1982).

18. The supposition that the peasantry was ready to rise in revolt formed the basis not only of radical ideas in the 1870s, but of official Serbian military doctrine as well. See Gale Stokes, "Serbian Military Doctrine and the Crisis of 1875–78," in Béla Király and Gale Stokes, eds., *Insurrections, Wars, and the Eastern Crisis in the 1870s* (Boulder Colo.: Social Science Monographs; New York: distributed by Columbia University Press, War and Society in East Central Europe, vol. 17, 1985), pp. 261–75.

19. Vaso Vojvodić, "Spomenica Miletićeve 'Srpske narodne slobodoumne stranke' i 'Glavnog odbora za srpsko oslobodjenje' kneževskom namesništvu u Srbiji o dizanju ustanka na Balkanu 1872," in Dušan Nedeljković, ed., *Naučni skup Svetozar Marković: Život i delo* (Belgrade: SANU, Naučni skupovi knj. 5, Odeljenje društvenih nauka knj. 3, 1977), p. 469. Vojvodić's article gives an excellent summary of Radical efforts to foment an uprising in 1871 and 1872 and of the sizable literature that has grown up around the question. See also docs. 115, 118–24 in V. N. Kondratjeva and Nikola Petrović, eds., *Ujedinjena omladina srpska i njeno doba, 1860–1875: Gradja iz sovjetskih arhiva* (Novi Sad and Moscow: Matica srpska and Institut slavianovedeniia i balkanistiki AN SSSR, 1977).

20. Vaso Čubrilović, *Politička misao u Srbiji XIX. veka* (Belgrade: Prosveta, 1958), p. 338.

21. Marković to Pašić, 2/14 Oct 72 (Novi Sad), Škorić collection, doc. 28. "I will probably be imprisoned in Požarevac [he was right, but in 1874], where prison is sufficiently bearable [he was wrong—it killed him]. . . . It makes no sense to stay here [i.e., in Novi Sad]. . . . If it were only a

question of earning a living, I could find a job here. . . . But that is not for me. *My work is in Serbia.* I have thought it over for a long time. In fact, I think mostly about that, and I have no other course" (letter to the Ninković sisters, 8/20 Jan 73 in Skerlić, *Svetozar Marković*, pp. 107–8).

22. Miroslav D. Popović, *Kragujevac i njegovo privredno područje* (Belgrade: SANU, Posebna izdanja knj. 246, Geografski institut knj. 8, 1956).

23. See the article "Topolovnica" in Stanoje Stanojević, *Narodna enciklopedija srpsko-hrvatsko-slovenačka* (Zagreb: Bibliografski zavod, 1928–29).

24. Vojvodić, "Spomenica Militićeve stranke," pp. 457–58, 466–67; Kondratjeva and Petrović, *Ujedinjena omladina srpska*, docs. 120–21; *Oslobodjenje*, 21 Jan/12 Feb 75; and Milorad Ekmečić, *Ustanak u Bosni 1875–78* (Sarajevo: Veselin Masleša, 1973), p. 64. The committee included Sava Grujić and wrote a statute of 23 paragraphs. In 1872 Jevrem was also laying plans for training Bulgarian officers in Serbia to assist with a Balkan-wide uprising (Hadidian, "Thought of Early Bulgarian and Serbian Radicals," p. 58n). This idea was similar to Prince Michael's Bulgarian Legion, which Jevrem had commanded.

25. Skerlić, *Svetozar Marković*, pp. 113–14; and Živanović, *Politička istorija*, 1:288. The society that created the press contained 101 persons (Živomir Spasić, "Uticaj Svetozara Markovića na srednjoškolsku omladinu u Kragujevcu [1874–1876]," in Nedeljković, ed., *Svetozar Marković, omladina i marksizam*, p. 130).

26. As in Germany at this time, the substantive editor of a newspaper was not usually its "responsible editor." The latter was the person who was legally responsible for the contents of the paper, whether he actually controlled it or not. Sometimes persons were hired for this position with the expectation that they would have to spend some time in jail for breaches of the press law in order to protect the political figure behind the paper. Dimitrije Stojković was the responsible editor of *Javnost.*

27. *Javnost* had 1,336 subscribers at its peak in 1874, a very high number for the time (Mitrović and Andrić, *Marković i njegovo doba*, p. 166).

28. Skerlić, *Svetozar Marković*, p. 111.

29. *Sabrani spisi*, 3:235–36; and McClellan, *Svetozar Marković*, pp. 203–4.

30. *Sabrani spisi*, 3:244, from *Javnost*, 20 Nov/2 Dec 73. Here, and in the following paragraphs, the italics indicate the specific passages for which Marković was sent to jail early in 1874. On Marković's trial, defense, and judgment, see Dragoje M. Todorović, *Sudjenje Svetozaru Markoviću* (Belgrade: Rad, 1974).

31. *Sabrani spisi*, 3:259–60, from *Javnost*, 17/29 Dec 73. The order of sentences has been rearranged. The word *favor* is italicized in the original.

32. *Sabrani spisi,* 3:262, from *Javnost,* 28 Nov/10 Dec 73.

33. *Sabrani spisi,* 3:274, from *Javnost,* 16/28 Dec 73.

34. McClellan is correct when he says Marković opposed the law, but errs when he says Marković found the arguments "in defense of it" worthless *(Svetozar Marković,* p. 220). Actually, Marković said "the main arguments which I heard in the skupština against this law, in my opinion, are worthless. And yet I still hold that this law will not insure national welfare in the future" *(Sabrani spisi,* 3:271).

35. VMO, 1:347, 369; *Sabrani spisi,* 3:267.

36. Todorović, *Sudjenje Markoviću,* p. 35, from *Javnost,* 29 Dec 73/10 Dec 74.

37. The correct term to apply to Marković (radical, socialist, uptopian, Marxist, narodnik with Marxist tendencies, or eclectic thinker) has been a main theme of all Marković scholarship. For a brief but clear exposition of this historiography, see Andrija Stojković, "Da li Svetozar Marković marksist," in Nedeljković, *Svetozar Marković, omladina i marksizam,* pp. 229–41.

38. On the zadruga see Robert F. Byrnes, ed., *Communal Families in the Balkans: The Zadruga* (Notre Dame, Ind.: Notre Dame University Press, 1976).

39. His articles "Opština," "Srez," "Srez i sreska uprava," "Sud i prava," "Sud," and "Financija," began appearing in *Javnost* in March, continued in *Glas javnosti* in August, and were completed in *Oslobodjenje* in January. They may be found in *Sabrani Spisi,* vols. 3, 4.

40. See Marković, "Narodna skupština," *Sabrani spisi,* 4:75–93, originally appearing in *Glas javnosti,* August and September 1874.

41. "Narodno pitanje," *Oslobodjenje,* 18/30 Jan through 26 Jan/7 Feb 75. See also "Opozicija u skupštini," 29 Jan/10 Feb; "Predlog za izmenu ustava," opposing Milutin Garašanin's conservative proposal, 2/14 Feb; and "Narodna partija," 5/17 Feb 75. These proposals did not differ greatly from the proposals of left-Liberals like Ljubomir Kaljević and were undoubtedly inspired by debate over the constitution then going on between the Conservatives and the Liberals in the skupština.

42. On Todorović see Velizar Ninčić, *Pera Todorović* (Belgrade: Nolit, 1956); Latinka Perović, *Pera Todorović* (Belgrade: Rad, 1983); and Slobodan Jovanović, "Pera Todorović," *Sabrana dela Slobodana Jovanovića. Političke i pravne rasprave* (Belgrade: Geca Kon, 1932), 1:301–403.

43. Perović, p. 20, quoting Lenka Zah-Paču, who knew Todorović in Zürich *(Samouprava,* 22 Jan 1937).

44. Sava Grujić, *Vojna organizacija Srbije* (Kragujevac: Kragujevačka društvena štamparija, 1874).

45. The original *Glas javnosti* began publishing 15/27 Jul 74 and shut down 1/19 Sep 74. Its non-Radical successor reopened 20 Oct/1 Nov 74, only to peter out before the end of the year (4/16 Dec 74 [*Crveni barjak*, 1:335]). *Istok* praised the non-Radical *Glas javnosti's* "decidedly healthy program," and congratulated the citizens of Kragujevac for "shaking off the foolishness [that] . . . was spreading communist principles" (6/18 Nov 74).

46. In "Sećanja Dj. Lazarevića na Nik. P. Pašića," in *Nikola P. Pašić* (Belgrade: Samouprava, 1938), Pašić's father is referred to as a baker (p. 228), but usually he is simply called a merchant.

47. The literature on Pašić is much less extensive than one would expect for such an important historical figure. Only in the last few years have the first serious studies based on primary sources appeared. They are two books by Djordje Dj. Stanković, *Nikola Pašić i jugoslovensko pitanje*, vol. 1 (Belgrade: Beogradski izdavačko–grafički zavod, 1985), which is broader than its title suggests, and *Nikola Pašić, saveznici, i stvaranje Jugoslavije* (Belgrade: Nolit, 1984). The earliest journalistic effort was Count Carlo Sforza, *Fifty Years of War and Diplomacy in the Balkans: Pashich and the Union of the Yugoslavs* (New York: Columbia University Press, 1940). Interesting but brief is Slobodan Jovanović *Moji savremenici* (Windsor, Canada: Avala, 1963). Alex N. Dragnich, *Serbia, Nikola Pašić, and Yugoslavia* (New Brunswick, N.J.: Rutgers University Press, 1974) is apologetic, and Momčilo Vuković-Birčanin, *Nikola Pašić 1845–1926* (Munich: by the author, 1978) is none too reliable. The most authoritative North American scholar on the young Pašić is Sofija Škorić of Toronto, but unfortunately Škorić has published most of her work only as typescripts or conference papers, except for "The Populism of Nikola Pašić: The Zürich Period," *East European Quarterly* 14 (1980): 469–85. For a discussion of these and other sources see Stanković, *Pašić i jugoslovensko pitanje*, 1:11–30. Because of the lack of primary data on this most important figure, I have annotated his youthful activities more extensively than might otherwise be required.

48. In the fall of 1867 competition to select six students, there were twenty-six applicants. The second Serbian student to study in Zürich, Čedomil Mijatović, was a member of the commission that selected Pašić, who had completed "three years of technical studies at our Velika škola with very good success." When his selection was approved in February 1868 Pašić signed the normal agreement by which he agreed to serve the state in his profession for the same number of years that he received his training (AS:MPS-1862-V-66: Min. Pros. to Rektor Vš 8/20 Dec 67; Vš selection

committee 12/24 Dec 67; Pašić's agreement 22 Feb/6 Mar 68; and Min. Pros. final approval 27 Feb 11 Mar 68). At this time Serbia had thirty-three students studying abroad, only four of whom were in engineering, the same number as in theology. Nine were studying medicine, eight law, and one each in philosophy, history, mining, forestry, economic administration, painting (the trade, not the art), natural sciences, and Turkish (ibid., report of 31 Oct/12 Nov 67).

49. For an excellent history of liberalism in Zürich, see Gordon A. Craig, *The Triumph of Liberalism: Zürich in the Golden Age, 1830–1869)* (New York: Charles Scribners' Sons, 1988). See also Karl Dändliker, *Geschichte der Schweiz* (Zürich: Schulthess, 1904), pp. 753–65.

50. Pašić to Min. Pros., 14/26 Mar 68. The minister turned down the request 23 Mar/4 Apr 68 (AS:MPS-1873-IV-53). Pašić arrived in Zürich on about 12 Mar 68 (Velimirović to Min. Pros., 12 Mar 68 [AS:MPS-1873-V-66]).

51. Information on the neighborhood in which the young Serbs lived is from Werner G. Zimmermann, "Südslavische Studenten in Zürich. Ein Beitrag zur Auswertung lokalen Quellenmaterials," in Richard George Plaschka and Karlheinz Mack, eds., *Wegenetz Europäischen Geistes* (Vienna: Schriftenreihe des Österreichischen Ost- und Südosteuropa-Instituts, band 8, 1983), pp. 326–37. Dr. Zimmermann lists sixty-seven Serbs who matriculated either at the Polytechnikum or the University of Zürich for the decade following the arrival of the first Serbian student in 1863. These included, besides Svetozar Marković, nine persons who later were ministers in Serbian government and the first Serbian woman to become a doctor of medicine, indeed, one of the first women in the world to complete a fully recognized course of university study for that degree, Draga Ljočić, the sister of Djura Ljočić and later wife of Raša Milošević.

52. In his memoirs the Swiss socialist Hermann Greulich mentions Pašić's presence at a meeting of "die Wilde Sektion" of the International (so called because it contained members from all over Eastern Europe). It consisted largely of Serbs, among them Pašić. Greulich reported that "they gave speeches in Serbian, of which I understood only the word revolution." Greulich continued that under the circumstances he thought it well "not to call any more meetings for the time being" (Zimmermann, p. 11, quoting *Das Grüne Hüsli. Erinnerungen von Hermann Greulich* [Zürich, 1942], pp. 52, 55).

53. These pocket notebooks are in the archive of SANU under inventory number 11721. They contain fragmentary and often enigmatic notes, summaries of letters, and lists, some as late as 1893. An undated page lists ten persons as "members of the society" in "January." The list can

be positively dated as 1871 by the matriculation dates of the students (Zimmermann, p. 330).

54. Škorić, "Populism of Nikola Pašić," p. 477; and Ljubica Ljotić, *Memoari* (Munich: Iskra, 1973), pp. 55–56. See also Aleksandr Vučićević, "Mladost i školovanje jednoga državnika," *Samouprava*, 5–9 Jan 1937, reprinted from *Politika*, 1927, which contains valuable personal recollections of Svetozar Vidaković, a youthful colleague of Pašić. Vidaković said that the printing press was the same one used by Vladimir Jovanović in the 1860s to publish *Sloboda*. Jovanović in turn had purchased the press with a loan from Alexander Herzen (Stokes, *Legitimacy through Liberalism*, p. 71).

55. Pašić to Ljotić, 2 Jul 70, AS:Varia-405.

56. Zimmermann, p. 334.

57. Personal communication from Werner Zimmermann, 8 Dec 1983.

58. Ljotić, *Memoari*, pp. 54–55.

59. Carl Landauer, *European Socialism: A History of Ideas and Movements from the Industrial Revolution to Hitler's Seizure of Power* (Berkeley: University of California Press, 1959), pp. 225–50.

60. Indeed, this is exactly the criticism the socialist Mita Cenić made of the Radicals in 1881, that they followed German socialism too closely (Perović, *Pera Todorović*, p. 73).

61. Stanković agrees that Lassalle had an important impact on Pašić, even quoting Svetozar Marković to that effect (*Nikola Pašić*, p. 41).

62. SANU notebooks. Also discussed by Škorić, "Populism of Nikola Pašić," pp. 475–76.

63. Pašić successfully completed all his coursework and received a certificate of completion, but he did not take the final examination for receipt of a diploma, and therefore technically did not graduate (Zimmermann, p. 329). This was not at all unusual.

64. Pašić to Min. pros., 8 Mar 72, AS:MPS-1873-IV-53.

65. Ranislav M. Avramović, "Nikola P. Pašić kao tehničar u politici i praksi," in Vukašin Životić, ed., *Spomenica Nikole P. Pašića 1845–1926* (Belgrade: Pavlović, 1926), p. 66.

66. Marković had proposed him for editor of *Javnost* in 1872 when Djura Ljočić quit, but Mita Cenić opposed him and Steva Milićević was appointed (Mitrović, "Djura Ljočić," p. 122).

67. On 17 Feb/1 Mar 75 the State Council approved expenses of Pašić and an otherwise unidentified J. Lutman for their trip through Ottoman lands (Škerović, *Zapisnici saveta*, p. 130).

68. *Dnevnik Kalaja*, 14 Dec 74, p. 623.

69. *Dnevnik Kalaja*, 18 Dec 74, p. 623.

70. *Dnevnik Kalaja*, 4 Jan 75, p. 629, 16 Jan 75, p. 632.

71. Private letter to Andrássy, early Jan 75, *Dnevnik Kalaja*, pp. 804–5.

72. *Vidovdan* tried to pin a Karadjordjević label on Svetozar Marković because he said Serbia had not followed a truly national policy since 1858 (Marković, *Sabrani spisi*, 4:107), and others claimed (correctly) that Jevrem Marković was in touch with former Prince Alexander (*Dnevnik Kalaja*, 7 Feb 75, p. 638). On 17/29 Jan 75 Čumić instructed all regional administrators to be on the lookout for Peter Karadjordjević, Alexander's son, who was rumored to be en route to Serbia through Bosnia posing as "Petar Djordjević" (AS:PO-84/49). For allegations of liberal connections with Montenegro, see *Dnevnik Kalaja*, 7 Feb 75, p. 639, 11 Apr 75, p. 649.

73. "Of what value to us are laws, a constitution, all the freedoms, when the government has the raw power to put a completely innocent man in jail," asked Nikola Krstić (Krstić's diary, 18/30 Jan 75). When the issue of Bošković's guilt became completely deadlocked later in the session, Milan solved it by publicly dropping all charges in what Milan Dj. Milićević called a "coup de téatre" (Milićević's diary, 12/24 Feb 75). This move temporarily gave Milan's popularity a considerable boost, although it did nothing to restore the credibility of the government

74. Krstić's diary, 21 Jan/2 Feb 75; and Milićević's diary, 21 Jan/2 Feb 75.

75. Krstić's diary, quoting Marinović, 13/25 Dec 75. "Parliamentarism is impossible in Serbia as long as the skupština does not stand alongside the government," Krstić quoted Marinović on another occasion (Krstić to Cukić, 23 Feb/7 Mar 75, SANU, 7966).

76. Milan also feared and distrusted the Liberals because he believed that among them were persons who had been involved in the assassination plot against Prince Michael (Krstić to Cukić, 4/16 Feb 75 [SANU, 7966]; Krstić's diary, 21 Jan/2 Feb 75; and Milićević, *Jevrem Grujić*, pp. 220–22).

77. Krstić's diary, 23 Jan/4 Feb 75; and *Dnevnik Kalaja*, 2, 3 Feb 75.

78. Krstić to Cukić, Sv. Jovana 75, SANU, 7699.

79. Jaša Prodanović, *Unstavne borbe u Srbiji* (Belgrade: Geca kon, n.d.), pp. 234–40; and VMO, 1:406–7. Even the Radicals wanted a constitutional convention. Milija Milovanović urged the proposal for a convention be declared urgent *(Istok*, 21 Feb/5 Mar 75). *Oslobodjenje* vigorously opposed Garašanin's proposal (2/14, 5/17, 7/19 Feb 75).

80. 16/28 Mar 75.

81. SB, 1875, 1907–67; Krstić's diary, 11/23, 12/24 Mar 75; *Dnevnik Kalaja*, 23/24 Mar 75, pp. 646–47; and Milićević's diary, 11/23 Mar 75.

82. If Svetozar Marković is well known among Western scholars, Adam Bogosavljević is not. McClellan, for example, calls him a Croat *(Svetozar Marković,* p. 254), Hadidian never mentions him in her dissertation about Serbian and Bulgarian Radicals, and Michael B. Petrovich says that at his death "he was closer to bourgeois liberalism than revolutionary socialism," when in fact Adam was neither (Petrovich, *History of Modern Serbia,* 2:409). The standard biography is Rastislav V. Petrović, *Adam Bogosavljević* (Belgrade: Rad, 1972).

83. The Društvo za poljsku privredu published a newspaper, *Težak* (Peasant) and for the first half of the 1870s pursued a vigorous, but not very successful, effort to improve Serbian agriculture. It received informal support from the government and from the establishment in general, although few of its members were actually peasants like Bogosavljević.

84. See his article "Glas se sela," in *Istok,* 1873, nos. 1, 14, 36, 37, 73, 90 (Petrović, *Bogosavljević,* pp. 39–41).

85. Svetozar Marković, *Sabrani spisi,* 4:103, from *Oslobodjenje,* 3/15 Jan 75.

86. SB, 1875, p. 162.

87. The source of most of the information on Tajsić is the very thorough and informative Dragoje M. Todorović, *Narodni tribun: Ranko Tajsić* (Belgrade: SANU, Posebna izdanja 550, 1983).

88. Todorović, *Ranko Tajsić,* p. 17, quoting Tajsić's own *Životopis* (Autobiography), a manuscript which remains in private hands.

89. The investigation brought on by Tajsić's accusation showed that the local srez office contained 512 undecided actions, some from as far back as 1867, 356 unfinished administrative subjects, 1,050 items not yet registered in the protocols, 201 unforwarded court appeals, and, among other things, five persons held in jail for from six to nine months without investigations. These inadequacies cost the local official his position, for which he naturally blamed Tajsić (Todorović, *Ranko Tajsić,* pp. 20–22).

90. Meeting of 19 Feb/3 Mar, reported in *Srpske novine,* 19 Apr/1 May 75. Bogosavljević responded to criticisms of his proposal by going on the attack. "Besides lessening pay, many more important things could be lessened, such as . . . the number of officials in all specialities, . . . [and] the standing army could be brought to a minimum too" *(Budućnost,* 2/14 Mar 75).

91. Petrović, *Adam Bogosavljević,* p. 52.

92. Todorović, *Ranko Tajsić,* p. 28.

93. *Sabrani spisi,* 4:94–98.

94. Petrović, *Adam Bogosavljević,* pp. 60–69.

95. During the skupština Bogosavljević complained that the government

was investigating him illegally, since he was an elected delegate and the skupština was in session. Stefanović vigorously denied the accusation, and he was right: the government was investigating Bogosavljević's nephew. Once the skupština was over, the investigation broadened to other associates of Bogosavljević in an effort to intimidate his followers (Petrović, *Adam Bogosavljević*, pp. 56–58).

96. Petrović, *Adam Bogosavljević*, p. 64.
97. Todorović, *Ranko Tajsić*, p. 39, quoting *Samouprava*, no. 58, 1882. Tajsić was held in jail for the month preceding the election, but was returned with a heavy majority anyway (AS:PO-84/25).
98. Stefanović to all načelnici, 21 Apr/2 May 75 (AS:PO-132/98); and *Istok*, 21 May/ 2 Jun, 31 May/12 Jun, 8/20 Jun, 11/23 Jun, 19 Jun/1 Jul, 5/17 Jul 75.
99. 22 Jul/3 Aug 75.
100. 14/26 Jul 75. By "abolishing marriage and the family" *Istok* meant that the Radicals advocated civil marriage and equality for women.

NOTES TO CHAPTER 3

1. As one historian put it, "many peasants were driven into revolt because, like Karadjordjević in the First Uprising, the bands [sent by the Serbian government] burnt their homes," in Vukoman Šalipurović, *Ustanak u zapadnom delu stare Srbije 1875–1878* (Titovo Užice, 1968), p. 79.
2. Milorad Ekmečić, *Ustanak u Bosni, 1875–78* (Sarajevo: Veselin Masleša, 1973), pp. 105–9; and Ljubomir Kaljević, *Moje uspomene* (Belgrade: Večernje novosti, 1908), p. 19.
3. The standard work on the diplomacy of the Balkan crisis of 1875–78 remains B. H. Sumner, *Russia and the Balkans, 1870–1880* (London: Archon Books, 1962, orig. pub. 1937). Very useful in this study have been two books by David MacKenzie, *The Serbs and Russian Pan-Slavism, 1875–78* (Ithaca N.Y.: Cornell University Press, 1967), and *The Lion of Tashkent: The Career of General M. G. Cherniaev* (Athens: University of Georgia Press, 1974).
4. Another purpose of the trip was to fix the engagement of Milan to Natalia Kechko, a wealthy eighteen-year-old Romanian heiress (VMO, 1:427). Since the couple was married October 17, some observers have attributed Milan's antiwar policy in the fall of 1875 as much to his desire to have a happy engagement and marriage as to political and military factors. Those factors were sufficiently weighty, however, to justify an antiwar policy, whatever Milan's personal motivations may have been.

5. Ekmečić, *Ustanak u Bosni*, p. 124.
6. Danilo Stefanović, "Šta je Srbska vlada radila za podpomaganje ustanka koji se je u Ercegovini meseca Juna ove 1875-te godine pojavio," 10 Oct 75, AS:PO-132/82.
7. Apparently the document cited in the previous note was not available to Slobodan Jovanović, because he attributes Stefanović's resignation to the Liberal electoral victory (VMO, 1: 430–31), relying on Krstić's diary, 5/17 Aug 75, and Krstić's letter to Cukić (3/15 Aug 75, SANU, 7966). Stefanović's letter of resignation mentions only his frustration with the prince and his military attaché, Kosta Protić (AS:PO-132/83).
8. Even Jevrem Marković was eventually returned from Jagodina, although not until a by-election in October *(Srpske novine,* 26 Sep/8 Oct 75).
9. 10/22 Aug 75.
10. Krstić's diary, 17/29 Aug 75.
11. Ibid., 10/22 Aug 75.
12. *Istok,* 31 Aug/12 Sep 75. The reluctant Milan had to be convinced to come to Kragujevac to open the skupština formally in the first place (MacKenzie, *Serbs and Russian Pan-Slavism,* p. 51).
13. Ristić to Milan, 2/14 Sep 75, AJR, 27/162 XXVII/5. Some familiar names voting for this proposal were Uroš Knežević, Panta Srečković (right-Liberal professor), Miloš Glišić, Paja Vuković (Radical kmet of Kragujevac), Milija Milovanović (close friend of Bogosavljević), Jovan Bošković, and Ljubomir Kaljević. Against risking war, but in favor of assistance, were Adam Bogosavljević and Sima Nestorović, among others (Jevrem Grujić, *Zapisi Jevrema Grujića* [Belgrade: Štamparija 'Skerlić,' 1923], 3:111–12).
14. Grujić, *Zapisi,* 3:109–10.
15. This sentiment evoked an enthusiastic response among the public (agent's report, 12/24 Sep 75, AJR, 3/1060 III/19). Matija Ban called the address "splendid" (Ban to Ristić, 11/23 Sep 75, AJR, 26/705 XXVI/12). Ristić calmed the foreign consuls by saying that "despite its lively expressions, . . . it did not contain an appeal to extreme measures" (9/21 Sep 75, AJR, 3/298 III/15). Nevertheless, the consuls handed Serbia an official note on 24 Sep/5 Oct 75 advising against any aggressive acts (AS:PO-28/267).
16. *Istok,* 11/23 Sep 75.
17. Grujić, *Zapisi,* 3:115–47.
18. *Istok,* 20 Aug/1 Sep 75.
19. For the committee members, see *Istok,* 2/14 Sep 75. Adam was defeated

328 : Notes

for the very last position on the committee on petitions and complaints by a certain Ivko Ostajić, a not otherwise distinguished delegate.

20. 27 Nov/9 Dec 75.
21. Ristić to Milan, 6/18 Sep 75, AJR, 27/190 XXVII/5.
22. "Memoari Alimpije Vasiljevića," p. 52 (AS:PO-102-136).
23. Milojković to Ristić, 12/24 Sep 75, AJR, 3/331 III/17; and Milan to Stevča Mihailović, 12/24 Sep 75, AJR, 27/193 XXVII/5.
24. Milojković to Stevča Mihailović, 12/24 Sep 75, AJR, 3/325 III/17; cabinet to Milan, 13/25 Sep 75, AJR, 27/194 XXVII/5; and Ristić to Milojković, 13/25 Sep 75, AJR, 3/260 III/12.
25. Ljubomir Kaljević, *Moje uspomene*, p. 13.
26. This description of Milan's entry into the skupština and talk with the skupština members is taken from "Memoari Alimpije Vasiljevića," p. 53. See also Kaljević, *Moje uspomene*, pp. 7–12; Krstić's diary, 24 Sep/6 Oct 75, and his letter to Cukić, same date (SANU, 7966); and "Memoari Avrama Petrovića," p. 8 (SANU, 10039), which has the story somewhat garbled, since Petrović was in Kragujevac, not Belgrade.
27. One exception was Ranko Tajsić, who proposed to the prince that the means necessary for war be achieved through savings, rather than loans. "Eh, Tajsić," the prince replied, "even I know that it would be best if we armed ourselves with cash, but there isn't any." "Let the skupština pass the proposals of me and my friends [to cut governmental salaries]," Tajsić said, "and we'll have the money." Since this implied a criticism of the prince's own extravagant habits, Milan was highly irritated at this suggestion (Todorovoć, *Ranko Tajsić*, p. 50).
28. Kaljević, *Moje uspomene*, p. 13.
29. Jovanović, Bošković, and Janković tried to organize a newspaper together in the early days of Prince Michael's reign. Significantly, they entitled it *Narodna skupština*. Michael simply arrested them (Stokes, *Legitimacy through Liberalism*, pp. 45–48).
30. Petar Milosavljević, "Pripreme Srbije za rat sa Turskom 1876. godine," *Balcanica* 9 (1978): 131–57.
31. The most thorough gathering of materials concerning the opština are by Ružica Guzina in her two books, *Opština u Kneževini i Kraljevini Srbiji, Prvi deo, 1804–1839* (Belgrade: Pravni fakultet u Beogradu, Institut za pravnu istoriju, 1966), and *Opština u Srbiji, 1839–1918* (Belgrade: Rad, 1976).
32. Milan Dj. Milićević, *Opštine u Srbiji* (Belgrade: Državna štamparija, 1878), pp. 27–38; and Vuk Stefanović Karadžić, *Srpski rječnik*, 3d ed. (Belgrade: Štamparija Kraljevine Srbije, 1898), under "kmet" and "knez."

33. Guzina, *Opština u Srbiji*, pp. 51–53.
34. Milićević, *Opštine u Srbiji*, p. 22. The kmet's assistants were permitted to tie up offenders until the kmet could come to administer the beating.
35. *Zbornik zakona* 28 (1976): 1–30.
36. The rule against selling papers in the street or in shops was not unusual in Europe at this time. Newspapers were not hawked in Prussia until the 1880s, for example, and even then it was considered somewhat vulgar (Robert H. Keyserlingk, *Media Manipulation: The Press and Bismarck in Imperial Germany* [Montreal: Renouf, 1977], p. 13).
37. Bjelica, "Borba za slobodu štampe," pp. 208–10. It is interesting to note that Milutin Garašanin formulated the final version of the law, according to Kaljević, even though he voted against it, supporting Bogosavljević's plan for a one sentence law (Bjelica, p. 208).
38. *Srpske novine*, 20 Dec 75/1 Jan 76.
39. "Memoari Avrama Petrovića," p. 7. Milica died of tuberculosis in 1881 but Anka lived until 1923. It is said that Milica and Pera never consummated their marriage, but Anka and Sreta did (*Politika*, 6 Jan 1980). Nonetheless, both Todorović and the Ninković family always spoke of Milica as Pera's real wife (Perović, *Pera Todorović*, pp. 28–29).
40. Dragnich, *Nikola Pašić*, p. 13.
41. "Memoari Avrama Petrovića", p. 7. "Everyone" meant Anka and Milica, their husbands, Pera Velemirović, Ilija Todorić (responsible editor), Nikola Pašić when he was in town, and Avram Petrović (*Crveni barjak*, 1:251).
42. *Staro oslobodjenje*, 10/22 Aug 75. See also his "Zašto se bori Hercegovina i Bosna," *Staro oslobodjenje*, 24 Oct/5 Nov, 26 Oct/7Nov 75.
43. Jovan Radonić, "Nikola Pašić i bosansko-hercegovački ustanak 1875," *Politika*, 20 May 1937, 14, 15, 16, 20 Apr 1938; and Stanković *Nikola Pašić i jugoslovensko pitanje*, pp. 43–44.
44. From Serbia Pašić recommended one Liberal and one Radical be sent. For the Liberal he recommended either Vladimir Jovanović, Gliga Geršić, Djoka Vlajković, or Milan Kujundžić, and from the Radicals Pera Velemirović or Jevrem Marković. See Nikola Pašić to Sima Popović, Kastelnovi, 31 Oct 75, Škorić collection, doc. 41.
45. Marinović also had a plan for self-administration in Bosnian opštinas, and the writer Matija Ban even proposed the Bosnians should fight a national guerrilla war. Serbian Conservatives were averse to radical options only when they involved internal reform, not when they concerned what they perceived as national interests outside Serbia's borders (Ekmečić, *Ustanak u Bosni*, pp. 126–27).

46. The program appeared in *Zastava*, 15/27 Jan 76 (Ekmečić, *Ustanak u Bosni*, pp. 135–37). Pelagić was director of the Banja Luka Seminary. In 1869 he was banished to Asia Minor for a protest against the Ottoman administration. He fled to Serbia and in 1871 signed the program put forward by Jevrem Marković, Aćim Čumić, and others. Very active both as an author and a politician, Pelagić became Serbia's first outright atheist author, and is remembered today as second only to Svetozar Marković among early Serbian socialists.

47. In Serbia itself the Radicals formally proposed a constitutional reform that went beyond the Kaljević measures. Jevrem Marković and eighteen others, including Adam Bogosavljević, Ranko Tajsić, and Paja Vuković put a draft constitution before the skupština just before it went home early in 1876 that would reorganize Serbia on the basis of the srez, as Svetozar Marković had proposed in 1875 (SB, 1875, pp. 1549–68).

48. Ekmečić, *Ustanak u Bosni*, pp. 23, 35.

49. Krstić's diary, 8/20 Dec 75; Slobodan Jovanović says that in Ćuprija only 14 voters showed up, even though there were 15 places to fill (VMO, 1:461); *Istok* ridiculed the voters of Kragujevac, only 270 of which showed up out of 1,700 (16/28 Nov 75); and *Staro oslobodjenje* responded by pointing out that this was a larger proportion than had turned out in Belgrade, where fewer than 400 out of 4,000 eligible voted (26 Nov/8 Dec 75).

50. Krstić to Cukić, 22 Feb/5Mar 75.

51. "The authorities should not mix in the elections for kmet in any way" (Kaljević to Čačak načelnik, 27 Oct/8 Nov 75, AS:PO-84/41).

52. Most of the following is taken from the sources reprinted in *Crveni barjak*. Only documents of special importance or interest are cited individually. The election results can be found also in AS:PO-73-48 and AS:PO-37-43.

53. One of the two was Pera Velimirović, heir to the small estate of Svetozar Marković. In 1874 a certain Pera Djordjević died, leaving a house and a plot of land to Svetozar Marković for the socialist cause. On his death, Svetozar left the holdings to Velimirović (*Crveni barjak*, 2:202, 1:48 n. 2).

54. 16/28 Nov 75.

55. Pera Todorović had already spent most of 1875 in jail for previous press violations (*Crveni barjak*, 1:386). Ilija Todorić was eventually sentenced to five years in jail, Pera to three years nine months as part of the larger trial over the Red Banner Affair (*Crveni barjak*, 2:339–40).

56. 26 Nov/8 Dec 75.

57. *Staro oslobodjenje*, 24 Dec 75/5 Jan 76, 28 Dec 75/9 Jan 76.

58. His lengthy article in *Staro oslobodjenje* (17/29 Feb 76) gives a typically vivid description of the events (*Crveni barjak*, 1:68–76).

59. The banner was approximately 6 feet by 4 feet in size (*Crveni barjak*, 1:88–90), and had been put together by Pera Todorović and a friend the previous evening (Perović, *Pera Todorović*, p. 34, reporting a reminiscence of Todorović's).

60. VMO, 1:278–79; and Ljubica Ljotić, *Memoari* (Munich: Iskra, 1973), pp. 100–105.

61. *Crveni barjak*, 1:1–21. For examples of outlandish plot rumors, see AS:PO-28-264, dated 29 Jun/11 Jul 74; and AS:PO-25-132, dated 15/27 Jan 74.

62. Kaljević, *Moje uspomene*, pp. 48–50.

63. The paper continued under the editorship of Mita Stojanović and with the help of Nikola Pašić, who was in Belgrade at the time of the demonstration and therefore not jailed (Pera Todorović, *Dnevnik jednog dobrovoljca* [Belgrade: Srpska književna zadruga, 1938], p. 138). Stojanović was killed in action in the war of 1876.

64. "Odziv na poziv," *Zastava*, 12/24 Apr 76, in *Crveni barjak*, 1:300–304.

65. Nikola Pašić to Miša Dimitrijević, 4/16 Apr 76, Škorić collection, doc. no. 53. The *okrug*, mentioned in this text, was the largest administrative division of Serbia, containing several *srezovi*.

66. Todorović's vigorous defense inspired his friends. Avram Petrović was moved to copy it out verbatim, for example ("Memoari Avrama Petrovića," p. 11). Pera's heroic stance included his refusal to answer any of the questions of the investigating magistrates. "Do what you will, condemn me, but I will not answer until I can answer before a commission or court in whose impartiality I have confidence" (*Crveni barjak*, 1:393).

67. Todorović's defense can be found in *Crveni barjak*, 1:336–97. The quotations in this paragraph are from pages 337, 362, 356–57, 360.

68. *Staro oslobodjenje*, 20 Feb/3 Mar 76 (*Crveni barjak*, 1:101).

69. *Crveni barjak*, 1:366, original emphasis.

70. Report from *Graničar*, an Austro-Hungarian newspaper that followed Serbian events closely, 6/18 Jun 76 (*Crveni barjak*, 2:314).

71. Velimirović was actually found innocent and the verdict was sustained on appeal. "Only on its third try did the government find a legal formula by which I could be condemned," Velimirović put it later (Velimirović to Jovan Ristić, 1/13 Jun 80, AJR, III/7 3/1344).

72. A few scattered strikes and protests had occurred previously, but the Red Banner Affair was the first demonstration involving workers that attained political significance (Mladen Vukomanović, *Radnička klasa Srbije u drugoj polovini XIX. veka* [Belgrade: Rad, 1972], pp. 271–82).

73. 14/26 Mar 76, quoted by MacKenzie, *Serbs and Russian Pan-Slavism*, pp. 78–79.
74. 8/20 Apr, 6/18 Jun, 22 Jun/4 Jul, 27 Jun/9 July, 17/29 Nov 75, 5/17 Jan 76.
75. 23 Jul/4 Aug 75, quoted by MacKenzie, *Serbs and Russian Pan-Slavism*, p. 33.
76. 6/18 Feb 76, quoted by MacKenzie, *Serbs and Russian Pan-Slavism*, p. 63.
77. E. g., *Šumadija*, 28 Mar/9 Apr 76; and MacKenzie, *Serbs and Russian Pan-Slavism*, p. 78.
78. MacKenzie, *Serbs and Russian Pan-Slavism*, pp. 66–67.
79. Protocol of the committee's first meeting, 21 Jan/2 Feb 76 (AS:NS, 1876, F. I, r. 3).
80. The committee had been discussing the conditions of the loan since mid-February, but approved it only after Ristić came to power. Committee meeting of 8/20 May 76 (AS:NS, 1876, F. I, r. 46).
81. AS:NS, 1876, F. I, r. 53.

NOTES TO CHAPTER 4

1. The next sentence, and several sentences from the following paragraphs, are taken in part from Gale Stokes, "Serbian Military Doctrine and the Crisis of 1875–76," in Király and Stokes, eds., *Insurrections, Wars, and the Eastern Crisis in the 1870s*, pp. 261–75.
2. Fikret Adanir, "Heiduckentum und osmanische Herrschaft," *Südost-Forschungen*, 41 (1982): 57; and Stephen Fischer-Galati and Dimitrije Djordjević, *The Balkan Revolutionary Tradition* (New York: Columbia University Press, 1981).
3. Memorandum to the Congress of Berlin, 12/24 Jul 78, in Mihailo Vojvodić et al., eds., *Srbija 1878: Dokumenti* (Belgrade: Srpska književna zadruga, kolo 71, knj. 473, 1978), p. 446.
4. Both Miloš and Milićević quoted by Milorad Ekmečić, "Srpska vojska u nacionalnim ratovima od 1876. do 1878.," *Balcanica* 9 (1978), rendered into English by Gale Stokes as "The Serbian Army in the Wars of 1876–78: National Liability or National Asset?" in Király and Stokes, eds., *Insurrections, Wars, and the Eastern Crisis*, pp. 277–78.
5. On the Serbian military tradition, see Wayne S. Vucinich, "Serbian Military Tradition," in Béla Király and Gunther E. Rothenberg, eds., *Special Topics and Generalizations on the 18th and 19th Centuries* (New York: Brooklyn College Press, distributed by Columbia University Press, War and Society in East Central Europe, vol. 1, 1979), pp. 285–324.

6. Sava Grujić, *Vojna organizacija Srbije* (Kragujevac: Kragujevačka društvena štamparija, 1874), pp. 66–67.

7. "National militia" seems to render the term *narodna vojska* best in English, but other translations, such as "popular army," would be equally correct. On Michael's reform see Milo Djurdjevac, "Narodna vojska u Srbiji 1861–83 godine," *Vojno-istorijski glasnik* 10 (1959), no. 4: 78–93, and the article "Vojska" in Stanoje Stanojević, ed., *Narodna enciklopedija srpsko-hrvatsko-slovenačka* (Zagreb: Bibliografski zavod, 1928–29). The standard work is now Života Djordjević, *Srpska narodna vojska, 1861–64* (Belgrade: Narodna knjiga, 1984).

8. Ekmečić, "The Serbian Army," pp. 281–82.

9. See the articles "Vojna akademija" and "Topolivnica" in Stanojević, *Narodna enciklopedija*, as well as Ekmečić, "The Serbian Army," p. 280. On the development of Balkan armies and their officer corps see Dimitrije Djordjević, "The Role of the Military in the Balkans in the Nineteenth Century," in Ralph Melville and Hans-Jürgen Schröder, eds., *Der Berliner Kongress von 1878* (Wiesbaden: Veröffentlichungen des Instituts für Europäische Geschichte Mainz–Abteilung Universalgeschichte, Beiheft 7, Franz Steiner Verlag, 1982), pp. 317–47.

10. Draga Vuksanović-Anić, "Uloga vojske u kulturnom životu Srbije i ratovi 1876–1878 godine," in Danica Milić, ed., *Srbija u završnoj fazi velike istočne krize* (Belgrade: Istorijski institut, Zbornik radova, knj. 2, 1980), pp. 309–24. Vuksanović-Anić quotes the Russian Colonel Bobrikov, not otherwise well disposed toward the Serbian army, as being impressed in 1877 with the "excellent capacities and military knowledge of the Serbian officers, who could serve proudly in the army of any Great Power" (p. 318). One should recall, however, that except in Prussia, military education in Europe was not particularly good. Michael Howard observes that "the standard of teaching at great military colleges [of France], at St. Cyr, Metz and Saumur, was deplorable, and the intellectual calibre of the senior officers in no way corresponded to their panache. . . . In 1870 the Germans were to be astounded at the illiteracy of the officers who fell into their hands." Michael Howard, *The Franco-Prussian War* (New York: Macmillan, 1962), p. 16.

11. The vote was 55–53 (*Istok,* 2/14 Dec 75).

12. See, e.g., Stokes, *Legitimacy through Liberalism,* p. 116; and MacKenzie, *Serbs and Russian Pan-Slavism,* p. 12.

13. See the comments of Michael Howard, *Franco-Prussian War,* pp. 6–7.

14. The best discussion of Serbia's war effort is Ekmečić, "The Serbian Army." For the purely military aspects see Petar Opačić, "Vojne operacije

u srpsko-turskom ratu 1876. godine," in Rade Petrović, ed., *Medjunarodni naučni skup povodom sto-godišnjice ustanka u Bosni i Hercegovini, drugim balkanskim zemljama i istočnoj krizi 1875–1878 godine* (Sarajevo: ANUBiH, 1977), 2:281–304. For a solid review of the Yugoslav historiography of the entire Eastern Crisis, see Milorad Ekmečić, "Rezultati jugoslovenske istoriografije o istočnom pitanju 1875–78. godine," *Jugoslovenski istorijski časopis* 16 (1977) nos. 1–2: 55–74. A complete bibliography through 1979 listing 836 titles is in Jelena Maksin and Anica Lolić, *Bibliografija jugoslovenske literature o velikoj istočnog krizi 1875–1878* (Belgrade: Istorijski institut, Gradja, knj. 20, 1979).

15. Breech-loading rifles came into common use in the 1860s, although they were known in the first half of the century. One of the most popular systems, which was used both for retrofitting muzzle-loaders and for constructing new rifles, was invented by Henry O. Peabody of Boston and was called the "falling block." Peabody rifles were adopted by Bavaria and Mexico, as well as by Serbia, and the falling-block idea became the principle on which the Martini-Henry rifle used by the Ottomans was constructed (so called because Friedrich von Martini, an Austrian lace manufacturer, invented the breech mechanism and Alexander Henry, an Edinburgh gunmaker, the barrel). The English adopted this weapon in 1871 and armed the Ottomans with it in time for the Eastern Crisis. The Ottomans were among the first to use the Winchester repeating rifle, the only weapon of its kind in actual use in the 1870s, devastating the Russians at Plevna with their superior firepower. See articles on "Breechloaders," "Berdan," "Martini-Henry," and "Winchester," in Harold L. Peterson, ed., *Encyclopedia of Firearms* (New York, 1964); and W. W. Greener, *The Gun and its Development*, 9th ed. (London, 1910), pp. 701–75.

16. MacKenzie, *Lion of Tashkent*, p. 165.

17. Colonel Djura Horvatović, for example, got excellent results with his troops by imposing ruthless discipline and placing his troops in good defensive positions. He put up a spirited defense of Knjaževac early in the war, and a dogged defense of Djunis at the end of the war. Kosta Protić also distinguished himself leading the Serbian troops at the only real Serbian victory at Šumatovac (VMO, 2:59–89).

18. Dimitrije Djordjević, "The Serbian Peasant in the 1876 War," in Király and Stokes, *Insurrections, Wars and the Eastern Crisis*, pp. 305–16, contains these two quotes and many other piquant examples that show the lack of interest in the war by the average Serb.

19. MacKenzie, *Lion of Tashkent*, p. 126.

20. Grujić, *Zapisi*, 3:194.

21. Ibid., p. 208. In 1875 some Serbs living in the area between Višegrad
    and Novi Pazar revolted and a volunteer corps from these rebels was
    formed for use on the Ibar front in 1876, but the movement was so small
    and disorganized it had little effect. See Šalipurović *Ustanak u zapadnom
    delu stare Srbije.*
22. MacKenzie, *Serbs and Russian Pan-Slavism,* p. 102.
23. Milosavljević, "Pripreme Srbije za rat sa Turskom 1876. godine," pp.
    131–57.
24. See the report of the Minister President Stevća Mihailović to the Council
    of Ministers of 14/26 Oct 76 in Grujić, *Zapisi,* 3:236–39.
25. VMO, 2:91.
26. Živanović, *Politička istorija Srbije,* 1:344.
27. Two days before the crucial session, the government and Milan agreed
    on a detailed schedule of twenty-five chronological steps for stage-man-
    aging the assembly, all of which were carried out exactly according to
    plan (Grujić, *Zapisi,* 3:281–83).
28. "Memoari Avrama Petrovića," p. 19, (SANU, 10039).
29. Andrija Radenić, "Topolska buna," in his *Iz istorije Srbije i Vojvodine 1834–
    1914* (Novi Sad and Belgrade: Matica srpska and Istorijski institut, 1973),
    p. 404.
30. Rastislav Petrović argues cogently against the standard view that the low
    number of votes for Bogosavljević represented a decline in strength.
    Actually, it was a result of a joint Radical/Conservative effort to maximize
    the strength of their opposition. Cf. Petrović, *Adam Bogosavljević,* p. 110;
    Miličević, *Jevrem Grujić,* p. 239; and VMO, 2:138.
31. "Memoari Avrama Petrovića," p. 119a.
32. Grujić, *Zapisi,* 3:293; and Petrović, *Adam Bogosavljević,* pp. 109–10.
33. See Karl Kaser, "Typologie der politischen Parteien Südosteuropas im
    neunzehnten Jahrhundert," *Österreichische Osthefte,* 1985, pp. 358–61.
34. Škorić collection, doc. 59. The minority's committee report, written by
    Uroš Knežević, was much more flowery and diplomatic than the draft
    Pašić had prepared for it. Knežević praised the birth of the royal heir,
    Alexander, at the beginning of his address, for example, whereas Pašić
    kept his mention of the royal birth to the end of his draft. The final
    statement by the minority left out all the peripheral demands and con-
    centrated on a return to the prewar laws (Škorić collection, doc. 60).
35. Some sources say twenty-six resignations took place, others twenty-five.
    A copy of the resignation preserved in the historical archives of the
    Serbian Academy of Sciences, however, lists twenty-two names (SANU,
    7203/1).

36. Petrović, *Adam Bogosavljević,* p. 113.
37. "Memoari Avrama Petrovića," pp. 18a, 19a.
38. Bogosavljević quixotically argued that the tax on beer encouraged the luxurious life style of the bureaucracy, since it was only the middle and upper levels of society that drank the newly stylish drink introduced from Austria. He thought that taxing an upper-class drink to give the bureaucracy higher wages had nothing to do with the welfare of the people (Petrović, *Adam Bogosavljević,* p. 116).
39. Young people as late as 1876 often were not even aware that party struggles were going on at all. See Živanović, *Politička istorija Srbije,* 1:345–46.
40. Generalstab der fürstlich serbischen Armee, *Der Serbisch-Türkische Krieg von 1877–78* (Belgrade, 1879), pp. 27, 65.
41. For the military aspects of the war see Savo Skoko, "Pregled operacija srpske vojske u srpsko-turskom ratu 1877–1878," in Petrović, *Medjunarodni naučni skup,* 2: pp. 257–80.
42. The best study on the Topola Mutiny *(Topolska buna,* which can also be translated "Topola Uprising" or "Topola Insurrection") is by Andrija Radenić, "Topolska buna," in *Iz istorije Srbije i Vojvodine,* pp. 367–424. It contains an excellent bibliography of primary sources and secondary works.
43. Ekmečić, *Ustanak u Bosni,* pp. 138–41, 196–97.
44. Ljubica Ljotić, *Memoari* (Munich: Iskra, 1973), pp. 119–33.
45. Nikola Krstić tried to convince Milan that cursing the government was not very serious. "Our people are used to speaking crudely, to swearing. They curse themselves, their father, their children, even their animals." Milan agreed Serbs cursed a good deal but did not accept Krstić's argument that it was nothing to worry about (Krstić's diary, 26 Feb/10 Mar 78).
46. Radenić, "Topolska buna," p. 396.
47. "Memoari Avrama Petrovića," p. 25.
48. Radenić, "Topolska buna," p. 409.
49. Ljotić, *Memoari,* pp. 56–57.
50. Here are some birth dates: Svetozar Marković (1846); Nikola Pašić (1845); Peter Karadjordević (1844); Vlada Ljotić (1845); Adam Bogosavljević (1844); and Pera Velimirović (1848). Jevrem Marković was a little older (? but c. 1840), and Pera Todorović a little younger (1852).
51. Gerard Francis Gould (British minister resident in Belgrade) to Marquess of Salisbury, 13 Sep 78, reported that Kaljević had mysteriously

disappeared from Belgrade followed by rumors that he was in touch with Peter Karadjordjević. Kaljević may have also been involved in financial difficulties (FO, 105/2, no. 153). See also Ljotić, *Memoari*, p. 117.

52. Peter Karadjordjević to Vlada Ljotić, n.d., Škorić collection, doc. 37 (Monastir Hilandar), quoted in part in Ljotić, *Memoari*, pp. 71–72, where the letter is dated 1874.

53. Personal communication from Sofija Škorić, summer 1983.

54. Ekmečić, *Ustanak u Bosni* p. 138.

55. Jovan Skerlić, *Svetozar Marković*, pp. 94–97.

56. In 1872, for example, opponents of *Radenik* liked to point out how Svetozar Marković's father participated in the revolt of 1842 that brought Alexander Karadjordjević to power, and how the elder Marković remained a vigorous Karadjordjevist until his death. Jevrem Marković's continued links with the Karadjordjevists also did not escape notice (Skerlić, *Svetozar Marković*, p. 80). It is also known that Peter Karadjordjević read *Oslobodjenje* (Ekmečić, *Ustanak u Bosni*, p. 138).

57. Radenić, "Topolska buna," p. 417n.

NOTES TO CHAPTER 5

1. "Da li nam je rat od koristi?" manuscript dated Kragujevac, 1877 (SANU, 13478).

2. Henryk Batowski, "Die territorialen Bestimmungen von San Stefano und Berlin," in Melville and Schröder, *Berliner Kongress*, p. 60.

3. Ristić memorandum to the Congress of Berlin, 12/24 Jul 78, in Mihailo Vojvodić et al., eds., *Srbija 1878: Dokumenti* (Belgrade: Srpska književna zadruga, 1978), p. 446.

4. Peter Sugar and Vladien N. Vinogradov have differed over whether Austrian imperialism toward the Balkans was purposeful or improvised, but the result was the same. See their contrasting articles in Király and Stokes, *Insurrection, Wars, and the Eastern Crisis*. For a discussion of the economic interests involved, see Emil Palotas, "Die wirtschaftlichen Aspecte in der Balkanpolitik Österreich-Ungarns um 1878," in Melville and Schröder, *Berliner Kongress*, pp. 271–85.

5. The decision was hotly debated, with liberals and Hungarians generally opposed, but the military argument that the territory was needed to protect Austrian holdings along the Adriatic Sea eventually won out.

6. The news of the agreement was greeted with resignation in Belgrade, but, as Milan Milićević agreed in his diary, "everyone said that without

these concessions we would never get Pirot and Vranje" (22 Jun/4 Jul 78).

7. The diplomatic history of these negotiations, as well as those that followed until Ristić's resignation in 1880, are so well known that they are not covered extensively here, although they constitute an essential background to internal Serbian political developments. As Milorad Ekmečić has put it, "The diplomatic history of the Eastern Question to 1878 has already become so sterile that qualitatively new results can no longer be anticipated" (in Melville and Schröder, *Berliner Kongress*, p. 427). Documents on the Congress of Berlin can be found in Vojvodić, *Srbija 1878* and Imanuel Geiss, ed., *Der Berliner Kongress 1878: Protokolle und Materialen* (Boppard am Rhein: Boldt Verlag, Schriften des Bundesarchivs, 27, 1978). For an excellent overview of Ristić's two-year minister presidency following the war, see VMO, 2:245–320, an English paraphrase of which appears in Michael B. Petrovich, *History of Modern Serbia, 1804–1918* (New York: Harcourt Brace Jovanovich, 1976) 2:402–6.

8. Krstić's diary, 26 May/8 Jun 78.

9. Grujić to Ristić, 1/13 Jul 78, Vojvodić, *Srbija 1878*, p. 553.

10. Ristić secret speech to the skupština, 13/25 Jul 78, in Vojvodić, *Srbija 1878*, pp. 585–91. Ristić did not mention Milan's threat to the Russians, which became public only later in a work on the Berlin Congress by Vladan Djordjević.

11. During the skupština that convened in December 1878, government supporter Panta Srećković scoffed at opposition claims that people were in real need. He knew of only two or three places where there was actual starvation, he said (SB, 1878, pp. 874–75).

12. *Straža*, 1879, pp. 521–26.

13. Of Matić, Pera Todorović said in *Straža*, ibid., that he was "softer than cotton and obedient to infinity *[do bezkrajnosti]*." Of Vasiljević, Milan Milićević said "he just smokes and hopes" (Milićević's diary, 21 Oct/2 Nov 78). In a letter to Ristić a year later V. Popović wrote that Mihailović was not reconciled to being out of power and considered Ristić's ministers nothing more than clerks (21 Dec 79/3 Jan 80, AJR, III/2 3/41).

14. Both *Straža*—the radical journal produced in Novi Sad by exiles Pera Todorović and Lazar Paču—and Radical interpellations in the skupština accused the government of setting the election at a time when it could be more easily controlled and of calling opponents into the militia and sending them off to the border so they could not vote. As to the first charge Milojković made the unlikely claim that he just did not think of this connection, and as for the second the English consul in Belgrade

reported that the entire militia had been disbanded except for the Šabac brigade, which had been sent from the Drina to the new regions, presumably to provide security for the upcoming skupština. Of course, transfer of the Šabac brigade could have been motivated in part politically, but the implication is that the government did not systematically march the urban brigades to the border to prevent them from voting for the Radicals (Straža, 1879, pp. 264–67; Protokoli, pp. 143–44; and Gould to Salisbury, 6 Nov 78, FO, 105/3). An example of how closely voters' choices were monitored is offered by a report from Valjevo stating that all teachers in the middle school (polugimnasium) there voted for Miloš Glišić and mentioning the votes and factional preferences of dozens of other individuals by name ([načelnik?] to Ristić, 29 Oct/10 Nov 78, ARJ, III/2 3/32).

15. Gould to Salisbury, 31 Oct 78, 17 Nov 78 (FO, 105/3, 221, 226). See also Gould's reports of 28 May 79, 23 Jun 79 in which Gould points out how difficult it is for the government when the prince is so far away and under the influence of his adjutant, Kosta Protić, whom Gould says "encourages . . . the Prince's naturally despotic tendency" (Gould to Salisbury, 28 May 79, 23 Jun 79, FO, 105/7 126, 165). Milan bought his estate (konak), which was located in the finest location of the Niš fortress, for the relatively small sum of 1,500 ducats. (Gould to Salisbury, 18 Aug 79, FO, 105/8 248; for the location of Milan's konak see the magnificent map of Niš forwarded in the 28 Nov 79 report of Vice-Consul Baker, Gould to Salisbury, 1 Dec 79, FO, 105/8 305), and furnished it with furniture confiscated from local Muslims and Jews (Gould to Salisbury, 3 Jul 79, FO, 105/7 180).

16. Among the ministers, only Stojan Bosković favored holding the skupština in Belgrade. The others were for the traditional city of Kragujevac. But since that city had been the site of the Red Banner Affair and held unpleasant memories from the previous skupština, Ristić insisted on Niš (Ristić to Milan, 13/25 Oct 78, AS:PO-20-130).

17. Regulations for Niš appeared 11/23 Nov 78 (AJR, XXXII/31 32/1485). Besides requiring a special passport to enter or leave the city and the region, it required, among other things, all pedestrians to carry a lantern after dark and not to smoke, and every store to clean the space in front of it on Wednesday and Saturday evenings.

18. Gould to Salisbury, 12 Nov 78, FO, 105/3 218.

19. Gould reported that Ristić identified the names of ten oppositionists on the skupština list, plus some other unknown persons (Gould to Salisbury, 15 Dec 78, FO, 105/3 254). Milićević says that Ristić estimated 12 to 15 oppositionists and 12 to 15 undecided (Milićević's diary, 14/26 Nov 78).

20. In old age Pašić wrote that "when I came to the skupština they offered
to take me into the ministry [presumably at a later date] if I would be a
temperate oppositionist, but I refused. For that reason they nullified the
election of twelve *[sic]* colleagues . . ." (Nikola Pašić, "Autobiografija,"
Politika, 4 Apr 1927, quoted in Petrović, *Bogosavljević*, p. 124).
21. SB, 1878–79, pp. 71–73, 384–85.
22. Geiss, *Der Berliner Kongress*, p. 396.
23. All quotations for this debate not otherwise cited are taken from *Protokoli*,
pp. 100–109, 116–39.
24. SB, 1878–79, pp. 413–16.
25. *Protokoli*, pp. 131–38. Ristić clearly defended censorship on the basis of
reasons of state in his speech to the July 1878 skupština. In discussing
Russia's abandonment of Serbia early in 1878, he said, "I dare say that
if we did not have a free press at that time we did not lose much,
because dissatisfaction would have penetrated through the press to the
[educated] public, which would have had an effect on the people, the
people on the government, and the government, under the influence of
such events, would have had to depart from its measured path" (Vojvodić, *Srbija 1878*, p. 589).
26. A related issue was the right of Jews to trade in the interior, which had
been prohibited since 1856. The Congress of Berlin required Serbia to
abolish this rule, which was part of the constitution of 1869. Although
Serbian traders were violently opposed to permitting Jews to trade in
the interior, the government finessed the issue by getting the skupština
to delete the offending sentence from the constitution by acclamation,
in order to avoid an embarrassing debate *(Protokoli*, p. 472). Since technically a Grand National Assembly was required to change the constitution,
the opposition had an opening on this issue to insist on convening one,
at which they hoped to introduce other changes as well.
27. The Merchant and Craftsman Committee of Smederevo printed a form
letter (23 Nov/5 Dec 79) for citizens to send to their skupština delegate
demanding protection from the influx of goods (AJR, III/2 3/39).
28. This is not to say that no Serbs understood at least some aspects of this
problem. Some who did were Prince Milan, Nikola Pašić, and Vladimir
Jovanović, and there were economists beginning to propose solutions as
well. But the overwhelming sense of public life was that the smallholding
peasantry must be preserved as the backbone of the Serbian nation.
29. *Protokoli*, p. 293.
30. Ibid., p. 406.
31. For a printed statement of the debt as of 1880, see AS:PO-27-167.

32. He outlined his program in an undated letter to Ristić in 1879 (AJR, III/ 8 3/172).

33. Jovanović suggested the packing plant in 1880 (IAB, K-XVII/II, 18, Jovanović, to načelnici, 22 Aug/3 Sep 80).

34. William H. Sewell, Jr., *Work and Revolution in France* (New York: Cambridge University Press, 1980), pp. 86–87.

35. *Le Moniteur Universale* (Paris, 1791), p. 397; Charles Gomel, *Histoire Financière de l'Assemblée Constituante* (New York: Burt Franklin, n.d., orig. pub. Paris, 1897), pp. 420–32; John Hall Stewart, *A Documentary Survey of the French Revolution* (New York: Macmillan, 1951), pp. 437, 554; and Vladimir Jovanović, "Politićki rečnik," unpublished manuscript, IAB, entry entitled "patentarina."

36. "Kaiserliches Patent vom 20. December 1859 wo mit eine Bewerbe-Ordnung . . . gesesst wird," *Reichs-Gesetz-Blatt für das kaiserthum Österreich* (Vienna, 1859), pp. 619–50.

37. On the continuing viability of guilds, see, e.g., *Videlo,* 29 Feb/12 Mar 80, which reports the suppression of a baker who tried making bread outside the baker's guild. The butcher trade, however, was free. *Videlo* pointed out how much better service was from the free butchers than from the guild-operated bakers. The basic law on guilds from 1847 remained on the books until 1910. See Nikola Vučo, *Raspadanje esnafa u Srbiji* (Belgrade: SANU, posebna izdanja 222, Istorijski institut knj. 5, 1954), p. 13.

38. *Zbornik zakona* 34 (1879–80): 151–70.

39. Pašić's income is taken from the patentarina tax rolls for 1879. Only a few of these rolls, along with some registration sheets, have survived. They can be found in seven unnumbered boxes in the Arhiv Srbije (AS) under the call number MF-A-1879-V-191 (hereafter UPIS). By chance one of the surviving registration books *(upisne knjige)* is for Požarevacka opština, where Pašić is shown under item 60. The only information that appears are his name, occupation *(inžinjer),* and salary.

40. For a history of taxation in Serbia see Leposava Cvijetić, "Poreski sistem Srbije 1835–1884. godine," Ph.D. diss., Belgrade University, 1956. Unfortunately, Cvijetić does not discuss the patentarina very thoroughly.

41. Pašić's taxes for 1877 are shown on two tax receipts in AS:MF-A-1882-I-55. Pašić complained that for various reasons he had been forced to pay two danaks that year, and eventually he received a refund.

42. SB, 1878–79, p. 721.

43. *Protokoli,* p. 205.

44. SB, 1878–79, pp. 1282–83.

45. *Protokoli,* pp. 302–3.

46. SB, 1878–79, pp. 1260–66.
47. Todorović, *Tajsić*, p. 89; and SB, 1878, p. 1306.
48. Jovanović calculated that per capita Serbs paid only 16 dinars of tax annually, whereas he listed figures from other countries that were much higher. E.g., Ottoman Empire 23 dinars; Germany 30 dinars; and France 78 dinars *(Protokoli*, pp. 412–13).
49. Pašić to Dimitrijević, 4/16 Apr 76, Škorić collection, doc. 53.
50. As a matter of fact, according to Vladan Djordjević, in 1878 Serbia lost 60,000 head of cattle to rinderpest (*Protokoli*, p. 309).
51. AS:MF-A: *Protokoli i registar*, 31 Jan/12 Feb 79.
52. UPIS: Državni savet decision of 19/31 Mar 79; and minister of finance to trgovački-zanatlijski odbori, 23 Feb/7 Mar 79.
53. UPIS: minister of finance to all načelnici, 26 Apr/8 May (two memoranda); and minister of finance to teachers of Kragujevac, 24 May/5 Jun 79.
54. UPIS: draft of minister of finance's instructions to the commissions, 8/20 May 79; and message to all načelnici, 22 May/3 Jun 79.
55. Report to Ristić from Kladovo, AJR, III/2 3/1305.
56. Report to Ristić from Ćuprija, AJR, XXXII/6 32/200.
57. E.g., AJR, XXVII/3 27/61, dated 17 Feb/1 Mar 79.
58. Milićević's diary, 18 Feb/2 Mar 79 (SANU, 9327).
59. Ristić to Milan, 17 Feb/1 Mar, AJR, XXVII/3 27/61.
60. This report, dated 2/14 May 79, is included with the records of the second revision of the patentarina completed after December 1879 (AS:MF-A-1880-XIX/3-49).
61. UPIS: Nikolić to minister of finance, 16/28 Jun 79. In an effort to discredit Popović, this report was read aloud in the skupština on 26 Nov/8 Dec 79 by Svetozar Milojević (SB, 1879, pp. 79–80).
62. UPIS: minister of finance directive 25 Jun/6 Jul 79; and commission to minister of finance, 10/22 Jul 79. Surprisingly, whistle-blower Nikolić was a member of the commission.
63. These figures were collated from the records in the UPIS collection and from the second revision file.
64. UPIS: *upisne knjige* for Požeski srez, opština Zdravčić, item 10.
65. E.g., UPIS: minister of finance to all načelnici, 30 May/11 Jun 79.
66. A large number of unsorted documents concerning Vladimir Jovanović's efforts to increase the income of the patentarina can be found in his papers, IAB, XVII/11-14, from which the information in this and the next paragraph of text is taken.
67. The crop in 1878 had been good (Gould to Salisbury, 20 Oct 78, FO, 105/5, Commercial report 5), but on December 22, 1879 Gould reported that

the situation was so bad that "in some districts they [the peasants] are already reduced to support themselves on the inner bark or rind of trees" (Gould to Salisburg, FO, 105/8 316). See also Gould's reports of 17 Aug 79 and 17 Sep 79 (FO, 105/8 259, 275), and *Protokoli* 1879–80, p. 339. Milićević's diary 28 Nov/10 Dec 79 complains about the bitterly cold weather, and Ristić's papers contain a report of 8/20 Dec 79 noting that the Danube was frozen over (AJR, XXXII/3 32/113). When Ranko Tajsić returned home to Dragačevo after the skupština session he found such severe hunger that he gave the opština's money out to peasants to buy bread so they could survive until spring (Todorović, *Tajsić*, p. 112). The 1880 crop was good.

68. Tucaković to Ristić, 2/14 Nov 79, AJR, XXVII/3 27/139; and cabinet to Ristić, 4/16 Nov 79, AJR, III/10 3/234.
69. Milan to Ristić, 4/16 Nov 79, AJR, III/10 3/233.
70. Ristić to Milan, 5/17 Nov 79, AJR, III/10 3/238.
71. Milan to Ristić, 5/17 Nov 79, AJR, III/10 3/239.
72. Ristić to Milan, 5/17 Nov 79, AJR, III/10 3/240.
73. Ristić to minister of internal affairs, 5/17 Nov 79, AJR, III/10 3/241.
74. SB, 1879–80, pp. 3–13.
75. VMO, 2:287.
76. Pašić letter of 29 Nov/10 Dec 79 (SANU, 11582).
77. There had been rumors about Jovanović's resignation since summer (Milićević's diary, 13/25 Jul 79), and even Jovanović himself said he was in poor health and needed rest (Dimitrije Matić to Ristić, 12/24 Aug 79, AJR, XXXII/3 32/102, and Jovanović to Ristić, 22 Aug/3 Sep 79, AJR, XXXII/30 32/172, by which Jovanović asked for a leave for health reasons). Jovanović would have liked to move from minister to state councillor, essentially a sinecure, which he believed Ristić owed him (Jovanović to Ristić, 11/23 Jun 79, 17/29 Jun 79, AJR, XXXII/6 32/198-199). But in fact he became director of the state accounting office, from which position he was appointed minister of finance once again in June 1880.
78. *Protokoli*, pp. 141–42.
79. SB, 1879–80, pp. 233–99.
80. *Protokoli*, pp. 645–46. Several other plans were drafted by the government, but none achieved much support (AS:MF-A-1880-XXI-3).
81. Eighty-five soldiers died from typhus in the Vranje area in the period February through May 1879, according to an answer to an interpellation of the oppositionists (*Protokoli*, pp. 257–59). See also the report dated 4/16 Feb 80 in which typhus and pneumonia among the poorly clothed

and housed troops of the Moravska corps had resulted in a "very high" mortality rate (AS:PO-25-179).

82. Djordjević's remarks here and below are taken from *Protokoli*, pp. 308–55.

83. *Protokoli*, p. 344.

84. Pašić's letter of 8/20 Dec 79 (SANU, 11763). In this letter Pašić discusses the difficulties he experienced when in this debate he called another member of the skupština a "nobody" *(nitkov)*. When he was threatened with censure and temporary expulsion, he apologized because not to do so, he thought, "would have damaging consequences, both in the skupština and for my constituents."

85. For a superb discussion of the historical development of property relations in these territories see Miroslav R. Djordjević, "Inostrani komentari zakona o uredjenju agrarnih odnosa u novooslobodjenim krajevima Srbije od 1880. godine," in *Leskovački zbornik* 18 (1978): 57–75.

86. Gould to Salisbury, 1 Dec 79 (FO, 105/8 305), encloses three lengthy reports on the situation in the newly acquired areas. In one of them Baker reports (20 Sep 79) that the Muslim population of Niš had dropped from 8,000 before the war to 300 in 1879 and Nicolaides (Baker's agent) reports (29 Oct 79) that the Albanian population of the region had dropped from 42,000 to 2,000. The Christian (Serbian) population of Niš went from 10,000 to 12,000, making Niš the second largest city in Serbia. Other data in this and the succeeding paragraph are taken from this report of Baker's as well as information in the following dispatches of Gould to Salsibury: 3 Jul 79 (FO, 105/7 180); 18 Aug 79 (FO, 105/8 248); and 17 Sep 79 (FO, 105/8 274).

87. The very smallness of this estate, taken over by one of Serbia's most successful generals, gives a good insight into the relative lack of social differentiation in Serbia. Serbs connected with the state or successful in business unquestionably rose above the ordinary peasant, but the distance was still small compared to that of the rest of Europe.

88. Alimpije Vasiljević noted in his memoirs how he and another Liberal opposed the ruthless clearing of Muslims from their homes, "but everyone else agreed with the prince that it was necessary to drive the Albanians *(arnaute)* out of the liberated lands" (AS:PO-102-136, p. 70).

89. Gould to Salisbury, 23 Feb 79 (FO, 105/6 56).

90. Gould to Salisbury, 1 Dec 79 (FO, 105/8 304).

91. VMO, 2:245.

92. "Memoari Avrama Petrovića," SANU, 10039, p. 29.

93. SB, 1879–80, p. 1089.

94. Slobodanka Stojičić, "Pravni i politički aspekt agrarnog pitanja u novo-oslobodjenim krajevima," *Leskovački zbornik* 18 (1978): 77–91. The army also tried to force the peasantry in the new territories to send recruits, and this provoked both resistance from the peasants and conflict with the civil authorities, who did not agree with this heavy-handed approach (AS:PO-64-230, report from Leskovac, 5/17 Feb 78).

95. A full account of the debate may be found in Slobodanka Stojičić, *Novi krajevi Srbije, 1878–1883* (Leskovac: Biblioteka narodnog muzeja u Leskovcu, knj. 20, 1975), pp. 33–56.

96. Details on the agrarian law are taken from Baker's excellent report of 23 Feb 80 enclosed in Gould to Salisbury, 29 Feb 80 (FO, 105/12 16).

97. For the Ottoman protest of 2/14 May 80 and Ristić's rejection of it see AS:PO-25-184.

98. Gould to Salisbury, 17 Sep 80 (FO, 105/82).

99. VMO, 2:248.

100. Leskovac and Vranje had been relatively strong textile craft towns under the Ottomans, but with the drawing of a new border that deprived them of easy access to their traditional markets to the south they suffered serious decline.

101. The line, to be built by the Hungarian state railroad (Magyar állami Vasutak—MAV), would compete with the line run by the Austrian state railroad (Österreichischen Südbahn—OSB), whose terminus since 1856 had been the Danube town of Bajzaš, which is in the Banat, just west of the westernmost Serbian border. The new line was in fact completed in 1883 (Ferenc Erdósi, "Zur Bedeutung des Eisenbahnbaus für die Entstehung der monozentrischen territorialen Struktur im Ungarn des 19. Jahrhunderts," *Ungarn-Jahrbuch* 16 [1988]:209).

102. VMO, 2:259.

103. *Protokoli*, p. 37.

104. *Protokoli*, pp. 65–66.

105. *Protokoli*, pp. 79–80.

106. VMO, 2:262.

107. *Protokoli*, p. 76.

108. Baron Herbert to Ristić, 16 Jun 80, and Ristić's response 2/14 July 80 (AS:PO-25-192).

109. Diary of Jovan Mišković (minister of war), which chronicles the actions of the ministry during the crisis, SANU, 7241, pp. 41–46.

110. Louis Gould (Francis's brother, who served as secretary to the legation while Francis was on home leave; citations to Gould alone always refer to Francis) to Granville, 26 Jun 80, FO, 105/12 49. Milan departed on his

three-month trip less than three weeks before his wife, Princess Natalija, was delivered of a stillborn boy (Gould to Granville, 16 Jul 80, FO, 105/ 13 53).

111. Milan Živanović, "Prilozi za proučavanje pitanja imperijalističkog prodiranja Austro-ugarske u Srbiju od Berlinskog kongresa (1878) do zaklju-čenja trgovinskog ugovora 1881." in *Mešovita gradja* (Istorijski institute) 12, no. 9 (1956):149. When Milan returned to Belgrade in March he dismissed his aide General Kosta Protić, who many saw as having had undue influence on him in Niš (Gould to Salisbury, 30 May 80, FO, 105/ 12 24). This was considered a step favoring Austria.

112. Milan to Ristić, 4/16 Jul 80, in Živanović, "Prilozi za proučavanje prodiranja Austro-ugarske," pp. 148–52.

113. Milan to Ristić, 1/13 Aug 80, in ibid., pp. 152–55.

114. Mišković's diary, 16/28 Sep 80. This visit occurred despite Milan's remark in June that Bulgaria was "a government of cynical chauvinism" (Gould to Salisbury, 23 Jun 80, FO, 102/12 47).

115. Ibid., 4/16 Oct 80. See also Mišković's notes for 24 Sep/6 Oct 80, 27 Sep/ 9 Oct 80, SANU, 7242/14; Milićević's diary, 2/14 Oct 80; and Gould to Granville, 11 Oct 80, FO, 105/13 89.

116. Mišković's diary, 24 Sep/6 Oct 80.

117. Ristić to Milan, 9/21 Oct 80, in Živanović, "Prilozi za proučavanje prodiranja Austro-ugarske," pp. 163–64.

118. AJR, III/5 3/92, the resignation, dated 14/26 Oct 80.

NOTES TO CHAPTER 6

1. The term "Young Conservatives" is well established in Serbian historigraphy and, therefore, probably must be used when referring to these persons. However, as we shall see, it is not a particularly enlightening phrase, since the Young Conservatives proved to be closer to classical liberalism than the Liberals themselves. British Consul Gould called them "in reality ultra-liberals" (FO, 105/13, Gould to Salisbury, 1 Nov 80). Later they adopted the name Progressives, which was not a bad word for the tendency they represented.

2. Slobodan Jovanović, "Milan Piroćanac," *Političke i pravne rasprave*, 2 (Belgrade: Geca Kon, 1932, orig. pub. 1910): 145–212.

3. Most of the details concerning the organization of *Videlo* are taken from Milićević's diary between 7/19 Oct 79 and 21 Feb/5 Mar 80.

4. The quotation is from VMO, 2:310. British consul Gould thought Gara-

šanin had "sterling qualities," perhaps a comment on Gould's analytical capacities (Gould to Salisbury, 4 Nov 80, FO, 105–13, no. 104).

5. Among the best known of the twelve were Stojan Novaković, Gliša Geršić, Čedomil Mijatović, Milan Kujundžić, and Milan Dj. Milićević (Milićević's diary, 4/16 Dec 79).

6. At least this was the information forwarded to Ristić by the editor of *Istok* (K. Mijatović to Ristić, 1/13/ Jan 80, ARJ, III/7 3/1326). The report also states that the first issue of *Videlo* was seized by the police.

7. Garašanin apparently believed the Young Conservatives were too liberal and wanted to maintain closer ties with the old conservatives like Jovan Marinović. This came out in a five-hour discussion among Garašanin, Piroćanac, Milan Milićević, and Čedomil Mijatović on January 23 (Milićević's diary, 11/23 Jan 80).

8. VMO, 2:350–51.

9. *Videlo*, 2/14 Jan 80.

10. For the English case see Abraham D. Kriegel, "Liberty and Whiggery in Early Nineteenth-Century England," *Journal of Modern History* 52 (1980):253–78.

11. *Videlo*, 8/20 Jan 80.

12. Milićević's diary, 29 Jan/10 Feb 80.

13. Ibid., 21 Feb/4 Mar 80. Already on 10/22 Feb 80 Milićević complained that he was about to be put on pension and that his new boss appointed for that purpose had moved his desk from the warm to the cold part of the room. When he complained, Ristić claimed no knowledge of any moves against him. "Arrogant, deceitful man!" responded Milićević—to his diary.

14. Pašić later called the cooperation of the Radicals and Young Conservatives at this time "a serious effort to organize the opposition into a national party" (Gunjac i opanak speech, 1882, Škorić collection, doc. 179).

15. The most succinct narrative of these events can be found in Petrović, *Adam Bogosavljević*, pp. 130–34.

16. *Videlo*, 5/17 Mar 80, reprinted in Petrović, *Adam Bogosavljević*, pp. 177–78.

17. *Videlo*, 19/31 Mar 80. Kosta Taušanovic immediately notified both Pašić and Glišić by telegram, copies of which were sent to Ristić by the telegraph service (AJR, XXXII/19 32/583).

18. For the following see Petrović, *Adam Bogosavljević*, pp. 135–39.

19. Pašić's telegram asking Dr. Jovan Danić to pick a colleague and attend the autopsy can be found in AJR, XXXII/19 32/585, although the catalogue card misidentifies the document.

20. E.g., SB, 1880–81, second session, pp. 242–44 (19/31 May 81).
21. *Videlo*, 30 Mar/11 Apr 80.
22. *Videlo*, 26 Mar/7 Apr 80. The other two members of the original committee were Sava Obradović and Steva Milićević.
23. *Videlo*, 30 May/11 Jun 80.
24. *Videlo*, 2/14 May 80. In 1882 Pašić described how the oppositionists at Niš in 1879 had given him the job of writing a program for them, so we can assume this was the result of that effort (Gunjac i opanak speech, 1882 Škorić Collection, doc. 179).
25. *Videlo*, 23 May/4 Jun 80.
26. K. Mijatović to Ristić, 1/13 Jan 80, AJR, III/7 3/1326.
27. This and the following from Mišković's notes of 23 Jun/5 Jul 80, 7/19 Jul 80, 11/113 Aug 80.
28. *Videlo*, 18/30 Jul 80, 20 Jul/1 Aug 80, 25 Jul/6 Aug 80, 13/25 Aug 80; Milićević's diary, 17/29 Jul 80; and Mišković's notes, 9/21 Jul 80.
29. Stojan Mitrović to Ristić, 5/17 Aug 80, AJR, III/7 3/126.
30. Milićević's diary, 10/22 Oct 80.
31. Ibid., and 11/23 Oct 80; and Mišković's notes, 10/22 Oct 80.
32. VMO, 2:306; Mišković's notes, 15/27 Oct 80; and Milićević's diary, 17/29 Oct 80.
33. A report to Ristić from Požarevac concerning a speech given there by an editor of *Videlo* mentions Garašanin's privileged access to the prince, 30 Aug/11 Sep 80, in AJR, III/7 3/126. A disgusted Milićević reported that Piroćanac "won't be anywhere other than first [*On nigde drukčije nego prvi*]" (17/29 Oct 80).
34. 15/27 Oct 80. One is reminded of Svetozar Marković's similar sentiments in 1875.
35. For an excellent discussion see VMO, 2:333–50.
36. *Videlo*, 26 Oct/7 Nov 80.
37. *Videlo*, 23 Nov/4 Dec 80, and also 29 Oct/10 Nov 80.
38. *Videlo*, 5/17 Nov 80.
39. *Videlo*, 16/28 Nov 80. Along with Pašić the signatories were Miloš Glišić, Paja (Pavle J.) Vuković, Jovan Jovanović, and Kosta Taušanović.
40. *Videlo*, 30 Nov/12 Dec 80, 5/17 Dec 80.
41. *Videlo*, 11/23 Jul 80.
42. *Videlo*, 30 Nov/12 Dec 80 reported on such meetings in Smederevo, Negotin, and Valjevo.
43. *Videlo*, 28 Nov/10 Dec 80; and Milićević's diary, 24 Nov/6 Dec 80.
44. Mišković's notes, 20 Oct/1 Nov 80, 25 Oct/6 Nov 80.
45. Ibid., 24 Nov/6 Dec 80.

46. *Videlo,* 7/19 Dec 80.

47. According to Milićević, Garašanin kept his promise not to interfere in the election. "Everywhere he is leaving the right to the people. If nothing else [should be accomplished by this government], this is a great gain" (Milićević's diary, 26 Nov/8 Dec 80).

48. "The result of the election surprised everyone," Jovan Mišković said in his notes. Still "[it was] decided not to do anything and to remain passive until the skupština" (Mišković's notes, 1/13 Dec 80).

49. Milićević's diary, 5/17, 7/19 Dec 80.

50. Todorović brought Milićević a note from his son, who was studying in Paris, and reported that the son was in good health, studying, and maintaining the family's good name (Milićević's diary, 26 Dec 80/7 Jan 81).

51. SB, 1881, p. 14.

52. Ibid., p. 20.

53. Ibid., pp. 34–37.

54. *Samouprava,* 8/20 Jan 80.

55. Stanković, *Pašić i jugoslovensko pitanje,* 1:69.

56. Quoted by Perović, *Pera Torodović,* p. 78.

57. *Samouprava,* 8/20 Jan 81.

58. Pera Todorović, "Krvava godina" (SANU, 13512), p. 1. Torodović and Pašić lived "on Kalemegdan" in an apartment attached to the Serbian Crown café.

59. Perović, *Pera Torodović,* pp. 90–93, and Ninčić, *Pera Torodović,* pp. 62–68. Ninčić declares that while in Paris Todorović became a "radical, a radical-jacobin" (p. 68) and that the Radical program of 1881 "was completely dependent on the West," except that it did not call for separation of church and state and for a republic (p. 75). Milan Protić supports this point of view, even though he also says that "it is virtually impossible to establish the exact paths by which French ideas came to Serbia" ("The Ideology of the Serbian Radical Movement, 1881–1903," Ph.D. diss., University of California at Santa Barbara, 1987, p. 125).

60. Todorović, "Krvava godina," p. 5.

61. Francois Furet, *Interpreting the French Revolution* (Cambridge: Cambridge University Press, 1981), p. 49.

62. For Cenić see Andrija Radenić, "Pogovor," in Mita Cenić, *Ispod zemlje ili moja tamnovanja* (Belgrade: Prosveta, 1983, orig. pub. 1881), p. 132.

63. On Taušanović see Milan Kostić, "Kosta Taušanović," *Samouprava,* 1938 (58), no. 569:7; and Živorad P. Jovanović, "Kosta S. Taušanović," *Delo,* 2/1940, no. 39:2.

64. Nikola Pašić, "Politička kronika," *Rad,* 1881, pp. 85–86, written 10/22 Oct 81.
65. In his memoirs Avram Petrović says that the main issue was the vice presidency of the skupština (p. 37).
66. Milićević's diary, 2/14 Jan 81 (but written 10/22 Jan 81).
67. Todorović, "Krvava godina," pp. 40–41.
68. Milićević's diary, 10/22, 11/23, 12/24, 13/25 Jan 81. According to Ranko Tajsić's unpublished memoirs, the Radicals met there too (Torodović, *Tajsić,* p. 126), although the Serbian Crown was a more likely spot.
69. *Videlo,* 18/30 Jan 81. *Istok* found the Progressive formula uncomfortably vague—basing one's program on the prince's speech to the throne? At least the Radicals were clear about what they were doing, *Istok* thought (23 Jan/4 Feb 81).
70. Milićević's diary, 11/23 Jan, 12/24 Jan 86.
71. Todorović, "Krvava godina," pp. 41–43.
72. Torodović, *Tajsić,* p. 127.
73. A bitter sniping campaign began soon after when *Samouprava* accused Glišić of writing the greetings he ostensibly received from the voters in his district. When Glišić responded with an "account clearing" in *Videlo,* Pašić pointed out it was Glišić who had changed his position, not the Radicals. As was the Serbian custom, when an older brother wanted to divide the zadruga, Pašić said, the others must enter in, and the Radicals were only too happy to do so (*Samouprava,* 19 Feb/3 Mar 81).
74. Other defectors included Sima Nestorović and Aca Milenković.
75. *Videlo,* 18/30 Jan 81.
76. 15/27 Jan 81.
77. *Samouprava,* 20 Jan/1 Feb 81.
78. sb, 1881: for Tajsić's comment and its resolution, a request that the government lower per diems within reason, pp. 38, 107–8, 202; for Milosević's complaint and a government promise to look into it, pp. 78, 154–57; for abolishing peasant shops, p. 290; and for the army's promise to buy in Serbia as well as it could, taking into account the approximately 15 percent higher price of goods, pp. 344–46. "All this is only that the interpellants can listen to themselves," complained Milićević (diary, 7/19 Feb 81).
79. *Videlo,* 21 Jan/2 Feb 81.
80. Ibid., 28 Jan/9 Feb 81.
81. *Istok,* 27 Jan/8 Feb 81.
82. *Samouprava,* 31 Jan/12 Feb 81.
83. Milićević's diary, 23 Jan/4 Feb, 26 Jan/7 Feb, 27 Jan/8 Feb, 30 Jan/11 Feb, 4/16 Feb 81.

84. Kristić's diary, 25 Jan/6 Feb 81. Krstić says he drafted a good deal of the bill. "A great demonstration of confidence," said Milićević (diary, 7/19 Feb 86). The bill as passed provided for a top salary of 7,500 dinars a year to the president of the highest appeal court, compared to 12,500 proposed in the original bill, and a salary of 2,500 dinars a year instead of 4,000 to a beginning member of the lowest (okrug) court *(Zbornik zakona* [1881–82] 37:222).

85. *Zbornik zakona* (1881–82) 37:249–64.

86. Ibid., 37:544–54. This law was similar to one passed in France by the republican government at almost the same time, June 30, 1881 (Tony Judt, *Socialism in Provence, 1871–1914* [New York: Cambridge University Press, 1979], p. 62).

87. *Samouprava,* 21 Feb/5 Mar 81.

88. For a history of railroads in Serbia see *Železnice u Srbiji, 1884–1958* (Belgrade: NIN, 1958), which, despite its title, begins with the first rumors of possible railroad building in 1851.

89. See Barnard Michel, "Zur Gründung der Länderbank. Planung und Einsatz französischen Kapitals im Donauraum (1880 bis 1882)," *Österreichische Osthefte* 28 (1986):440–51.

90. The "existing kike-riddled [*očivućenih*] institutions" is the exact wording used by Filip Hristić in his letter to Jovan Ristić on the matter *(Pisma Filipa Hristića Jovanu Ristiću, 1868–1880,* Grgur Jakšić, ed. [Belgrade: SANU, Posebna izdanja 206, 1953], letter from Vienna of 8/20 Oct 80, p. 359).

91. Vojislav J. Vučković, "Pad Generalne unije i proglas kraljevine (1882)," *Glas* SANU, 118 (1956):50. This article is the standard source for the question stated in its title, and is one of the finest articles on Serbian history ever written.

92. The question of bribery in the Bontoux affair is murky. No smoking gun has ever been found, but it is the opinion of such careful analysts as Slobodan Jovanović and Vojislav Vučković that a great deal of bribery took place, most of it either with the support of Prince Milan or with his knowledge. See VMO, 2:437–53, where Jovanović concludes "Rozen conducted the indirect negotiations, Bontoux provided the money—the price of individual consciences was calculated by Milan." Vučković simply states that Bontoux, through Rozen, bribed both Radical and Progressive leaders (p. 50).

93. This paragraph is from VMO, 2:387–405. Summaries in English include Petrovich, *History of Modern Serbia 1804–1918,* pp. 419–22; and Charles Jelavich, *Tsarist Russia and Balkan Nationalism: Russian Influence in the Internal Affairs of Bulgaria and Serbia, 1879–1886* (Berkeley: University

of California Press, 1962), pp. 169–70. For some piquant details, see Živanović, *Politička istorija Srbije*, 2:174–79.

94. This second loan was passed separately by the skupština only after the main deal was approved.

95. The debate is in SB, 1881, pp. 1421–1718. Speeches of the Radical opponents can be found in *Govori radikalaca protiv železničkog ugovora u skupštini za 1880/1* (Belgrade: Štamparija zadruge štamparskih radenika, 1881).

96. The Radicals did not believe that Serbia was legally obligated to build a railroad, since no international agreement had been reached by the commission of four (Bulgaria, Ottoman and Habsburg Empires, and Serbia) on how the Serbian line would connect to the south (*Samouprava*, 7/19 Mar 81).

97. Milićević reported to his diary that the loan sailed through the Progressive Club almost unanimously, although there were rumors that the Radicals were going to walk out of the skupština (3/15 Mar 81).

98. Later it was alleged that Pašić and other Radicals were bribed not to leave the skupština, but they denied it, saying they could not get enough signatures of resignation to make it work (*Samouprava*, 11/23 Jan 83). In his diary Piroćanac says Bontoux told Mijatović he had given Pašić 20,000 dinars not to walk out (SANU, 9989, 19/31 Oct 80, but obviously written months later). By Pašić's account, 34 signatures were obtained (*Samouprava*, 20 Jun/2 Jul 81). Alimpije Vasiljević alleges that General Cherniaev, who was intriguing for the concession, told Raša Milošević and Kosta Taušanović that by resigning and walking out, they could stop Bontoux. They are supposed to have said then that they could not afford the trip home (Taušanović lived in Belgrade, Milošević was a delegate from Pirot, far to the south). Cherniaev asked how much they needed. Twenty thousand dinars, they replied. Cherniaev claimed he gave them the money, but in any event they did not walk out (AS:PO-102-136, p. 87; on Cherniaev's efforts to obtain the concession see Mackenzie, *Lion of Tashkent*, chapter 14). In 1889 Dimitrije Katić said that when the Radicals could not muster enough resignations among themselves, they approached the Liberals, who agreed to resign with them. When the moment came, however, the Liberals did not walk out (Todorović, *Tajsić*, p. 402 n. 66). In his dissertation Todorović said Katić was probably telling the truth (p. 24 of notes), but in the published version he is noncommittal.

99. Milićević's diary, 7/19 Mar 81.

100. Baker's report of 23 Mar 81 (FO, 105/19).

101. *Samouprava*, 7/19 Mar 81; and Milićević's diary, 4/16 Mar 81.

102. *Govori radikalaca*, p. 144.

103. Ibid.

104. Todorović's reaction to the Bontoux affair was a sarcastic poem in *Samouprava* (28 Feb/12 Mar, 9/21 May 81) about Big Bontoux and Little Serbia, for which he eventually had to serve a month in jail (Ristić's old law was still in effect when the poem was published). *Samouprava* said the Progressives were "practicing" for how they would enforce their new press law (10/22 Mar 81). However, see also Krstić's diary, 16/28 Apr 81, where Milan became annoyed with Krstić because the appeals court overturned another conviction of *Samouprava* on procedural grounds.

105. *Govori radikalaca*, p. 141.

106. SB, 1881, pp. 2391, 2393, 2340. The Radicals presented their position more fully in *Samouprava*, 11/23 Apr 81. This new patentarina, it said, was on gross not net income, and actually was a turnover tax regardless of profit.

107. In fact, the three taxes raised between 2 and 3 million. See Lampe, "Financial Structure and the Economic Development of Serbia," p. 140.

108. SB, 1881, second session, pp. 116–235; VMO, 2:321–33.

109. Cvijetić, "Poreski sistem Srbije," p. 227. Cvijetić points out what an important negative impact the agreement had on Serbia, since it removed the old "sales tax" by which Serbia had been effectively taxing Austrian imports since 1869. On kerosene (*špiritus*), for example, the tax had been 100 percent, so that when the new agreement went into effect the amount of kerosene imported into Serbia from Austria jumped from zero in 1881 to 442,000 kilos in 1882 (p. 245).

110. Mihailo V. Vujić, *Naša ekonomna politika* (Belgrade: Državna štamparija, 1883), p. 15 and passim. For a discussion of Vujić's economics see Obren Blagojević, *Ekonomska misao u Srbiji do drugog svetskog rata* (Belgrade: SANU, Posebna izdanja 525, 1980), pp. 157–206.

111. For Mijatović as an economist, see Blagojević, *Ekonomska misao u Srbiji*, pp. 126–57.

112. Once they came to power in 1889 the Radicals did not hesitate to bribe the peasantry by means of a tax collection policy in the countryside that Michael Palairet characterizes as "positively cavalier" (Michael Palairet, "Fiscal Pressure and Peasant Impoverishment in Serbia before World War I," *Journal of Economic History* 39 [1979]:736).

113. SB, 1881, special session, p. 183.

NOTES TO CHAPTER 7

1. For the following see Jean Mousset, *La Serbie et son Eglise (1830–1904)* (Paris: Librairie Droz, 1938), pp. 315–64; and VMO, 2:406–21. The basic documents concerning the affair can be found in AS:PO-78-322.
2. The five dioceses of the Serbian Orthodox Church in 1881 were the archbishopric of Belgrade and the bishoprics of Šabac, Žiča, Timok (Negotin), and Niš (Mousset, *La Serbie et son Eglise,* p. 311).
3. Baker's report of 7 Apr 81, FO, 105/19 40. Two weeks later Baker reported that Milan fed the Radicals information to help them in their perennial efforts in the skupština to get the Metropolitan's salary reduced (20 Apr 81, FO, 105/19 52).
4. Mousset, *Le Serbie et son Eglise,* p. 318.
5. Živanović, *Politička istorija Srbije,* 2:188.
6. Mousset, *La Serbie et son Eglise,* pp. 337–39.
7. Ibid., p. 363, quoting from *Srpska nezavisnost,* 15/27 Aug 82.
8. *Samouprava,* 9/21 Apr 81.
9. See Andrija Radenić, "Radnik (1881)," in his *Socijalistički listovi i časopisi u Srbiji 1871–1918* (Belgrade: Rad, 1977), pp. 368–406; and on Cenić see the same author's "Afterword," in Mita Cenić, *Ispod zemlje ili moja tamnovanja,* pp. 123–50.
10. *Radnik,* 19/31 Jul 81, quoted by Radenić, "Radnik," p. 368.
11. Radenić, "Radnik," p. 393.
12. *Samouprava,* 16/28 Jun 81.
13. *Samouprava,* 18/30 Jun 81. Paču vehemently denied writing this article (*Samouprava,* 20 Jun/2 Jul 81), but it is now generally accepted that in fact he did (Radenić, "Radnik," pp. 390–91).
14. Pašić to Ranko Tajsić, 26 Oct/7 Nov 81, AS:PO-100-33.
15. VMO, 3:13.
16. Andrija Radenić, "Policiski (*sic*) izveštaji o dogadjajima u Beograda početkom osamdesetih godina XIX. veka," *Godišnjak grada Beograda* 4 (1957): 415–31.
17. *Radnik*'s subscription rate was 2 dinars a month and actual production costs were at least 2,040 dinars a month, not counting editorial salaries (Radenić, "Radnik," pp. 405–6). See also Radenić "Policiski izveštaji," p. 422.
18. The Radicals scoffed at this lineage: "Whoever knows the decisions and work of the St. Andrew's skupština," *Samouprava* said on 8/20 Oct 81, "knows that the program that the Bureaucratic-Liberal Party now presents in *Srpska nezavisnost* is nowhere near or equivalent to the program of the liberal party" of 1858.

19. "Program of the National-Liberal party," *Srpska nezavisnost*, 1/13 Oct 81.
20. Živanović, *Politička istorija Srbije*, 2:189.
21. "Spisak akcionara 'družine za potpomaganje srpske književnosti,' " 28 Nov/10 Dec 81, AJR, VIII/2 8/38.
22. Financial report of the society, 5/17 Jan 82, AJR, VIII/3 8/42.
23. Apparently *Novi vek* had as much trouble surviving as *Radnik*. It was saved, according to an Austrian agent in Zemun, by financial help from Russia (Radenić, "Policiski izveštaji," p. 417). This would be consistent with Russian policy in the early 1880s, which supported the Russophile Liberals.
24. *Srpska nezavisnost*, 1/13 Oct 81.
25. E.g., *Samouprava*, 2/14 Jul 81, "Jugoistočna Jevropa i njen preporodjaj na osnovu narodnosti."
26. Radenić, "Policiski izveštaji," p. 426.
27. Živanović, *Politička istorija Srbije*, 2:191. Živanović tells how Ristić saved the rock for a long time as a reminder, as he put it, "of contemporary political toleration."
28. "Memoari Avrama Petrovića," p. 38.
29. Report from Vranje dated 6/18 Oct 81, AJR, VIII/3 8/40. The Radicals never did have much success in Vranje. In March 1883 the Radical committee there reported a membership of only 11 and commented that its work was very poorly known (SANU, 9783/56).
30. Ristić's speech to the second meeting of the society, 17/29 Oct 82, AJR, I/25 1/28.
31. Milićević's diary, 3/15 Sep, 8/20 Sep 81.
32. *Videlo*, 25 Sep/7 Oct, 30 Sep/12 Oct, 4/16 Oct 81.
33. Undated note, AJR, VIII/3 8/48.
34. Invitation from the srez clerk of Golubac to join the Progressive Party, 10/22 Nov 81, enclosed in clerk's letter to Garašanin, 27 Nov/9 Dec 81, AS:MG-63. Letter to Garašanin from his nephew in Kruševac mentions trying to recruit "illustrious" citizens, but it seems many of them were already Liberals (AS:MG-175).
35. AS:MG-53. The list is dated only with the year, not the month or day.
36. "Memoari Avrama Petrovića," p. 38.
37. Milićević's diary for October 1881 discusses this situation in at least six entries.
38. Later in the year the government sent Čumić to Paris as its representative to General Union (Nikola P. Škerović, ed., *Zapisnici Sednica ministarskog saveta Srbije, 1862–98* [Belgrade: Archiv Srbije, 1952], pp. 400, 403, 406). Kaljević had headed the government in 1875–76, of course, but during

the wars he was forced into exile and was able to return only after the Progressives came to power. In Milićević's view he had "declined a great deal" (Milićević's diary, 2/14 Oct 81). Later that year he was named ambassador to Romania *(Videlo,* 25 Nov/7 Dec 81).

39. Škorić collection, doc. 138. The speech was given 2/14 Jun 81 and became one of the classics of Radical political literature.

40. *Samouprava,* 22 Dec 81/3 Jan 82.

41. Pera Torodović, "Krvava godina" (SANU, 13512), p. 44.

42. Radenić, "Policiski izveštaji," p. 423.

43. This according to Slobodan Jovanović, VMO, 3:12.

44. Perović, *Pera Todorović,* p. 69. Of the eight members of the editorial board of *Rad,* five were teachers at either the Velika škola or the Belgrade gymnasium.

45. Pašić, "Politička kronika," *Rad* (1881), pp. 210–11.

46. Todorović, "Krvava godina," p. 44. Pašić to Tajsić mentions Pera's illness (26 Oct/7 Nov 81, AS:PO-100-33). On 20 Sep 81 an Austrian agent in Zemun noted that "for some time Todorović has worked very zealously on the formation of Radical clubs in the interior, and toward that end he often travels. . . . All of them have rather many members" (Radenić, "Policiski izveštaji," p. 426).

47. *Samouprava,* 8/20 Sep, 17/29 Oct 81. During the month of September the lament "O tempora, o mores" appears in the paper several times, almost with a sigh.

48. Pašić to Tajsić, ibid.; Mladen Žujović (Knjaževac) to Garašanin, 10/22 Nov 81, AS:MG-95.

49. *Samouprava,* 7/19 Nov 81.

50. Quoted in Živanović, *Politička istorija Srbije,* 2:192.

51. *Samouprava,* 15/22 Nov 81.

52. Ibid., 3/15 Dec 81. The statutes were dated 15/27 Nov 81.

53. VMO, 3:2–3.

54. Memoirs of Alimpije Vasiljević, p. 89 (AS:PO-102-136).

55. N.d., but received by the Central Committee 16/28 Feb 83 (SANU, 9783/ 24). See also SANU, 9783/25.

56. SANU, 9782/72, list of local committees with officers.

57. For a list of the thirty-nine persons who paid their memberships in the local Belgrade party unit see SANU, 9781/3. Nikola Pašić not only paid 10 dinars instead of 6 for his membership, but contributed the significant sum of 240 dinars as well. Kosta Taušanović, a successful tobacco merchant, contributed only an extra 50 dinars. *Samouprava* reported that fifty voting persons showed up at the first meeting to form the local committee (8/20 Dec 81).

58. The skupština had to convene at least once each calendar year. Usually the prince and government waited until the last possible moment, which in the case of the skupština for 1881 meant until December 30 (o.s.). Even this date was in actuality postponed until January 7, 1882 (o.s.).

59. *Samouprava*, 11/23 Dec 81.

60. *Samouprava*, 12/24 Dec 81.

61. Diary of Jovan Mišković, 13/25 Dec 81. The government candidate received 915 votes, Cenić 188, the Liberal 148, and Banković 108.

62. Milićević's diary, 10/17 Jan 82; and Čedomil Mitrović and Miloš N. Brašić, *Jugoslovenske narodne skupštine i sabori*, (Belgrade: Narodna skupština Kraljevine Jugoslavije, 1937), pp. 94–95.

63. Mišković's diary, 22 Nov/4 Dec 81; and *Samouprava*, 22 Dec 81/3 Jan 82. Pašić stopped attending after the first meeting (Milićević's diary, 17/29 Dec 81). The commission decided to recommend taxing the peasants 10 dinars and having the state build roads rather than relying on the old system of peasant labor (Milićević's diary, 19/31 Dec 81).

64. "It was wonderful to see how Milutin and Radivoj sat one next to the other," said Milićević. "Milutin offered Radivoj a cigar, and the latter provided the light" (diary, 20 Dec 81/1 Jan 82).

65. For a review of the debate see Todorović, *Tajsić*, pp. 149–52.

66. The reasons the Radicals cited for not signing the address went beyond procedural matters. They included their irritation with Milan's coldness toward Russia and his closeness to Austria, the Bontoux affair, a desire for closer relations with Bulgaria, with those liberals the Radicals kept in close touch, and, naturally, Serbia's growing tax burden (*Samouprava*, 14/26 Feb 81).

67. SB, 1881–82, pp. 303–4; *Samouprava*, 19/31 Jan 81; and Locock to Granville, 30 Jan 81, FO, 105/32 15.

68. VMO, 3:28–39; SB, 1881–82, pp. 258–59; and Locock to Granville, 2 Feb 81, FO, 105/32 18.

69. *Samouprava*, 9/21 Jan 81.

70. The description that follows is a paraphrase of the definitive account presented by Vučković, "Pad General unije."

71. "Why?" asked Milićević. "Because Čedo has a soft heart and does not know how to refuse anything to anyone" (diary, 22 Jan/3 Feb 82). Mijatović had switched from foreign affairs to finance in October 1881, when Piroćanac became foreign minister.

72. *Samouprava*, 7/19 Jun 81; and Locock to Granville, 3 Jul 81, FO, 105/19 42. On May 12 Sidney Locock, formerly British representative in Guatemala, replaced Gould, who was reassigned to Württemberg (FO, 105/19 68).

73. Radenić, "Policiski izveštaji," pp. 423, 425; and *Samouprava*, 5/17 Sep 81.
74. Radenić, "Policiski izveštaji," p. 424; and Pašić to Tajsić, 26 Oct/7 Nov 81, AS:PO-100-33.
75. *Samouprava*, 6/18 Aug 81.
76. On this revolt see Hamidija Kapidžić, *Hercegovački ustanak 1882* (Sarajevo: Veselin Masleša, 1958).
77. *Samouprava*, 8/20 Apr 81, commented that permitting the nuns to gather contributions was outrageous, since we "very well know that they will educate children in the stupid Catholic faith and then let them into the world to stab their brother Serb, who is not Catholic, in the breast, exalted by religious fanaticism."
78. Milićević's diary, 23 Jan/4 Feb 82.
79. Todorović, *Tajsić*, p. 152.
80. Quoted by Todorović, *Tajsić*, p. 153.
81. Locock to Granville, 7, 8 Feb 81, FO, 105/32 19, 20.
82. Gould to Granville, 14 Apr 81, FO, 105/19 49.
83. In April Mr. Baker, described by Gould as "the official pamphleteer of the Servian government, and one of Mr. Ristić's staunchest and ablest adherents," was given two months' leave of absence to write a pamphlet favoring raising Milan to the rank of king (Gould to Granville, 18 Apr 81, FO, 105/19 50).
84. Locock to Granville, 20 Jan 82, FO, 105/32 5.
85. Locock to Granville, 6 Mar 82, FO, 105/32 45. Milićević reported, "Tumultuous, endless cries of 'Long Live the King' shook the hall" (diary, 22 Feb/6 Mar 82).
86. Three of the most obstreperous Radicals, Ranko Tajsić, Raša Milošević, and Aca Stanojević, did not attend the king's reception, but took a walk in Topčider instead, since, as they said, "it was such a lovely spring day" (Todorović, *Tajsić*, p. 158).
87. *Zbornik zakona* (1881–82) 37:79; and Milićević's diary, 19/31 Apr 82.
88. Locock to Granville, 14 Mar 81, FO, 105/32 64. *Samouprava* entitled its explanatory article "Čaša strpljenja prepunjena je," 4/16 Mar 81.
89. Škorić collection, docs. 165, 166, 167.
90. Ibid., doc. 168.
91. *Samouprava*, 5/17 Mar 81; and Locock to Granville, 17 Mar 81, FO, 105/32 67.
92. *Samouprava*, 18/30 Mar 81, reported that Pop Marinko gave his public accounting to 200 persons, despite police efforts to prevent it. On the other hand, *Samouprava*, 17/29 Apr 82, reported that local authorities prevented many meetings.

93. *Samouprava,* 18/30 Mar 81. Pašić gave his report to a crowd of 400 persons, and even fielded questions, such as why did the Radicals not resign to prevent the original Bontoux agreement? His answer: there were too few of us.

94. Škorić collection, note to doc. 170.

95. E.g., Raša Milošević, one of the most extreme Radicals, was relieved of his duties as kmet of Pirot (*Samouprava,* 10/22 Apr 81).

96. Reprinted in *Samouprava,* 1/13 Apr 81.

97. *Samouprava,* 3/15 Apr 81; and V. Djordjević, teacher, to central committee, 28 May/10 Jun 81, SANU, 9782/6.

98. *Samouprava,* 18/30 Mar 81.

99. *Samouprava,* 27 Apr/9 May, 1/13 May 81.

100. VMO, 3:48.

101. The Radicals had constructed several archway signs with such messages as "Bosnia and Hercegovina must be ours," and "Through here lies the road to Bosnia," with which they hoped to stir anti-Austrian sentiment and unsettle Milan's meeting with the visiting Austrian representative (Locock to Granville, 4 May 82, FO, 105/32 87).

102. Milićević's diary, 28, 29, 30 Apr/10, 11, 12 May 82; Locock to Granville, 12 May 82, FO, 105/32 88; and VMO, 3:50–53, discusses the two events mentioned in this pararaph.

103. Todorović, *Tajsić,* pp. 163–67 gives a full description of the arms incident.

104. The following from Todorović, *fi÷ć,* pp. 167–68.

105. Figures vary in different sources. These are taken from Lockock to Granville, 29 May 82 (*sic*), FO, 105/33 93.

106. Ibid.; and Locock to Granville, 1 Jun 82, FO, 105/33 95.

107. Milićević's diary, 10/22 May 82.

108. Ibid., 14/26 May 82.

109. Ibid., 15, 16, 17/27, 28, 29 May 82.

110. VMO, 3:58.

111. For this paragraph see Milićević's diary, 21–26 May/2–7 Jun 82.

112. On June 6, for example, Gornji Milovanac responded that the party should remain resolute, not enter a joint cabinet, and not form a cabinet until the party achieved a majority (SANU, 9782/7). On June 26 Predvorica responded that "our party [should] not relent even a hair from its program" (SANU, 9782/9).

113. Mišković's diary, 24 May/5 Jun 82.

114. Živanović, *Politička istorija Srbije,* 2:206.

115. At its meeting of 30 May/11 Jun, the central committee noted that the

party's local organizations agreed that Radical delegates should not come
to the skupština (SANU, 9777).

116. Mišković's diary, 26 May/7 Jun 82.

117. Todorović, "Krvava godina," p. 49.

118. Milićević's diary, 31 May/12 Jun, 2/14 Jun 82.

119. Locock to Granville, 13 Jun 82, FO, 105/33 108.

120. Avram Petrović recalled that when the two-voters passed through Radical villages on their way to Belgrade the villagers greeted them by bang-
ing on pots and pans ("Memoari Avrama Petrovica," p. 41). The central
committee of the Radical Party advised its delegates not to come but to
send their credentials to the central committee. Those who were close
could come to consult on how to handle the government's unconstitutional acts (Minutes of 1/13 Jun 81, SANU, 9777). Many delegates came
anyway.

121. Milićević's diary, 30 May/11 Jun, 3/15 Jun 82; and Todorović, *Tajsić*, pp.
169–70.

122. Central Committee Minutes, 8/20 Jun 82 (SANU, 9777).

123. *Zbornik zakona* (1881–82) 37:97–98.

124. Ibid., 1881–82, pp. 91–96.

125. *Samouprava*, 24 Jun/6 Jul 82. Three versions of this paper are preserved
in the Svetozar Marković (Belgrade University) Library, one showing
some blank spaces, a second complete copy, and a third with almost
the entire paper white and the word "banned" printed across the
columns.

126. *Zbornik zakona* (1881–82):171–72.

127. Milićević's diary, 10/22 Jun 82.

128. Ibid., 11/23 Jun 82.

129. Central Committee Minutes, 4/16 Jul 82, 13/25 July 82 (SANU, 9777).
The trip lasted from June 28 through July 16.

130. "Zapisnici glavne godišnje skupštine radikalne stranke 1882," report on
credentials (SANU, 9779/4). The next largest proportion of delegates, at
12 percent, were traders (*trgovic*); a category that did not include numerous others in business such as storekeepers, pubkeepers, or tobacco
merchants, for example. Nikola Pašić listed himself as a writer (*knji-
ževnik*).

131. In June Pop Milan Djurić, a Radical who was close to the Progressives
through his business ties with Aleska Popović, told the Progressives twice
that he feared civil war (Milićević's diary, 23 May/4 Jun, 6/18 Jun 82).

132. *Samouprava*, 31 Jul/12 Aug 82.

133. VMO, 3:64.

134. SANU, 9779/7, 9779/9.

135. A gunj, or gunjac, is a traditional jacket worn by Serbian male peasants, and the opanak is a traditional sandal with a distinctively turned-up toe. Pašić started eleven consecutive sentences with the phrase, but only seven are reproduced here.

136. Škorić collection, doc. 179.

137. "Baja" is a affectionate term of respect used in the Timok region to denote someone with substantial life experience, a person "who has been to the well three times and the market twice" (Miodrag B. Petrovich, "Timočka Krajina and the Radicals," unpublished paper given at the University of Toronto, May 15, 1981, p. 10). The late Professor Petrovich marked his paper "Not for citation or reproduction," but since the papers for this conference were never published and since Professor Petrovich in the interim has passed away, I have taken the liberty of citing it.

138. From the start of 1882 the party had received 3,462 dinars and spent 1,731 on party business. It had also loaned 750 dinars to *Samouprava*. The report noted that 1,357 dinars had accumulated in the Adam Fund, and it recommended that amount simply be placed in the party treasury. In addition, the party received 2,535 dinars in donations to help persecuted party members, although it had given out only 970 dinars in loans and aid. By far the biggest item was the publication of *Samouprava*, which from mid-January 1881 through the end of July 1882 had taken in 38,282 dinars and spent 38,462, or an average of 2,136 dinars a month. These expenses included about 14,000 dinars to maintain an apartment for the editors and to pay honoraria, postage, and other small expenses. Also included was a loan of 302 dinars to *Čosa*, a radical satirical paper (SANU, 9779/20).

139. This is Slobodan Jovanović's description, VMO, 3:68–69.

140. *Samouprava*, 2/14 Sep 82.

141. Quoted by VMO, 3:66–67.

142. *Samouprava*, 30 Sep/12 Oct 82.

143. Ibid., 28 Sep/10 Oct 82.

144. Ibid., 2/14 Oct 82.

145. Ibid., 25 Sep/7 Oct 82.

146. Ibid., 7/19 Aug 82.

147. Ibid., 25 Sep/7 Oct 82.

148. Central Committee Minutes, 3/15 and 11/23 Aug 82.

149. Ibid., 28 Aug/9 Sep 82.

150. Ibid., 28 Aug/9 Sep 82.

151. Ibid., 4/16 Sep 82; and *Samouprava*, 27 Mar/8 Apr 82.

152 Central committee to local committees, 15/22 Sep 82, AS:MG 276.

153. Report from Metriš, 17/29 Aug 82 (SANU 9782/28).

154. Report from Valjevo, 19/31 Sep 82 (SANU, 9782/31).

155. Reports from Čačak, Užice, Kragujevac, and Valjevo all seemed to understand the issues well, whereas those from smaller places like Branešci, Čajetina, Banja, and Tunava found it difficult to deal with any sort of legal or theoretical issue, although they forwarded specific complaints about party members who were imprisoned and so forth (SANU, 9782/34–50).

156. Report from Niš, 22 Sep/4 Oct 82 (SANU, 9782/33).

157. Central committee's letter of 15/27 Sep 82 (AS:MG-276).

158. SANU, 9782/37.

NOTES TO CHAPTER 8

1. VMO, 3:80–83.

2. *Samouprava* printed the transcript of the trials starting 21 Dec 82/2 Jan 83.

3. Milićević's diary, 29 Sep/11 Oct 82.

4. VMO, 3:70–73.

5. The following is taken from Locock to Granville, 23 Oct 82, FO, 105/33 140; Raša Milošević, *Timočka buna 1883. godine* (Belgrade: Drag. Gregorica, 1923), pp. 55–60; Mišković's notes for 1882 (SANU, 7242/16); the diary of Paja Mihailović; and *Videlo,* 12/24 Oct 82.

6. Earlier in the year the Radicals held a memorial service for Svetozar and Jevrem attended by many Radicals at which Ilka played a prominent role (*Samouprava,* 1/13 Mar 82).

7. VMO, 3:75; and Stokes, *Legitimacy through Liberalism,* pp. 141–45.

8. Milošević, *Timočka buna,* p. 60.

9. *Samouprava,* 12/14 Oct 82; Central Committee Minutes, 11/23 and 14/26 Oct 82. The day before the assassination attempt the central committee, afraid that the Progressives were going to call a sneak election while intensifying their efforts to jail active Radicals, decided to print all the cases of such jailings in the paper, but when the assassination attempt took place they changed their minds (Minutes 10/22 Oct 82). See also *Samouprava,* 18/30, 19/31 Oct 82.

10. *Videlo,* 20 Oct/1 Nov 82.

11. *Samouprava,* 23 Oct/5 Nov, 28 Oct/10 Nov 82.

12. Milićević's diary, 29 Oct/11 Nov 82.

13. Central Committee Minutes, 4/16 Nov 82; *Samouprava,* 8/20 Nov 82.

14. Mišković's notes for 1882, 15/27 Oct 82 through 24 Oct/6 Nov 82.

15. AJR, 1/25 1/28, for Ristić's speech (17/29 Oct 82), and AJR, VIII/3 8/41, for the protocols of the second sitting, which included the visit to court (18/30 Oct 82).

16. *Samouprava*, 19/31 Oct 82; and Stojan Protić, *Odlomci iz ustavne borbe* (Belgrade: Dositije Obradović, 1911), p. 105.

17. VMO, 3:78; and Locock to Granville, 17 Nov 82, FO, 105/33 155.

18. The possibility of being fined 1,000 dinars, which was about 40 percent of Nikola Pašić's good salary as a junior engineer in 1876, for example, caused the Radicals a great deal of confusion. One of their members wrote in despair that he had received only one vote and was now being told he had to come to the skupština or pay the fine, and he could not even afford the trip to Belgrade! At first the central committee said those elected should come; then it told local committees to try and ensure a unanimous vote for the Radical candidate, but if that was not possible to make sure their candidate did not come in second; and finally it decided that since the skupština was illegal anyway, Radicals simply should not attend it, whatever the consequences. See Central Committee Minutes, 18/30 Nov, 27 Nov/9 Dec, 28 Nov/10 Dec 82; complaint of Sima Pavić, 13/25 Nov 82 (SANU, 9782/53); and Central committee to local committees, 29 Nov/10 Dec 82 (SANU, 9782/57).

19. Locock to Granville, 13, 15 Dec 83, FO, 105/33 166,167.

20. 9/21 Dec 82. Milićević also commented on the unusual smoothness of the session—no interruptions, no fights (Milićević's diary, 24 Nov/6 Dec 82).

21. *Zbornik zakona* 38 (1882–83): 280–315.

22. For the following, see *Videlo*, 11/23 Mar through 20 Mar/1 Apr 83. The law on which this was based was dated 30 Mar/11 Apr 81.

23. *Samouprava*, 22 Jan/3 Feb, 23 Jan/4 Feb 82.

24. Todorović, "Krvava godina," pp. 61–62.

25. Milićević's diary, 20 Mar/1 Apr 82.

26. Coverage of this event, based on the trials that followed, began in *Samouprava*, 28 Jun/10 Jul 83.

27. This is what Pera Todorović relates, at least ("Krvava godina," p. 62).

28. Secret logbook of King Milan, 22 May/3 Jun through 16/23 Jun 82 (AS:PO-27-183). This potentially valuable source exists only for the first few months of 1883. The Niš Radical committee notified the central committee in Belgrade that the 14th and 15th battalions of the standing army had departed under arms (26 May/7 Jun 82, AS:MG-607). This indicates that the Radicals were rather well informed. It also could easily

be interpreted by the government as a suspiciously keen interest by the Radicals in troop movements.

29. E.g., Mihailo Nikolić, president of the Krajina Radical committee, to Anta Rajičić in Salaš, 14/25 Jan 83 (TB, 2:613).

30. *Samouprava*, 5/17 Jul 83. This did not prevent the local načelnik from seeing in Pop Marinko's statement that the peasants had the right to delay the registration, or at least to petition for a delay, as subversive (*Videlo*, 23 Aug/4 Sep 83).

31. Report of Krajina committee to Central Committee, 8/20 Feb 83 (SANU, 9783/17).

32. E.g., report of the Negotin Radical committee of 12/24 Feb 82, complaining that traders who used to cross the Timok from Bulgaria now went to Vidin, and those who did come were subjected to pettifogging regulations they could avoid only by paying a napoleon or two. As regards Austria, the committee complained that the Negotin merchants were still paying the high tariffs from Ristić's time, whereas Austrian traders were paying the lower tariffs of the new trade agreement, thus hurting the Serbs (SANU, 9782/2).

33. Jelavich, *Tsarist Russia and Balkan Nationalism*, pp. 191–93.

34. Milošević, *Timočka buna*, p. 47. In 1883 Raša married Draga Ljočić, sister of Djura Ljočić (see chapter 4) and Serbia's first female medical doctor. Since the Ljočić family had close connections with the Karadjordjevićes, Milan could easily have assumed his supposition was correct about Milošević; but Milošević, in a letter to Ranko Tajsić, said that Draga's family was against the marriage and she had broken off relations with them. On the other hand, since this letter is found today in Milutin Garašanin's papers, its contents may well have been known to the prince (Milošević to Tajsić, 9/21 Feb 83, AS:MG-738). In the same letter Milošević mentions that Pera Velimirović had married the daughter of Milan Milovuk, a Russophile.

35. Milan's secret logbook, 30 May/11 Jun 82.

36. Ibid., 1/13 Aug 83.

37. Report of Austrian agent Heinrich Welsch, Zemun, 7 Jul 84 (IAB: Box 3599–Zemunski Magistrat, 1880–1883, poverljivi spisi). Welsch reported that Svetozar Nikolajević contacted Ristić on behalf of the Radicals, but in general Ristić wanted to stay aloof from any negotiations and left contacts in the hands of a three-man committee consisting of Alimpije Vasiljević, Stojan Bošković, and Nikola Krsmanović. Joca Jovanović wrote Kosta Taušanović on 15/27 Feb 83 that cooperation between the Liberals and Radicals in the event of an election to the Grand National

Assembly was imperative in Šabac, despite differences between the parties, so that each could win two seats rather than split the vote and permit the Progressives to win all four (SANU, 9783/22).

38. Central committee to local committees, 8/15 Feb 83, AS:MG-604.

39. Zaječar committee to central committee, 7/19 Mar 82. This view did not reach the central committee in time for its decision.

40. SANU, 9783 contains the responses, documents, nos. 21–54. A review of the list of for and against (SANU, 9783/104) does not reveal any particular regional or urban/rural pattern to the responses; central committee to local committees, 4/11 Mar 83 (AS:MG-604); and Central Committee Minutes 4/11 Mar 83 (SANU, 9778).

41. On 12/24 Jul 83 Milićević wrote in his diary, "The Radicals are talking with both the Liberals and with us. Whoever gives more will be the one!"

42. Piroćanac's letter of appointment, 9/21 Dec 81 (SANU, 7220).

43. On 18/30 Jul 83, Milićević wrote in his diary, "The ministers are discussing the draft of a constitution and of other laws that they are preparing for a Grand [National] Assembly."

44. Piroćanac's notes along with several constitutional drafts can be found in SANU, 10048. The Progressive constitutional proposal can be found in Prodanović, *Ustavne borbe*, pp. 254–65.

45. Locock to Granville, 10 Aug 83, FO, 105/39 28.

46. Todorović, "Krvava godina," p. 67.

47. Welsch's report of 7 Jul 83.

48. These meetings began 22 Mar/3 Jun 82, and ran nightly until 2/14 Apr 82 (Central Committee Minutes, SANU,9778). The main participants were Pašić, Djaja, Milošević, Taušanović, Todorović, Paču, Nikolajević, Svetozar Milosavljević, Paja Mihailović, Mijailo Vujić, Joca Simić, Kosta Borisavljević, Milan Protić, and Radoslav Nešković. For the invitation, which asked as well that local committee representatives bring membership lists and dues, see SANU, 9731, and for the initial banning of the meeting see Milan's secret logbook, 3/15 Apr 82.

49. Central Committee Minutes, 5/17 Apr 83.

50. Central Committee cover letter, 7/19 Jul 83 (SANU, 9732).

51. Central Committee Minutes, 26 Jun/8 Jul 83. Extraordinary care was taken with the drafts. Pašić kept a list of the recipients of each copy and the central committee outlined the route each person would take when he distributed them around the country (SANU, 9783/105; and Central Committee Minutes, 2/14 Jul 83). Despite these efforts, the government knew the messengers were delivering copies of the draft constitution and followed their progress through the country. E.g., reports from

Kruševac on Raša Milošević's arrival and contacts, Milan's confidential logbook, 17/29, 18/30 Jul 83. "As is well known," the načelnik wrote, "he brought a copy of the constitution and explained it to those who think as he does."

52. Russian consul Persiani believed the maneuvers were only a pretext and that Milan was going to Austria and Germany for political consultations. "There is no doubt," Persiani informed his government, "that the fate of the government and the direction of Serbian politics depends on the answer the king receives" (dispatch of 3 Aug 83, quoted by Danica Milojević, "Ruski konzul A. I. Persijani o prilikama u Srbiji početkom druge naprednjačke vlade," *Istorijski časopis* 31 [1984]: 241).

53. Milićević's diary, 2/14/ Jun 83; and Locock to Granville, 11 Oct 83, FO, 421/55 no. 29.

54. Welsch's report of 7 Jul 83.

55. *Videlo*, 29 Apr/11 May 83.

56. Živanović, *Politička istorija Srbije*, 2:223–24.

57. Milićević's diary, 4/16 Aug 83.

58. Milićević's diary, 13/25 Aug 83.

59. Todorović, "Krvava godina," p. 72. The Battle of Kosovo between the invading Ottomans and the medieval Serbian state took place on Vidovdan (June 28) 1389. The Serbs suffered a great defeat, but the memory of the battle and the Serbian medieval state that was crushed on that occasion lived on in oral epics and remains today as much an emotional focus of Serbian national feeling as it was in the nineteenth century.

60. *Samouprava*, 18/30 Aug, 20 Aug/1 Sep 83.

61. Milićević's diary, 20 Aug/1 Sep 83.

62. *Videlo*, 4/16 Sep 83.

63. Todorović, "Krvava godina," p. 75.

64. Ibid., p. 73.

65. *Samouprava*, 25 Aug/6 Sep 83. Almost this entire issue was blanked out.

66. Milićević's diary, 4/16 Sep 83.

67. Todorović, "Krvava godina," p. 80.

68. Ibid., pp. 80–81. It is not possible to reproduce fully the bantering tone of this interchange and the derogatory character of the terms the two men used to describe each other's voters.

69. The figures vary. The first vote in the skupština showed 84 in favor of the opposition's point of view, 65 in favor of the government, with 16 delegates yet to appear (Krstić's diary, 15/22 Sep 83). Živanović says that *Srpska nezavisnost* reported the election of 24 Progressives, 34 Liberals, 62 Radicals, along with 8 persons of unknown affiliation and 6 elections

incomplete *(Politička istorija Srbije,* 2:225); Milićević counted 61 Radicals, only 11 Liberals, 34 Progressives, and 7 without affiliation (8/20 Sep 83); after the appointment of 44 persons to the government positions in the skupština, Locock reported to Granville a first gathering of the skupština consisting of 65 Progressives and 85 opposition (27 Sep 83, FO, 105/39 45); this is the same number Milićević has, except he says there were 64 Progressives (15/27 Sep 83); and *Samouprava* reported that of the 146 delegates that appeared at the skupština, only 22 were Progressives who had actually won election rather than being part of the government's delegation (16/28 Sep 83).

70. Krstić's diary, 16/28 Sep 83; and Milićević's diary, 13/25 Sep 83. Milićević showed his usual moderate good sense. Even though he did not like the Radicals, he concluded that perhaps the best thing in the long run would be simply to let them come to power. But he was a minority among the Progressives.

71. Krstić's diary, 10/22 Sep 83.

72. Ibid., 9/21 Sep 83. The Radicals believed that by this decree Milan effectively told the Progressives that they had his unlimited confidence and were free to do whatever was necessary to win the election ("Izjava emigranta Nikole Pašića, Ace Stanojevića, Žike Milenovića i Djoke R. Lazarevića," 1/12 Dec 83, Škorić collection, doc. 234 [SANU, 7885/1], p. 7).

73. Milićević's diary, 3/15 Sep, 9/21 Sep 83; and Piroćanac's diary, 10/22 Sep 83 (SANU, 9989).

74. Piroćanac's diary, 8/20 Sep 83.

75. *Samouprava,* 10/22 Sep 83.

76. Ibid., 13/25 Sep 83.

77. Ibid., 15/27 Sep 83.

78. Krstić's diary, 16/28, 17/29 Sep 83.

79. Pera Todorović was particularly worried about this, and it remains an open question whether the opposition could have maintained its majority had the skupština run its full course, since the Liberals quickly got irritated at what they saw as a Radical effort to exclude them from any important positions (Todorović, "Krvava godina," p. 85; Milićević's diary, 16/28 Sep 83; and Krstić's diary, 16/28 Sep 83).

80. Locock to Granville, 27 Sep 83, FO, 105/39 45; report of Credentials Committee, 19/31 Sep 83, TB, 1:12–14; and Krstić's diary, 18/30 Sep, 22 Sep/4 Oct 83.

81. Piroćanac's diary, 16/28 Sep 82.

82. Ibid., 20 Sep/2 Oct 83. A week earlier Piroćanac had told Milićević, "I

will give the king a resignation, but I won't give him advice" (Milićević's diary, 14/26 Sep 83).

83. *Videlo*, 9/21 Sep 83.

84. Todorović, "Krvava godina," p. 84; and Locock to Granville, 4 Oct 83, FO, 105/39 58.

85. Todorović "Krvava godina," p. 83.

86. Pirоćanac's diary, 10/22 Sep 83. Milićević was less concerned—he did not even read the draft when it came into his hands (diary, 9/21 Sep 83).

87. Locock to Granville, 23 Sep 83, FO, 105/39 43.

88. Todorović, "Krvava godina," p. 87.

89. Locock to Granville, 6 Oct 83, FO, 105/39 58.

90. Živanović, *Politička istorija Srbije*, 2:241; and Krstić's diary, 23 Sep/5 Oct 83.

91. Locock to Granville, 6 Oct 83, FO, 105/39 59.

92. Milošević, *Timočka buna*, pp. 137–41. On the reliability of this source, see VMO, 3:517–34.

93. Todoгоrić, "Krvava godina," p. 89.

94. E.g., *Videlo*, 25 Sep/7 Oct 83. After saying how the immaturity and political boneheadedness of the Radicals shone forth from every article of its constitution, *Videlo* concluded: "Serbia! You stand on the verge of betrayal! Watch out!" Two days later *Samouprava* complained that *Videlo* offered only rhetoric, not real criticism. "We expect from you serious criticism of our draft. . . . You are politically dead, and await only an autopsy."

95. Locock to Granville, 20 Oct 83, FO, 105/40 64.

96. Todorović, "Krvava godina," p. 92.

97. "Izjava emigranata," Škorić collection, doc. 234, p. 11.

98. Lampe, "Financial Structure and Economic Development of Serbia," p. 122. On 21 Oct/2 Nov 83, *Videlo* reported that subscriptions had passed 36,000 shares, when only 20,000 were issued.

99. The government ordered 100,000 mausers at 70 dinars each in 1881 (SB, 1881, 2254).

100. TB, 1:3–6.

101. TB, 1:6–10, from *Samouprava*, 30 Jul/11 Aug 83.

102. Milošević, *Timočka buna*, p. 148.

103. The description that follows relies heavily on Andrija Radenić, "Timočka buna 1883," in his *Iz istorije Srbije i Vojvodine 1834–1914*, pp. 439–556, which is the standard work on the subject and contains not only a superb description and analysis, but a comprehensive bibliography. The best account in English is Dimitrije Djordjević, "The 1883 Peasant Uprising in Serbia," *Balkan Studies* 20 (1979): 235–55.

104. Locock to Granville, 11 Oct 83, FO, 105/40 61. When the uprising broke out, the Austrian government instructed its consul in Belgrade to urge Milan to show mercy, but, as the consul reported, "The king and Nikola Hristić greeted this peasant uprising as a welcome opportunity to free themselves from an unpleasant situation and to wipe out the accursed radicalism. Now the government has the chance to break up all the Radical committees and to clap all the leaders of the party in jail" (Radenić, "Timočka buna," p. 553, quoting the Austrian consul's secret report of 5 Nov 83).

105. TB, 1, docs. 15–19. The Radicals pointed out later the contrast between the wars of 1876 and 1877, when the pay of the officer corps had been cut in half while fighting the Ottomans, and the example of 1883, when its pay was doubled to put down Serbs ("Izjava emigranata", Škorić collection, doc. 234, p. 22).

106. Nikola Krstić and Milan Milićević, both well connected and often well informed, note in their diaries that they knew nothing of what was happening in the interior.

107. The article, by Pera Todorović, was entitled "Disarming"—reminiscent of Pašić's article of three months earlier. On October 22 the leadership also received a letter from Aca Stanojević that got through police surveillance by Aca addressing it to Raša Milošević's wife (Milošević, *Timočka buna*, p. 149).

108. Todorović, "Krvava godina," p. 107.

109. The other members of the central committee were: Gliša Geršić, professor of law at the Velika škola, later minister of justice who had a great influence on the constitution of 1888; Paja K. Mihajlović, secretary in the ministry of finance and former associate of Svetozar Marković; Jovan Djaja, gymnasium professor, translator of Manzoni's *The Betrothed* into Serbian, and later minister of education; Andra Nikolić, professor of law at the Belgrade gymnasium and subsequently many times minister of education and foreign affairs; Jovan Simić, printer; and Stevan Stevanović, merchant (TB, 2:136).

110. Milojević, "Ruski konzul Persijani," p. 242.

111. Todorović, "Krvava godina," p. 110. Vračar is a section of Belgrade and Topčider is a hill and park then just outside the city.

112. VMO, 3:125.

113. Locock to Granville, 7 Nov 83, FO, 105/40 78.

114. Mišković's notes from 1883, SANU, 7242/17.

115. Locock to Granville, 7 Nov 83, FO, 105/40 76.

116. Djordjević, "The 1883 Peasant Uprising," pp. 246–47.

117. TB, 2:200.

NOTES TO CONCLUSION

1. See, e.g., Anthony Fletcher, *The Outbreak of the English Civil War* (New York: New York University Press, 1981).
2. David Cannadine, "The Context, Performance and Meaning of Ritual: The British Monarchy and the 'Invention of Tradition', c. 1820–1977," in Eric Hobsbawm and Terrence Ranger, *The Invention of Tradition* (Cambridge: Cambridge University Press, 1983), p. 109.
3. Fletcher, *The Outbreak of the English Civil War*, p. 407.
4. Benedict Anderson, *Imagined Communities* (London: Verso, 1983), pp. 77–78.
5. The term "His Majesty's Opposition" was coined in England only in 1826, and the inability of nineteenth-century parliaments throughout the world to conduct their business decorously was so notorious that in 1904 Georg Jellinek was moved to write, "Parliamentary obstruction is no longer a mere intermezzo in the history of this or that parliament. It has become an international phenomenon which, in threatening manner, calls into question the whole future of parliamentary government" (*Political Science Quarterly* 19 [1904]: 579). For the phrase "His Majesty's Opposition" see J. C. D. Clark, *Revolution and Rebellion* (Cambridge: Cambridge University Press, 1986), pp. 134–35, citing Archibald S. Ford, *His Majesty's Opposition, 1714–1830* (Oxford: Oxford University Press, 1964).
6. See Karl Kaser, "Typologie der politischen Parteien Südosteuropas im neunzehnten Jahrhundert," pp. 331–65. Kaser argues that the Radical Party was the only fully realized Balkan political party because it was the only one characterized by organizational continuity, regular links between local and national levels, the ability to take power, and organized efforts to mobilize the electorate.
7. Raša Milošević, *Organizacija sreza na načelu samouprave i izbornog prava* (Belgrade: Zadruga Štamparskih radnika, 1883), p. 5. Milošević said that "the Radical Party was not at all a ruling party. It differs fundamentally from all other *political* parties. . . . The only goal of its political life is to realize its program, and nothing more."
8. On the lack of benefit to the Balkan peasantry from railroads see Peter Sugar, "Railroad Construction and the Development of the Balkan Village in the Last Quarter of the Nineteenth Century," in Melville and Schröder, *Berliner Kongress*, pp. 485–98.

BIBLIOGRAPHY

MAIN ARCHIVAL COLLECTIONS CONSULTED

Archive of the Historical Institute of the Serbian Academy
    Mihailović, Paja (Pavle K.): Diary
    Ristić, Jovan: Papers
Archive of Serbia
    Garašanin, Milutin: Papers
    Vasiljević, Alimpije: Memoirs
    and other sources
Archive of the Serbian Academy of Sciences
    Krstić, Nikola: Diary
    Milićević, Milan: Diary
    Mišković, Jovan: Diary and notebooks
    Pašić, Nikola: Notebooks and letters
    Petrović, Avram: Diary
    Piroćanac, Milan: Diary
    Todorović, Pera: "Krvava godina"
    and other sources
Historical Archive of the City of Belgrade
    Jovanović, Vladimir: Papers; including unpublished volumes of "Politički rečnik"
Public Record Office, Kew
    Consular Dispatches, 1878–83

NEWSPAPERS CONSULTED

Budućnost
Glas javnosti
Istok

Javnost
Oslobodjenje
Rad
Radenik
Samouprava
Srpska nezavisnost
Srpske novine
Staro oslobodjenje
Straža
Težak
Videlo
Vidovdan
Zastava

PRINTED WORKS CONSULTED

Adanir, Fikret, "Heiduckentum und osmanische Herrschaft," *Südost-Forschungen* 41 (1982): 43–116.

Aleksić-Pejković, Liljana, *Politika Italije prema Srbiji do 1870. godine.* [Italy's Policy toward Serbia to 1870] (Belgrade: Istorijski institut, 1979).

Anderson, Benedict, *Imagined Communities* (London: Verso, 1983).

Avramović, Ranislav M., "Nikola P. Pašić kao tehničar u politici i praksi" [Nikola P. Pašić as an Engineer in Politics and in Practice], in Životić, *Spomenica.*

Batowski, Henryk, "Die territorialen Bestimmungen von San Stefano und Berlin," in Melville and Schröder, *Berliner Kongress*, pp. 51–62.

Besarović, Risto, *Vaso Pelagić* (Sarajevo: Svijetlost, 1969).

Bitković, Blagoje and Živomir Spasić, eds., *Crveni barjak u Kragujevcu 1876: Gradja* [The Red Banner in Kragujevac 1876: Materials] (Kragujevac: Istorijski arhiv Šumadije, 1976).

Bjelica, Mihailo, "Borba za slobodu štampe u Kneževini Srbiji" [The Struggle for Freedom of the Press in the Principality of Serbia], *Istorijski časopis* 24 (1977): 191–222.

———, *Velike bitke za slobodu štampe* [The Great Battles for a Free Press] (Belgrade: Narodna knjiga, 1985).

Blagojević, Borislav, "Uticaj francuskog gradjanskog zakonika na srbijanski zakonik" [The Influence of the French Civil Code on the Serbian Code], *Prava misao* 5 (1939), nos. 11, 12: 477–93.

Blagojević, Obren, *Ekonomska misao u Srbiji do drugog svetskog rata* [Economic

Thought in Serbia to the Second World War] (Belgrade: SANU, Posebna izdanja 525, 1980).

Byrnes, Robert F., ed., *Communal Families in the Balkans: The Zadruga* (Notre Dame, Ind.: Notre Dame University Press, 1976).

Cannadine, David, "The Context, Performance and Meaning of Ritual: The British Monarchy and the 'Invention of Tradition,' c. 1820–1977," in Hobsbawm and Ranger, *The Invention of Tradition*, pp. 101–64.

Cenić, Mita, *Ispod zemlje ili moja tamnovanja* [Under Ground, or My Imprisonments] (Belgrade: Prosveta, 1983, orig. pub. 1881).

Ćirić-Bogetić, Ljubinka, "Antibirokratske i samoupravne koncepcije Raše Miloševića, poslanika za grad Pirot (1880–83)" [The Anti-Bureaucratic and Self-Management Conceptions of Raša Milošević, Representative for the City of Pirot, 1880–83], *Pirotski zbornik* 3 (1971): 57–69.

Clark, J. C. D., *Revolution and Rebellion* (Cambridge: Cambridge University Press, 1986).

Craig, Gordon A., *The Triumph of Liberalism: Zürich in the Golden Age, 1830–1869* (New York: Charles Scribners' Sons, 1988).

Čubrilović, Vasa, *Politička misao u Srbiji XIX. veka* (Belgrade: Prosveta, 1958).

Čubrilović, Vasa, ed., *Timočka buna 1883. i njen društveno-politički značaj za Srbiju XIX veka* [The Timok Rebellion of 1883 and its Sociopolitical Significance for Serbia in the Nineteenth Century] (Belgrade: SANU, Naučni skupovi 29, Odeljenje istorijskih nauka 7, 1986).

Cvijetić, Leposava, "Poreski sistem Srbije, 1835–1884. godine" [The Tax System of Serbia, 1835–84] (Ph.D. diss., Belgrade University, 1956).

Dändliker, Karl, *Geschichte der Schweiz* (Zürich: Schulthess & Co., 1904).

Dimitrijević, Sergije, *Socialistički radnički pokret u Srbiji 1870–1918* [The Socialist Workers Movement in Serbia, 1870–1918] (Belgrade: Nolit, 1982).

Djordjević, Dimitrije, "The 1883 Peasant Uprising in Serbia," *Balkan Studies* 20 (1979): 235–55.

———, "The Role of the Military in the Balkans in the Nineteenth Century," in Melville and Schröder, *Berliner Kongress*, pp. 317–47.

———, "The Serbian Peasant in the 1876 War," in Király and Stokes, *Insurrections, Wars, and the Eastern Crisis*, pp. 305–16.

Djordjević, Miroslav R., "Inostrani komentari zakona o uredjenju agrarnih odnosa u novooslobodjenim krajevima Srbije od 1880. godine" [Foreign Comments on the 1880 Law to Regulate Agrarian Relations in the Newly Liberated Regions of Serbia], *Leskovački zbornik* 18 (1978): 57–75.

Djordjević, Vladan, "Gornji dom Srbije: Rad velikog ustavnog odbora" [Serbia's Upper House: Work of the Great Constitutional Committee], *Otadžbina*, 1890.

Djordjević, Života, *Srpska narodna vojska, 1861–64* [The Serbian National Militia, 1861–64] (Belgrade: Narodna knjiga, 1984).

Djurdjevac, Milo, "Narodna vojska u Srbiji 1861–83 godine" [The National Militia in Serbia, 1861–83], *Vojno-istorijski glasnik* 10 (1959), no. 4: 78–93.

Dragnich, Alex N., *Serbia, Nikola Pašić, and Yugoslavia* (New Brunswick, N.J.: Rutgers University Press, 1974).

Državopis Srbije [Serbian Almanac] for 1889.

Durković-Jakšić, Ljubomir, "Istorija zakonodavstva i sudstva o braku u oslobodjenoj Šumadiji do 1888. godine" [A History of Legislation and Legal Judgments concerning Marriage in Liberated Šumadija to 1888], *Zbornik radova pravoslavnog-bogoslovnog fakulteta* 1 (1950): 175–91.

———, "O boravku Svetozara Markovića u Švajcarskoj za vreme školovanja" [Svetozar Marković's stay in Zürich during his Schooling], *Zbornik Istorijskog muzeja Srbije* 13–14 (1977): 99–104.

Eddie, Scott, "The Changing Pattern of Landownership in Hungary, 1869–1914," *The Economic History Review* 20 (1967): 293–310.

Ekmečić, Milorad, "Nacionalna politika Srbije prema Bosni i Hercegovini 1844–75" [The National Policy of Serbia toward Bosnia and Hercegovina 1844–75], *Godišnjak Bosne i Hercegovine* 10 (1959): 197–219.

———, "Rezultati jugoslovenske istoriografije o istočnom pitanju 1875–78. godine" [The Results of Yugoslav Historiography on the Eastern Question, 1875–78], *Jugoslovenski istorijski časopis* 16 (1977) nos. 1–2: 55–74.

———, "Die serbische Politik in Bosnien und Herzegowina und die Agrarrevolutionen 1848–1878," in Melville and Schröder, *Berliner Kongress,* pp. 427–44.

———, "Srpska vojska u nacionalnim ratovima od 1876. do 1878.," *Balcanica* 9 (1978): 97–130. English version: "The Serbian Army in the Wars of 1876–78: National Liability or National Asset?" in Király and Stokes, *Insurrections, Wars, and the Eastern Crisis,* pp. 276–304.

———, *Ustanak u Bosni, 1875–78* [The Uprising in Bosnia, 1875–78] (Sarajevo: Veselin Masleša, 1973).

Erdósi, Ferenc, "Zur Bedeutung des Eisenbahnbaus für die Entstehung der monozentrischen territorialen Struktur im Ungarn des 19. Jahrhunderts," *Ungarn-Jahrbuch* 16 (1988): 203–15.

Fischer-Galati, Stephen, and Dimitrije Djordjević, *The Balkan Revolutionary Tradition* (New York: Columbia University Press, 1981).

Fletcher, Anthony, *The Outbreak of the English Civil War* (New York: New York University Press, 1981).

Furet, Francois, *Interpreting the French Revolution* (Cambridge: Cambridge University Press, 1981).

Garašanin, Ilija, *Pisma Ilije Garašanina Jovanu Marinoviću* [Letters of Ilija Garašanin to Jovan Marinović], 2 vols. (Belgrade: SKA, 1931).

Geiss, Imanuel, ed., *Der Berliner Kongress 1878: Protokolle und Materialien* (Boppard am Rhein: Boldt Verlag, Schriften des Bundesarchivs, 27, 1978).

Generalstab der fürstlich serbischen Armee, *Der Serbisch-Türkische Krieg von
1877–78* (Belgrade, 1879).

Geršić, Giga, "Nekoliko ustavnih pitanja: Gornji dom," [Some Constitutional
Questions: The Upper House] *Rad* (1881), pp. 35–46, 136–42, 300–314.

Gomel, Charles, *Histoire Financière de l'Assemblée Constituante* (New York: Burt
Franklin, n.d., orig. pub. Paris, 1897).

Govori radikalaca protiv železničkog ugovora u skupštini za 1880/1 [Speeches of the
Radicals against the Railroad Agreement in the Skupština of 1880–81]
(Belgrade: Štamparija zadruge štamparskih radenika, 1881).

*Gradjanski i trgovački zakonik sa zakonima o sudjenju i o zakonima po kojima će se
suditi u prisajedinjenim predelima za knjažestvo Srbije* [Civil and Trade Law
Code with Laws concerning Legal Proceedings and Concerning Laws by
which Proceedings will be Run in the Annexed Regions of the Principality
of Serbia] (Belgrade: Državna štamparija, 1879).

Greener, W. W., *The Gun and its Development*, 9th ed. (London, 1910).

Greulich, Hermann, *Das grüne Hüsli: Errinnerungen von Hermann Greulich* (Zürich, 1942).

Grujić, Jevrem, *Zapisi Jevrema Grujića* [The Notes of Jevrem Grujić], 3 vols.
(Belgrade: Štamparija "Skerlić," 1923).

Grujić, Sava, *Vojna organizacija Srbije* [The Military Organization of Serbia]
(Kragujevac: Kragujevačka društvena štamparija, 1874).

Grujić, Vladimir, "Obrazovanje i udžbenici na pravnom fakultetu velike škole
u Beogradu" [Education and Textbooks at the Law Faculty of the Belgrade Academy], *Istorijski glasnik* (1976), pp. 131–42.

Guzina, Ružica, "Istorijski osvrt na karakter i značaj srpskog gradjanskog
zakonika od 1844. godine." [A Historical Review of the Character of the
Serbian Civil Code of 1844], *Istorijski glasnik* 2 (1949): 22–37.

——, *Opština u Kneževini i Kraljevini Srbiji, Prvi deo, 1804–1839* [The Opština
in the Principality and Kingdom of Serbia: Part 1, 1804–1839] (Belgrade:
Pravni fakultet u Beogradu, Institut za pravnu istoriju, 1966).

——, *Opština u Srbiji, 1839–1918* [The Opština in Serbia] (Belgrade: Rad,
1976).

——, "Opštine u Srbiji XIX. veka kao uporišta političkih stranaka u borbi
za vlast" [Opštinas in Nineteenth-Century Serbia as the Foci of Political
Parties in the Struggle for Power], *Anali pravnog fakulteta u Beogradu* 21/
2 (1973): 53–64.

Hadidian, Ellen Claire, "A Comparison of the Thought of Early Bulgarian and Serbian Radicals, 1867–1876," Ph.D. diss., University of Wisconsin at Madison, 1980.

Hauptmann, F., "Politika Austro-Ugarske, trojecarski savez, i tajna konvencija sa Srbijom 1881." [The Policy of Austria-Hungary, the Three Emperors' League, and the 1881 Secret Convention with Serbia], *Godišnjak Bosne i Hercegovine* 9 (1958): 57–72.

Hobsbawm, Eric, and Terrence Ranger, *The Invention of Tradition* (Cambridge: Cambridge University Press, 1983).

Howard, Michael, *The Franco-Prussian War* (New York: Macmillan, 1962).

Hristić, Filip, *Pisma Filipa Hristića Jovanu Ristiću, 1868–1880* [The Letters of Filip Hristić to Jovan Ristić, 1868–80], edited by Grgur Jakšić (Belgrade: SANU, Posebna izdanja 206, 1953).

Humo, Avdo, et al., eds., *Socijalistički pokret u Srbiji i crveni barjak* (Belgrade: Institut za političke studije, Fakulteta političkih nauka, 1977).

Ignjić, Sretan, "Narodni tribun račanskog kraja Sima Milošević" [Sima Milošević: National Tribune of the Rača District], *Užički zbornik* 3 (1974): 103–18.

———, *Užice i okolina 1862–1914* [Užice and its Surroundings] (Titovo Užice: Vesti, 1967).

Isović, K., "Austro-Ugarsko zaposedanje novopazarskog sandžaka 1879. godine" [The Austro-Hungarian Occupation of the Sadnjak of Novi Pazar in 1879], *Godišnjak Bosne i Hercegovine* 9 (1958): 109–37.

Ivanović, A. P., "Opisanije okružija krainskog" [Description of the Krajina Okrug], *Glasnik DSS* 5 (1853).

Ivić, Aleksa, "Istorija radikalne stranke" [History of the Radical Party], *Vreme*, July 2–26, 1928.

Jakšić, Grgur, *Iz nove srpske istorije: Abdikacija kneza Milana i druge rasprave* [From Modern Serbian History: The Abdication of Prince Milan and Other Studies] (Belgrade: Prosveta, 1956).

Janković, Dragoslav, "O političkim prilikama u odnosima u Srbiji uoči 'Crvenog barjak' " [Political Conditions in Serbia on the Eve of the 'Red Banner Affair'], in Humo, *Socijalistički pokret u Srbiji i crveni barjak*, pp. 181–86.

Jelavich, Barbara, *History of the Balkans*, vol. 1 (Cambridge: Cambridge University Press, 1983).

Jelavich, Charles, *Tsarist Russia and Balkan Nationalism: Russian Influence in the Internal Affairs of Bulgaria and Serbia, 1879–1886* (Berkeley: University of California Press, 1962).

Jellinek, Georg, "Parliamentary Obstruction," *Political Science Quarterly* 19 (1904): 579–88.

Jovanović, Miloš, *Dragiša Stanojević* (Novi Sad: Matica srpska, 1971).

———, "Jedna polemika Dragiše Stanojevića i Mite Cenića" [A Polemic Between Dragiša Stanojević and Mita Cenić], *Književnost* 29 (1959): 306–12.

Jovanović, Slobodan, "Carigradski put Kneza Milana" [Prince Milan's Trip to Istanbul], *Srpski književni glasnik*, n.s., 16 (1925): 44–49.

———, "Milan Piroćanac," *Političke i pravne rasprave* (Belgrade: Geca Kon, 1932, orig. pub. 1910), 2:221–302.

———, *Moji Savremenici* [My Contemporaries] (Windsor, Ont.: Avala, 1963).

———, "Pera Todorović," *Političke i pravne rasprave* (Belgrade: Geca Kon, 1932), 1:301–403.

———, "Svetozar Marković," *Političke i pravne rasprave* (Belgrade: Geca Kon, 1932, orig. pub. 1903), 1:61–298.

———, *Vlada Milana Obrenovića* [The Reign of Milan Obrenović], 3 vols. (Belgrade: Geca Kon, 1934).

Jovanović, Živorad P., "Kosta S. Taušanović," *Delo* 2 (1940), no. 39:2.

Judt, Tony, *Socialism in Provence, 1871–1914* (New York: Cambridge University Press, 1979).

Kaljević, Ljubomir, *Moje uspomene* [My Reminiscences] (Belgrade: Večernje novosti, 1908).

Kállay, Benjamin, *Dnevnik Benjamina Kalaja*, [The Diary of Benjamin Kállay], edited with commentary by Andrija Radenić (Belgrade: Istorijski institut and Novi Sad: Institut za istoriju Vojvodine, 1976).

Kapidžić, Hamidija, *Hercegovački ustanak 1882. godine* [The Hercegovina Uprising of 1882] (Sarajevo: Veselin Masleša, 1958).

Karadžić, Vuk Stefanović, *Srpski rječnik* [Serbian Dictionary], 3d ed. (Belgrade: Štamparija Kraljevine Srbije, 1898).

Karpat, Kemal, "The Social and Political Foundations of Nationalism in South East Europe after 1878: A Reinterpretation," in Melville and Schröder, *Berliner Kongress*, pp. 385–410.

Kaser, Karl, "Typologie der politischen Parteien Südosteuropas im neunzehnten Jahrhundert," *Österreichische Osthefte*, 1985, pp. 331–65.

Keyserlingk, Robert H., *Media Manipulation: The Press and Bismarck in Imperial Germany* (Montreal: Renouf, 1977).

Király, Béla, and Nándor F. Dreisziger eds., *East Central European Society in World War I* (Boulder, Colo.: Social Science Monographs; New York: distributed by Columbia University Press, War and Society in East Central Europe, vol. 19, 1985).

Király, Béla, and Gale Stokes, eds., *Insurrections, Wars, and the Eastern Crisis in the 1870s* (Boulder, Colo.: Social Science Monographs; and New York: distributed by Columbia University Press, War and Society in East Central Europe, vol. 17, 1985).

Király, Béla, and Gunther E. Rothenberg, eds., *Special Topics and Generalizations on the 18th and 19th Centuries* (New York: Brooklyn College Press, distributed by Columbia University Press, War and Society in East Central Europe, vol. 1, 1979).

Kondratjeva, V. N., and Nikola Petrović, eds., *Ujedinjena omladina srpska i njeno doba, 1860–1875: Gradja iz sovjetskih arhiva* [The United Serbian Youth and its Era, 1860–1875: Materials from Soviet Archives] (Novi Sad and Moscow: Matica srpska and Institut slavianovedeniia i balkanistiki AN SSSR, 1977).

Kostić, Milan, "Kosta Taušanović," *Samouprava*, 1938 (58), no. 569:7.

Kriegel, Abraham D., "Liberty and Whiggery in Early Nineteenth-Century England," *Journal of Modern History* 52 (1980): 253–78.

Kundaković, Z., *Sedam i po decenija jedne fabrike, 1884–1959* [Seven-and-one-half Decades of a Factory, 1884–1959] (Niš, 1959).

Lampe, John M., "Financial Structure and the Economic Development of Serbia, 1878–1912," Ph.D. diss., University of Wisconsin, 1971.

———, "Serbia 1878–1912," in Rondo Cameron, ed., *Banking and Economic Development: Some Lessons of History* (New York: Oxford University Press, 1972), pp. 122–67.

Lampe, John M., and Marvin R. Jackson, *Balkan Economic History, 1550–1950* (Bloomington: Indiana University Press, 1982).

Landauer, Carl, *European Socialism: A History of Ideas and Movements from the Industrial Revolution to Hitler's Seizure of Power* (Berkeley: University of California Press, 1959).

Lazarević, Dj., "Sećanja Dj. Lazarevića na Nik. P. Pašića" [Dj. Lazarević's Memories of Nikola P. Pašić], in the memorial publication of the Radical Party, *Nikola P. Pašić*.

Ljotić, Ljubica, *Memoari* [Memoirs] (Munich: Iskra, 1973).

Lovčević, Stojan, *Pisma Ilije Garašanina Jovanu Marinoviću*, vol. 2 (Belgrade, SKA, 1931).

Lunzer, Marianne, *Der Versuch einer Presselenkung in Österreich 1848–1870* (Vienna, 1954).

McClellan, Woodford, *Svetozar Marković and the Origins of Balkan Socialism* (Princeton, N.J.: Princeton University Press, 1964).

MacKenzie, David, *Ilija Garašanin: Balkan Bismarck* (Boulder, Colo.: East European Quarterly Press, 1985).

———, *The Lion of Tashkent: The Career of General M. G. Cherniaev* (Athens: University of Georgia Press, 1974).

———, *The Serbs and Russian Pan-Slavism, 1875–78* (Ithaca, N.Y.: Cornell University Press, 1967).

Maksin, Jelena, and Anica Lolić, *Bibliografija jugoslovenske literature o velikoj istočnog krizi 1875–1878* [Bibliography of Yugoslav Literature on the Great Eastern Crisis 1875–1878] (Belgrade: Istorijski institut, Gradja, knjiga 20, 1979).

Marinković, Dimitrije, *Uspomene i doživljaji Dimitrija Marinkovića, 1846–1869* [The Reminiscences and Experiences of Dimitrije Marinković], edited by Dragoslav Stranjaković (Belgrade: SKA, Posebna izdanja 126, 1939).

Marjanović, G., "Ekonomska publicistika Srbije krajem XVIII. veka pa do 70-tih godina XIX veka" [Economic Publications in Serbia from the End of the Eighteenth Century to the Seventies of the Nineteenth Century], *Ekonomska misao* I/1 (1968): 171–78.

Marković, Svetozar, *Sabrani spisi* [Collected Writings], vol. 1, edited by Najdan Pašić (Belgrade: Kultura, 1960); vols. 2–4, edited by Radovan Blagojević (Belgrade: Prosveta, 1965).

Melville, Ralph, and Hans-Jürgen Schröder, eds., *Der Berliner Kongress von 1878* (Wiesbaden: Veröffentlichungen des Instituts für Europäische Geschichte Mainz–Abteilung Universalgeschichte, Beiheft 7, Franz Steiner Verlag, 1982).

Michel, Bernard, "Zur Gründung der Länderbank. Planung und Einsatz französischen Kapitals im Donauraum (1880 bis 1882)," *Österreichische Osthefte* 28 (1986): 440–51.

Milić, Danica, "Ekonomski položaj radnika u Srbiji 60-th i 70-th godina 19. veka" [The Economic Position of Workers in Serbia in the 1860s and 70s], in Bitković, *Crveni barjak*, pp. 161–78.

———, "Značaj metarskog sistema za privredu Srbije" [The Significance of the Metric System for the Serbian Economy], *Katalog Galerije* SANU 23 (1974): 131–49.

Milić, Danica, ed., *Srbija u završnoj fazi velike istočne krize* [Serbia in the Final Phase of the Great Eastern Crisis] (Belgrade: Istorijski institut, Zbornik radova, knjiga 2, 1980).

Milićević, Jovan, *Jevrem Grujić: Istorijat svetoandrejskog liberalizma* [Jevrem Grujić: A History of Serbian Liberalism in the Mid-Nineteenth Century] (Belgrade: Nolit, 1964).

———, "Opozicija u Srbiji uoči stvaranja organizovanih političkih stranaka (1878–1881)" [Opposition in Serbia on the Eve of the Creation of Organized Political Parties, 1878–81], *Istorijski glasnik* 2 (1969): 9–27.

———, "Prilog poznavanju porekla srbijanskog parlamentarizma" [Contribution to the Understanding of the Origin of Serbian Parliamentary Practice], *Zbornik filozofskog fakulteta* 11/1 (1970): 609–26.

Milićević, Milan Dj., *Opštine u Srbiji* [Opstinas in Serbia] (Belgrade: Državna štamparija, 1878).

————, "Pregled zadružnog stanja srba seljaka" [A Review of the Zadruga among the Serbian Peasantry], *Glasnik* DSS 9 (1857).

Milisavac, Živan, ed., *Ujedinjena omladina srpska: zbornik radova* (Novi Sad and Belgrade: Matica srpska and Istorijski institut, 1968), pp. 105–32.

Milojević, Danica, "Ruski konzul A. I. Persijani o prilikama u Srbiji početkom druge naprednjačke vlade" [The Russian Consul A. I. Persiani on Conditions in Serbia at the Beginning of the Second Progressive Government], *Istorijski časopis* 31 (1984): 239–48.

Milosavljević, Petar, "Pripreme Srbije za rat sa Turskom 1876. godine" [Serbian Preparations for War with the Ottomans, 1876], *Balcanica* 9 (1978): 131–57.

Milošević, Raša, *Organizacija sreza na načelu samouprave i izbornog prava* [The Organization of Srezes on the Principle of Self-administration and the Electoral Law] (Belgrade: Zadruga štamparskih radnika, 1883).

————, *Timočka buna 1883. godine* [The Timok Rebellion 1883] (Belgrade: Drag. Gregorica, 1923).

Milutinović, Dragutin C. *Industrija i njeni činioci u Srbiji* [Industry and Its Factors in Serbia] (Novi Sad: n.p., 1877).

Mitchell, B. R., *European Historical Statistics, 1750–1975*, 2d revised edition (London: Macmillan, 1981).

Mitrinović, Čedomil, and Miloš N. Brašić, *Jugoslovenske narodne skupštine i sabori* [Yugoslav National Legislatures and Synods] (Belgrade: Narodna skupština Kraljevine Jugoslavije, 1937).

Mitrović, Djordje, and Savo Andrić, *Svetozar Marković i njegovo doba* [Svetozar Marković and His Times] (Belgrade: Rad, 1978).

Mitrović, Jeremija D., "Djura Ljočić," *Zbornik Istorijskog muzeja Srbije* 13–14 (1977): 105–28.

Mousset, Jean, *La Serbie et son Eglise (1830–1904)* (Paris: Librairie Droz, 1938).

Naujoks, Eberhard, *Die parlamentarische Entstehung des Reichspressegesetzes in der Bizmarckzeit (1848/74)* (Düsseldorf: Droste, 1975).

Nedeljković, Branislav M., *Istorija baštinske svojine u Novoj Srbiji od kraja 18 veka do 1931* [The History of Private Property in New Serbia from the End of the Eighteenth Century to 1931] (Belgrade: Geca Kon, 1936).

Nedeljković, Dušan, ed., *Naučni skup Svetozar Marković: Život i Delo* [Scholarly Conference—Svetozar Marković: His Life and Work] (Belgrade: SANU, Naučni skupovi knjiga 5, Odeljenje društvenih nauka knjiga 3, 1977).

————, *Svetozar Marković, omladina i marksizam* [Svetozar Marković, the Omladina, and Marxism] (Belgrade: SANU, Naučni skupovi knjiga 14, Odeljenje društvenih nauka knjiga 4, 1982).

Nikčević, Tomica, *Postanak i pokušaj prerade gradjanskog zakonika kneževine Srbije*

[Origin and Effort to Adapt the Civil Code of the Principality of Serbia] (Belgrade: SANU, *Spomenik*, v. 119, 1971).

Nikić, Fedor, *Lokalna uprava Srbije u XIX. i XX. veku* [Local Administration in Serbia in the Nineteenth and Twentieth Centuries] (Belgrade, 1927).

Nikola P. Pašić (Belgrade: Samouprava, 1938).

Nikolić, Milen M., ed., *Timočka buna* [The Timok Rebellion], 2 vols. (Belgrade: Državna arhiva NR Srbije, Gradja, 1954).

Nikolić, V., "Arhivski prilozi za izučavanje etničkih, socijalnih, i ekonomskih promena u Prokuplju 1877–78" [Archival Materials for the Study of Ethnic, Social, and Economic Changes in Prokuplje, 1877–78], *Arhivski almanah* (1962) 4:135–59.

Nikolić-Stojančević, Vidosava, *Leskovac i oslobodjeni predeli Srbije 1877–78 godine* [Leskovac and the Liberated Regions of Serbia, 1877–78] (Leskovac: Biblioteka narodnog muzeja, 1975).

Ninčić, Velizar, *Pera Todorović* (Belgrade: Nolit, 1956).

Obradović, Stojan, "Opisanije okružija užičkog" [Descriptions of the Užice Orug], *Glasnik* DSS 10 (1858).

Opačić, Petar, "Vojne operacije u srpsko-turskom ratu 1876. godine," in Petrović, *Medjunarodni naučni skup*, 2:281–304.

Palairet, Michael R., "Farming in Serbia c. 1830–1875: Impoverishment Without the Help of Malthus," forthcoming from the East European Program of the Woodrow Wilson Center, Washington, D.C.

——, "Fiscal Pressure and Peasant Impoverishment in Serbia before World War I," *Journal of Economic History* 39 (1979): 719–40.

Palotas, Emil, "Die wirtschaftlichen Aspecte in der Balkanpolitik Österreich-Ungarns um 1878," in Melville and Schröder, *Berliner Kongress*, pp. 271–85.

Pašić, Nikola, "Politička Kronika," *Rad*, 1881, pp. 85–86.

Perović, Latinka, *Pera Todorović* (Belgrade: Rad, 1983).

Peterson, Harold L., ed., *Encyclopedia of Firearms* (New York, 1964).

Petrić, Vera, "Poreklo srpskog gradjanskog zakonika i njegov značaj u stvaranju pravnog sistema buržoaske Srbije" [The Genesis of the Serbian Civil Code and Its Significance in the Creation of the Legal System of Bourgeois Serbia], *Zbornik istorijskog muzeja Srbije* 5 (1968): 79–91.

Petrović, Rade, ed., *Medjunarodni naučni skup povodom stogodišnjice ustanka u Bosni i Hercegovini, drugim balkanskim zemljama i istočnoj krizi 1875–1878 godine* [International Conference on the Occasion of the 100th Anniversary of the Uprising in Bosnia and Hercegovina and in Other Balkan Lands, and the Eastern Crisis of 1875–78], 3 vols. (Sarajevo: ANUBiH, 1977).

Petrović, Rastislav V., *Adam Bogosavljević* (Belgrade: Rad, 1972).

Petrovich, Michael B., *A History of Modern Serbia, 1804–1918*, 2 vols. (New York: Harcourt Brace Jovanovich, 1976).

Petrovich, Miodrag B., "Timočka Krajina and the Radicals," unpublished manuscript, presented as a paper at the University of Toronto, May 15, 1981.

Popov, Čedomir, *Srbija na putu oslobodjenja, 1868–1878* (Belgrade: Naučna knjiga, 1980).

Popović, Mihailo, *Filosofski i naučni rad Alimpija Vasiljevića* [The Philolosphic and Scholarly Work of Alimpije Vasiljević] (Novi Sad: Matica srpska, 1972).

Popović, Miroslav D., *Kragujevac i njegovo privredno područje* [Kragujevac and its Economic Region] (Belgrade: SANU, Posebna izdanja 246, Geografski institut, knjiga 8, 1956).

Popović-Petković, R., "Osnivanje družine za veštinu i zanate u Beogradu 1874. godine" [The Formation of a Society for Skilled Crafts in Belgrade in 1874], *Istoriski časopis* 9–10 (1959): 439–49.

Poznanović, Rade V., "Razvitak užičke zanatlijske čaršije posle izlaska Turska" [The Development of the Craft Trades in Užice after the Departure of the Ottomans], *Užički zbornik* 1 (1972): 19–50.

Prodanović, Jaša, *Istorija političkih stranaka i struja u Srbiji* [The History of Political Parties and Currents in Serbia] (Belgrade: Prosveta, 1947).

————, *Ustavne borbe u Srbiji* [Constitutional Struggles in Serbia] (Belgrade: Geca kon, n.d.).

Protić, Ljubiša, *Razvitak industrije i promet dobara u Srbiji za vreme prve vlade kneza Miloša* [The Development of Industry and Trade in Serbia during the Reign of Prince Miloš] (Belgrade: Rad, 1953).

Protić, Milan, "The Ideology of the Serbian Radical Movement, 1881–1903," Ph.D. diss., University of California at Santa Barbara, 1987.

Protić, Stojan, *Odlomci iz ustavne borbe* [Fragments from the Constitutional Struggle] (Belgrade: Dositije Obradović, 1911).

Prvanović Svetislav, *Timok i Timočani* [The Timok Region and its Inhabitants] (Zaječar: Razvitak, 1963).

Radenić, Andrija, *Iz istorije Srbije i Vojvodine 1834–1914* [From the History of Serbia and the Vojvodina] (Novi Sad and Belgrade: Matica srpska and Istorijski institut, 1973).

————, "Pogovor" [Afterword], in (Cenić, *Ispod zemlje ili moja tamnovanja*, pp. 123–50.

————, "Policiski (*sic*) izveštaji o dogadjajima u Beogradu početkom osamde-setih godina XIX. veka" [Political Reports about Events in Belgrade in the Early 1880s], *Godišnjak grada Beograda* 4 (1957): 415–31.

————, *Socijalistički listovi i časopisi u Srbiji 1871–1918* [Socialist Newspapers and Journals in Serbia, 1871–1918] (Belgrade: Rad, 1977).

————, "Svetozar Marković i Ujedinjena omladina," in Milisavac, *Ujedinjena omladina srpska,* pp. 105–32.

Radonić, Jovan, "Nikola Pašić i bosansko-hercegovački ustanak 1875" [Nikola Pašić and the 1875 Uprising in Bosnia and Hercegovina], *Politika,* May 20, 1937, April 14, 15, 16, 20, 1938.

————, "Pašićev izbor na velikoj školi pre pedeset godine" [Pašić's Election to the Belgrade Academy Fifty Years Ago], *Vreme,* December 8, 1928.

Radosavljević, Mata, *Evolucija srpske zadruge* [The Evolution of the Serbia Zadruga] (Belgrade: Državna štamparija, 1886).

Raičević, Jovan, *Železnice u Srbiji, 1884–1958* [Railroads in Serbia, 1884–1958] (Belgrade: NIN, 1959).

Rakić, Lazar, "Radikalna stranka u Vojvodini" [The Radical Party in the Vojvodina], *Istraživanje* (Novi Sad: Insitut za izučavanje istorije Vojvodine, 1975), 4:133–260.

Ristić, Jovan, *Pisma Jovana Ristića Filipu Hristiću* [The Letters of Jovan Ristić to Filip Hristić], edited by Milan Hristić and Slobodan Jovanović (Belgrade: SKA, 1931).

Šalipurović, Vukoman, *Ustanak u zapadnom delu stare Srbije 1875–1878* [The Uprising in the Western Part of Old Serbia 1875–78] (Titovo Užice, 1968).

Saradnja izmedju srba i grka za vreme svojih oslobodaličkih pokreta 1804–1830 [Cooperation between Serbs and Greeks during Their Liberation Movements, 1804–30] (Thessaloniki: Institute for Balkan Studies, 1979).

Šarić, Dragoslava, "Bibliografija ekonomske literature XIX. i početka XX. veka u Srbiji" [Bibliography of Economic Literature in Serbia in the Nineteenth and Early Twentieth Centuries], *Ekonomski anali* 20 (1966): 150–66.

Sewell, William H., Jr., *Work and Revolution in France* (New York: Cambridge University Press, 1980).

Sforza, Count Carlo, *Fifty Years of War and Diplomacy in the Balkans: Pashich and the Union of the Yugoslavs* (New York: Columbia University Press, 1940).

Skerlić, Jovan, *Svetozar Marković, njegov život, rad i ideje* [Svetozar Marković, his Life, Work, and Ideas] (Belgrade: Prosveta, 1966, orig. pub. 1910).

Škerović, Nikola P., ed., *Zapisnici sednica ministarskog saveta Srbije, 1862–98* [Minutes of the Meetings of the Council of Ministers of Serbia, 1862–98] (Belgrade: Arhiv Srbije, 1952).

Škorić, Sofija, "The Populism of Nikola Pašić: The Zürich Period," *East European Quarterly* 14 (1980): 469–85.

————, "The Populist Adventure of Nikola Pašić," typescript, 1978.

————, "The Role of Serbia as a Piedmont according to an Early Study by Nikola Pašić," typescript, 1978.

Skoko, Savo, "Pregled operacija srpske vojske u srpsko-turskom ratu 1877–1878" [A Review of the Operations of the Serbian Army in the Serbian-Ottoman War of 1877–78], in Petrović, *Medjunarodni naučni skup*, pp. 257–80.

Spasić, Živomir, "Uticaj Svetozara Markovića na srednjoškolsku omladinu u Kragujevcu (1874–1876)" [The Influence of Svetozar Marković on Middle-School Youth in Kragujevac, 1874–76], in Nedeljković, *Svetozar Marković, Omladina i Marksizam*, pp. 129–44.

————, "Život i politički rad Miloja Barjaktarovića" [The Life and Political Work of Miloje Barjaktarović], *Zbornik Istorijskog muzeja Srbije* 13–14 (1977): 129–44.

Stanković, Djordje Dj., *Nikola Pašić i jugoslovensko pitanje* [Nikola Pašić and the Yugoslav Question], vol. 1 (Belgrade: Beogradski izdavačko-grafički zavod, 1985).

————, *Nikola Pašić, saveznici, i stvaranje Jugoslavije* (Belgrade: Nolit, 1984).

Stanojević, Stanoje, ed., *Narodna enciklopedija srpsko-hrvatsko-slovenačka* (Zagreb: Bibliografski zavod, 1928–29).

Stewart, John Hall, *A Documentary Survey of the French Revolution* (New York: Macmillan, 1951).

Stojičić, Slobodanka, *Novi krajevi Srbije, 1878–1883* [The New Regions of Serbia, 1878–83] (Leskovac: Biblioteka narodnog muzeja u Leskovcu, knjiga 20, 1975).

————, "Pravni i politički aspekt agrarnog pitanja u novooslobodjenim krajevima" [The Legal and Political Aspect of the Agrarian Question in the Newly Liberated Regions], *Leskovački zbornik* 18 (1978): 77–91.

Stojković, Andrija, "Da li Svetozar Marković marksist," in Nedeljković, *Svetozar Marković, omladina i marksizam*, pp. 229–41.

————, *Filozofski pogledi Vladimira Jovanovića* [The Philosophical Views of Vladimir Jovanović] (Novi Sad: Matica srpska, 1972).

————, *Milan Kujundžić Aberdar: Filozofska i društveno-politička shvatanja* [Milan Kujundžić Aberdar: Philosophical and Sociopolitical Conceptions] (Novi Sad: Matica srpska, 1977).

Stokes, Gale, *Legitimacy through Liberalism: Vladimir Jovanović and the Transformation of Serbian Politics* (Seattle: University of Washington Press, 1975).

————, "Nikola Pašić i Svetozar Marković do 1875" [Nikola Pašić and Svetozar Marković to 1875], *Zbornik istorijskog muzeja Srbije* 23 (1986): 77–91.

————, "Prince Milan and the Serbian Army before World War I," in Király and Dreisziger, *East Central European Society in World War I*, pp. 555–68.

————, "Serbian Military Doctrine and the Crisis of 1875–78," in Király and Stokes, *Insurrections, Wars, and the Eastern Crisis*, pp. 261–75.

————, "Svetozar Marković in Russia," *Slavic Review* 31 (1972): 611–25.

Sugar, Peter, "Austria-Hungary and the Balkan Crisis: An Ingenious Improvisation," in Király and Stokes, *Insurrections, Wars, and the Eastern Crisis*, pp. 66–85.

————, "Railroad Construction and the Development of the Balkan Village in the Last Quarter of the Nineteenth Century," in Melville and Schröder, *Berliner Kongress*, pp. 485–98.

————, *Southeastern Europe under Ottoman Rule, 1354–1804* (Seattle: University of Washington Press, 1977).

Sumner, B. H., *Russia and the Balkans, 1870–1880* (London: Archon Books, 1962; orig. pub. 1937).

Todorović, Dragoje M., "Mesto i uloga Ranka Tajsića u političkom životu Srbije krajem 19. veka" [The Place and Role of Ranko Tajsić in the Political Life of Serbia at the End of the Nineteenth Century], Ph.D. diss., Belgrade University, 1972.

————, *Narodni tribun: Ranko Tajsić* (Belgrade: SANU, Posebna izdanja 550, 1983).

————, *Sudjenje Svetozaru Markoviću* [The Trial of Svetozar Marković] (Belgrade: Rad, 1974).

Todorović, Pera, *Dnevnik jednog dobrovoljca* [Diary of a Volunteer] (Belgrade: Srpska književna zadruga, 1938).

————, *Izabrani spisi* [Selected Writings], edited by Latinka Perović (Belgrade: Rad, 1987).

————, "Krvava godina; dnevnik jednog roba" [Bloody Year: Diary of a Slave] *Male novine*, January 1–December 31, 1880 (citations in the text are to the manuscript version, not to this published version).

————, "Uspomene na Kralja Milana" [Memories of King Milan], *Male novine*, 1901.

Veljković, Stojan, "O apsanama" [On Jails], *Glasnik* DSS 10 (1858).

Vinogradov, Vladien V., "The Congress of Berlin, 1878: An assessment of Its Place in History," in Király and Stokes, *Insurrections, Wars, and the Eastern Crisis*, pp. 319–29.

Vojvodić, Mihailo, et al., eds., *Srbija 1878: Dokumenti* [Serbia 1878: Documents] (Belgrade: Srpska književna zadruga, kolo 71, knjiga 473, 1978).

Vojvodić, Vaso, "Spomenica Miletićeve 'Srpske narodne slobodoumne stranke' i 'Glavnog odbora za srpsko oslobodjenje' kneževskom namesništvu u Srbiji o dizanju ustanka na Balkanu 1872" [Commemoration of (the Proposal of) Miletić's "Serbian National Freethinking Party" and "Main Committee for Serbian Liberation" to the Prince's Regency in Serbia about the Raising of an Uprising in the Balkans 1872], in Nedeljković, *Naučni skup Svetozar Marković: život i delo*, pp. 447–86.

Vučićević, Aleksandr, "Mladost i školovanje jednoga državnika" [Youth and Schooling of a Young Statesman], *Samouprava*, January 5–9, 1937, reprinted from *Politika*, 1927.

Vucinich, Wayne S., "Serbian Military Tradition," in Király and Rothenberg, *Special Topics and Generalizations on the 18th and 19th Centuries*, pp. 285–324.

Vucinich, Wayne S., ed., *The First Serbian Uprising, 1804–1813* (Boulder, Colo.: Social Science Monographs; New York: distributed by Columbia University Press, War and Society in East Central Europe, vol. 8, 1982).

Vučković, Vojislav J., "Pad generalne unije i proglas kraljevine 1882" [The Fall of General Union and the Proclamation of the Kingdom, 1882], *Glas* SANU 118 (1956): 45–91.

Vučo, Nikola, *Položaj seljaštva. I: Eksproprijacija od zemlje u XIX. veku* [The Condition of the Peasantry. I: The Expropriation of Land in the Nineteenth Century] (Belgrade: Privredni Institut ekonomskog fakulteta, 1955).

———, *Raspadanje esnafa u Srbiji* [The Breakdown of Guilds in Serbia] (Belgrade: SANU, Posebna izdanja 222, Istorijski institut, knjiga 5, 1954).

———, *Razvoj industrije u Srbiji u XIX veku* [The Development of Serbian Industry in the Nineteenth Century] (Belgrade: SANU, Posebna izdanja 533, Odeljenje istorijskih nauka, knjiga 7, 1981).

Vujić, Mihailo V., *Naša ekonomna politika* [Our Economic Policy] (Belgrade: Državna štamparija, 1883).

Vukomanović, Mladen, *Radnička klasa Srbije u drugoj polovini XIX. veka* [The Serbian Working Class in the Second Half of the Nineteenth Century] (Belgrade: Rad, 1972).

Vuković, M. Gavro, *Istorijski razvitak prava svojine od rimskog doba pa do danas* [The Historical Development of the Law of Property from the Roman Period to Today] (Belgrade: Državna Štamparija, 1873).

Vuković-Birčanin, Momčilo, *Nikola Pašić 1845–1926* (Munich: by the author, 1978).

Vuksanović-Anić, Draga, "Uloga vojske u kulturnom životu Srbije i ratovi 1876–1878. godine," [The Role of the Army in the Cultural Life of Serbia, and the Wars of 1876–78], in Milić, *Srbija u završnoj fazi velike istočne krize*, pp. 309–24.

Železnice u Srbiji, 1884–1958 [Railroads in Serbia, 1884–1958] (Belgrade: NIN, 1958).

Zimmermann, Werner G., "Südslavische Studenten in Zürich. Ein Beitrag zur Auswertung lokalen Quellenmaterials," in Richard George Plaschka and Karlheinz Mack, eds., *Wegenetz Europäischen Geistes: Wissenschaftszentren und geistige Wechselbeziehungen zwischen Mittel- und Südosteuropa vom Ende des 18. Jahrhunderts bis zum ersten Weltkrieg* (Vienna: Schriftenreihe des Österreichischen Ost- und Südosteuropa-Instituts, Band 8, 1983), pp. 326–37.

Živanović, Milan, "Prilozi za proučavanje pitanja imperijalističkog prodiranja Austro-ugarske u Srbiju od Berlinskog kongresa (1878) do zaključenja trgovinskog ugovora 1881." [Contribution to the Study of the Question of Austria-Hungary's Imperialist Penetration of Serbia from the Congress of Berlin (1878) to the Conclusion of the Commercial Agreement of 1881], *Mešovita gradja* [Istorijskog instituta] 12, no. 9 (1956): 121–66.

Živanović, Živan, *Politička istorija Srbije u drugoj polovini devetnaestog veka* [The Political History of Serbia in the Second Half of the Nineteenth Century], vols. 1, 2, and 4 (Belgrade: Geca Kon, 1923).

Životić, Vukašin, ed., *Spomenica Nikole P. Pašića 1845–1926* [In Memory of Nikola P. Pašić, 1845–1926] (Belgrade: Pavlović, 1926).

Index

Action ministry: First, 77–80, 85; Second, 104–6, 115

Adam committees: disposition of, 361 n. 138; formed, 185–87, 193, 194, 230

Address to the throne: 1871, 16; 1873, 24–25; 1874, 37–39, 62, 68; 1875, 77–80; 1876, 116; 1877, 119; 1878, 142; 1879, 160; 1880, 195–96; 1882, 234–35

Agrarian law. *See* Newly acquired territories

Albanians, 165–66, 344 n.86, 344 n.88

Aleksinac, 58, 289

Alexander II, Tsar of Russia, 18, 139

Alimpić, Ranko, 140, 171

Anastasijević, Miša, 22

Anderson, Benedict, 293

Andjelković, Sreta, 89

Andrássy, Gyula, 20, 76, 137

April uprisings in Bulgaria (May new style), 105, 114

Arandjelovac, 47

Army in Serbia, 196, 271, 363 n.28; early evolution of, 108–9, 111; Miloš and, 109–10; officer training in, 109, 334 n.15, 368 n.99; reorganization of, 77, 124,

264, 281, 306; weapons of, 112, 324 n.15

Artillery Academy, 109

Asiatic Department (Russia), 104

Assembly, freedom of. *See* Constitutional issues

Austria. *See* Serbia: relations with Austria-Hungary

Avakumović, Jovan, 130, 134

Babeuf, 58

Baker, Augustus, 165, 358 n.83

Bakunin, Mikhail, 57, 133

Ban, Matija, 329 n.45

Banja, 284, 285, 286, 288

Banković, Tasa, 233, 357 n.61

Battenberg, Alexander of Bulgaria, 175

Belgrade, 46, 47, 237, 369 n.111; artillery academy in, 109; gymnasium, 9, 55, 356 n.44; political cafes, 122, 128, 203, 226, 245, 274, 349 n.58, 350 n.68; railroad, 169, 172. See also Vračar

Belgrade Academy. *See* Velika škola

Belimarković, Jovan, 21, 28–30, 32, 39, 124

Berlin, Treaty of, 168, 169, 186, 207, 209, 213, 338 n.10;

394 : Index

117–22; of 1878, 138, 142–54; of
1879, 159–65, 167–69, 179, 183,
184; of 1879 (special), 170–72,
186–87; of 1880, 195–96, 205–11;
of 1882, 233–35, 240, 244, 246–
48; of late 1882 ("two-voter"),
263–64, 280; of 1883 ("five-minute"), 272, 277, 279, 367 n.79;
Marković on, 49–50, 53–54; obstructive methods in, 65–66, 119–
20, 209, 239–40, 245, 295, 357
n.66; tradition and role of, 6, 7, 9,
11; unicameral versus bicameral,
12–14, 65, 181, 251, 271
Slavic Committees in Russia, 104,
106, 112
Sloboda, 132, 151, 323 n.54
Smederevo, 93, 127
Socialism, Serbia, 43, 44, 46, 54. *See
also* Cenić, Mita
Society for Agricultural Improve-
ment, 67, 325 n.83
Society for Serbian Unification and
Liberation, 46
Society for the Support of Serbian
Literature, 224, 227, 262. *See also*
Liberal Party
Spasić, Damjan, 128
Srbadija (student club), 66
Srbija, 16, 179
Srećković, Panta, 143, 153, 338 n.11
Srez, definition of, 82
Srpska nezavisnost, 219, 220, 225,
237, 241, 249, 261, 354 n.18
Srpske novine, 141
Stanojević, Aca, 285, 288, 289, 358
n.86, 369 n.107
Stanojević, Dragiša, 132
Staro oslobodjenje, 70, 71, 89, 92, 95,
97, 102, 103, 105–6
Starvation in Serbia. *See* Serbia: star-
vation in
State Council, 22, 155; appointments
to, 35; background of, 6, 7, 9, 12,

13, 19; Radicals on, 196, 233;
Svetozar Marković on, 45, 54
Stefanović, (Uncle) Danilo, 64–66,
71–72, 75–76, 85, 89, 111, 327
n.7
Stevanović, Stevan, 369 n.109
Stojković, Dimitrije, 319 n.26
Straža, 229, 338 n.14
Šumadija, 103

Tajsić, Ranko, 140, 229, 230, 303,
343 n.67; acts on behalf of the
Radicals, 240, 246; early life, 68–
69, 325 n.89, 326 n.97; relations
with Milan, 72, 241, 243, 328
n.27, 358 n.86; in skupština, 70,
120, 152, 205, 350 n.78
Tariffs, 17, 26, 142, 152, 190, 302;
agreements with European states,
173; German tariff law of 1877,
137; possibility of tariff war in
1880, 175–76, 298; relations with
Austria, 142, 143, 170–71, 364
n.32; union with Bulgaria, 175
Taušanović, Kosta, 202, 246, 248,
270, 275, 279, 287, 290, 352 n.98,
356 n.57
Težak, 325 n.83
Three Emperors' League, 30, 76,
81, 191
Timok Rebellion, 4, 264, 283–90,
291, 303
Timok region, 42, 56, 71, 112, 139–
40, 265–66, 283–85, 287, 361
n.37, 364 n.32
Todorić, Ilija, 95, 100, 102, 329
n.41, 330 n.53
Todorović, Pera, 4, 62, 68, 140, 203,
220, 233, 238, 247, 262, 270, 273–
74, 283, 300, 303, 338 n.14; and
assassination attempt on Milan,
260–61; in crisis of 1883, 280, 286,
287, 288, 289; early life, 55–56;
illness of, 280, 356 n.46; influenced